The
Sisterhood

Acclaim for
The Sisterhood
and
Marcia Cohen

"Marcia Cohen's *The Sisterhood* had me avidly turning pages. These were the girls who couldn't fit into the demure role ordained for women in the 1950s, people who wanted to run things, to be the center of attention, often at any cost."
—Laura Miller, Editorial Director, Salon.com

"*The Sisterhood* is one of my favorite books."
—Gail Collins, Columnist, *The New York Times*

"She tells the story behind the story."
—Howard Blum, Author of *Pledge of Allegiance*

"It's a thrilling story—a fine blend of history and moving portraits."
—Betty Rollin, Author of *Last Wish*

"This is a benchmark book that I want to nail to my daughter's bedside table, read out loud to my sons."
—Phyllis Theroux, Author of *Peripheral Visions*

"Her pages crackle with such energy they almost turn themselves."
—*The Kirkus Reviews*

The
Sisterhood

The Inside Story of the Women's Movement
and the
Leaders Who Made It Happen

Marcia Cohen
With a New Foreword by the Author

SUNSTONE
PRESS

SANTA FE

Sunstone books may be purchased for educational, business, or sales promotional use.
For information please write: Special Markets Department, Sunstone Press,
P.O. Box 2321, Santa Fe, New Mexico 87504-2321.

Cover design by Vicki Ahl
Printed on acid free paper

Library of Congress Cataloging-in-Publication Data

Cohen, Marcia.
 The sisterhood : the inside story of the women's movement and the leaders who made it happen
/ by Marcia Cohen ; with a new foreword by the author.
   p. cm.
 Earlier ed. published in 1988 as: The sisterhood : the true story of the women who changed
the world.
 Includes bibliographical references and index.
 ISBN 978-0-86534-723-6 (softcover : alk. paper)
 1. Feminism--United States--History--20th century. 2. Feminists--United States. 3. Feminists-
-United States--Biography. I. Title.
 HQ1426.C626 2009
 305.420973'0904--dc22
                              2009039684

WWW.SUNSTONEPRESS.COM
SUNSTONE PRESS / POST OFFICE BOX 2321 / SANTA FE, NM 87504-2321 /USA
(505) 988-4418 / ORDERS ONLY (800) 243-5644 / FAX (505) 988-1025

To the Memory
of
Belle and Morris Friedlander

Foreword to this Edition

Today everything seems possible for women. As I write this, in the year two thousand and nine, a brilliant, ambitious woman, having come within a hair's breadth of winning the most powerful leadership position on our troubled planet, has refused appeasement with anything less than an international role of historic proportions. Hundreds of strong women have achieved more than any of us even dreamt of in the 1980s, when this book was first written. Today, women reign across the globe as doctors, lawyers, police chiefs, ministers, heads of our most prestigious educational institutions, CEOs of major corporations, chairs of important government agencies, highly regarded media pundits, powerful members of Presidential cabinets. Today, we can marry or not, reproduce as we choose, even switch genders if we so desire. We function on an equal plane with men in nearly every walk of life.

How did this astonishing transformation happen to "the weaker sex"?

Probably, the seeds of this change were sown by the much maligned Eve or the Biblical Deborah, then fed over the decades by the prescient writings of an Afra Behn, a Susan B. Anthony, the courageous suffragists, the feisty, beloved Eleanor Roosevelt, a few fair-minded men like John Stuart Mill plus plenty of grassroots, back-fence conspiring over eons of misanthropic oppression.

Certainly, though, the most immediate and notable impetus was the explosive women's revolution of the 1960s and 70s, which is the subject of *The Sisterhood*.

Most of us recognize the names of the major players in *The Sisterhood*— Gloria Steinem, Betty Friedan, Kate Millett, etc.—but how many of today's brilliantly successful women consciously credit these feminist icons on whose shoulders we all stand? Even some of us who were witness to the blazing fireworks of those neon-bright mid-twentieth century years barely remember—or pay homage to—the struggles and humiliations every one of those passionate revolutionaries endured.

Does it matter?

"Those who cannot learn from history are doomed to repeat it." That was George Santayana's dire prediction, and if it holds true, we could be condemned to hear once again such directives from the pulpit as "God forbids the woman to teach . . . not to usurp authority over the man, but to be in silence," or such innocent maternal bromides as "Keep your ankles crossed and your skirt below your knees."

By the 1940s and 50s, to our detriment, we females were silently enduring:

> "We don't hire women because men support families."
> "You can't play. Only boys' sports teams can be funded."
> "No trousers in this office: women should look like women."
> "Here's the form for your insurance (mortgage, savings account). Take it home and have your husband sign it."

As well as such intimidating threats as:

> "Day care will irreparably damage your child."
> "There's only one career for girls (this from my own college dean): to raise educated, cultured children."

And then, by the late 1950s, as early feminist ideas began to seep into public awareness:

> "Feminists are all lesbians; too ugly to get a man."
> "Rape? She asked for it. Boys will be boys, y'know!"

Proclamations of authoritative scientific misinformation filled our books and magazines:

> "Clitoral orgasm is a sign of penis envy and immaturity."
> "Women aren't suited for repetitive tasks."

Those were still the days of:

> "You're so cute when you're mad."
> "Fly me. I'm Barbara."

Thus, the inevitable explosion, a sweeping rebellion that eventually spread to every part of the globe, if not fully succeeding in those distant societies where chadors and clitorectomies still ruled, at least making inroads in a few of these rigidly superstitious places, insinuating the messages of liberation, declarations of independence—the shocking notions of the F-word of the day: Feminism.

In America, demonstrations were held, and against fierce resistance, perfectly crafted new laws against sex discrimination were passed. This wasn't the first time the ideas of women's rights had been raised, of course, but it was the first time such a supremely powerful vehicle as the 1960s media took notice and spread those revolutionary notions to every newspaper, magazine and television screen in the world.

Media-power was a relatively new, barely understood force on the horizon then, but somehow, many of the super-smart, well-educated new feminists were media-savvy as well as dazzlingly dramatic. They became leaders because they believed so fervently that the time had come for women to raise their voices, and they became celebrated stars because they knew how to make themselves noticed and heard. Like so many women, they harbored years of suppressed, simmering anger, and they found their audience by fighting passionately against what they cleverly coined "sexism," "male chauvinism," and "sexual harassment."

Also, because they were distinct individuals with distinct opinions, they argued with each other.

After all, this highly verbal women's movement was the only social revolt in history to deal with every single component of human life—fair employment, money, spousal abuse, sexuality, marriage, law, health, medicine, art, literature, in fact, the preservation of the species—a perfect orgy of provocative issues.

Given this incredible range, the women who fueled the explosion simply had to be intelligent and communicative, to say nothing of complicated and idiosyncratic. Each and every one of these charismatic rebels was a fascinating mixture of flaws and strengths, flamboyance and charm. They talked and wrote and wrote and talked and in this process of internecine intellectual turmoil, they raised many of the thorny issues that still plague us today, when too many of these heroic women are already in their graves. I do often picture them troubling deaf heaven, irascibly pummeling away at such deceptively simple axioms as:

"Equal pay for equal work."
"The personal is the political."
"Anatomy is not destiny."
"A woman needs a man like a fish needs a bicycle."

These were movement slogans, and some of them worked mainly for one segment or another of the overall movement, for single women, for instance, or ambitious careerists.

And today, even in our highly developed countries, as blatantly unequal pay scales between men and women still enrage, we find women pooled in low paying segments of the economy, in non-profits, for instance, or teaching small children.

Often, this is the choice of the women themselves, mothers, for the most part, a women's movement conundrum never thoroughly studied or unraveled, including, as a corollary, the highly ambiguous differences between men and women, anatomical, biological, or psychological, a subject too threatening to examine back in those days when feminists and all feminist principles were under siege.

In 2009, as the United States (and the globe) writhes in the grip of financial and climatic crisis, even when the United States was headed by a man who gives the lie to racial—and, by implication—all human prejudice, no observer can miss the fact that few, if any women are among the recipients of the obscene "golden parachutes," the billions of dollars in salaries and bonuses that have accrued to men in the corrupt and corrupting financial world.

Even women who have not retired to the supposedly safe role of "stay-at-home Moms" have usually opted for outside employment far beneath their abilities, jobs that are undemanding enough and close enough in proximity to their homes to allow them to attend to their children's sudden injuries or offer much needed psychological support.

The problem of full respect for those women (or men) who raise children, children with needs, special or not, children whose talents deserve and require careful nurturing, leads directly to the complex questions of equal—or, more to the point, "fair" pay. Top jobs in our competitive capitalistic world require top, i.e. full, undivided—attention. And from there, the sustenance money still flows.

Indeed, like most revolutions, the women's movement, raising ideas that were complex and difficult, left certain problems unsolved, such as, for example, whether feminists should vote for a woman because she is a woman or because she espouses the principles of feminism; i.e. which to support, the gratifying presence of a woman candidate or utterly essential issues themselves.

And yet, so much has indeed changed for women, and for so many men who have finally been given permission to act on their "maternal" instincts.

Perhaps the revolution has merely transmogrified into an evolution, which is the most hopeful sign of all, because far beneath the radar of the current popular media, in the far corners of the globe, strong, liberated women are helping less confident women become stronger. In such a poverty and conflict-stricken country as Nepal, for instance, a young American journalist is teaching intelligent but oppressed women how to become journalists themselves. These Nepalese women want to tell the stories that have been hidden in their restricted culture, and soon they will do so. When this miracle happens, their words will reach the eyes and ears of the world just as the heroes of the "Sisterhood" did. I believe that women will even reverse the threatening dangers to our painfully overpopulated, precipitously heating planet; a new, confident, empowered sisterhood will soon arise to rescue Mother Earth.

So whether or not our heroic politicians attain the pinnacles they aim for, it seems time to take another look at how we happened to get here, even tangle with a few of the brutal and bizarre injustices—the stoning of women in undeveloped countries, the shameful rape of female soldiers in our own armed forces, the ideological disputes that still remain. There is good reason, after all, why thousands of women still pack auditoriums, grasping each others' hands and cheering a great leader like Gloria Steinem, all of us aware that we must thank our lucky stars or—as *The Sisterhood* records—Betty, Gloria, Germaine, Kate, et al—that the whole women's conflagration of words happened at all.

—Marcia Cohen
Santa Fe, New Mexico 2009

Contents

CONTENTS

What is the matter with Mary Jane?
She's perfectly well and she hasn't a pain!
What is the matter with Mary Jane?

—A. A. Milne, When We Were Very Young

PART I

1

THE WAY
OF THE WORLD
AT LUNCHTIME

So where *was* she? Where in God's name was Betty?

They were freezing out here on the sidewalk, in spite of their fur coats. Their fingers were numb on the stems of the picket signs: "Wake Up Plaza! Get With It NOW!" Across the street, Central Park loomed white as a wedding cake, a frosted swirl of snow drifts. Directly before them (an increasingly nervous, red-cheeked group of two dozen or so) was the target: the Plaza Hotel.

Already, right on time, the press was beginning to troop in. One by one, they straggled past the tall globe standards, the discreet P etched in the hotel's facade. The print reporters with their coat collars turned up against the cold, eyes alert to this opulent haunt of the rich. The photographers, pausing to snap some preliminary shots. There was the reporter from the *New York Post,* and over there, the *Daily News,* even the *New York Times.* Now the cameramen, the TV grunts lumbering up the wide, carpeted steps with their clumsy equipment. My goodness, wasn't that network television? Weren't those people from the "Today" show?

It was February 12, 1969, the birthday of the Great Emancipator, Abraham Lincoln. A great blizzard had been raging for days, blanketing the East. Maybe the press was sick of writing about the snow, of trotting out the synonyms for cold-white-wind. They had come out in spite of the weather, or perhaps because of it . . . merely grateful for something new.

Whatever the reason, to judge purely by the growing media parade, this impudent, brazen protest was actually going forward. Here and there among the picketers (who included two brave men) stomach muscles tightened, a few breaths were sharply drawn in.

They were going to invade the Oak Room of the Plaza Hotel.

The moment Betty Friedan arrived, that is.

But how strange that she was so late!

Not that punctuality was among their forty-eight-year-old leader's most sterling qualities. Many the conference or meeting when this five foot two inch, buxom, hot-blooded, cocky little rebel would come pounding in at the last minute, her straight brown hair flying over her ears, satchel bulging with a bird's nest of papers, and, within seconds, focusing those heavy-lidded dark eyes on whoever was assembled, let loose a barrage of roiling, extemporaneous rhetoric.

Terrific, except that this was hardly the occasion for one of those huffing, puffing, last-minute entrances of hers. This was no neatly structured press conference with folding chairs set all in a row. This was an incursion. Enemy territory. You couldn't control it, and least of all could you control the press. If anyone knew that, Betty did.

So what could possibly have happened to her?

When this protest was so hugely important. When it was not, after all, some dreary government office in Washington, D.C., they were hitting. Not some seamy, smelly side street off Times Square. It was a citadel, a gilded edifice of a million soapsuds dreams, a trusted domicile to more celebrities—not to mention royalty and aristocracy—than any fan magazine could cover in a year. This well-protected fortress, this sumptuous dwelling for the rich and accomplished, from the Vanderbilts to the Kennedys, from Diamond Jim Brady to the Beatles, was a movie set, literally, in *North by Northwest.* (*The Way We Were, The Great Gatsby* yet to come.) The Plaza . . . ranking arbiter of propriety, decorum, taste.

Yet that taste did not extend to permitting women to enter (let alone sit down in) its dignified, clublike, white-clothed Oak Room at lunchtime, from twelve till three, just before the stock exchange closed—the hours, in short, of serious (that is, male) negotiations. Which meant that female executives (such as there were in 1969) would be excluded from certain essential business meetings. Which meant, as well, even if you weren't an executive, an affront—at the very least, a symbolic slur.

Not that anyone complained, of course. You wouldn't dare. Even Betty, just five years before, had not dared.

Much had transpired in those intervening years, and Betty had surely grown stronger. Even back then, though, this mother of three had shown her stuff. She had already published her groundbreaking polemic *The Feminine Mystique*; she had already appeared on television talk shows around the country. And on one particular day in 1964 she had been invited to lunch by an influential editor. At the Plaza Hotel. Right here in the Oak Room of the Plaza . . .

The austere, quiet German Renaissance room—a popular publishing hangout—had been a natural choice. The editor was Clay Felker, the ingenious force who would soon create *New York* magazine. At that moment in 1964, Felker was a consultant to *Ladies' Home Journal*, and he was interested in this angry, provocative, new feminist perspective of Betty Friedan's. Perhaps it might heat the veins, jack up the flagging sales of the magazine. Perhaps, as he had suggested to Betty on the phone, she might like to edit an issue of the magazine.

Betty had hustled in eagerly from the suburbs. Arriving at the Plaza, she headed for the Oak Room bar.

The headwaiter stopped her cold.

"No, madam," said he impassively, "you cannot wait at the bar. Women are not allowed."

Well, in that case, Betty answered, she would wait at Mr. Felker's table.

"I'm sorry, madam," came the reply, "we do not serve women in the Oak Room at noon."

Oh.

She hadn't known. And so she said . . . absolutely nothing.

The usually unquenchable voice of Betty Friedan had been totally silenced.

High-decibel visionary, analyst, rebel, Betty had already squared her shoulders and faced down—yelled back at, in fact—a spate of public attacks on her book. Yet the forces arrayed here, the years of convention embodied in this smartly black-tied waiter, this *sniffy* dismissal, had somehow unnerved, rendered her mute. To Betty, as to most women, so many of them, like her, suburban housewives, the rules of the "real" world, the world of commerce, of business lunches

—the world, in short, of men—were mysterious. In this terra incognita, she had responded as millions of other women would have in those days. Oblivious to the possibility that the essential rightness of the Plaza Hotel might be questioned, Betty had assumed, reflexively, that the problem must be hers.

Her clothes, perhaps. Or somehow, just *her,* she figured, as off she slunk to less august quarters where, presumably, she could not intrude on any serious business negotiations. Such as, of course, the hard proposition she was about to be offered—a free hand at editing a full section of a magazine with over six million readers, one of the most lucrative advertising magnets in the world.

Clay Felker, who also did not know, who had never before *noticed* the absence of female faces in the lunchtime lantern glow of the Oak Room, had eventually found his luncheon companion, the best-selling author, in another dining room entirely. He found her chastened and subdued, unable even to believe that he actually meant his offer.

A searing memory which, by all logic, should have brought Betty speeding to this morning's scene, this nervy, jazzy little coup at the Plaza.

Where, at 11:30 this frosty morning, the shivering brigade of NOW members—the New York contingent of the National Organization for Women—awaited their avenging angel.

"Is she here yet?" For at least the tenth time, Muriel Fox, NOW's public relations chief, left her press duties inside, dashed to the front entrance, and called to the picketers out on the sidewalk.

No, they called back. And again, no.

Finally, the corps, tired by now of stamping about in the cold, trooped inside, following Muriel back through the huge glass doors. They all looked just fine, decked out, as they were, in their best coats, in as many furs as they could round up. The point being to leave no grounds for exclusion, they had dressed as if they belonged. No frizzy-haired hippies. No cranky Cinderellas. No refugees from the dropout set.

Once inside, they divided into smaller groups, marched briskly into the pink-and-green lobby with its shimmering chandeliers, its gold-encrusted walls, down the long, graceful corridor, and into . . .

An incredible crush! The narrow hallway outside the Oak Room was a teeming zoo. More reporters had arrived through another entrance; two of them, it seemed, for nearly every demonstrator. The wire services, the foreign press, every television and radio station in the city—fifty, sixty press people wedged in front of the Oak Room. They were lolling behind the potted palms, slouched beside the massive vases with their huge bouquets of pink and white flowers. Camera cables snaked treacherously across the thick, patterned carpets. Blinding bright lights slashed through heavy cigarette smoke. A media blitz!

Except that . . . nothing was happening.

The streets were clear. Traffic was moving. So what could be holding up Betty? Was it possible, some of the women began to whisper, that she wasn't coming at all?

The moment that suspicion was voiced, Dolores Alexander, a *Newsday* reporter and NOW member who had played a major role in orchestrating this event, began a litany of steady, calming reassurances. Betty was indeed coming; there was no question about it. Dolores was sure. She sounded so sure, in fact, that they couldn't help believing her. As if she knew *something* that the rest of them didn't.

Which, as it happened, was true. Dolores had learned of the problem early that morning, moments after Betty's anguished voice came on the phone. Betty was calling, she had said, to tell Dolores that she could not come to the Plaza that day.

Not come? Dolores simply could not believe what she was hearing. She knew very well how much Betty cared about this one.

"Betty," she answered, "you *have* to be there!"

But no. Though obviously saddened, Betty was adamant. She definitely could not make it. There was nothing to be done.

"But why?" Dolores asked, and then, in the way of friends, began to press. Betty was an integral part of this action. The Plaza was only a ten-minute cab ride from her apartment. What could possibly stop her? Had something happened?

And slowly, as Dolores gently prodded, she learned that something had indeed happened.

This wasn't the first time, Betty told her. Carl had done it before, especially before important events.

Her face was bruised. Visibly. There had been an argument, and Carl had . . . done it. Whatever that meant to Betty personally was not the issue. The problem was that the bruises, the blackened eye, could be seen. By her co-workers, by the Plaza people, by the reporters, and by, of course, the cameras.

Dolores's heart sank. With sympathy for her friend, with disappointment for them all, for the entire protest. Who could replace Betty Friedan?

And yet, even as Dolores resisted, she also realized that Betty was right. She could not appear at the Plaza. The famous symbol of this struggling new movement simply could not issue forth before reporters and cameras to be projected on TV screens across the world as (though it would be years before the world was familiar with this term) a battered wife.

Already, at *Newsday*, Dolores had been on the lookout for the quality of the image Betty presented. Often, when Dolores heard that a NOW story was running, she had picked over the photos of Betty to find, as best she could, a decent one. It did seem, sometimes, that Betty was just too busy to give much care to her appearance. And, it had to be admitted, she was not exactly photogenic. Furthermore, the male editors, if not preempted, seemed to relish choosing the worst possible, the ugliest pictures, the ones where Betty's mouth was open or her fist raised, or some shots that emphasized her substantial nose.

Unflattering, however, was one thing. A black eye was another. Yet as Dolores listened, commiserating with her friend and mourning their high hopes for the Plaza demonstration, a possible solution began to suggest itself. Jean Faust, the first president of New York NOW, had been active in the theater and was highly skilled at makeup. Perhaps . . .

"Look, Betty," Dolores ventured. "You trust Jean, don't you?"

"Yes."

"Well, she's very good with cosmetics. What if I called her and asked her to come to your apartment? Maybe she can fix you up. Maybe she can cover it over. Would that be okay?"

There had been a second or two of silence at the other end of the phone, then Betty's familiar upbeat, decisive tone.

"Okay, that's a very good idea!"

And that, as far as Dolores knew, was what was happening right now. That was why Betty was late.

But why this late? That makeup job seemed to be taking forever. The reporters were shuffling around, the NOW women growing edgier by the minute. The press had been alerted for eleven o'clock. It was already past twelve. They wouldn't wait forever.

"She's not coming," somebody said. "Let's start."

"Please," begged Dolores. "She's on her way. I *know* she'll be here soon."

"We made reservations. The reporters will leave . . ."

"Please. Let's wait, please."

Until (though, of course, Dolores would not reveal this) Jean had finished carefully camouflaging Betty's eye and the dark, swollen lump on her cheekbone.

It was painstaking work. Carefully, skillfully, Jean was smoothing on layer after layer of makeup. Clearly, she thought, as she daubed on the stuff, *someone* had wanted to prevent Betty from appearing that day.

And all the while that Jean was painting, Dolores held the fort, for as long as she could, while the women—and the press—milled about, less than patiently, in the hot, smoky hallway of the Plaza.

Just a few minutes . . . a few minutes more.

Dolores had positioned herself directly in front of the french doors. It was still a bit early for the lunch-hour crowd, and beyond the doors, where the ordinarily dark Oak Room was flooded with television lights, there were few patrons.

Now, however, Dolores caught a glimpse of a woman. One of their group had managed to get inside and sit down at a table.

And so, she realized sadly, the action had begun. There was no use waiting anymore. She turned away then to motion to the rest, reassuring herself as she did so: After all, there were others. Someone else besides Betty *could* speak to the press. Muriel had already been explaining the issues. Dolores herself or any one of the women . . .

Which was exactly when, suddenly, directly at Dolores's side, there before her eyes was Betty.

Dolores was so stunned she could barely absorb the sight.

Betty's chunky body was elegantly encased in mink. Even her hair was smooth and neat, cut short in the back in the current Sassoon style. Just as if nothing had gone awry, as if Betty herself had precisely arranged this moment. The overture. The curtain . . .

"Oh, thank heavens," Dolores whispered. "Thank heavens you're here. Are you all right?"

"How do I look? Do I look okay?"

"Fine," Dolores answered, although, in truth, on careful inspection, she wasn't so sure.

Betty was wearing dark glasses. They would photograph horribly,

19

making Betty look like some monstrous blind owl. Knowing what she knew, of course, Dolores said nothing. She just worried and wondered. Would Betty take them off? Would she risk it?

For now, ready or not, the great Oak Room engagement commenced.

The manager and the headwaiter, well prepared, stood like sentinels at the door. Behind them, the hallowed halls of the sanctum sanctorum itself. The high Gothic arches, the heavy oak carvings, the fleur-de-lis and oak heraldry festooning the walls, the bronze chandelier and burgundy carpet, the brown leather chairs with shiny brass studs. Opposite the deep easy chairs for the men stood the inevitable smaller, stiffer ones, evidence that women were allowed in this grand emporium *sometimes.*

And they were just in time—before the arrival of the regular patrons, so they could not be accused of disrupting business. (And, not incidentally, well within range of the evening news.) Most of the tables were still empty, thus forcing the manager to announce his intentions, which he quickly did.

It was a "sixty-year-old tradition at the Plaza," he intoned, "to ban women from the Oak Room from the hours of twelve to three."

"We have reservations," one of the women replied.

"We have the Edwardian Room for you ladies. It's a beautiful restaurant."

"And we consider that," came the riposte, as the women filed resolutely past him, "separate but unequal."

Television cameras, set up at the doorway, followed their passage. Print reporters, hustling behind them, scribbled in their notepads.

The women sat down at two round tables near the center of the room. And waited. One of them waved her arm in the direction of a group of handsomely black-tied waiters standing nearby, waiting for the real customers.

No one came.

"Waiter! Waiter!"

Still no response. Some friendly discussions ensued, waiters to women, women to waiters, expressions of sympathy on the merits of the case, but they had their orders.

"Waiter! Waiter!" For nearly half an hour, they troubled deaf ears until the refusal of service was unmistakable and the point had been made.

Then, with dignity, the well-appointed women rose. With nary a fuss, they serenely departed the well-appointed room. Mission accomplished; it had all clicked along like a scene from *Major Barbara*.

Out in the hallway, inches from the grand marble reception desk, Betty held forth on Section 40E of the New York State Civil Rights Act. An innkeeper cannot refuse service without just cause (and so on), proving that the dignified, sophisticated Plaza was, in fact, violating the law. Perhaps she would even take them to court!

"This is the only kind of discrimination that's considered moral, or, if you will, a joke," she proclaimed.

Which was what the reporters wrote, and the cameras recorded. Betty proclaiming, eyes blazing.

She had removed her dark glasses!

Dolores looked carefully. Nothing was visible. Thanks to the skillful ministrations of the first president of New York NOW, not a bruise was visible. Not even, it would turn out, to the sharp, professionally curious eyes of the overflowing press corps.

Among them, in fact, Muriel would remember meeting that day, for the very first time, a stunning young reporter with a glamorous, slinky figure and long, dark hair, the political columnist from Clay Felker's new, slick, and trendy *New York* magazine. Muriel would remember introducing herself to Gloria Steinem and wondering what she thought, hoping that this highly placed journalist would understand their issues.

But though Gloria Steinem would not write about the climactic scene at the Plaza, many others would, the acerbic Harriet Van Horne among them.

"For a woman to stroll into a men's bar at lunchtime and demand service seems to be as preposterous as a woman marching into a barbershop and demanding a hot towel and a haircut," Van Horne chided in her *New York Post* column two days later. "This storming of the Oak Room was . . . a shrewish, attention-seeking stunt. . . . Women lose so much—beginning with charm, dignity and a certain mystery—when they carry on like strumpets in foolish causes. Ultimately, this can only have a bad effect on the men. . . .

"A sexual ban in this context can hardly be termed illegal or immoral.

"It is simply the way of the world at lunchtime."

It had been, of course, the way of the world for millennia, and many women—empathizing with Harriet Van Horne—believed that it should remain that way.

Their values, they knew, were the right ones.

You stayed at home and raised your children. You polished the kitchen floor until it shone, and then you polished it again. You insisted always that you had no unseemly, unfeminine ambitions—no big ego, artistic or otherwise. You helped your husband to further his career. You were auxiliary and you were muse. You waited a lot, as women throughout the ages had always done. For your children to come home from school, for your men to come home from work. Or from war.

And so maybe you were depressed a little too often. Or you drank a little too much or, just now and then, took a few extra tranquilizers.

You did not, at least, make a damned fool of yourself. You did not harangue people in public. You did not push yourself where you weren't wanted—no more than you ran down the street with your breasts bouncing. Would any decent man put up with that sort of behavior? Nothing, after all, was more unappealing than a pushy woman; nothing less attractive than an angry one.

Picketing. Demonstrating. Intruding. Showing off!

And at the Plaza Hotel!

My God, who *were* these women?

2
VOICES

*In public . . . the committed change innovators are
the ones who seem to play for the future. But in private, they follow this zigzag course, like we all do.*

—Ellen Goodman, *Turning Points, How People
Change Through Crisis and Commitment,* 1979

They were, in many ways, women just like the rest of us.

Like the schoolteacher in Gary, Indiana, who worked twice as
hard as the male in the next classroom, but was paid so much
less. No matter how many years she labored, she would not be promoted to principal of the school. That job, she knew, would go to a
man.

. . . the female student, one of a very few, at Harvard Law School
who had to travel completely across the campus to use a bathroom,
even in the midst of an exam. In the classroom, once a semester, on
"Ladies' Day," as the professor called it, she was directed to a group
of high stools specially set up for this purpose, and there she was
quizzed—not on the usual cases to which the male students had been
responding all term, but on specially chosen, embarrassing lawsuits
replete with sexual innuendo.

. . . the cocktail waitress in San Francisco who was not allowed in
the main dining room.

23

... the secretary in Austin, Texas, who could be fired for wearing a pantsuit.

... the University of Michigan "coed," as female undergraduates were described, who night after night was dropped off at her dormitory at "women's curfew hour" as her date (and his buddies) proceeded to the pizza parlor.

... the talented athlete in Omaha, Nebraska, unable to train because there were no funds for "girls' " sports.

... the forty-year-old married woman in Seattle who could not have a charge account in her own name.

... the fine science student at Muhlenberg College in Pennsylvania who was told by her adviser that she must not apply to medical school because she might be usurping the place of a male student who had to support a family.

... and the thousands of others who were refused jobs simply because the employer, perfectly legally, didn't hire women. Or were grudgingly hired, but at half a male's pay. Or were treated, in the law, as chattels of their husband. Or denied a seat on juries. Or raped, and disbelieved. ("She asked for it.")

Few of these women would carry a picket sign; few would push their way into a restaurant. Instead they hid their anger beneath forced smiles, buried it deep in mountains of trivia, or, more dangerously, swallowed it with alcohol or pills—a discontent so deeply suppressed that few responded (outwardly, at least) to such typical insults as:

"Fly me, I'm Barbara."

"Women are basically emotional creatures."

"Keep her barefoot and pregnant."

"The female sex is best suited to repetitive tasks."

"Women go to college to collect their Mrs."

"I don't touch your woman, you don't touch my car."

And so, of course, in so many, the rage smoldered. The wounds were festering, the pot steaming, and, sooner or later, it was bound to explode.

The Second Wave of Feminism, some historians would call it, the first being the early-twentieth-century battle for suffrage. Others would regard it as the Third Wave, considering, in this view, women's polemics of the eighteenth and nineteenth centuries. Still other scholars would note that feminism had probably been with us since Eve.

And yet *this* time, unlike the others, the women's rebellion would not merely strike and withdraw in lonely volleys or dissipate quickly after one salient issue was solved. This time, whether labeled "women's rights," "women's liberation," or "the women's movement," the battle for justice would sweep the world. We would hear the voices of millions, but, above all, we would hear the voices of a few.

Gloria Steinem. Kate Millett. Germaine Greer. Susan Brownmiller. Betty Friedan. Women who had been affected, in their formative years, by World War II. Women who also had lived through, were still living through, their own crucibles, their own personal versions of what Betty would call "the problem that has no name."

Betty herself—a housewife, born in Peoria, Illinois, who had migrated with her husband and three children to the suburbs of Rockland County, New York. She had been offered a prestigious fellowship that would have launched her career, but, fearing the loss of a conventional married life, she had turned it down. Gloria Steinem, the beautiful young woman from Toledo who wore miniskirts and aviator glasses and was beginning to make a splash in the big city: She had risked her life in an illegal abortion. Kate Millett, the loquacious, struggling artist and college lecturer vilified for her sexual preference. Susan Brownmiller, stung by the assumptions of male superiority in the civil rights movement. Shulamith Firestone, Florynce Kennedy, Ti-Grace Atkinson, the sexy, eloquent Germaine Greer—all of them women who chafed at the restraints, the insults, the denial of their human equality, and, perhaps most of all, of their potential.

It would have happened without these soon-to-be-celebrated women, of course, because the time was right, if only because of the booming post–World War II economy with its passion for home consumption, its pressure on women to maintain their domestic roles.

It would have happened without these particular women because there were so many others—brushfires burning, a grass-roots movement. Even on that wintry day when Betty and her nervy crew entered the Oak Room of the Plaza Hotel, dozens of other women—small, isolated groups across the country—protested as well. At the Polo Lounge in the Beverly Hills Hotel in Los Angeles, at the Retreat in Washington, D.C., at McCarthy's Men's Bar in Syracuse, New York, at Stouffer's Restaurant in Pittsburgh, at McSorley's Men's Bar in downtown Manhattan. By then, women had already been agitating, picketing, demanding, and legislating for several years, selfless labors by unsung heroines, their names barely mentioned outside of their own locales.

What most of the world heard, however, what hit the newspapers as far away as Hong Kong, was:

The Oak Room . . . the Miss America protest . . . the sit-in at the *Ladies' Home Journal.*

The Feminine Mystique . . . The Female Eunuch . . . Against Our Will . . . The Women's Room.

Best-sellers. Their authors talking and talked about on radio and television, in magazines and newspapers, becoming noted feminist oracles in what was, in truth, a "Golden Age of Feminism." Women just like the rest of us and yet, somehow . . . different.

Intelligent and quick-witted, they had all been—as children—avid readers. They were also highly educated, and their expectations for themselves were equally lofty. They were, in short, ambitious, and their sense of self-esteem not easily gained, far from satisfied by a floor well polished or a "helpmate" role well played. They were as well—through either family upbringing or actual dramatic training— verbal, theatrical, naturally given to public expression. Skilled communicators, they were writers and talkers at a time when the media explosion was paramount.

Whatever the direct influences on this women's revolution, whether the youth / civil rights / antiwar movements of the sixties, technology in general, or the birth control pill in particular, among them surely was the powerful communications boom. In 1950 only 4.4 million of the nation's homes had television sets; by 1960, the number had grown to 45 million. Any doubt that skill in front of those ubiquitous cameras could be an instrument of political power and persuasion was dispelled by the Kennedy-Nixon debates, that coup in which a handsome young Catholic captured an audience— and the election—with "charisma" (that sixties word) and skill in communication, which was coming to mean the same thing.

And which, in fact, these ardent feminists possessed as well—some to a dazzling degree.

Corralled as students into the liberal arts, where the ultimate dream was to become a writer, most of them had found their way into some form of journalism, a field not altogether inhospitable to women. Through this connection to the media, they learned how to attract its attention, to maneuver and to manipulate. They learned, in short, to use the media just as the Irish had used politics, the blacks had used sports, the Jews the professions, the Italians construction. And just as the civil rights and antiwar leaders had used the media to convey social demands, so did these feminist oracles speak, not just for themselves, but for *all* women.

And perhaps, given their talents, their outrage, their needs, and their willingness to risk, the women did it better, for across the country and around the world, as we watched and listened, we began to respond. So many of us found ourselves nodding our heads: "Amen." Whispering, sighing: "Right on." "At last."

"You are not alone," their messages told us, and with that the storm broke. The false smiles on pretty faces, the quiet endurance, the deceptively still waters turned to a torrent. This upheaval would leave nothing untouched—not business, art, law, medicine, morals, certainly not love or marriage.

All would be changed forever.

3

SITTING
ON A FORTUNE

Her essential quality is castratedness. She absolutely must be young, her body hairless, her flesh buoyant, and she must not have a sexual organ. No musculature must distort the smoothness of the lines of her body, although she may be painfully slender or warmly cuddly. Her expression must betray no hint of humor, curiosity or intelligence, although it may signify hauteur . . . or smoldering lust . . . or, most commonly, vivacity and idiot happiness. Seeing that the world despoils itself for this creature's benefit, she must be happy; the entire structure would topple if she were not.

—Germaine Greer, *The Female Eunuch*, 1970

On January 29, 1939, bushfires tore across the coastal belt of Australia, from the Great Australian Bight to southern New South Wales. A pall of smoke so thick that it darkened the sun at noon hung over Melbourne, over Mercy Hospital where Margaret May Mary LaFrank Greer labored over the birth of her first child. Heat from the oven-breath wind poured into the room, mingling with the cloying smell of Madonna lilies, and the birth—a high forceps delivery—was so difficult that Peggy Greer slipped a disc during labor. Or so, at least, her daughter Germaine was later told.

Peggy was bedridden in her comfortable suburban flat during much of the following year, according to the family story. She breastfed her new daughter while a nurse saw to her other needs. The war was looming, the Axis powers menacing, and Germaine's father, Eric Reginald Greer, was already housed in army barracks. By September, the German army would attack Poland, and a formal declaration of war would be issued from the British Empire.

In the years to come—"for the duration," as it was called—Peggy, like so many young wives of servicemen, would wait. She would not go back to her work as a model. Instead she would play the role of war wife, entertaining the American soldiers who stopped off in the charmed middle-class oasis of Melbourne en route to the battlefields of the Pacific.

And the Americans, as Germaine would remember it, were thoroughly entertained. That Peggy Greer was some knockout, the soldiers often remarked. Didn't she look a lot like Rita Hayworth, though? With her hair hennaed a glowing auburn and her luscious, toasty tan. Peggy spent hours on the great white beaches of Melbourne, sunning herself amid her admirers, usually taking Germaine along so that the child, too, learned to love the sunshine. What she learned not to love, however, to actively despise, in fact, was what she would describe—when she was much older—as Peggy's flirtatiousness.

For Peggy, in Germaine's memory, "flirted with every man, wore tons of makeup . . . big red lips. All those handsome young air force men made her feel like a million dollars and all she had to do was go to Hollywood."

Eventually, Germaine Greer would analyze flirtatious, manipulative behavior with her own dramatic flourish. She would shock and entrance with her graceful, philosophical account of warped female sexuality, labeling it the performance of a "female eunuch."

But back then, during those war years, the little girl simply watched and waited, with her mother, for the return of the dashing officer whose face smiled out at them from the photograph on the mantelpiece: "Reg" Greer, the high-level intelligence officer who never once came home on leave and whose whereabouts, so much of the time, they could only guess at. They waited as the Germans overran all of Western Europe, bombed London, and stormed across Africa toward

29

Cairo, while Australian troops, attempting to stop them there, took heavy losses at the hands of the Afrika Korps. They waited until the tide turned in favor of the Allied nations, and after the final victory, they waited still longer.

Germaine was almost six years old when word came that her father would finally return. Peggy took her along to meet him at the station, a meeting that would provide Germaine's first memory of her father, of a crowded station, of mother and daughter rushing eagerly through the building, looking for the tall, heroic father, the vigorous, good-looking husband.

"We went up and down that station," Germaine would recall, "peering at everyone who passed by."

The man in their photograph was nowhere to be seen.

After a while, they stepped back from the crowd to make a more careful study. And then Germaine noticed, to her utter confusion, that Peggy was carefully studying one particular man. Not the handsome man in the picture certainly, but an old, bent soldier in a steely-blue army greatcoat.

Now her mother moved toward this strange man, her head tilted to the side like a bird.

"Reg?" Peggy whispered.

The man nodded, tears streaming down his face.

And the little girl watched them, stunned.

Could this be true? Was this old man, this terrible old man with thin hair and missing front teeth, actually her father?

In fact, Reg Greer, his teeth lost to starvation, was returning home after a two-year stay in a hospital. He was suffering, Germaine would learn much later, from severe anxiety neurosis, the aftermath of battle shock and wartime deprivations in Egypt and Malta. He was taking sedatives, and he would need some form of medication for the rest of his life.

"He was hanging on to normal life by a very, very thin thread," Germaine would come to believe. "But I didn't know that then. . . . He never let on because he's English. He never, ever said, 'I'm only just keeping this show on the road. There are some things I can't help you with.'"

In time, however, the former intelligence officer resumed his position as advertising manager of a local newspaper. Germaine, who adored him, was aware only of his reserve and his distance from her.

Eventually, two more children—a girl, Alida Jane, and a boy, Barry

John—were born. The clean, easy, blissful middle-class life of Australia, the life the Allied soldiers had fought so desperately to preserve, resumed. Germaine grew very tall and strong like her father, with high, rounded cheekbones, gray-green eyes, thick chestnut hair. She was verbal, spontaneous, endlessly curious . . . and she did not get on well with her mother.

Peggy, in the racy, impudent language Germaine would eventually weave through her erudition, was "mean as cat's piss."

Germaine would remember beatings. Not frequent, just once or twice a year, but "passionate . . . and for no good reason. I wasn't a bad child!"

One day, for example, when Germaine was still small, no more than six, she was upstairs in the playroom with her friend John when the two children hit upon a plan to go into the closet and examine things. To be specific, "his dick, his prick, his cock . . . in the cupboard," the grown-up Germaine would deadpan.

Unfortunately, Peggy discovered the culprits and lost her temper.

"I got beaten half to death then," Germaine would remember. "With a copper stick, the stick that's used for pulling up boiling laundry from the copper pot. The steel ferrule had broken off and left this little jagged point. And sometimes, not quite by accident, I got ploughed with the point."

Peggy didn't strike Germaine often, but when she did, Germaine thought, she aimed for the face. . . .

"And you can't hit me now, even in fun, because I have a completely uncontrollable response. I just burst into tears. Even if we're just playing a game and somebody fillips me, especially in the face. I can't bear it; I just can't bear it. I suddenly feel utterly tiny and crushed and humiliated."

Her mother simply didn't like her, the child concluded. If she lost a ball or a coloring book, Peggy would never allow her to have another. That was that. And so her imagination began to paint possibilities. Perhaps she was not really her mother's child. She didn't feel like Peggy's child.

"I thought about the children who did, obviously, not only love their mothers, but actually like them, hang out with them. . . . I thought they were faking. I thought it was a thing you did for outsiders. You pretended to be good chums."

Peggy was not a "chum," and it would never do for Germaine to tell her mother about her lovely afternoons in the beachfront park.

Not that there was anything much to tell. To Germaine, those pleasant moments signified nothing more than an exchange of warmth and friendship.

"Come here, little girl," the old men in the park would say. Then they'd unzip their flies.

"Oh, that's cute," thought the youngster, and because they asked her, she'd hold on. The old men's organs never got hard; they just lay there "like warm slugs," as Germaine would remember it. She was eighteen years old before she realized that the male organ would stiffen to perform sexual intercourse.

Nor did relations with her mother improve as Germaine grew older. Peggy's dramatic appearance and behavior ("flamboyant and outrageous," in her daughter's view) embarrassed her, and she would have preferred a different sort of mother entirely.

The mother she dreamed of, the sort of woman the world-renowned feminist Germaine Greer would still admire in later years, appeared in her life, quite by accident, when she was fifteen.

In 1954, a reluctant Germaine was sent by train to a farm miles from Melbourne, to recover from a bout of food poisoning. The farm, which belonged to a family with eight children, was in a flatlands, a wheat-growing area on the edge of Victoria, New South Wales, on the Murray River, and immediately upon her arrival Germaine found it easily as grim as she had suspected it would be. Not a single tree in sight, no shady streets, no cozy corner shops, no busy city social life. It all looked, to her adolescent eyes, "terrible." She was to stay with the family in their big white clapboard house and—even worse—share a room with one of the daughters, "a great big, sleepy-eyed farm girl," she would recall, named Ann.

Germaine's first night at the farm was indeed a shock. Barely asleep in her strange new bed, she was jolted awake by a loud thumping within inches of her head. Whatever it was, she realized, was actually inside the wall of the bedroom!

"Oh, it's only possums," soothed her roommate as Germaine cowered in her bed, terrified.

The farm, a large property of 52,000 acres, was run by Ann's three big brothers and, promptly the next morning, they informed Germaine of her duties. She was to shoot galahs and dig ditches with Ann and her brothers, and, furthermore, she was to cook their breakfast. To do this, she was to put twelve eggs in an enormous iron frying pan "so heavy," Germaine would remember, "I couldn't even lift it."

She was directed to put the brothers' socks in the oven to warm because the mornings were cold, and she was also supposed to help pull in the cows and milk them.

That first morning, Germaine settled on a stool beside one of the cows and struggled with the rough teats for hours, till her hands ached. For all her pulling and squeezing, only a small stream of the thick yellowish stuff trickled into the pail.

Of course, it was not much better the next day or the day after that, but gradually the warm, creamy bubbles began to fill the pails, the twelve eggs came cracking into the pan without a sliver of shell. The city-bred girl was beginning to feel, well, almost *capable,* when one day, as she was sweeping the veranda, she suddenly froze in terror. Directly in front of her was an enormous, poisonous funnelweb spider.

"I'd never seen one before . . . this great gray spider who was getting up on his back legs ready to jump at me."

"Just kill it!" came a cry from the ubiquitous Ann.

Germaine's arms went weak. She swung the broom with a wobbly *thonk,* missing the spider, the broom landing useless as a dry spray of wheat.

"Oh, for Crissakes," Ann muttered.

Calmly, the husky girl ambled toward the insect, placed one substantial foot on its back, and just stood there. Within seconds, she removed her foot, and there lay the monster, dead on the wooden floor.

It was days before Germaine's flush of shame subsided to the point where she could give the whole incident sober thought. There was a lesson to be learned here, after all, perhaps even a guide for female deportment.

"Why make a fuss?" was the gist of it. "No one is going to give you any prizes for being girlish."

And indeed, by the close of her stay at the flatland farm, Germaine's ease with the world of nature and physical labor had reached new heights, rivaled only by her enormous respect for the farm women, for their vigor and strong sense of integrity, their generosity, for what she had come to regard as an unadorned love of family.

"You know, Dad," she told her father when she returned home, "I just met a completely different sort of women. They're terrific. They're not mischievous. They wouldn't know what all this intrigue and buggering people up and making trouble is all about."

Completely different, she meant, from her mother.

She had found new heroines, new inspiration. The farm women, in her view, were authentic; they communicated with people. And she was certain, though she didn't tell her father this, that these women, though dignified and reserved, had strong, even torrential sexual desires. The fuss of flirtation and capitulating to a man was nowhere in their repertoire, but, she was sure, if a man reached them, "touched the button," they would respond with a deep and profound sexuality.

In contrast, Germaine began to doubt that her mother had sexual desires at all. Peggy's flirtatiousness, she concluded, was a put-on. She saw Peggy as "a glamour puss" who deployed her sexuality in a cold and calculating way—never forgetting it, always "using" it. Years later, she would point to what she regarded as a contradiction between Peggy's provocative clothing and her complaints about men touching her.

"My mother used to say," Germaine would recall, "that when men walked along the street, they swung their hands so that they hit her in the pussy."

By the eighties, Germaine would fit her picture of Peggy into a social context: "Mother was a gorgeous model before the war and then a bobby soxer. She really thought she was Zelda Fitzgerald and Daddy was Scott Fitzgerald and that they were going to dance on ocean liners and play Randolph Hearst and all that. She didn't have a career, and being a mother meant nothing to her; the family meant nothing. She had nothing to build and nothing to make, no idea of what role a woman might play.

"Then suddenly it was all over. There she was with a squalling brat. Women like her had big ideas about what they might do with their lives. They thought they were sitting on a fortune. But they didn't know how to regulate the one thing that was essential, which was their fertility."

Sex and fertility. They were subjects Germaine would explore in great depth in the years ahead.

Meanwhile, the teenager, who was growing into a noticeable beauty, began to collect new models of womanhood. A movie star heroine, Anna Magnani. And, above all, the nuns at the Star of the Sea Convent, in Gardenvale, Victoria, outside Melbourne, where, for several years, Germaine was at school.

Many women writers, Simone de Beauvoir and Mary McCarthy

among them, would recall their parochial school days as cool inter-
ludes of restriction. For Germaine, they were just the opposite. Somehow, the convent sisters managed to impress her with the possibility
of another way of life.

"Not that it had to be *theirs*," she would remember, "following *their*
rules." Just that there *was* another way.

In part, what Germaine observed was a simple sense of community,
a particular kind of sisterhood. The nuns were women alone, living
in a female society. They were committed to their teaching and had
no husbands or children on their minds. Not unlike the farm women
Germaine had taken to her heart, the sisters worked together; they
were intelligent and respectful of one another.

Furthermore, to the inquisitive, impressionable Germaine, these
dedicated women possessed a wonderful arrogance—the holy arrogance of the children of God.

"The nuns were," she would come to conclude, "too *big* and too
special to be some man's menial. Certain women could only be satisfied with God Himself!"

And there at the Star of the Sea Convent, the tall, strong-boned,
adventurous young woman whose heavy dark hair flashed reddish in
the Australian sunlight, and whose green eyes seemed so openly
searching, began to construct a new and wondrous idea.

If she could only become a great artist, or a great singer, or a great
something, she would never have to become one man's woman, one
man's concubine. There would surely be sacrifices, of course. Perhaps
great ones. The sisters, after all, made many. But if she *really wanted
to*, she, Germaine, could be many men's woman.

"I could have *lovers in every town!*"

And so it happened that the celibate nuns in the Star of the Sea
Convent became Germaine's guides to a more emancipated way of
life.

The sisters understood her in a way, she was certain, her mother
never had.

"They knew that I was easily ruled by love, that my naughtiness
was mere ebullience," Germaine would remember, and that, though
the road might be bumpy, they'd be proud of her in the end. They
encouraged their irrepressible charge, and when the class lumbered
too slowly for her imaginative mind, they offered her something else
to do. Something to draw, for instance.

One of these little pictures, in fact—a piece of calico adorned with poster paint—the nuns would wisely save. Many years later, the Star of the Sea Convent would honor that significant treasure as the altarpiece for their Centenary High Mass. Meanwhile, the entire atmosphere offered the support Germaine did not sense from her mother, a woman who, in her daughter's eyes, "had no respect for truth, logic, dignity or grace or consistency," but instead "a completely improvised sort of intellectual system."

Many years after she had made her final escape, Germaine would still be at odds with Peggy and would still insist: "It's all battle in there . . . terrible din of rubbish. There's no talking to her. She does not even obey the simplest conventions of communication. You think you're talking about something, and she's suddenly talking about something else. And you no sooner think maybe you've cottoned on to that one, and she's done it again. There's a sheet of glass. The whole logical order of the universe is being attacked. The whole thing's going to pieces. I feel like screaming. I have nothing to say to her because she can make me so crazy. Within seconds I feel desperate."

Germaine was seventeen years old when she ran away from home.

It was the summer after she was graduated from the convent. She had begun classes at the University of Melbourne; she was living at home and the term had been difficult. Since the family's income level excluded Germaine from most scholarships, and since, as she would still angrily note years later, "Peggy refused to pay for my schooling," she had taken a teachers college grant, which offered a small allowance. Out of that—and not without resentment—she paid her mother a small sum for room and board.

One day, while reading a paper aloud in class, Germaine began to hear noises in her head, "a tolling of bells," as she would put it, so loud that she was unable to continue. The attending physician at Melbourne Hospital across the street diagnosed "nervous exhaustion" and prescribed a sedative. He phoned her parents, Germaine would recall, to report that he could not discover what was wrong with the girl, and to suggest that "you just give her a moment's peace. Let her take her medication and let her rest."

A friend drove her home after the doctor's examination but, en route, Germaine began to question the prescription. She was determined to get a "first" in her exams, which she couldn't very well accomplish befuddled with sedatives.

"I've lost my battle," she worried. "I've lost control of myself." She was now, in her view, "in the hands of the quacks and drugs and everything else."

"This isn't going to work, is it? These bloody pills and all," she announced to her friend, and threw the pills out the window, watched as they scattered over the road. Then, in an early instance of what would prove to be outstanding academic achievement, Germaine went on, in the following weeks, to excel in her exams.

"But I still felt unsteady," she would remember, and she was determined not to take a job that summer, which seemed to irritate Peggy even further.

One day that summer, as Germaine would tell it, she opened the refrigerator and reached for a glass of milk.

"Leave that alone. That's for my children," Peggy snapped. And at that, the wounded, furious seventeen-year-old made her move. Into her school briefcase went the essential items—a hairbrush, a sample bottle of Schiaparelli perfume, a copy of Ovid's *Metamorphosis*. No time for clothes, but the thought that what she was wearing that moment was all she would have for the days ahead only added to her exhilaration.

"I sat on Mentone Railway Station waiting for the train, and I thought, 'Someone's going to appear, that mad McGarra is going to appear saying *Come home! Where do you think you're going?*' . . . and then the train came. . . . It was just as if the sky had shot up about a million miles. It was the most wonderful feeling! . . . I thought: 'I don't have to sleep at home. I never have to go home!' "

The fantasy of running away forever sustained Germaine through a month at an off-campus house not far from the university. That fantasy and the scenario that played in her head:

"Reg: Why did Germaine leave?

"Peggy: Oh, I don't know.

"Reg: Well, she wouldn't leave for nothing would she?

"Peggy: Well, just because I wouldn't let her eat anything. I mean, where's my rent?"

It was a delicious—if imaginary—squaring of accounts. But the housing Germaine found provided no supervision; she was still underage, and the whole adventure was against school rules. A few days before the opening of the new term, she trundled home with her heart in her mouth. As she would remember that moment, Peggy was out back in the garden. Germaine heard the door downstairs open and her mother's voice:

"Who let all the flies in?"
And then: "Oh, it's you. You're home."

Well into the eighties, Germaine would remember that story angrily and there would be implicit blame in her confession: " I guess, at bottom, I've always thought I was unlovable."

Back then, however, since her mother refused to pay for her schooling, she continued to piece together scholarships, to work hard at her studies, and, in fact, far from minding that labor, to thrive on it.

One day, she was sure, she would leave for good. She thought about that often, especially when she stood at Port Melbourne, as she had since she was twelve years old, gazing out at the horizon, her long, dark hair tossing in the wind . . . watching the ships sail off to foreign ports.

One day, she knew, she would have an entirely different life. One day, she would leave the country.

4

BEHIND
HER EYES

If men could menstruate, abortion would be a sacrament.

—Gloria Steinem, early 1970s

From the day the United States entered the war—on December 7, 1941, when the Japanese attacked Pearl Harbor—the headlines in America were relentless. Bataan, Tunisia, Guadalcanal, Anzio, Iwo Jima, the Marshall Islands. Food prices doubled. The Japanese were reported to be using poison gas. The federal government lowered the draft age to eighteen. The covers of *Life* and *Time* carried photographs of generals. The Allies invaded Italy and, in 1944, France. D-Day.

The best relief was entertainment, both overseas, where stars like Bob Hope traveled to cheer up the troops, and at home, where the war years were also the era of the big bands, Glenn Miller, Tommy Dorsey, Benny Goodman, and swing. Frank Sinatra and Bing Crosby, who sang with these full, sweet orchestras, were called "crooners" or "boy singers." Peggy Lee, Frances Langford, and Dinah Shore were the "girl singers." In spite of skintight dresses, bright red lipstick, lots of curls, pompadours, and snoods, there was, apparently, a crying need to distinguish between the sexes. In the movies, Betty Grable peeked back girlishly over her shoulder to become the world's number one pinup, and Paulette Goddard, Dorothy Lamour, and Veronica

Lake (with long blond hair spilling over one eye) summed up wartime fashions as they sang "A sweater, a sarong, and a peek-a-boo bang" in a Paramount movie called *Star Spangled Rhythm*.

In time, the little girl who, toward the close of those wartime years, lived in a dilapidated two-family house in a working-class section of East Toledo, Ohio, would become, in her own way, as great a star, as well known to the American public (and much of the world), as any of these performers. The day would come when Gloria Steinem's entrance at a New York opening—in a dazzling, wide-shouldered white coat and a long cascade of shimmering blond hair—would cause a moment's intake of breath not unlike the arrival of one of the grand stars of the forties; when she would be welcomed into the homes of the rich and mighty; when, as a famous and glamorous feminist, a great gala in the grand ballroom of the Waldorf-Astoria would be thrown in her honor and a silvery "birthday book" would carry an inscription from Alice Walker, a protégée of editor Steinem and a Pulitzer prize–winning author: "Surely the earth can be saved for Gloria."

Like the luminous halos of those singers and actresses, the Gloria star would entertain, charm, and seduce. Unlike them, it would transform minds. At a time of drastic social upheaval, it would flash a kaleidoscope of messages, colored by the outcries of many women, tinctured and toned by Gloria's own past.

She was in her early teens in the forties, which were fine days for show business. The stars, though far fewer than there would be after the advent of television, were revered by the press. The great magazines—*Saturday Evening Post, Collier's, Life*—never deigned to reveal the seamy side of life in Hollywood. Even fan magazines hid any whiff of scandal behind photo layouts of stars and their "perfect" families at play. If Joan Crawford was mistreating her children, America was worshipfully unaware of it. Hardly anyone knew anything *real* about the stars, any more than they knew that the president of their country was crippled.

To Gloria's father, the sweet, sentimental, fun-loving Leo Steinem, the world of show business was the just-over-the-horizon pot of gold. His substantial Jewish family had neglected, somehow, to imprint any sobering sense of the realities of life, and the route to success was never, to his mind, a career.

"My father had two points of pride," Gloria would one day quip. "He never wore a hat and never had a job."

Though terribly clever with words—Leo was an inveterate punster and had been editor of his school paper at the University of Toledo— he had never seen fit to finish his studies. Instead, he had schemes. Making it big, fast and easy.

Show biz. That was the ticket!

Leo had met his wife, the tall, auburn-haired Ruth Nuneviller, at the local university. Ruth was as liquid tongued and witty as Leo, though she came from an entirely different background, a modest French Huguenot family, many of them schoolteachers, her own father a locomotive engineer, unable to afford Ruth's final years at Oberlin College. The "mixed marriage" enraged both sides, with the important exception of Leo's mother, Pauline. Nonetheless, the elder Steinems bought the newlyweds a fine house, and in the comfortable early days before the Depression, Leo's father always covered his imaginative, promotional-minded son's bad debts. Their first child, Susanne, was born in 1925, and, for a while, Ruth kept her job as society reporter and editor at one of the Toledo newspapers. "Mama Einie," as Susanne called her grandmother Steinem, took care of the child so Ruth could work.

In the 1970s, when such miracles as feminist scholars would come to pass, one of them would send a monograph on Pauline Steinem to Gloria's office in New York. Pauline had been, as it turned out, not only an effective feminist who addressed Congress on behalf of the women's vote, but she was also the first female member of a school board in Ohio and had helped to found the first vocational high school in that state. Deeply involved in civic and world affairs, during the war she sent money—more money than the Steinem family deemed appropriate, in fact—to rescue European relatives from Hitler's death grip.

Pauline Steinem was, by all accounts, including that of her granddaughter Susanne, a remarkable woman, a pioneer whom most any mid-century feminist might proudly claim as an ancestor.

Gloria, however, would seldom mention her grandmother, nor would she respond to the feminist monograph on Pauline with any sense of filial or religious ties.

"I don't believe in either religion," she would say. "When I'm around Jews who feel there's something good about being exclusively Jewish, I emphasize the non-Jewish side of the family. When I'm around Protestants who think there's something good about being Protestant, then I emphasize the Jewish side."

Nor would she "feel that connected to family."

The Steinem family, Gloria would offer by way of explanation, had not emphasized Pauline's nonconformist public actions. Instead they had extolled her kosher table, her ability to "cook all these meals for her four antifeminist sons. And all these things my mother admired very much. She was presented with what she must have thought of as a vision of superwoman. And she had too many inadequacies already. It just didn't really help."

It didn't help, Gloria meant, to prevent the disintegration that loomed for her mother.

"Whither thou goest I shall go," Ruth would say in regard to her much-admired mother-in-law, but where Pauline went, Ruth somehow would not be able to follow.

Still, in the beginning at least, the young Steinems' marriage must have seemed jolly enough. Leo and Ruth were so determined to enjoy life that they set off for motels in California or Florida whenever Ohio's winter wind began to whistle round the corners of the house. (The Steinems did their own thing, Ruth would one day convince a reporter, before anyone knew what that meant.) Summers were spent at a resort in Clarklake, Michigan, which Leo had bought as a surefire show biz center, big bands and all. Susanne, when she wasn't off on one of those trips, went to an exclusive private school.

It was a sunshine house of cards, destined to collapse. By 1930, both the country and Ruth were in trouble. Ruth had, or so she believed, the excessively rapid heartbeat known as tachycardia. Much later, when Susanne discovered that her mother had diagnosed her disorder herself, from a medical column, she surmised that Ruth's problem may have been, even then, psychological. Financially squeezed by the crash (though not destitute—Leo had inherited some property upon his father's death), they soon bought a small, silver-colored vacation trailer for those Christmas to April escapes. Eventually they sold their house and moved permanently to the Michigan resort.

It was here that Ruth suffered her first "nervous breakdown."

Susanne was five years old when her mother entered the sanatorium, where a physician who was a fraternity brother of Leo's prescribed a compound of chloral hydrate and potassium bromide, also known as "knockout drops." How much of the torment Ruth suffered in later years was caused by this drug—"Doc Howard's medicine," as Ruth would call it—would be forever a matter of speculation.

For a long time, though, in spite of that short stay in the sanatorium, the depth of Ruth's malady remained hidden. Susanne would remember, from those earliest days, before Gloria was born, a mother both competent and clever, a tennis court built by the side of the house, the crowds that flocked to the resort to listen and dance to the famous bands. She was nine years old on March 25, 1934, when Gloria, the sister she had wished and prayed for, arrived.

The child was adorable and adored. Whatever their financial difficulties—always more distressing to Ruth than to Leo—Gloria was supplied with ballet and piano lessons, an accordion, puppies, and, when she developed a passion for horses, even one of her own, with a western saddle. ("They bought him for seventy-five dollars," Gloria would remember fondly. "His name was Rusty.")

And, through the thirties, the family continued to travel, Susanne transferring from high school to high school, Gloria, for all practical purposes, hardly attending school at all. Neither child spent one full year in a classroom. Gloria absorbed a facility for language from her sharply verbal parents and learned to read, as she would tell a reporter years later, "from candy wrappers and Burma Shave signs."

"I learned to detect bill collectors at a very early age," she would remember. "My father would send me to the door and what's a guy going to do with a three-year-old kid?"

If a truant officer came knocking, which happened occasionally, Ruth could always brandish her teacher's certificate. Why bother with school? Gloria certainly didn't need inoculations or vaccinations, according to Ruth's special reasoning, if everyone else had them. All Gloria needed (this from Leo's point of view) was to marry a rich man.

As he himself once was and would be again, surely.

"I fell in love with instability," Gloria would recall. "I always thought that the worst thing would be to know what was going to happen next year. Because if you didn't know, it could be wonderful!"

Probably, real soon, Leo would invent a new orange drink that would sweep the country. Maybe he'd produce a dance show. Anything was possible.

To Gloria, Leo was wonderful fun, a grand, lovable father—like a kid himself, as ready to sneak out and catch a movie as she was. A big man, about six feet tall, with a prominent V, a sort of widow's peak, at his forehead, Leo was handsome—large, aquiline nose, long, tapered fingers (which Gloria inherited)—but, like most members of the Steinem family, he had a weight problem. He neither smoked nor drank, but food was another matter. Leo just loved to eat, and he weighed, at one time, three hundred pounds.

In short, Gloria's naive, warmhearted father was hooked. On food and on dreams.

Susanne, too, would eventually weigh over three hundred pounds, although, with Gloria's ministrations and the help of a diet center, she would lose more than one hundred of them. "My sister always kind of blamed my father," Gloria would recall, "because he took care of her while my mother was in the hospital, and they went out and ate ice cream and all." And Gloria herself would become a scrupulous dieter, sometimes insisting on nothing but hot water and lemon for both breakfast and lunch, keeping practically nothing in her refrigerator, but binging on Sara Lee cakes.

"There's no stopping for me," she would confess years later. "It's exactly the same as being an alcoholic, so it's serious business. If I have a little sugar, then I just binge. It's very hard."

Never "fat," in spite of her claims to the contrary, by the mid-seventies Gloria would become so stylishly thin that reporters would describe her as a "compulsive noneater."

As a child, though, she was healthily rounded, her pudgy cheeks attracting more than their share of benign pinches. She was dark-haired, but otherwise not altogether unlike America's sweetheart, the pretty, golden-tressed, cute-as-a-button Shirley Temple. And, in fact, a family story points out a certain connection.

"According to my mother," Gloria would recall, "I was once looking at a magazine with an article about Shirley Temple and, suddenly, I threw the magazine away and burst into tears. My mother asked why and I told her it was because I wanted to *be* Shirley Temple," who was, in Gloria's view, "spunky and usually played a part where she was a waif or orphan or had to look after her father."

During the war years, Gloria, too, began performing, playing small parts in civic operettas and plays around Toledo, tap dancing for a local men's club, and, eventually, entering the popular "Ted Mack's Amateur Hour" contest. By that time, Susanne was attending Smith College, and she would remember spending a good part of one summer vacation driving back and forth sixty miles every night to deliver little Gloria for one or another local performance.

By then, however, Leo's resort had fallen victim to wartime gas rationing and his antique trading, once something of a hobby, had become essential to the family income. The Steinems were able to manage Susanne's tuition at Smith College, but Leo's charm was now heavily invested in cajoling the officers at various loan companies, taking Gloria along, sometimes, to wait patiently in the bland outer offices while Leo worked his wiles. Traveling was now a necessity as, ever cheerful, Leo plied his new trade as an itinerant antiques dealer, singing war songs as he drove, making more plans. How about a movie? Maybe he'd cut a record. . . .

Eventually, though, the flimsy net of this peripatetic family began to shred. There were quarrels and Ruth, always excruciatingly anxious about money, given to saving her pennies in a cookie jar and pridefully paying her bills on time, grew more and more distraught. She was furious when she found that Leo, without consulting her, had mortgaged the pier at the lake for one of his promotional deals, and she could be devastating with her barbs.

And so, in 1945, Ruth and Leo divorced. Although America's divorce rate was on the rise (only to drop again in the conventional fifties), such a breakup was far from the social norm. By then, though, Ruth was an awful field of psychic devastation. Leo could not, he explained, handle both Ruth and the exigencies of making a living, and the always amenable Gloria understood, never—consciously— blaming him for leaving. After a year in a rented house in Amherst, Massachusetts, seven miles from Susanne's college, Ruth and Gloria moved back to East Toledo, to 747 Woodville, a rundown house Ruth's family had owned. Gloria was deemed able to care for the disturbed Ruth.

And so began what Ruth would call—though refuse to discuss— the "bad years in Toledo." For Gloria, they were the tender years— from ages eleven to sixteen—the ones she would focus on whenever she discussed or wrote about her childhood. Suddenly, she was the sole caretaker of her painfully, confusingly ill mother.

The poverty was ugly, and years later, after Gloria had catapulted to stardom as one of New York's "beautiful people," she would talk about the rats, about waking up at night and pulling her toes in under the covers in fear, about actually being bitten by one of them.

Not everyone quite believed her. Not everyone could reconcile this smoothly manicured, sophisticated young woman with the rough slum origins she described. And Ruth, by then at least partly recovered, insisted that the house in East Toledo was certainly no slum. The rats, she told a reporter, came from an old garage on the property that had been demolished. The story had gotten exaggerated in the telling.

But Lillian Barnes Borton, who as a teenager had lived downstairs in the same house, remembered the rats. She remembered a house in terrible shape and, in fact, overrun with them. Rats in the beds at night, in the kitchen range, the sink cabinet, once even jumping up on the dinner table. Lillian remembered the rats biting Gloria, and she remembered Ruth crying when it happened.

In 1983, after Ruth died, Gloria would write, in the best-selling *Outrageous Acts and Everyday Rebellions,* a moving tribute to her mother. "Ruth's Song" is laced with a gentle shower of detail, of heartbreaking incidents. Ruth, in this portrait, is frightened, abstracted, terribly sad, and if, as some critics suggested, she is not altogether convincing, she is, certainly, utterly pitiable, "an invalid who lay in bed with eyes closed and lips moving in occasional response to voices only she could hear."

Terrified, Ruth spends most of her days in bed, unable to function even to the point of cleaning the house, consumed with loving protectiveness and fear.

And Gloria tries to assuage those fears. "Has your sister been killed in a car crash?" Ruth asks. "Are there German soldiers outside?"

Once she loses track of the time her daughter is due home and sends the police, sirens blaring, to Gloria's after-school job—to the child's pained embarrassment. Gloria yells at her and Ruth answers pitifully, "I'm sorry, I'm sorry."

Once, Ruth thrusts her arm through a window, thinking to protect them both from the evil outside. And once, too, Gloria takes her to a doctor who recommends a state hospital. Afraid that her mother would be mistreated there, Gloria brings Ruth back home to their shabby apartment.

But Ruth apparently adored her daughter, for Lillian saw love shining from the mother's eyes whenever she looked at Gloria. Ruth never raised her voice to her child. "Brought her up," Lillian would remember with admiration, "like a little lady princess."

Yet there, Lillian thought, Ruth's beneficence ended. To Lillian, Ruth seemed to be two separate people—one to Gloria and one to everyone else.

"Ruth was spooky, frightening to look at," in Lillian's recollection.

"She was a tall, masculine-looking woman with raw bones like a hillbilly, big knuckles, elbows, wrists. She usually kept her sort of reddish hair pulled back in a braid. She never wore anything but a cotton housedress that should have been a rag ages ago and a pair of felt slippers. She always scowled. I never once saw her smile. And she had such an evil look on her face all the time, I thought she was a witch. She would stand up on the porch upstairs and scream and curse at the kids who came in the yard . . . no matter who was around. And in those days, ladies didn't curse! I was scared to death of her. All the kids in the neighborhood were scared."

Ruth had "a big, black, nasty chow dog," according to Lillian. "And she wouldn't take him outside. Down at the bottom of their front stairs, in the vestibule just outside my mother's bedroom . . . Well, this is where Ruth would bring her chow dog instead of taking him for a walk like she should have. Then about once a week or once every two weeks, she would put on a yellow slicker and a rain hat and knee-high rubber boots, get a shovel and a broom and a wheelbarrow, and clean out that front entrance and put it in the yard."

The place, Lillian would recall, smelled awful, but given her fireman father's salary, Lillian's family couldn't manage a move for a couple of years. So they endured.

In future years, as one of the best-known feminists in the country, a "transformational leader," as author Gail Sheehy would call her, Gloria would stir millions with her inspirational speeches. And she would also achieve what few leaders can muster: a close following of women and men whose affection and loyalty were unshakable. "Anyone who dislikes Gloria," her friend the feminist Letty Cottin Pogrebin would say, "has to be truly, seriously ill."

Yet not one of these co-workers (or, in some cases, ex-boyfriends) could be a more devoted admirer of Gloria Steinem than the little girl who lived downstairs in East Toledo.

To Lillian, who, in the years to come, would tenaciously follow Gloria's accomplishments in the newspapers and on television, the beautiful "little lady princess" upstairs was her heroine, her idol, her own version of a star—not like Shirley Temple, by then, but, in Lillian's memory, "like Elvis Presley."

Just a few months younger than Gloria, Lillian was awed by Gloria's smashing clothes—especially the tartan-plaid pleated skirts with fringe down the front, held smartly in place by an oversized safety pin, especially her spanking-clean white blouses and blazers. Gloria always looked so pretty, so perfectly poised, and always, thought Lillian, "carried herself like a lady."

Though both girls were barely twelve when they met, about fourteen when Lillian finally moved away, Lillian would be utterly convinced that her little friend who was in such command of herself was "born thirty-five years old." Gloria never played Red Rover with the other kids, never got all dirty, never ever ran around barefoot. She was always sweet and kind, always reading books. "She wasn't a kid or a girl like my sister and me. She was a lady." Unlike Ruth, who, according to Lillian, was less the gently pathetic creature Gloria would describe than seriously disruptive, often "plowing in our door without knocking, letting us know that it was *her* house.

"Once when my mother and father had company, we suddenly heard a great *bang, bang, bang* down the back stairs. When we went to look, there was Ruth at the top of the stairs. She had thrown a bowling ball down. And then when that didn't get enough attention, she threw herself down, slamming into the walls, getting all banged up and scraped. 'Are you all right?' my mother asked. But Ruth didn't say a word. Just marched back upstairs.

"Once we were all listening to a suspense play on our big floor-model Zenith radio. Ruth marched in and snapped it off. 'I don't like that program,' she said. My father turned it back on and it went back and forth like that. On. Off. On. Off. Finally, my father reached out his arm to Ruth and said: 'You'd better not do that again, Ruth.' Then she got scared and went back upstairs.

"Once my mother was dressed to go out and sitting in front of her mirror, putting on makeup. Suddenly my sister yelled, 'Mom, look what Mrs. Steinem is doing!' We looked over and Ruth was painting our windows over with black paint. She said that if my mother was going to display herself to the neighbors, she was going to cover the windows. But my mother was fully dressed!

"And once, my mother had a miscarriage and she had to stay in bed. She was told to take a spoonful of mineral oil and she had this big jug of it standing on the bureau. Ruth walked in and asked, 'What's that for?' My mom told her and then Ruth said, 'Oh, in that case, you want to take it this way,' and she proceeded to pick up that bottle and chugalug. Nearly the whole quart!

"We laughed because, after a while, the things Ruth did got to be kind of funny."

Few people, in Lillian's memory, ever came to visit Ruth and Gloria. Lillian never saw Susanne, who did, in fact, return occasionally. Like Leo, though, Susanne was sure that if she remained in that house in Toledo, her chances of surviving in the business world—where, by now, she was training to be a gemologist—would have been nil.

And so the mother became the child and the child tried to become what no child can ever be—the mother. Gloria brought the meals, such as they were, and never, in Lillian's recollection, showed any anger. She kept her sense of humor, responding with a beautiful, wide smile whenever someone made a joke, and deeply impressing Lillian, who would have given just about anything to look and talk and act just like her idol. (Once, Gloria wore a black patch over her eye. So dramatic! So dignified! Lillian gave hours of consideration to what she could do to her own eye so that she might wear a patch, too.)

Almost every day for more than two years, the two girls walked to school together but, to Lillian's great disappointment, Gloria always went directly inside after school with her books, and never played in the yard with the rest of the kids. Lillian longed to get close to her heroine and she would ask Gloria questions. Why, for instance, Ruth was . . . well, why she was the way she was.

"My mother is sick," Gloria would answer softly. Or, "My mother has a problem." If Lillian pressed, Gloria would just look at her and then turn her head, letting her friend know, without a word, that she had gone too far.

Once Lillian asked about the divorce and Gloria said that her father didn't like her mother. That was all.

"I could never get behind her eyes," Lillian would remember. "She was different from anybody else I ever knew. With Gloria, you knew when you had said too much. When she decided to shut up, that was it. She'd turn the switch off. I kept trying but never got any further. I knew that if I went too far, Gloria would tell me to go to hell."

And, in the years to come, Gloria would confound reporters as well, even friends, who tried to "get behind her eyes." Always gracious, generous, and apparently honest with the press (for by then she would be press herself), perhaps, some interviewers came to feel, this was truly all there was. If her answers were glib—which they sometimes would be—or contradictory, or elliptical, perhaps it was because, as even her friend Letty would admit, Gloria would "never peel the onion."

But Gloria would put it this way: "I have trouble expressing anger."

Or, on another occasion: "I could never quite understand the Freudian tradition of blaming one's parents. Intellectually, I understand it. Emotionally, I don't. When people were doing essentially the best that they could, I find it hard to get angry at them."

Perhaps, as Lillian believed, "Gloria just didn't want anyone to know what Ruth was like." Or perhaps, Gloria didn't quite want to know herself, for, as she would write in "Ruth's Song," "My ultimate protection was this: 'I was just passing through, a guest in the house.'"

And so the protective shell was already in place, the psychological detachment that would, in time, free Gloria to act in the world, to translate personal problems into social causality, and perhaps, somehow, to dissolve them entirely.

"I sometimes imagined that I had been adopted and that my real parents would find me," she would write, quickly adding, typically, a line that blanched the personal agony by translating it into global terms, into the reductive notion that she was no different from anyone else: "a fantasy I've since discovered is common. (If children wrote more and grown-ups less, being adopted might be seen not only as a fear but also a hope.)"

The causes Gloria would describe in this memoir—the reasons Ruth was the way she was—are not in any way personal, or even psychological. They are the social problems that would, in fact, ignite the great women's rebellion of the sixties and seventies. Ruth was forced to leave the newspaper job she loved; she was isolated and lonely at the resort; she feared the stigma of divorce and the selfishness implicit in any notion of pursuing her career. And, given the evil-smelling "Doc Howard's medicine," she was among the "pioneers of modern tranquillizers."

It was because of these forces, Gloria would write, that Ruth would be incarcerated in a mental hospital with the diagnosis of "anxiety neurosis" with spells of agoraphobia. "Her spirit had been broken." When asked about her mother's "mental illness," she would answer: "My mother was not mentally ill. She was defeated by a biased world . . . Her fate was not uncommon for women."

By then, too, Gloria would have cheered on thousands of women with such slogans as:

"We have become the men we wanted to marry."

"A woman needs a man like a fish needs a bicycle."

And if, as one mulled over these lively, creative notions in the dark of the night, the logic seemed a bit strained, it mattered little. Those verbal shocks to the system, these wake-up alarms, would be as welcome as Gloria's rhetorical method for dealing with a biased world—the trick of simply reversing the genders:

"In fact," she would say in regard to her mother, "it's so usual for women that we almost have to consider how a man would respond to it to understand how unjust it is. What if a man had his name and identity taken away from him—the work that he loved the most, all of his friends, and had to live in isolation? Naturally he would be depressed and perhaps enter a fantasy world by way of escape, which is what my mother did."

As for her own youthful fantasies of escape during "those awful years": "I was trying to tap-dance my way out of Toledo."

And though Gloria would remember a childhood resistance to performing, an "attack of the shies," Lillian would recall her friend's serious preparation for a show biz career. The Bortons would often hear Gloria practicing her tap dancing and playing the accordion upstairs. The racket was deafening because, Lillian would recall, there were no carpets in the Steinem apartment or, for that matter, any furniture, except for a rocking chair and a spinet piano in the living room. In Gloria's bedroom, just a mattress and box spring on the floor and a wooden packing crate for her clothes.

Sometimes, Lillian would yell upstairs to Gloria:

"What are you doing? Why all the noise?"

"I'm practicing," came the reply.

"For what?"

"Someday I'm going to be a big star," Gloria would answer solemnly. "And big stars have to practice."

A statement which, in Lillian's eyes, made it bound to happen. Because Gloria didn't joke or play or kid around. "She was serious."

Rescue—of a quite different sort—did finally come. In 1951, the house in East Toledo, which Ruth owned and had been trying to sell, was suddenly bought by the church next door for the decent sum, at that time, of $8,000.

Ruth and Gloria would have to go *somewhere* and, according to Gloria, it was Susanne, home for a summer visit, who conceived the plan. She would get Leo, who was also in Toledo at the moment, to assume the care of Ruth so that Gloria could live with her sister in Washington.

"Forget it," Gloria said. "He's not going to do that. They're divorced."

At breakfast with Leo and Gloria the next day, Susanne broached the subject, and Leo answered just as Gloria expected.

"Absolutely not."

In years to come, the chronology of Gloria's own personal history would often blur, but this moment, this morning's breakfast in East Toledo, would remain clearly in her mind. Susanne, Gloria would remember, rose angrily and left the restaurant. Gloria and her father remained sitting there for a few minutes, just looking at each other, each of them sadly understanding the situation. Father and daughter then left the restaurant and Leo drove Gloria to the first day of her summer job at a department store.

On their arrival, Gloria opened the car door and then, suddenly, burst into tears. In spite of herself, secretly, the tinder of hope had caught.

Leo was overwhelmed. What was this? ("I *never* cried," Gloria would remember.)

And just as suddenly, the sentimental father capitulated.

"All right, all right," he said quickly. "I'll do it."

But, he added: "We're synchronizing our watches. One year and that's all."

So it happened that the teenage Gloria spent her senior year of high school in Washington, D.C., with Susanne, and eventually, at Susanne's urging, applied to Smith College.

She was accepted but, as Susanne would tell it, Gloria quickly grew apprehensive. She had met a wealthy young woman ("You know, the kind who wears a different cashmere sweater every day of the week"), and she began to fret. If this rich girl was going to Smith in the fall, could that possibly be the right place for her? Would she fit in? Perhaps she belonged somewhere else.

"Gloria was always intimidated by people who had a lot of money," in Susanne's memory.

Susanne had no such worries. You'll be fine, she assured her sister. None of that matters.

And so in the fall of 1952, Gloria entered the ivy-covered walls of Smith College—exactly one decade after another young woman, whose fate would be deeply entwined with hers, had departed.

Both "Smithies" would graduate Phi Beta Kappa and with high honors. Both would be known throughout the world as the major oracles of the Golden Age of Feminism. Yet few personalities could differ more radically, and, to many who knew them well, few would be regarded as more implacable rivals.

By then, though—the early seventies—the names and faces of a chorus of new feminists would dance and flicker across the nation's television screens so often that many in the outside world would confuse these two. And it would be then that an excited, flustered hairdresser at one of Manhattan's toniest beauty salons would point to a woman in a nearby chair and whisper tremulously to his client:

"Look, there's Gloria Steinem!"

And the woman under the dryer would be, in fact, Betty Friedan.

5

IF THEY
DON'T LIKE ME

*If I am right, the problem that has no name stirring
in the minds of so many American women today is not
a matter of loss of femininity or too much education,
or the demands of domesticity. It is far more important
than anyone recognizes. It is the key to these other
new and old problems which have been torturing
women and their husbands and children, and puzzling
their doctors and educators for years. It may well be
the key to our future as a nation and a culture. We
can no longer ignore that voice within women that
says: "I want something more than my husband and
my children and my home."*

—Betty Friedan, *The Feminine Mystique,* 1963

Seven books were at least three too many, no matter what they said
at the public library in downtown Peoria. Harry Goldstein, Betty's
father, was clear on that point.

Not that Harry wasn't extremely proud of his smart, bookish little
girl. Oh, he definitely was! Everyone in the family could see that—
his sleekly attractive wife, Miriam; Amy, who was a year and a half
younger than Betty; even the girls' kid brother, Harry, Jr.

They would all remember those cerebral exercises in the dining room of the house on Franklin Street, the grace of the room itself, with its french doors, cream-colored drapes, and beautiful, rose-and-blue Oriental rug—Harry, Sr., sitting at one end of the table, Miriam at the other, where her invariably well-shod foot could reach the buzzer to surreptitiously call the maid from the kitchen. And the table, so grand it could hold twelve without leaves, always set for six, just in case Grandfather came by.

Whether or not Grandfather arrived, however, Father held forth with the questions. On math or politics or *something*—an exercise which bothered sister Amy a good deal.

"The serious questions about what was going on in the world would always be directed at Betty and the frivolous ones at me," Amy would remember. "And in that way we began to build our sense of who we were."

Harry, Sr., was a voracious reader, and believed in challenging the children. Seconds after he posed the problems, Betty would invariably pop up with the right answers, convincing her brother that his eldest sister was "not going to be just an ordinary person."

But Peoria, Illinois, in the thirties was not the best place or time for the extraordinary. It was distinctly unsuitable for Betty, a teenager on the verge of debut as an acceptable upper-middle-class "lady," to be seen trudging up Main Street Hill, lopsided and clumsily burdened with her bulky literary load. Or so, at any rate, the carefully conforming Goldsteins believed.

It was 1936, midway through the Great Depression, and Betty Naomi Goldstein, who would eventually, in the time-honored tradition, change her name to her husband's—Friedan—was an impressionable fifteen.

Born on February 4, 1921, Betty spent her adolescence in the days of the Works Progress Administration and the Civilian Conservation Corps, when "that man in the White House," as Franklin Delano Roosevelt was so often called, was welding the federal government tight as an iron joist to the Puritan American work ethic. The dreary spectacle of breadlines was not yet safely behind the beleaguered American psyche, and what was craved, more than anything, was security, safety, and permanence. Recreation was almost a patriotic duty—games, sports, new hobbies such as amateur photography—and that year, *Life* magazine burst on the scene, taking even its founder, Henry Luce, by surprise with its runaway popularity. People flocked to the movies, especially on Dish Nights, when you could win glass dishes, and nearly every film had a happy ending.

The point was to lift one's spirits. "The only thing we have to fear is fear itself" was the president's magic slogan. Confidence was the order of the day, and if the tenor of life in Peoria—as in hundreds of other towns across the country—was as cheerfully bland as a Jell-O commercial on the radio, that was okay, too. The news weekly *Time* magazine spoke for midwestern sentiments to a T: conservative, staunchly Presbyterian, patriotic to the near edge of boosterism, relentlessly upbeat.

Betty's life, however, was far from upbeat. Her own personal disaster had shattered her heart as painfully as the earlier small-town bankruptcies and bank failures had shaken the adults. In Betty's view —adolescent, thin-skinned, as she was—she had suddenly become an outcast.

That fall, she had been abandoned by all her upper-middle-class grade school friends as they flew off to the pack cruelty of high school sororities. No blacks were allowed in these social clubs, not that there were many in Peoria, and no Jews. Betty was no more acceptable to the pubescent Greek-lettered societies than her father was welcome at the Peoria country club. Added to that, a change in scheduling had put Betty's old schoolmates in entirely different time slots, so that in class the intense, heavy-lidded, dark-eyed little girl was with strangers. Out of school, she felt completely alone.

Well into the eighties, some of Betty's high school classmates would deny that it ever happened, insisting that "we didn't have isolation in our high school," or that Betty, who by then had publicly described her youthful misery, had "exaggerated" the anti-Semitism, that she "wanted to be thought of as put-upon."

But Betty's younger sister, Amy, too, would remember its effect. "You didn't talk about it. You had to act as if it didn't bother you," Amy would recall, "and since nobody was there to say that there was something wrong with these other people, you thought: 'There's something wrong with me because they don't want me.'"

And so, nearly every day, Betty despondently marched her small-boned, roundly filled little frame up the steep hill from the library, laden down like a sort of literary pack mule. She read indiscriminately, almost anything she could get her hands on—*Little Women*, "Nancy Drew"—but especially her beloved English fantasy books, about children who went out on sailboats and had all sorts of adventures.

She lugged her cache up toward home, the "bluff area" above the busy Illinois River, past upholstery shops, taverns, and appliance stores, small, two-story hotels and funeral homes, past the traffic of Main Street, with its electric streetcars rumbling beside her as the cars moved in and out of the crowded city below.

Some days, when the weather was good, she would wend her way to a park, or an old, overgrown cemetery.

Ah, if only she had a bicycle!

"It was a great sorrow that my parents were overprotective and wouldn't let me have a bicycle," Betty would remember. "I was never good at regular sports, team sports, but I had a great yen for nature. I loved Girl Scouts and hiking and canoeing and camp, longed to go out in the country, exploring."

She settled instead for the cemetery, which provided, at least, a setting for the fantasy of romance. It was practically Byronesque to sit there for hours, teary-eyed, until the sun set. Betty could dream about a wonderful boy, about the great actress she might someday become; she could sigh wistfully and compose poems of lyrical love.

But those were just dreams.

In the meantime, Betty's erstwhile friends wore their brightly striped pledge ribbons—their badges of acceptance—pinned to their blouses, and given the choice, the gregarious youngster would have flung herself into their chummy, sunny life with its roadster trips to the hamburger stand and its sorority bashes in less than a second. She was hurt, more introspective than she ever wanted to be, and, in typically workmanlike fashion, she made a vow, a pact with herself of the sort that would become something of a lifetime habit. This one asked a great deal of fifteen-year-old Betty from Peoria: "If they don't like me," she said to herself, "then someday, by God, they're going to respect me!"

"And I sure as hell delivered!" a gray-haired Betty would chuckle years later.

Which, even back then, wouldn't have surprised her kid brother, who was positive—and always would be—that his eldest sister's brain, when she died, would turn out to be "bigger than Lenin's" and who was, in short, "the most brilliant person I've ever known in my life."

If not the most even-tempered, placid, or, even, to put it very mildly, controlled.

For at home, the battles raged. Especially between Betty and her mother, Miriam.

Miriam, the daughter of a Peoria physician and pillar of the Jewish community, had been a society reporter on the Peoria newspaper, but she had given up the job for the more respectable role of middle-class matron, the wife of the owner of the finest jewelry shop in downtown Peoria. She was a handsome woman; "striking" was the word that most often came to mind.

"She always looked as if she stepped right out of Bergdorf's window," Amy would remember. "People turned around to look at her in the street. She was a fashion leader and people imitated her. She prided herself on that and her immaculate grooming."

The grooming. For Betty and her mother, it was a major bone of contention that would not wither with the ages.

"Betty is not the most beautiful creature in the world—she has my father's nose," her brother would remark years later, "and my mother still thinks Betty had worked as hard as she could to make herself as ugly as possible."

To which Amy would chorus: "There is no reason why Betty should be so unattractive. It's more in the way she has taken care of herself, a matter of"—and there it would be again—"*grooming.*"

Back then, the teenage Betty responded to such cutting criticism with a shatteringly high-decibel level of rage. She certainly could scream! brother Harry would remember. And Harry—who thought of himself as Peck's bad boy—would also confess to peeking through the keyhole of the room the two sisters shared, trying, actually, "to catch one of them nude. . . .

"Betty chased me, threw a book. She was screaming and she scared the hell out of me! Betty was volatile; she had a short fuse and could get wild when she lost her temper."

And that room, too, was a source of bloody conflict. Miriam would scold about its messiness, far beyond the scope of the maid. About once a month, in the middle of the night, Betty would suddenly switch on the light and take off on a whirlwind cleanup.

"Boy, when I grow up," she would announce, "I'm going to be rich so I can hire somebody to clean the room."

Sister Amy, on the other hand, harbored the opposite goal. When she grew up, she hoped, she would be poor. If Amy and her husband-to-be had no money at all, she imagined, there would be nothing to argue about.

For, by then, money was a major issue in the Goldstein household. The children would remember the arguments between their mother and father, remember Harry very angry, his face reddening, banging his fist on the table, storming out of the room.

Life-style mattered to the Goldsteins, especially to Miriam. Maintaining their gracious, large home with its impressive front porch, the salaries for the maids, the man who would sometimes act as butler or chauffeur. And Miriam herself brought an array of talents to the family's social position. Terrifically energetic and bright, she was known in Peoria as a fine hostess and was adept at nearly every skill valued in an upper-middle-class housewife of the day—at decorating, entertaining, wearing clothes, at golf and tennis (as Betty definitely was not), at civic affairs, at a busy array of charity work.

Living and dressing well were not unimportant to Harry, Sr., either. Seventeen years older than his wife, an immigrant whose mastery of English was not perfect, he was warm, affectionate, sentimental, a man of integrity, but a man who, in Amy's recollection, "just couldn't say no and stick to it."

Yet the fact was that "Goldstein's," that "Tiffany's of Peoria," was not what it had been before the Depression years. Harry had built the business from a street-corner collar-button stand, but now the store was suffering badly.

And so, at home, there were fights.

All three children would remember their father's suffering, his anxiety, his battle to generate the finances that would support the Goldstein life-style. Miriam's only son would not fault his mother for the pressure she put on his father, seeing her as a woman who was simply struggling to maintain a middle-class standard of living, but both Betty and Amy would.

Years later, Betty would contend that her mother "belittled, cut down my father because she had no place to channel her terrific energies." By then Betty would see her mother's "impotent rage" in feminist terms, a simmering frustration that was a typically female disorder. Miriam, like so many other women who "didn't have any power outside the family . . . had to have too much in it."

But Betty would also remember, and frankly express, her own adolescent dependency.

"I was very dominated by my mother," she would confess. "She was very critical of me and made me feel very insecure. I went through a period where a critical word from my mother or father and I would just dissolve into tears. Schoolwork was my only escape. I was good at it and I loved it."

What she was not good at, and what she surely did not love, was her mother's ability to "put on the charm." For that charm, in Betty's eyes, was pure hypocrisy.

"I saw all the phoniness about my mother," Betty would remember. "She was so unctuous on the telephone . . . 'My dear sweet darling' and so on, when you knew that the next thing she would say would be 'that bitch.'

"As a result, I virtually say 'that bitch' on the phone. Everybody gets on me for my telephone manner because I'm so brusque." (And "brusque" would be, in fact, something of an understatement.)

Betty would remember, too, that Miriam fostered a certain degree of unhealthy competitiveness, that the two girls were "compared in destructive ways." And though Betty would not dwell on the subject, Amy would be quick to discuss this "sibling rivalry" in great detail. Betty's attitude toward her younger sister, Amy would insist, "dripped with hostility toward what she called 'my feminine wiles.'" Amy would remember that Miriam dressed both girls alike until Betty reached junior high school, that when they were about five and six years old, Miriam took them to a psychologist at Bradley Polytechnic Institute for tests, I.Q. tests included.

"My mother told us afterward that Betty was a genius and that I was very artistic," Amy would recall. "I thought that artistic was just sort of nothing to be. . . .

"I was the pretty one, cute and pretty with naturally curly hair. She was ugly and I was dumb. Which in neither case is true. I'm certainly extremely intelligent and there was no reason why Betty should be so unattractive, unkempt. . . . When you see her in person she often leaves a great deal to be desired.

"We don't look at all alike. Everybody thinks I look at least ten years younger than she does."

By then—the mid-eighties—Amy would be divorced; she would have supported herself and her two sons as a schoolteacher, sold one of her own paintings to the Rockefeller Institute and be taking classes in creative writing. But she would be, as she put it, "a totally unknown person." Betty would be a world-renowned feminist author, and the two sisters would see very little of each other.

"Because of Betty's unresolved sibling rivalry," Amy, now in her early sixties, would state flatly. "I once wrote her a note that said, 'I don't in any way mean to diminish your accomplishments, Betty, but the person I'm interested in is the human being not the public figure. I have the impression you don't care to get together. It's your loss because I'm a terrific person.' I wanted her to know that the emperor wasn't wearing clothes and that I knew it.

"She speaks to me with contempt in her voice, so I wrote her another letter and I said: 'The person you were speaking to was not I. You don't really know me. You don't know the person I am.'

"To Betty, I'm just not very bright. But if I were rich or famous, I'm sure she'd be seeking me out."

Still, the cause of all this tension in the Goldstein family, at least according to Amy, was Miriam's social ambitions and pretensions, her "complete inability to nurture. . . . We really absolutely did not have a mother loving us." And, on discovering an old photograph of the two girls as children, Amy would conclude that if she had been the mother of those two cute little girls, "Betty wouldn't have grown up thinking she was ugly."

A fantasy which would, perhaps, project a different world. Certainly a different Betty—one who would not be quite so surprised (as Betty would be years later) when one of her children found a high school picture of an attractive, strong-featured young woman and announced: "But Mother, you were pretty!" Or when an old school chum remarked: "Betty could sure fill a sweater!" Or, even back then in Peoria, when a boy told her she looked like Bette Davis.

For eventually, there *were* a few dates. And bright new friends she made in the last two years of high school, when she was writing a column for the school newspaper. Friends who helped her start a school magazine, and looked on sympathetically as she worried frantically about her grades and her deadlines and all manner of agonies. Friends who thought that Betty "could talk your leg off on any subject" and "sometimes just wanted to look smarter than anyone else." But friends who also loved the liveliness of her—alternately bullying and beseeching, threatening and opening her heart.

"My whole personality changed," Betty would remember. "I stopped being so miserably self-conscious."

Often now, the gang gathered at the house on Franklin Street, where, one of them would remember, the lively Betty "held court." Sometimes, they went downtown to the Madison or the Palace or the

Rialto movie theaters. There, for just twenty cents, you could watch the real Bette Davis devour the screen as the half-crazed, venal waitress in *Of Human Bondage*, or Myrna Loy pilot an airplane and win her beloved Cary Grant. Or Joan Crawford with glamorous shoulder pads capping her image of supreme competence. Or Merle Oberon. (Once someone said Betty looked like Merle.) As dictated by the Hays Office, the plots of the movies had to end in marriage or the doom of these women was sealed, but these heroines were, unlike some others, at least vital, accomplished.

Betty hated Shirley Temple (who was, after all, so terrifically wholesome, so flirtatious, so exactly the image of what every mommy and daddy in Depression America wanted their little girl to be), but these feisty stars were another matter. She was mad about them and finally, in her senior year of high school, Betty Goldstein became a star herself.

It was a very short performance, but she won the school actress award for her stellar portrayal of the madwoman in *Jane Eyre*.

"What terrific screaming!" her classmates cheered.

And Betty loved every second of it.

"I guess I was always a ham," she would remember. "I think that if, in those days, there had been actresses like Barbra Streisand, you know, if the ideal of beauty hadn't been Betty Grable . . ."

Then, perhaps, Betty might have pursued her dreams of Broadway; she might not have set off, as she did in 1939, to Smith, the college Miriam had chosen for her.

"Betty has the most outstanding record of any student ever matriculated at Smith," a college administrator told her family at graduation. "Her thesis is an original contribution to the field of behavioral science. It could stand for a Ph.D."

But it didn't, for, as it would happen, Betty would not only relinquish her dreams of the theater but, far more seriously, this valedictorian of her class, this remarkable summa cum laude student, would fail to pursue her studies.

And yet she had adored college, had been swept up in a thumping, roiling love for the place.

"After Peoria," she would remember, "Smith, for me, was that whole thing of the passion of the mind."

The newspaper. She was editor-in-chief of *that*. The magazine. She was managing editor of *that*. Everybody knew her not only as Betty "the psychology brain," but as Betty the outspoken patriot, the throaty social conscience, who argued, always, for justice, for the poor, for the disadvantaged. Learning, doing, talking, meeting, writing, until, in her sophomore year, she landed in the hospital with a collapsed lung. With asthma, a condition that would plague her for much of her life.

Her illness took months of recuperation, but even so, she had managed to pull off all A's and, to top it off, get elected to Junior Phi Beta Kappa.

So it wasn't that, the asthma, that stopped her. Nor was it, certainly, lack of interest.

Betty spent nearly every summer of her college years working in her field. At the University of Iowa, with behavioral psychologist Kurt Lewin. At other universities, with more of the country's top social scientists. Even an internship at a Westchester County, New York, mental institution.

At graduation, she won a fellowship in psychology at the University of California at Berkeley and went off to study with the well-known analyst Erik Erikson. There she won another, even more prestigious fellowship, this one with a large stipend that could easily carry her through to a professional career as a psychologist.

But then—most surprisingly—this ambitious, intelligent young woman turned her back on it all. She refused the grant.

In years to come, journalists would colorfully recount the sad, romantic tale of how Betty Goldstein had turned down the fellowship of her dreams. All because of a boy, they said. They would write about homely Betty, with all A's and few dates, who finally fell in love, about too-smart Betty who finally found a boy to love her back, who picnicked idyllically with cucumber sandwiches and wine, and who then told this long-awaited sweetheart about her fellowship.

Instead of cheering her on, the boy had said: "You can take that fellowship, but you know I'll never get one like it. You know what it will do to us."

And then the accounts would relate how the love-torn "Mother Superior to Women's Lib" had given up the grant, all for *him*, and they would quote Betty to the effect that such an either-or situation was her constant burden in life; either she pursued her career or sublimated her wishes to a man's.

Thus, Betty would later complain, "making me into a cliché."

"It was merely an anecdote," she would insist. The boy hadn't been all that important, "just someone I fancied myself in love with at the moment."

But the fact remained that she had indeed refused the grant (friends would report, and Betty would never exactly deny, that she was passionate—often infuriatingly passionate—in her pursuit of men), and almost instantly, having turned down that fellowship, she was wrenched with asthmatic spasms. Coughing, wheezing, convulsively gasping for breath, she fled to New York, leaving academia *and* the boy behind.

There, in what she would call "the pit of asthma, terrible shape," Betty entered psychoanalysis. And there, for the first time, she began to focus on her own rage, her anger at her mother.

She would return to therapy off and on over the years, whenever the asthma broke out. Well into the eighties, however, after Betty had raised a family of her own, she would still have difficulties with her mother, who was by then living in a retirement community on the West Coast.

Once Betty stayed with Miriam for about five days, and found that her mother still got on her nerves terribly.

"She asked if I was still driving a car," Betty would recall, "and when I answered that I was, she said, 'Well, Betty, I don't know if you should be. You know what a bad driver you are.' " And at that memory, Betty, dressed smartly in a dark, flowered dress, her gray hair smoothly combed, would cough into her wadded-up handkerchief as she added: "A friend was with us and said, 'I get the whole picture.' "

Back in the early forties, though, during her college years and even afterward, Betty seldom returned to her home in Peoria.

In 1943, her father died. "Of overwork," all Harry's children would agree.

"After that," Betty would remember, "I became very estranged from my mother, very critical of her. Part of it was normal growing up, becoming aware of one's own self. But I had to do it more than most."

Meanwhile, in New York, as the asthma eased and she felt strong again, she began to enjoy the big city. She renewed acquaintances with old buddies from college. She roomed with a group of classmates in a Greenwich Village apartment. She began working for the Federated Press, a small labor newspaper, got involved in left-wing causes.

By then, World War II was drawing to a close. In April 1945, Roosevelt died of a cerebral hemorrhage. In May, Germany surrendered; in July, a new world organization called the United Nations came into being; in August, an "atomic bomb," which, it was said, "harnessed the basic power of the universe," was dropped on Hiroshima; and in September, Japan surrendered unconditionally.

World War II became, in the words of the *New York Times*, "a page in history." The world had changed irrevocably, but no one quite knew how, or how to cope with such concepts as "basic power of the universe." But what was most important, of course, was that after years of deprivation and anxiety, those who had survived the war— "the boys"—were coming home.

Subtly, America's focus turned inward, toward love and comfort and luxuries, some of them as yet unimagined, all long denied by the austerities of war. Lacking battle headlines and brilliant reportage from the front, the editors of newspapers and magazines began to examine American life itself. A few self-conscious "human-interest" stories began to appear on their pages, the first signs of what would eventually swell into an enormous industry devoted to probing and advising Americans in regard to their homes, their culture, and the guardians of both these essentials—women.

"The American Woman? Not for This GI" was the title of a 1946 diatribe in the *New York Times Magazine*. European girls were "much nicer," wrote the author, a former *Stars and Stripes* correspondent. "Parisiennes," for example, were "there for the sole purpose of being pleasant to the men," and had the good sense to "go into peals of laughter at the right moments." Unlike the Americans, no European women offended this young man with any extraneous interests. Instead these infinitely more appealing ladies were interested in "the fundamental business" of getting married and having children.

It was not the first time that American women had been put on notice, their minds and characters examined to no great credit. The 1941 film based on Kurt Weill's musical *Lady in the Dark* had brought the supposedly amoral force of psychiatry to bear by using a psychoanalyst to lecture a top female fashion editor: "You've had to prove you were superior to all men; you had to dominate them." The only solution to this career woman's "problem," according to the analyst, was to find "some man who'll dominate you."

In 1942, Philip Wylie's *Generation of Vipers* had chipped away at women's self-esteem with the epithet "Momism," and in 1946, *Fortune* magazine recruited anthropologist Margaret Mead for an early investigation.

"What Women Want" was the title of the article, presumably an answer to Sigmund Freud's query. Soberly, Mead put forth a remarkable cross section of issues that would inhabit literally thousands of books, articles, and talk shows three decades later. Women, Mead wrote, are taught in school to value the same things as men—that is, variety, choice, and freedom—yet are isolated and lonely at home with the refrigerator and the washing machine. They have no choice, no variety, no stimulation, simply "semi-voluntary slavery" and its resultant dulling of the mind. Limiting human activity according to the biological fact of childbirth is inconsistent with the expansive aims of modern civilization. Working mothers have an impossible double burden, and men should share equally in housework and childrearing. Day-care centers are imperative. Women want to be regarded as "persons" first and women second and should not be presented with the "unbearable choice" of family or career.

Nobody paid much attention to this prescient piece, except, perhaps, to the blame it placed on women themselves. It was cast in the era's typical "what's-wrong-with-women" probe. More than a quarter of the women in America are "disturbed," Mead wrote in the first paragraph. They are "uncertain about their role," "discontent," and therefore "destructive." Angled this way, the article seemed yet another attack on that dangerous "neurotic," the ambitious achiever.

And indeed, one by one, Betty's Greenwich Village crowd began to leave their jobs for the blissful, accepting, infinitely praised life of the suburbs, to marry and to break up the gang. Thus leaving Betty, once again, alone, with that dread of isolation that harked back, at the least, to her high school days in Peoria.

"A pathological fear of being alone," as she would describe it—a loneliness that lasted until Carl moved in.

A friend had introduced the two, and Betty was delighted with this amusing man. He was dark-haired, good-looking—quite conventionally so—and well built, though not much taller than she. He was a charming host, could mix a martini and cocktail chatter with skill and warmth. He told jokes with éclat, he had lots of imagination, and most of all, he made Betty laugh.

"He made me feel," Betty would remember, "not alone."

A flamboyant promoter, Carl Friedan had only just returned to the States after running an army show in Europe, and what he was going to do next was to open a summer theater in New Jersey. He had tons of ideas.

In June of 1947, Betty and Carl were married. Two years later, she gave birth to their first child, Danny. On a leave of absence from her editorial job at the labor paper, with enormous pride, Betty devoted herself to making a home and breastfeeding her baby, judiciously reading all the women's magazines for helpful hints.

The powerful women's magazines were just beginning to extend the psychological advice, the emotional how-tos that would provide the publishing industry with billions of dollars in revenue in the decades to come. The rationale for this sort of counsel was well summed up in a popular book called *Modern Woman: The Lost Sex*, by Ferdinand Lundberg and Marynia F. Farnham, M.D. (Farnham, though listed second, was the psychiatrist *and* a woman—thus, for the women's magazines, a tailor-made "authority.")

The book, with over 100 pages of explanatory appendix, was a direct assault on women whose interests extended outside the home. "The independent woman," it stated flatly, "is a contradiction in terms." A female's desire for success in the world of work was an unmistakable sign that she was a "masculine aggressive woman," afflicted with such distorted fantasies as an "unconscious wish herself to possess the organ upon which she must . . . depend" for sexual satisfaction. That satisfaction was impossible if the sex act itself was experienced either as "erotic play or sexual 'equality.' The sex act," according to this guidebook, "is primarily concerned with having children . . . women who don't want children, whether they have them or not, fail to derive maximal satisfaction from the sexual act." A woman's fulfillment could be achieved only through "receptivity and passiveness, a willingness to accept dependence without fear or resentment, with a deep inwardness and readiness for the final goal of sexual life—impregnation."

All else was sick, unhappy, neurotic, the woman "wholly or partly incapable of dealing with life," thus the root cause of the "destruction of the home" and most social ills, including Nazi Germany.

In this authoritative view, the modern woman's most profound disturbance could be seen in her desire for clitoral stimulation, an infantile denial of femininity which was "disturbing to the marital relation because it contributes to a feeling of insufficiency in the man and is derogatory of his organ." Also to frigidity. Also, as described in a footnote citing Dr. Helene Deutsch, to the "malicious orgasm," in which the woman's "rhythmic contractions follow their course in complete disregard of the man's rhythm," evidence that the "masculine aggressive" woman is engaged in a competitive "duel" with the man.

Bolstering the argument were short resurrections of a few long-dead feminists, with an analysis of their lives as "psychiatric case histories," fraught with the "libidinal chaos" of "penis envy," the "shadow of the phallus lying darkly, threateningly" over every move they made.

You could find this warning, simplified and homogenized, in all the women's magazines Betty was reading. Even the fiction steadfastly aimed in the same direction: The loving housewife triumphs over the callous career woman. After the devilish temptation of the outside world, the heroine discovers her only true happiness at home.

Betty would, in fact, remember one short story in particular well enough to repeat the plot. It was a tale about a little girl who lives with her hard-working mother, a divorced "know-it-all" psychologist. The child visits her father and his new wife in the country, where the three make bubbly cheese omelettes, grow flowers, and revel blissfully in the domestic scene. The child, of course, never wants to go back to her lonely, pathetic mother in her lonesome cold apartment again.

Not long after she read this story, Betty ran into an old friend who had married a man she had picked up on the subway and given up her own practice as a psychologist.

"And I understood," Betty would eventually write, in a self-mocking account, "because in 1949, I was also becoming infected by the mystique, that it almost didn't matter who the man was who became the instrument of your feminine fulfillment. I was awed by the strength and sincerity of her new psychological awareness, that she would even find him on the subway."

And so, ironically, Betty, too, was determined to find her fulfillment through a man. Unlike her mother, who was always so discontent with her husband and with herself, Betty would experience total happiness in her home and family. Unlike Miriam, she would joyfully accept her dependency, her "receptivity," as the psychology of the day had it. If women were to blame for their discontent, then she would try harder to be happy.

And so, with the tearing energy of the rebel she was, with the full force of her intelligence and strength, Betty threw herself into her new career: the home.

She moved her little family to a garden apartment in Queens, one that had french doors which opened onto a common lawn where all the children could play and the young families could share chores and entertainment. She took classes at the local maternity center, at a cooking school, wheeled Danny in the supermarket carts. Carl made martinis, which both parents drank their share of, and cooked hamburgers on the new barbecue grill, and Betty, who, like her mother, had a flair for decorating a home, if not for cleaning it, made everything cozy. She read Dr. Spock, noting carefully the section which, two decades later, the doctor would rewrite, but which then decreed that a mother of small children not go to work, that she would, in fact, harm her child if she did.

Nonetheless (and perhaps because she was never fully convinced), Betty did return to work after her year's maternity leave was up, but when she found herself pregnant once again, she was fired. Given the received opinion of the day, it was a relief. A woman wasn't considered good for much around a business office anyhow, and now she could do *the right thing* by her family. Yet, sure enough, once again, she was wracked by asthma. Again, she sought therapy.

It was true, of course, that her marriage was growing stormy, that during arguments, *things*—sugar bowls, books, and the like—seemed to fly. Carl, who had been managing an Off Broadway theater, switched to advertising after their second child, Jonathan, was born, and though the family's finances improved, Carl's one-man operation kept their income erratic.

Roots, Betty thought. What they needed was roots.

("Women should begin especially to look with critical eyes at the present physical framework of 'home' as represented by the cramped 'efficient' apartment . . . an expression in bricks and stones of modern woman's reduced status": Lundberg and Farnham, M.D.)

She began her search for roots by moving her family to a stone barn in Sneden's Landing, across the Hudson River in Rockland County, and from there to a charming old Victorian house in Grandview.

"It was a wonderful house," Betty would remember. "It was on a knoll and had a view of the Hudson River. It had woods in the back and a bank of daffodils and a boxwood hedge maze. Once, when we were terribly broke, I sold off the boxwoods. . . . Never could stand the smell of them anyway."

They bought the house for just $25,000, $2,500 down plus Carl's

G.I. mortgage. The front porch was even longer and wider than the one where she had played as a kid. And there were lovely arched windows.

Betty hurled herself into restoration, spent months stripping the staircase down to its original wood, restoring the marble on the fireplace. She put luscious, sexy red wallpaper in the bedroom, purple in the living room to complement the beautiful woodwork. She did battle, every third Saturday, at a nearby auction, bought a stunning chair for $3, and, her grandest purchase by far, an ornately carved loveseat for $25, the exact twin of one in the Museum of the City of New York.

"I'm no great expert," she would later admit, "but I'm good at houses. Every year or so, the kids made a pilgrimage to that one to show their friends where they grew up."

She began to make a few dollars on several educational projects for kids in the area and to do some free-lance work for the women's magazines, writing according to the formulas she had learned.

Given, as Betty was, to making pacts with herself, she made one more. Each article would have to bring in more money than she paid the part-time maid she had hired to clean and care for the kids while she worked. And then, after a while, another rule was added. She was breastfeeding her third child, Emily, by then, and the sources for the articles had to be in the immediate neighborhood.

Which is how she happened to write "The Coming Ice Age." Lamont Geological Observatory was near her home and once, as Betty was watching Jonathan in his play group, she heard another mother —a scientist—chatting about her work in carbon atoms and geological cores. This woman's investigations, she thought, might make a convenient, though difficult piece.

"I hadn't had physics since high school," she would recall, "so I had to prop a textbook at the breakfast table every morning just to prepare for the interviews."

When "The Coming Ice Age" appeared in *Harper's* magazine, however, it was so solidly written that an editor—George Brockway, at the prestigious publishing firm W. W. Norton—phoned Betty to ask if she might like to do more, if she might, in fact, like to write a book.

It was a lovely compliment. And a fine opportunity, one that most free-lance writers would have seized immediately.

But Betty, with three small kids, was having enough trouble getting her articles written, let alone a book.

70

And then there was the other reason.

The book George Brockway had in mind was an expansion of "The Coming Ice Age," which meant that Betty, who had set out from Smith on a social science career, would be writing an entire book about what was, essentially, another scientist's work. It was almost— or so it seemed to her—"ghostwriting," and this former recipient of a major fellowship had tried that before. She had not, she found, liked that "behind the scenes" role in the slightest.

And so once again, she refused an enticing career offer. But this refusal was different. This one had a bit of the fire, a bit of the old spark of a Betty Goldstein, valedictorian, editor, actress, "psychology brain."

No, thank you, she replied to the soft-spoken Brockway. "If I'm ever going to write a book," she announced firmly, "it's going to be about my own work!"

6

A
TERRIBLE WORD

Freud assumed that the female's discovery of her sex is, in and of itself, a catastrophe of such vast proportions that it haunts a woman all through life and accounts for most aspects of her temperament. His entire psychology of women, from which all modern psychology and psychoanalysis derives heavily, is built upon an original tragic experience—born female.

—Kate Millett, *Sexual Politics*, 1970

Like Gloria and Germaine, Kate Millett was born in the thirties, those years when Betty was already wrestling with her tumultuous adolescence. And though trauma—far more painful, according to her account, than anything these other young women had experienced—loomed in her future, through the war years Kate's childhood had been close to idyllic.

To a degree, all of America had been insulated from the battle. No television cameras followed the soldiers onto the bloody fields, and not until the war ended and newsreels of concentration camps appeared in movie theaters did Americans have any notion of the unspeakable horrors of the Nazi regime.

St. Paul was, perhaps, even more protected than the rest of the country. In those days, the whole town was almost exclusively immigrant Irish, conservative, and, as Kate would remember it, nineteenth century in its politics, concerned more with the 1922 rebellion, with Queen Victoria and the Great Famine than with Hitler's march through Europe. Most of these staunchly Catholic children, Kate among them, attended parochial school with pride and made sport of their elite status. Going to public school meant joining the rest of America, they joked, and who wanted to do that?

On fine spring afternoons, Kate could jump on her bike and speed down the river road past the sweet, green budding elms to the banks of the great, rolling Mississippi. Tomboy Kate, in her black serge accordion-pleated skirt and saddle shoes (the Derham Hall parochial school uniform), her long, dark braids flying behind her. Once she reached the banks, she would check round carefully for the dangerous "bums" everyone said hung out by the river (though she never saw any) and make her way out on a promontory. Perched there, her bike with its clumsy balloon tires propped against a tree, she would gaze out at the endlessly fascinating river. She would watch and listen to the strong musical waters, poke at the washed-up branches, give sober attention to everything that moved . . . or didn't. She might dream that she was an Indian or perhaps, drawing on her current favorite, Mark Twain, that she was Huckleberry Finn and that she, too, had a raft that would take her far away, to unimaginably exciting adventures. Or she might give sober consideration to the remarkable differences between the two grown-up women she knew best: her sensitive mother, Helen, and her bewitching aunt, Christina, from the wealthy Millett side of the family.

Kate was the second of three daughters. She was born on September 14, 1934, to Helen Feely and James Albert Millett, her mother the daughter of a farmer, her father, though not wealthy himself, a member of a family that was considered, in that part of the country, a genus of landed Irish gentry. James Millett, an engineer and contractor, worked for the state highway department, and his wages provided the family with a charming, three-bedroom stucco home not far from the river. The house, with its bright geraniums at the windows and its gabled roof, looked a bit like an English cottage and sat just behind St. Thomas College, on Selby Street. Not so fashionable an address as the grander Summit Avenue, not nearly so elegant as Aunt Christina's home, with its fine chambers and full library of valuable, leather-bound volumes, but still, the Selby Street house, as Kate would remember it, was carefully kept—"real cream in all the dishes, butter delivered in two stone crocks to the back door"—and immaculately cared for by Celia, a kindly farm woman whose Tollhouse cookies and ample sympathy were always available for Helen Millett's girls.

Yet Kate, along with her sisters—Sally, who was five years older, and Mary, five years younger—could hardly avoid an infatuation with their father's family, the wealthy Milletts, especially the dazzling, aristocratic Aunt Christina. Unlike Helen, from whose humble background rose deeply felt social concern and a personal focus on moral and ethical issues, Christina was widely educated, a private scholar who traveled and skied, lived for her own amusement and pleasure, and did exactly as she wished.

The grand feasts at the homes of Kate's Millett relatives seemed a wonder of endless parties. Gaiety, music, celebration. A blazing fire, glittering crystal and glowing mahogany, presents in gold and silver foil with wide, bright ribbons, the grown-ups drinking and laughing, singing songs they made up themselves, clowning, arguing about Governor Stassen. Once, just for Kate, a balloon shaped like a whale was floated down from the balcony by the butler. And the dinner-table conversation was wonderfully witty and bookish. It was fun, in that challenging gabble, to brag about the grand legacy of the great Irish literary figures, to suggest, in jest, that Shakespeare himself, according to the latest evidence, was undoubtedly as Irish as they themselves were, as Irish as the nuns at Derham Hall.

Books were important at home as well, though life there was lived on a much simpler scale. Helen had been the only member of her family to attend college, graduating from the University of Minnesota with a major in English literature. Always aware of how long the Irish had been kept illiterate, of how their own Gaelic language had been taken from them, Helen placed great value on education and the tolerance that she was convinced accompanied it. She was repelled by all forms of bigotry and refused to permit the endemic ethnic jokes to be told in her house. Never fully accepted by the Irish gentry into which she had married, she was acutely conscious of her own—as well as others'—victimization.

"You wouldn't believe what I was just reading," Kate would remark as she set the table.

The book in question might have been a history of the Jews which Kate had proudly purchased with the pocket money she earned from collecting Coke bottles. And she would proceed to recount, in tough, hard-line newspaper style to hide the brimming tears, a horror story of pogroms and other atrocities.

"It's unbelievable, just unbelievable what these people have been put through."

"Yes, my dear," Helen would respond. "This is what I've been trying to tell you."

In the Millett world, books were so highly treasured it was almost inevitable that, before long, big sister Sally ("the brain," as she was called) and then Kate, as well, would get hold of the wrong ones, those that were called, in this deeply Catholic world, "Protestant books." Hendrik Willem van Loon's intimations of evolution, for example. How utterly fascinating, thought the insatiable explorer of rivers and ideas. Now what does all this imply?

Soon, like the sophisticated Millett side of the family, Kate was making fun of more recent doctrines such as the Immaculate Conception and the Assumption.

And her mother was not pleased.

Those all-too-clever witticisms at the expense of the Church were, to Helen's mind, nothing more than "smart-aleck" foolishness.

But Kate's inner struggle with those heretical ideas would prove to be more profound and tumultuous than her pious mother imagined.

By the time she reached high school, she had taken to throwing herself into short periods of frenzied piety (joining the Schola, rising in the predawn hours to sing the exquisite Gregorian chants, to admire the nuns as they took Communion, replaced their veils, and skimmed back past the children with the veils afloat) that alternated with heretical phases. Back and forth until, finally, there was no returning. A profound rebellion had taken root, a rebellion that was both thrilling and terrifying, as stirring to the blood as one of those mammoth, sleek-finned Cadillacs Kate coveted, as risky as a fast skid on a rain-slick curve. The authority of the Church was everywhere, in every part of her life, and to challenge it was to dare all.

Among the seeds of this rebellion—tiny and scattered in the gale-force winds of her religious heresy—were her own schoolgirl's observations that she would still remember years later, complaints she shared with her sister Sally:

"Men were the popes. Priests had all power over the nuns."

"Boys get to serve Mass. They get to wear little red skirts and sing the Tenebrae in Latin."

"And they don't have to make their beds and they get the snow fort. We helped to build it but they won't let us in."

"It isn't fair."

If Kate took complaints like these to any adult, even her mother, whose alert antennae were so finely tuned to injustice and who was proud to have been among the first generation of women to exercise the vote, the answer would be the same. "Oh, well, *fair* . . . That's just how the world is. There's nothing to be done about it."

For even in this rich literary world, the writings of the great feminists of past centuries were deeply obscured. The suffragists were almost forgotten. Susan B. Anthony's battle for women's right to vote was a fuzzy image practically interchangeable with Carry Nation's escapades of breaking saloon windows. Both of them nothing more than faint objects of ridicule.

But for a while, Kate had in Sally ("Elder," as she often called her) an intellectual ally and guide, until, eventually, big sister went off to college.

By then, the country was solidly immersed in the undramatic postwar years under Harry Truman's stewardship. Millions of women who had gone to work in war-related industries had returned to full-time homemaking. Two decades later, Betty Friedan would point out angrily that these women had been forced out of their jobs by the driving ambitions of big business interests, the economics of retooling, and the need to create a housebound market for new products. Added to that, though less helpful to the feminist argument, was the pining, longingly romantic mood of the times.

For all the cheery wartime esprit, American hearts and minds had never been far from a pervasive, romantic yearning. "I'll see you again," the pop singers had warbled. "All or nothing at all," crooned the skinny teen idol Frank Sinatra.

Wives had been desperate to see their husbands safe at home. Single women had missed the fun of flirtation, of having boyfriends. "They're either too young or too old; they're either too gray or too grassy green. . . . What's good is in the army. What's left will never harm me," warbled Betty Garrett in the Broadway musical *Call Me Mister*. At the same time, far away, on the battlefields of blood, American men had woven idealized fantasies of the world they had left behind, the America worth dying for. Rosey the Riveter, though cheered on the cover of *Life* magazine, was a good sport indeed to have backed up the war effort, but what the "weary fighting men," as they were so often described in print, truly wanted on their return "stateside" was the happy home they had pictured over and over in the foxholes, the white frame house with its shady front lawn and its familiar creaky gate, the inner tube swinging from the elm tree: "The House I Live In." Tucked inside: the patient, waiting wife, the "perfect" family of their wartime dreams.

And then the dreams had met the reality.

The Best Years of Our Lives, a poignant commemoration of the returning troops, appeared in American movie theaters in 1946. In the film, one soldier, who had lost both hands, was greeted with a certain queasiness by his teenage girlfriend. The wife of a second soldier had been unfaithful. The third soldier, powerfully portrayed by Fredric March, was deeply shaken by the independence of his wife and children. They can "handle things," his daughter said, wrenching his heart with the implication that the family could get along without him.

Contrary to the foxhole fantasies, nothing was perfect in these, and many other real-life, families.

Guiltily, postwar America rushed to the rescue, erecting an emotional defense. The family would have to be as they dreamed it, worthy of the terrible sacrifices of the war. Reality must be willed into an exact replication of the fantasy.

The "perfection" of family life was hardening into social maxim at just about the same time—1948—that Jim Millett left home.

Kate's charming father—who could dance and sing and tell stories and who would, on bright occasions, deposit Kate on a bar stool at his side when, in bursts of gregarious joy, he bought drinks for his friends—"Jamie," the much-loved but, to Kate, always-distant father, simply left. A "mistress" was involved.

Helen was devastated. Terrible scenes, torrential tears ensued. Many years later, in a rambling, self-revelatory book called *Flying,* Kate would describe this as "the time of recriminations." Her mother crying: " 'We have no money. We will starve. Everyone in St. Paul knows about his drinking. You can be darn sure they talk about how he's left us. And the two of you are Jim Millett for sure. Took up right where he left off.' "

Kate would recall her own adolescent confusion and jagged, imploding resentment: "And still now we are poor. I cannot make her rich. And she says I am as bad as him. The man I should hate, my father, that bully. Underneath I'm even worse, still, hanging on to my infatuation with him and all the Milletts. Does that mean I am one of them? If I'm like my father am I still a girl?"

And she would confess disloyal thoughts: "Wouldn't it be wonderful if I could get adopted?" But she scrambled above them with a determination to be strong for her mother, to earn money so that the three of them could survive. "Now I realized I was my mother's man, opening car doors, driving for her, taking her arm across the ice."

In high school, she worked in a department store, babysat (by then, a big business among the bobby sox set), and took over management of the family finances, paying the bills, warding off creditors. One semester, she worked in a mental institution, was horrified by the brutality, never dreaming then what import that experience would have for her in later years. And as Helen's early efforts to sell insurance by phone met constant rejection, Kate worried that her mother would take her own life. It made her sick at heart. And angry. And no less voluble about the injustices of the world.

With Sally gone, Kate turned to Mary but, much as she loved her kid sister, many a battle line was drawn. In a newspaper account years later, Kate would admit that she and her sister (who was present during the interview) had only recently learned to "hack it with each other."

"I was smart and ugly," Kate would say, "and you were dumb and beautiful. I did the being-a-good-girl-in-school act because they had convinced me I was so ugly I couldn't make it any other way. I did my shuffling that way."

But Kate was not ugly, and she was making new friends to fill in for Sally. One, especially, that she adored, with whom she gossiped, played games, rode bikes, talked for hours on the phone.

It was a crush. Soon there were kisses.

And one day . . .

Sally's college beau, "the nice one," as Kate would remember, who had taught her how to draw horses, was visiting with Helen in the living room. Kate was in another room on the phone, yakking away, as usual, to her beloved friend.

"You should realize . . ." She heard the young man's voice as he talked to her mother.

Then suddenly, snaking through the polite conversation, she caught the sound of a terrible word. She had never heard that word spoken aloud before, and yet immediately she understood. And she understood the young man's tone. What he was talking about was something very bad. It was sexual. And it was as foul as—maybe it actually was—a disease.

"You should realize," he said coldly, as she listened, her ears far more alert to the threatening sound of his voice than to the schoolgirl gossip on the phone.

"Your daughter is a lesbian."

And, after that, in Kate's mind, there was no hope of returning to the Church or of absolution.

Helen demanded nothing less than that Kate's unspeakable behavior, whatever she had done that could lead to such disgraceful talk, should cease immediately.

Frightened, for several years Kate obeyed.

Even in her senior year in high school, when, chatting upstairs in Kate's bedroom, her friend reached for her with love.

No, Kate told her. Such things were dirty. Such things were wrong.

In 1952, Kate set off for her mother's alma mater, the University of Minnesota. For all the trials of her adolescence, her soul had begun to stretch. Making money, the clear sense that she could survive on her own, had given her a heady feeling of independence. Her rebellious spirit and passion for justice were undaunted. Minneapolis— though just across the river—seemed a world apart from insular St. Paul. All sorts of new ideas, new thinkers and writers flooded her mind.

She joined a sorority, Theta Sigma Chi, but in her junior year, with an impassioned speech, she resigned. Certain "kinds" of girls—in this case, Hawaiians, she had learned—would not be accepted. Kate raged, flexed her polemical muscles. Exclusion on the basis of race or religion received the full crescendo of her budding adversarial skills.

And then, as Kate would remember it, she began to pound the drums for a far more bizarre idea. Women's equality. Shocking her classmates, she voiced her doubts about the rigidly housebound role assumed for women, about her own future, about theirs. Where was it written that every one of them would find ultimate happiness solely and exclusively in caring for a family? Why should it be assumed that women were deficient, inherently inferior to men, that any attempt to forge a career perverted the "holy mission" of femininity?

These were indeed strange ideas for a "coed" of the fifties. And certain ideas, certain questioning of the status quo, the America of the postwar world had come to understand, were actually dangerous.

By then, U.S. forces were blocking the Communist expansion in Korea, but at home, to many Americans, the menace seemed even greater: Communist thought. That political ideas were dangerous was made abundantly clear by the Army-McCarthy hearings on the amazingly powerful new medium known as television. That sexual ideas —or the printed words that conveyed them—were equally threatening was evidenced by the fact that author Henry Miller's books, banned in this country, had to be smuggled in from France, that the film version of *The Moon Is Blue* was refused Hollywood's seal of approval because the word "virgin" was spoken aloud.

While Senator Joseph McCarthy was intimidating witnesses with political rhetoric ("Are you now or have you ever been a member of the Communist party?"), Kate's Minnesota classmates, it seemed to her, attacked with a not dissimilar but stunningly popular new weapon: "You ought to see a therapist."

These crazy ideas were Kate's sickness, her obsession, her "hobby-horse," as they called it.

And indeed, though Kate's bobby sox were properly rolled, her Lanz dresses with their tiny flowered prints and her Peter Pan collars roundly appropriate, she had begun to feel more and more eccentric. More out of place.

Different from the others.

By her senior year, the "difference" assumed alarming proportions. For Kate herself and for her family. To Helen's great joy, Kate was graduating from the university magna cum laude and Phi Beta Kappa. To the horror of the entire family, she had also fallen in love with and was now living with a woman.

PART II

7

THE
FEMININE
MYSTIQUE

*It was a strange stirring, a sense of dissatisfaction,
a yearning that women suffered in the middle of the
twentieth century in the United States. Each suburban
wife struggled with it alone. As she made the beds,
shopped for groceries, matched slipcover material, ate
peanut butter sandwiches with her children, chauf-
feured Cub Scouts and Brownies, lay beside her husband at night, she was afraid to ask even of herself the
silent question—"Is this all?"*

—Betty Friedan, *The Feminine Mystique*, 1963

Her so-called "brilliant career"! Not much had come of that, Betty
thought miserably as she trudged back to her beloved Smith College
for her fifteenth reunion. The great promise her professors had seen
—that eager, whirling intellectual energy—had come to nothing
more than a couple of women's magazine articles. Hardly "brilliant."
Hardly even worthy of the term "career"!

Betty—the class of 1942's hortatory, patriotic, tough tomato, al-
ways ready to take on an argument and, more often than not, *win* it.
That same plump little girl who was so determined, way back in
Peoria, to make her snooty contemporaries "respect her," who had set

out, in her younger brother Harry's words, "to be somebody important . . ."

She was now, in 1957, returning to the alma mater that had been, for her, such a glory, an affirmation, "that whole thing," as she would put it years later in her gruff, gravelly voice, "of the *passion* of the mind." And she was coming back not as the professional psychologist they must all have expected, but as, well, "just a housewife" with a few articles to her credit.

"It rankled me," she would remember, "because I hadn't lived up to my brilliant possibilities."

But the undergraduates on campus, she found, were not the slightest bit interested in such "possibilities," and she was shocked by their distracted answers to her questions. Questions about, naturally, their scholarly interests, what ideas or professors they were "passionately excited about."

"They looked at me," she would recall, "as if I were speaking a foreign language. 'We're not excited about things like that,' they said. 'All we want to do is to get married and have children and do things with them, like go ice skating . . .' "

But it was now, of course, the quiet Eisenhower era, the gritrock pit of what would be viewed in retrospect as the heavy-duty husband-hunting years. "I chased her until she caught me," was a standard husband's joke, though the truth probably lay as much in the male youth's intent on settling down as the female's. The house in the suburbs, the station wagon bursting with kids and collie dogs, the ability to provide for a family proved manhood as much as home-making proved femininity, and testified as well to those most important virtues of the decade: "adjustment," "maturity."

By now psychology was a preoccupation. Freud's vaunted theory of "penis envy" and Deutsch's interpretation of the achieving, intellectual woman as "masculinized . . . her warm, intuitive knowledge . . . [having] yielded to cold unproductive thinking," hinted of maladjustments to be avoided at all costs. The idea that woman's true nature, reflecting her anatomy, was passive and could be fulfilled only through renouncing her goals and "sublimating" to a male had taken firm root in the American ethic.

The women's magazines, growing ever more powerful as advertising pages and circulations mounted, had been pounding the message home for nearly a decade. Women, as Lundberg and Farnham had written, needed propaganda to keep them *in* traditional homemaking tasks, such as cooking or decorating, and *out* of those "fields belonging to the male area"—that is, "law, mathematics, physics, business, industry and technology." And indeed, the magazines invariably portrayed women as, above and beyond all else, housewives and mothers. If an interview subject happened to be an actress or dancer (two acceptably feminine undertakings), the editors quickly clarified: She was merely dabbling, taking a breather from her real work—and life —at home.

Nor was this notion purely the province of the popular press. Great citadels of learning were equally convinced and convincing. In most eastern women's schools, "gracious living" was the order of the day. This meant, on the whole, little more than learning to pour tea from a silver-plated samovar. But to carry out this future mission, give or take a samovar, you had to have a life of gentility, with, of course, a husband. Most college women, even those who never stood their turn at the tea kettle, knew beyond a shadow of a doubt that marriage— not a career—was their primary goal in life. Running a close second was the psychological health of their children, who were likely to erupt into neurotic misfits, psychologists warned, should Mother attempt any serious work outside the home.

Admittedly, the female's focus on marriage had an extra edge. The birth rate was soaring and given their dependent condition, women needed to be supported financially. The status gap of the thirties— between the gracious, respected matron, cared for by her breadwinner husband, and the lonely, forlorn working girl—was revived and slickly refurbished. Rare indeed was the college counselor who, by discussing the job market, would damn a female graduate to the latter state.

Some women left college without graduating. (Might as well get on with it. What's the point of waiting, anyhow?) Most collected a "Mrs." after or with their undergraduate degrees. You understood that you were marrying not just a husband but "a life," and this wholesale effort seemed at the time to blur class distinctions. Women cooked pot roast everywhere.

That there were, in fact, differences—in both class and interests— would eventually create knotty problems for feminists of the future. Many women, not only working-class women but also those with less defined intellectual appetites, very much enjoyed their roles as homemakers, household decision makers, disciplinarians, or managers, preferences that would eventually set them at odds with the revolutionaries of the sixties.

At the moment, though, like it or not, most women were preparing for the esteemed role of "auxiliary."

If, for instance, a woman was married to a doctor, she would join the hospital "auxiliary," have dinner ready when the doctor got home, and subscribe to a magazine called *Doctor's Wife.*

It was a given, in those days, that a young woman with a burning interest in the law should marry a lawyer. She would help him develop his practice and live the life of a lawyer's wife, mother of a lawyer's children. Or an engineer's, or a writer's, or a pharmacist's, or a retailer's—or especially a corporate executive's. That the deportment of an executive's wife had a major influence on her husband's advancement was a lesson clearly delivered, not just in an announcement from Radcliffe College of an Institute for Executive Wives, but in Jean Negulesco's popular film pointedly entitled *Women's World.*

In this 1952 movie, Lauren Bacall—no longer the sultry siren of the forties—played a devoted wife who, along with two others, June Allyson and Arlene Dahl, was summoned to corporate headquarters in New York, where their husbands were about to audition for top honcho.

"The best couple for the job," the company owner frankly informed the men, "will win. Your wife is under observation. She must never compete with the company. If there is a choice between wife and work, it must be work."

As the husbands in this "women's world" proceeded with their unmemorable politicking, the motivations (and "qualifications") of the wives were quickly established. June was frightfully anxious to rush home to her kids in the Midwest. Lauren fretted that the job might exacerbate her husband's ulcer. Arlene, on the other hand, was so delighted by the prospect of life in New York that she overreached by flirting with the owner, thus proving that she had missed not just one, but several commandments dosed out in the dialogue.

I: "What's important to him is important to me."

II: "You must convince him that you're perfectly happy even if you feel like screaming."

III: "The man who gets the job must have a wife who loves him very much."

IV (the overriding theme): "A man is working for the children, and they're your children so it's a *woman's world.*"

And if, in the end, it's Arlene's man who does win the job, this plot twist occurs only after her restrained, expressionless husband has impressed the owner by dispensing with his "handicap": his ambitious, brazen, childless (and therefore dispensable) wife.

Though heavy-handed, the movie accurately reflected a large segment of the women's world of the fifties, where back in the suburbs wives quickly buried ambitions of the sort (vicarious or not) that plagued the unfortunate Arlene.

Few could imagine, in the expanding economy of the post–Korean War years, that among these selfless wives would be many who would find themselves, twenty and thirty years hence, in the wake of defunct marriages or financial belt-tightening, pounding the pavements, or training for jobs that could bring in much-needed cash or restore flagging self-esteem.

There were, of course, exceptions. A few remarkable college graduates *did* pursue professional careers. Among them, ironically—though barely noticed at the time—was an assertive, achieving Illinois woman who, in 1952, ran for Congress. Phyllis Schlafly, who would eventually stand forth as the new feminism's most vocal enemy, who would sound the alarm for women's return to the home, was among those who were not, at the moment, at home.

For even then, in spite of the social propaganda, many women, including those from middle-income families, were quietly moving into the workforce—so many, in fact, that they soon accounted for 60 percent of its growth in that decade. Among them were many single women, including college graduates who, as they waited for Mr. Right, took jobs as "Gal Fridays" in ad agencies, or as researchers, "helping" a reporter on a news magazine. Many took speed-writing or shorthand courses so they could be secretaries and thus avoid the typing pool, jobs for which there was plenty of call under "Female" in the help-wanted columns. The men who ran America's industries knew better than to give their girls (as in "Call my girl, she'll make an appointment for you") dangerous notions about careers. "Gal Fridays," summa cum laude be damned, ran errands and made coffee. They were lucky, they were told, to be hired at all, since it was a given that they wouldn't be around for long. If they were "normal," they would soon drop out to get married, have babies.

And if they were "normal," they were known to be emotionally delicate as well, not cut out for the rough-and-tumble of the business world. Bless their hearts, said the men, and *vive la difference!*

A "difference" to be as carefully cultivated as it had been during the war years.

If, for example, a wife was working outside the home, she retained her auxiliary, ladylike status by referring to her job as unimportant and transitory, a diversion, never a "career." She was helping out—just for the moment—with the family finances. She was subdued and modest. She strolled, seldom ran, let alone worked up a sweat. She knew better than to enter one of those rare girls' track meets, where young men guffawed to each other on the sidelines: "Nice tits" or "Some ass." She aspired, if not to June Allyson's saccharine self-sacrifice, to the controlled charm of Doris Day, the elfin poise of Audrey Hepburn, the serene aristocracy of Grace Kelly.

Any sign of ambition was disaster. What would be known in the seventies as "abrasive" in the fifties was a "castrating bitch."

Simone de Beauvoir's *The Second Sex,* a brilliant feminist polemic, was published in this country in 1953, but nobody in America talked about it much. The revolutionary Kinsey Report on *Sexual Behavior in the Human Female,* documenting the fact that women enjoyed sex both emotionally and physically pretty much the same way men did, went barely noticed in America's heartland. As the lure of television swept the country, people watched "Ozzie and Harriet" and "Father Knows Best," images of the perfect American family. Blacks appeared on the screen almost solely as servants; women, as wives and mothers. It was the age of "conformity," or, as probably suited best, the "silent generation."

And yet . . .

Anyone with an ear to the quiet, frozen lake of the mid-fifties might have heard the rumble, the growl and surge of a riptide beneath the ice. In the late forties, Holden Caulfield, J. D. Salinger's sensitive hero of *Catcher in the Rye,* inspired thousands of young fans by limning the hypocrisy he saw around him. (No one yet used the term "drop out," but Holden seemed destined to do it.) In 1954, the Supreme Court ordered desegregation in all public schools, an act that would not only change the paper-white face of the country, but may well have precipitated the enormous upheavals to come. In 1955, the sensitive, introspective James Dean struck a chord of disaffection in *Rebel Without a Cause.* Elvis Presley had begun to heat up and transform the soul of pop music. Writers Jack Kerouac in *On the Road* and Allen Ginsberg in "Howl" were giving voice to a strange youthful ennui, a rough-timbered, off-balance sense of disillusionment.

In 1953, *Playboy* magazine—with a nude calendar photo of Marilyn Monroe—was launched. Being the "party organ," as feminist writer Barbara Ehrenreich would one day call it, of the male, hedonistic rebellion, it had nothing good to say about collie dogs, station wagons, church picnics, or the family. It was billed as Hugh Hefner's answer to conformity, to "home, family and all that jazz," as he put it, and to "togetherness"—the resoundingly successful advertising slogan of *McCall's* magazine, the symbol of the happy, glorified home with Daddy at work, Mommy in the kitchen, and 2.5 children as total fulfillment.

"The Togetherness Woman" was, in fact, the title of the article Betty had promised *McCall's*. She had taken the assignment simply to justify the months and months she had spent on a questionnaire that Smith had asked her to prepare for her class reunion.

Betty had labored mightily over the thing, even brought a couple of her friends in to hash over the questions. She had worked so hard, in fact, that her classmates at the reunion had giggled about how *long* the form was. How involved, how detailed the questions.

"What difficulties have you found in working out your role as a woman?" "What are the chief satisfactions and frustrations of your life today?" "How do you feel about getting older?" Leave it to Betty, the psychology buff, they joked, to dream up all that stuff!

Yet all she had been trying to do was prove one little point, just a corollary to the women's home-is-all psychology of the day, a sort of reassurance to her classmates and herself.

"All I was trying to do with that questionnaire," Betty would remember, "was to show that an education wasn't *bad* for a woman, it didn't make her *maladjusted* in her role as wife and mother." That academic learning was not, in short—as so many psychologists were then implying—an actual hindrance to femininity.

"I didn't realize it at the time," she would recall, "but I was asking the questions that were beginning to concern me." For indeed, skilled as she was in social science, and guiltily restless, Betty had designed the sort of query that took dead aim at the secrets of the heart—including her own.

"How have you changed inside?" she asked. "What do you wish you had done differently?"

And when, finally, she sat down to analyze the results for *McCall's*, she discovered that the responses raised more questions than they answered. Why was it, for example, that those of her classmates who were not active outside their homes were not especially happy at all? That they seemed, in fact, just as restless as she was?

They had written about a strange sense of emptiness—how like her own!—or a gnawing guilt, or shame, an uncertainty about who, exactly, they were: Jim's wife? Sally's mother? Betty found turmoils of indecision among these stay-at-home moms, and ennui, feelings of failure, despair, depression—even, for some, alcohol and drugs. And, most striking of all, from those isolated posts in suburbia, the uneasy sense that, because they had these feelings, they were unquestionably "neurotic."

So clearly Betty was not, as she had once thought, alone with these feelings. She was not, as she had also thought, a "freak."

But was education the villain, as all the psychologists and anthropologists and social scientists and magazine writers were more or less subtly suggesting?

That was, quite simply, a premise that the intense, verbal, thirty-six-year-old sometime writer, with her longings for intellectual achievement, could not accept. And as Betty read and reread and searched and analyzed, she discovered yet another piece to the puzzle.

"I found," she would remember at a later, much calmer time of her life, "that the women who seemed the strongest were not quite living this complete image of the housewife and feminine fulfillment. And that education had made them not willing to settle. . . ."

She was on to something!

Slowly but passionately, she began to write. Words and sentences began to fill the pages, words that bore no resemblance to "Millionaire's Wife," or "Two Are an Island," or anything she had ever written before. No panaceas, no hopeful methods of adjusting to the status quo, of finding total fulfillment in the home, poured forth from her pen. Instead of praising the homemaking role, she attacked the endless, monotonous, unrewarding housework it demanded. Instead of soothing her potential readers into the "feminine role" prescribed by the magazine she was writing for, she blasted the notion of vicarious living through husband and children. Rather than touting the "togetherness" so precious to *McCall's*, she indicted the slogan as a fraud.

She had to be kidding.

The male editor of *McCall's* summarily rejected "The Togetherness Woman."

A nasty shock for Betty Friedan. Never in her life had anything she had written been turned down. Quickly, she interviewed more women, then sent the piece to *Ladies' Home Journal*. There, sure enough, it was accepted, but . . .

"They rewrote it," she would remember years later, with the anger and dismay still in her voice, "to make the opposite point! That education *did* make women maladjusted in their role as women!"

Betty refused to allow the magazine to publish the article, retrieved it, and made one last try.

Bob Stein, then editor of *Redbook*, said he would indeed be interested in a piece based on Betty's Smith class questionnaire if it was greatly expanded to include younger women, and other, more extensive data.

Betty was already talking to younger married women and they weren't changing her view of the problem at all. In fact, she was beginning to think, the situation for women who graduated from college after 1942 seemed to be even worse than it was for her classmates. Given that domestic fantasy she had already seen among members of Smith's graduating class, even fewer women in their twenties and early thirties were active outside their homes; even *more* seemed vaguely unhappy.

She hadn't yet been paid for the article, of course, and she was violating that "enough-money-to-pay-the-maid" pact with herself. But still, since Bob Stein had asked—and since she was fascinated herself —she did more interviews. She rewrote the piece, integrating the new material, and shipped it off to the editor.

Who was, he would remember, stunned.

"I liked Betty a lot," Bob Stein would recall. "She was a solid, trustworthy writer, a bit argumentative maybe, but so were most writers worth their salt. I had been looking forward to 'The Togetherness Woman,' but when I read it, I could only wonder what in God's name had come over Betty Friedan. It was a very angry piece. I didn't think that our readers would identify with it at all."

The *Redbook* editor—like all successful editors of women's magazines—was fully aware of the link binding readers to *their* magazine, the great umbilical, as some called it, the trust which, if broken, could doom both magazine and its boss. And Betty was, Bob Stein would remember, "very sensitive about her writing. . . . Luckily, I'd never had to reject her work before." But this?

In years to come, Bob Stein would find himself on television and radio talk shows with Betty, defending her, if only because, as he would put it, "the opposition was so impossible," but admitting, too, that he hadn't realized "that the feelings dammed up out there were so strong." At the moment, though, he could only call Betty's agent and report regretfully: "Look, we can't print this. Only the most neurotic housewife would identify with this."

And that, perhaps, might have been the end of it.

Redbook had been Betty's last hope, and in the weeks that followed, she was very depressed. She wrote nothing and dropped out of an important writer's seminar because it met the same night of the week that she served as assistant den mother for her son's Cub Scout troop. She had already chastised herself, had an asthma attack, in fact, over missing some of those Scout meetings.

One night, though, just as a prop to her ego, just to make herself feel like a professional writer again, she made the trek in from Rockland County to hear the successful author Vance Packard talk about his book *The Hidden Persuaders,* an exposé of the sinister effects of advertising. Packard had written it, he said, after an article on the subject had been turned down by every major magazine.

And then—not long afterward, as Betty would remember it—she was riding the bus into Manhattan, taking the kids to the dentist, mulling it over . . . The juggernaut women's magazines, with their fingers on the commercial pulse, had been feeding the domestic palate to ever-rising profit margins . . .

"Damn it all," Betty suddenly realized, "I was right! Somehow what I was saying had gone against the grain of the women's magazines."

And now she knew she couldn't let it go.

In some deep place in the psyche of this impatient, demanding, worrisome, dedicated, prickly, volatile woman, a quiet vision was forming. Inside, as she would later write, she felt "this calm, strange sureness, as if in tune with something larger, more important than myself that had to be taken seriously."

It would be a book. Like *The Hidden Persuaders,* "The Togetherness Woman" could be a book. She would call that editor who had wanted her to expand "The Coming Ice Age," and this time she would tell him yes. Yes, she would write a book for W. W. Norton. But just as she had said before, it would not be about someone else's work. It would be hers. Her own research, her own social science, her own accomplishment in her field.

The Togetherness Woman.

And why not? said George Brockway, who immediately saw the potential.

The affluence of the fifties had permitted—even stimulated—critical examinations of contemporary life. *The Man in the Grey Flannel Suit, The Hucksters, Executive Suite, The View from the 40th Floor* had all been big sellers. *The Togetherness Woman,* the editor thought, would make a fine parallel to the latest sharp attack on the rage for conformity, William H. Whyte's *The Organization Man.*

And this woman had the fire in the belly.

"She was incredibly ambitious," Brockway would remember. "The most ambitious woman I had ever met. She said that she didn't know what to call the subject exactly, but that it had something to do with a lack of identity, that women weren't being told . . . they aren't being allowed . . ."

Betty talked on and on at that meeting, half her thoughts, as usual, dropping off mid-sentence, her mind going even faster than her tongue. She had been interviewing so many women. She didn't know quite how to put it, but . . .

There was *something* very wrong with the way women were feeling these days.

And, over the barrage, the furtive insights, the distress, George Brockway honed in.

"Ride it," he told Betty. "You've got the idea, now ride it, ride it!"

How long did she think it would take?

Well, she said, it took her about a month to do an article, so figure a chapter a month . . .

"A year," she said, "I'll have it done in a year." Oh, and yes, she supposed a thousand dollars now would be okay, with the rest of the $3,000 to come in installments.

It was years later—more research was required, a mysterious block arose—before Betty even *began* to write. She worked three days a week in the Frederick Lewis Allen Room of the New York Public Library and then, when her allotted time there ran out (and the maid quit), in her favorite spot at home, the beautiful dining room with windows on the garden.

"Neither my husband nor my publisher nor anyone else who knew about it thought I would ever finish it," she would write. "When the writing of it took me over completely . . . I wrote every day on the dining room table, while the children were in school, and after they went to bed at night. (It didn't do any good to have a desk of my own; they used it for their homework anyhow.)"

She worked against patronizing jokes about a "woman's book." Against guilt. Against fear. Given the resistance she had already encountered to her views, there must be *no* holes in her argument or her documentation, *no* room for attack.

But slowly, if not steadily, the chapters, scribbled on a legal pad, began to pile up in an old china cupboard in the corner of the dining room. In them, her thesis emerged.

At rock bottom, it was economics, if not to say greed. After World War II, women had been pushed back into the home as industrialists assessed the housewife's valuable role as the prime consumer of household products. The marketing of toasters, washing machines, cosmetics, and the like was the true purpose behind the hard sell of "femininity." Educators, sociologists, psychologists—and, of course, the women's magazines, with their hunger for the advertising dollar —followed suit.

One by one, Betty took them all on, both the current crop and their historical forebears.

Freud and his "sexual solipsism": "It is a Freudian idea . . . hardened into apparent fact, that has trapped so many American women today." Freud and his Victorian bias had perpetrated the greatest sin in psychotherapy; he had infantilized women, denied them their ability to grow, cut them off from "the zest that is characteristic of human health."

Margaret Mead: "The role of Margaret Mead as the professional spokesman [sic] of femininity would have been less important if American women had taken the example of her own life, instead of listening to what she said in her books."

Contemporary educators: They induced women into the superficial comfort of the home, thus depriving them of their function in society, consigning millions of women "to spend their days at work an eight-year-old could do."

As for the women's magazines, which offered that fraudulent home-as-religion editorial content: "I helped create this image. I have watched American women for fifteen years try to conform to it. But I can no longer deny its terrible implications. It is not a harmless image. There may be no psychological terms for the harm it is doing."

And, of course, "togetherness": "The big lie . . . the end of the road . . . where the woman has no independent self to hide even in guilt; she exists only for and through her husband and children."

It was this vicarious existence that caused educations to "fester," caused housewife's fatigue, ennui, depression. Not neurosis. It was society—not women—that was sick!

Like Lundberg and Farnham, Betty resurrected earlier feminists, but instead of damning them as sick souls, she sang their praises as heroines. Mary Wollstonecraft, Margaret Fuller, Elizabeth Cady Stanton, Lucy Stone, Susan B. Anthony. Anatomy, she agreed, with a somewhat cursory bow to Simone de Beauvoir's evocative phrasing in *The Second Sex,* is not destiny. Women were not simply their biology. They also had *minds.* And, "as if waking from a coma," they were beginning to ask, "Where am I? What am I doing here?"

She answered the hyperbole of Lundberg and Farnham with some of her own. The isolated suburban home, she wrote, was a "comfortable concentration camp," the women trapped within them cut off, like prisoners, from past adult interests and their own identities. It was a new neurosis, this modern ache, and you could read it in the hundreds of interviews and psychological tests she had accumulated —among them, one test that must have been reassuring, since it suggested that "the high-dominance woman was more psychologically free" than one who was "timid, shy, modest, neat, tactful, quiet, introverted, retiring, more feminine, more conventional." And perhaps, Betty herself speculated, only an "ugly duckling adolescence" or an unhappy marriage could fuel the ambition to resist the deadening, conformist pressure.

For "the problem lay buried, unspoken, for many years in the minds of American women." It was a problem, she wrote, "that had no name," a problem that was caused by the pervasive social pressure relegating women to the four walls of their homes, a pressure whose weapon was an image: "the feminine mystique."

Five years from the time Betty had signed the contract, four years late, *The Feminine Mystique* was published.

It was February 1963, and the New York newspapers, including the *Times,* were on strike. With no review in the *Times,* the chances that a book—even this thunderous polemic—would reach a substantial public were practically nil. And there was plenty of competition.

Morton Hunt had just published a gentle, affectionate paean to women's role *outside* as well as in the home. His book was called *Her Infinite Variety*, and it was moving off the bookstore shelves at a frighteningly rapid pace.

Betty was beside herself. And so, for that matter, was Carl. Never had the state of their marriage been worse, never stormier than during the last year she was writing, when, Carl would complain to friends, he would come home from work and "that bitch," instead of cooking dinner, was writing away at the dining-room table. Betty, friends would whisper, was writing out the problems of her marriage, writing a book instead of leaving Carl. His one-man advertising and public relations firm was far from a booming success, and now this. Who would even hear of *The Feminine Mystique*, let alone buy it? Where, after all these years, was the payoff?

"Betty would come in with ideas to promote the book," George Brockway would recall. "You could tell Carl was behind them, saying, 'Tell 'em to do this, tell 'em to do that.'

"One day she told me that Carl wanted to know what could be done to make *The Feminine Mystique* as big a seller as *Gifts from the Sea*." (This popular book was written by Anne Morrow Lindbergh, the wife of the heroic aviator.)

" 'Tell Carl,' I told her, 'that he can fly the Atlantic solo.' "

Irascible Carl, George would call him—the low-key editor being far from charmed by what he regarded as Carl Friedan's "sharp and nasty" tongue.

But Betty thought her husband knew his business. She would always remember that it was Carl who had persuaded Norton to hire a publicist. Eventually, in fact, she would switch to another publishing house, leaving Brockway entirely.

"I remember him pleading with me," Betty would tell a reporter, "and I remember looking him right in the eye and saying, 'George, you made me feel Jewish for trying to sell that book. Go fuck yourself.' "

But, with the help of the publicist, excerpts from the book began to appear, and articles ran in major news magazines about Betty as an "angry battler for her sex." She began bouncing around the country for speaking engagements, crusaded enthusiastically on radio and that potent new vehicle, the television talk show.

After one of these appearances—outside Rockefeller Center—she met another author who had just taped a show herself. She was just about Betty's age, a former copywriter who had performed the remarkable feat of hitting the nonfiction best-seller list the year before.

The woman was Helen Gurley Brown, and her book, *Sex and the Single Girl,* aimed, obviously, at the burgeoning singles market, had actually set down in print the startling notion that it was perfectly all right to have "an affair." Even with a married man.

For those who would, in retrospect, regard the sexual revolution as either intrinsic to or actually the wellspring of the Golden Age of Feminism, it would be hard to ignore the pioneering role of Helen Brown. Most feminists, however, would manage to do just that.

It was a matter, in part, of philosophy. In even greater part, perhaps, of style.

Sex and the Single Girl was a typical how-to of the women's magazine genre. It offered advice on decorating your apartment, diet, clothes, and money—not, however, for the purpose of hooking a man into marriage, but for getting him into your bed.

Helen Brown didn't protest much of anything—least of all society's ills. She only wrote about, as she herself insisted, what was already going on anyhow. Single women having sex with men, married or not. She simply made them feel better about doing it. Like the women's magazines, and in a similarly blithe, not to say giddy style, she was reassuring and helpful. The major difference—the shocker—was that while the women's magazines were still righteously committed to the double standard, continually warning their readers of the dire consequences of sex without marriage, Helen Gurley Brown wrote that this was perfectly okay. "Nice single girls *do* have affairs and they don't necessarily die of them." *Sex and the Single Girl*—aimed, unlike underground erotica, at a mass audience—was undoubtedly something of a relief.

The single life the book touted was one of supreme independence, satisfying work, fashion and success and money—a life, in short, that most married women were bound to envy. The single woman was sexy, Helen had written, "because she lives by her wits." She was not "a parasite, a dependent, a scrounger, a sponger or a bum." And when, in 1965, Helen would take over the Hearst Corporation's ailing *Cosmopolitan,* the appeal of that view, and the skill of its pragmatic, meticulous editor, would eventually triple the magazine's circulation.

On television, Helen was, from the beginning, flirtatious, supremely tactful, frankly manipulative, an open disciple of male-flattering femininity. "Helen Gurley Girly," some viewers called her.

She was a former secretary who had never gone to college and didn't plan to, a "girl" for whom *work* was the given, the man in one's life the pleasure to be sought. She had written her book at the suggestion of her husband, movie producer David Brown, and she had no hesitation about saying so.

And yet, in spite of Helen's flirtatiousness, and the focus on sex, which, Betty had written, was totally irrelevant, actually damaging to women's struggle for independence, the two women liked each other.

"We talked about business, promotion, all that," Helen would remember. "We became friends . . . and we've been friends ever since." They differed, but, in spite of her passionate nature, Betty would often differ with someone and still remain a loyal friend.

Unlike Helen Brown, however, Betty wasn't "cool"; her personality was not tailor-made for television. Often, in impatient, enthusiastic pursuit of an idea, she would talk so fast that hardly anyone could understand her. Or leave sentences dangling. Or angrily demand time. Her publicist would remember her screaming at hostess Virginia Graham on "Girl Talk": "If you don't let me have my say, I'm going to say orgasm ten times."

But Betty had been provoked.

Virginia Graham, Betty would one day explain, had coaxed the camera: " 'Girls, how many of us really need bylines? What better thing can we do with our lives than to do the dishes for those we love?'

"Well, I knew that her agent fought for every foot of the size of her byline on the television screen, and I wondered when the last time was she'd done the dishes for someone she loved. I turned to the camera and said, 'Women, don't listen to her. She needs you out there doing the dishes, or she wouldn't have the captive audience for this television program, whose byline she evidently doesn't want you to compete for.' "

Betty never was, never would be, any talk show host's favorite guest. She was confrontational, often tactless, and not—by any standards—a TV beauty.

But neither was she a phony. And there was something about this woman, who looked like everyone's *gemütlich* Aunt Minnie, something about what she proclaimed, in her hell-for-leather style, that made hundreds of viewers attend.

Scores of Americans, of course, including many women, were outraged. They could scarcely believe what they were hearing. A woman's career could be as important as a man's? A woman should go out in the world and compete with men? Make Casper Milquetoasts out of them?

One Smith alumna, writing in *Reader's Digest* about "the feminine *mistake*," saluted the housewife's "small acts of domesticity" with the good Scout cheer: "Well, sure! That's what we signed up for!" And when the *New York Times* got around to reviewing the book—in a short blurb under "Digest"—Lucy Freeman, who had written a bestseller on her own conquest of mental illness, zapped it as "superficial. . . . The fault, dear Mrs. Friedan, is not in our culture, but in ourselves."

"*Where*," wailed a letter writer in *Commonweal* magazine, "are all these women to go, having fled their homes? And *what* are they to do?"

In the midst of it all, Betty brought Carl and the kids back to Peoria for her twenty-fifth high school reunion. There, instead of praise, she found herself sitting alone at the banquet table. She stayed with a friend, and the next morning found the tree outside her door festooned with toilet paper.

Yet the sales of *The Feminine Mystique* were beginning to climb, and there was no stopping Betty now. Especially since hundreds of letters, expressing enormous gratitude, were starting to pour in. Letters from women who said they had no idea, until they read her book, that anyone else had such strange feelings. They had felt, they wrote, like sexual freaks, or like "appliances," insecure in their dependence, unable, much longer, to keep up the "act" of selflessness. She had given them courage, they wrote, to go back to school, to begin careers.

For threaded through the social criticism of *The Feminine Mystique* was also a message of Emersonian self-reliance and responsibility. This message was not, at bottom, altogether unlike Helen Brown's, but it was one that would set Betty at odds with many women who might have been her allies. Since, as Betty wrote, the women she was addressing were not those beset by dire poverty or disease, they were not, therefore, *completely* at the mercy of an unjust society.

"In the last analysis," Betty had written, "millions of able women in this free land choose themselves not to use the door education could have opened for them. The choice—and the responsibility—for the race back [to the] home was finally their own."

Not every new feminist, she would discover before the decade was out, would agree.

8

I WAS A
PLAYBOY BUNNY

Literally millions of women seem to have been taken to Deep Throat *by their boyfriends or husbands (not to mention prostitutes who were taken by their pimps) so that each one might learn what a woman could do to please a man if she really wanted to. . . . Of course, if the female viewer were really a spoilsport, she might identify with the woman on screen and sense her humiliation, danger and pain—but the smiling, happy face of Linda Lovelace could serve to cut off empathy, too.* She's there because she wants to be. Who's forcing her? See how she's smiling? See how a real woman enjoys this?

—Gloria Steinem, *Outrageous Acts and Everyday Rebellions*, 1983

The same year that Betty published *The Feminine Mystique*, another book—by Gloria Steinem—appeared in the bookstores. It was called *The Beach Book*, and had nothing to do with feminism. It was an anthology of excerpts from literature about beaches, including Gloria's own suggestions of things to do while sunbathing, fantasies one might have, for instance: "A landing party from Aristotle Onassis' yacht has just come ashore to ask you to join them. You say no." Or

"You share a ham sandwich with a gaunt, gray-haired man who turns out to be Huntington Hartford. 'Such kindness should be rewarded,' he says. 'Here is the deed to Paradise Island.' "

With its emphasis on money and good looks ("What a tan will do is make you look good, and that justifies everything"), Gloria's jazzy copy read, in places, not unlike *Sex and the Single Girl*.

For a young single woman in New York, which Gloria was, the sparkling, silver-foiled book—its cover a sun reflector—was perfectly in tune with the times. The city, in the early sixties, was such a post-college party town—so brimming with single "guys and girls" meeting each other in front of Picasso's *Guernica* at the Museum of Modern Art, at P. J. Clarke's or the White Horse, or, weekends, at ski lodges and Fire Island Pines—that Joan Didion wrote a cool-eyed article about the scene for *Mademoiselle*. For the unmarried, New York was all "red balloons," in her view, a *Great Gatsby* fantasy, "an endless snowbound houseparty." It was a "great reprieve," a long holiday, a way for "girls to postpone commitment."

It was also Kennedyesque, ebulliently alive with the promise of the handsome new president and his princess—the aristocratic Jackie, who wore, with such impeccable style, exquisitely tailored designer clothes and her much imitated pillbox hat. Richard Burton was playing in *Camelot*, the musical hymn to royalty that was a favorite of the Kennedy clan. Films like *The Apartment* and *Never on Sunday* were gently loosening public inhibitions. "Banned in Boston," a catchword of the fifties, disappeared as the courts lifted bans on such books as *Lady Chatterly's Lover*.

Conformity (or at least the appearance of it) was as out of style as cinch belts and crinolines. Life, the youth of America was beginning to protest, had to mean something more than the dreary pursuit of the organization man's paycheck. Unlike most of their parents, these affluent young people had traveled. They had trekked across Europe, worked in the lumber camps of Finland or the *kibbutzim* of Israel, and they had seen *more*. Something nobler was required, something more honorable and open-hearted than lounging beside a suburban barbecue pit while their neighbors, in Bermuda shorts, gingerly asked the sole invited "Negro" if he knew Jackie Robinson.

The civil rights movement was taking over the news columns, and "We Shall Overcome" thrilled the heart. Since 1961, when a crowd of two hundred southern whites had attacked a busload of biracial northern activist youths, a bloody, heroic legend was in the making.

Not just Roy Wilkins and Whitney Young were heard from now, but Martin Luther King, Jr., as well. Not only the NAACP (the National Association for the Advancement of Colored People), but a string of far more militant organizations such as CORE (Congress of Racial Equality) and SNCC (Student Nonviolent Coordinating Committee).

Since that day in 1957 when Betty Friedan first stacked her treasure trove of college questionnaires on her dining-room table through those six long years of furious thinking and scribbling, the whole country had been transformed. The thick ice of the fifties had cracked and the flow of change—obsessional, courageous, angelic, anarchic, and, for the moment, mostly visionary—would, by the end of the decade, thunder like a cataract.

The civil rights movement was certainly the spearhead, but from another direction came a surge of creativity that, in publishing at least, centered in New York. Sophisticated "hip" new magazines, wittily irreverent, verging sometimes on the hysterical, were proudly "underground"; others were grander, slicker, more glossily artistic.

For Gloria, a young woman with a future, New York was the place to be. Getting there, however, had not been simple. The route she had taken to that city of possibilities had been circuitous, both adventurous and chancy.

Synchronize watches! her father had said. He would take charge of his ailing, hallucinating ex-wife for exactly twelve months, and then back she went to her daughters.

This time, Susanne had shouldered the load. Married by then and living in Washington, D.C., Gloria's older sister had taken Ruth into her home. (And from there, eventually, to a carefully chosen mental hospital.) Gloria could enjoy her college years free of serving her mother's meals or worrying about when the next dose of chemicals could put Ruth to sleep.

And she *had* enjoyed them.

"If I deplored girls who left college to marry and live in Westchester," she would one day recall, "it wasn't because I thought they were buying security or marrying too young . . . but because I couldn't understand their wanting to leave a nice place like Smith where people gave you wonderful books to read and cooked your meals for you."

Gloria, her cheeks rounded by the ten pounds that she would

always complain she *should* have lost then, was nonetheless stunningly beautiful. Five feet, seven inches tall, straight-backed, long-legged, she often wore her dark hair pulled neatly back (only much later would it flow straight below her shoulders and be streaked blond). Always, there was the brilliant, even smile, the soft look of vulnerability, of acceptance. And she was agreeable, never supersensitive or touchy; bright but never the prickly pear that so many young, intellectual females seemed to be. Modest, poised, tactful, Gloria, as a legion of admirers would attest, was a dream girl.

"She was self-contained," her classmate Joanna Barnes would recall. "She was self-aware in a way that few college kids are, and it set her apart. She may not have known where she was going but she sure seemed to know she was going *somewhere.* I thought she would be a dancer. Or a writer. She seemed to be mulling it over . . . as though she knew she could make a difference."

And finding a man, in those matchmaking days, was hardly a problem for Gloria.

"I'd hate to get into heated combat with Gloria over a man," Joanna would add, and Joanna, a beauty herself, who would eventually embark on a successful television and writing career, would compare Gloria to "a mermaid. Men would wreck their ships."

And yet, as the fifties moved toward a loosening of the male sexual ethic, Gloria, like most other young women, was caught in a peculiar squeeze.

The new, free *Playboy* mentality had done little to change the social strictures for women. (Anatomically, of course, it put in its order for bigger, whiter breasts.) Young men were beginning to expect and demand more of them sexually, yet young women were still considered either promiscuous "bad girls" on the one hand, or the uncompromised future wives and mothers of America, on the other.

Using a diaphragm—even venturing to a doctor's office to get one—had indecent overtones. It implied that the young woman was not, as she professed, simply swept away, like Jennifer Jones in *Duel in the Sun.* It meant that she had actually premeditated the act of sex, a calculation that immediately threw her into the unmarriageable category of "slut."

Furthermore, in the fifties, as in millennia past, to be unmarried and pregnant was its own form of hell. An unwed mother brought disgrace on a family, no less heinous than a criminal son. A young woman in a small town was whisked off to a secret place, gossiped about in coffee klatches, and when she returned, that hapless girl might as well have been wearing a scarlet letter.

Abortion—even the word itself—was taboo. When, in the popular movie *Summer Place,* teen idol Sandra Dee found herself "in the family way," such a solution was never even suggested. Marriage or tragedy was the only possible outcome.

But if, as the psychoanalyst Carl Jung claimed, a collective racial unconscious is passed generationally among peoples, the subliminal memory of all women must include images of untold abortions.

Of blood and violence. Of desperately poor married women, afraid they could not provide for a child, perhaps the third, the fourth, or the fifth, thrusting wire coat hangers, twigs, roots, knitting needles into their own wombs, drinking turpentine, lye, bleach. Or of unmarried women seeking back-alley abortionists; finding filth, the foul table, the unscrubbed instruments.

And of death.

Whatever their views about the legalization of abortion, most women would own these tribal memories.

"I got pregnant out of dumbness," Gloria would recall. "Lack of knowledge about contraception, really."

She had been dating Blair Chotzinoff, the son of a music publishing scion, in her senior year, was even engaged to him for a while. On and off actually, as, in sudden clutches of resistance, she changed her mind. Something about marriage frightened her. Her mother's life, perhaps. Or the finality, the end of adventure, of the hope for something better, of the possibility—Leo's endless faith—that "something wonderful" was yet to happen.

As luck and talent had it, in 1956, by the time she graduated from Smith, magna cum laude, a Chester Bowles scholarship to India had settled the issue. Gloria wrote Blair a note telling him she was sorry and, one night, she left it, with her engagement ring, on his pillow. Then she quickly sailed to England, to wait for her travel papers there.

It was cold and rainy in London that winter, and her Indian visa seemed, for some bureaucratic reason, to be taking forever. She took odd jobs around town, worked as a waitress.

Perhaps it was that. The cold or the change in the water. Or traveler's imbalance. Her period was a week late.

But then it was two weeks, three . . . and she knew.

"It was terrible," she would remember years later. Her large, dark eyes, almost Indian themselves in their sad slope at the corners, would seem to pull earthward even further. "I had no money. It was awful. I saw my whole life going, the total value in my life would be over."

Everything, she would remember, just slipping away.

Gloria knew who the father was and though, well into the eighties, she would not identify him, she would hint: "It's funny," she would remark, "he never put it together—the timing and all."

But the boy would have married her, she would recall. He would have "done his duty," as upstanding young men were supposed to do in such circumstances, give or take a shotgun. Gloria could certainly be saved from shame, the stigma of illegitimacy, the grief of an "orphaned" child. He would give her his name, a home, a "life." That was the idea, wasn't it? Women everywhere were busily, greedily "trapping" men into marriage, it was said. Pregnancy was supposed to be the cleverest bait of all. That was all every woman wanted.

In fact, it was exactly what this *man* wanted; the young *woman*, not at all.

"I later discovered that this was sort of purposeful on his part," Gloria would recall, "because he thought we would have to get married."

And though she believed this, she would not remember feeling angry. Only frightened, full of dread. Alone, barely reasoning, like legions of women before her, Gloria searched frantically for a remedy.

She rushed to the library. What about . . . she looked it up . . . horseback riding? She had heard that riding could cause a miscarriage.

No, nothing there. What else? What else?

And she read until, finally, she gave up. There was only what she already, of course, knew.

Abortion.

"I was naive about it," she would remember, "but I had heard enough to know that though it was risky, a person didn't *necessarily* die."

Then she would get one! She would go to . . . Paris. That was it! Paris had everything. Everyone knew it was the Sin City of the world. If she could only save enough money to get to Paris. And she would tell no one, of course, not even her college classmate who was married and living in London.

"I don't know why," she would confess. "It's silly but I couldn't. I just couldn't."

Meanwhile, though, with faint hope, she would go to a doctor. She would tell him a lie. She would not say that she didn't want to marry her boyfriend. Hearing that brazen rejection of a decent arrangement, the doctor was bound to deem her promiscuous or, worse, utterly selfish, and he would refuse to help her. So instead Gloria would tell him a story—long, involved, heart-rending.

The doctor—who had turned out to be a gentle, kindly old man—listened sympathetically.

"So you see," Gloria said at the end of her tale, "he won't marry me."

The old physician nodded. Whether or not he believed her, he had no solution. He would give her some medicine. If she was not pregnant, it would bring on her period. If she was, it would harm neither her nor the baby. That was all.

And back to her flat she went, only to find that the medicine, unsurprisingly, had no effect.

As the weeks dragged on, Gloria's depression grew heavier, and she began to speculate about something she had never in her life thought of before.

"It was the only time," she would remember. "The only time in my life. If I have any breath in me, I want to be there, but then . . . yes, I thought about suicide."

And if she had given birth to this baby? Thinking of that, for one moment, the burnished brown mirror of her eyes, that reflecting glass, would shatter. As if a Tarot card had been read, and what she had seen there was too terrifying to contemplate.

"I don't know what I would have done. I really don't know . . . If I had to come home and got married and had a child . . . Maybe I would be functioning, maybe I would have survived, but I don't see myself surviving . . . not in any real way . . .

"I can only imagine going quietly crazy . . ."

Then she would quickly switch focus. Her calm gaze would return as she shifted the emphasis—and the significance—of her pregnancy from her own feelings to global principle.

"It was like being colonized," she would say. "It's your ability to decide not to, as opposed to man's ability to force you to do that." And she would quote an Egyptian friend "who thinks that legal abortion is the single thing that changes the balance of power between women and men."

Meanwhile, though, in London, through the fog of her depression, she continued to move about the city. To work, to go to parties.

One night, at a literary gathering, help arrived from an unlikely source—an American playwright, supercilious and overbearing, who was entertaining the company by recounting the trials he had endured while casting his play. To add to his misfortunes, he rambled on, two of his actresses were pregnant, and he was forced to get them abortions.

Gloria suddenly paid close attention.

"Where?" she asked the playwright politely. "In France?"

"Of course not," he snickered. Didn't she know that France was a Catholic country? London was the place. In London, if you get two doctors to sign . . .

The next day, Gloria rushed back to the old physician. Yes, he agreed, if she got another doctor to sign (what, exactly, they were signing she never did find out), he would help. He would send her to another physician, on Harley Street, who would perform the abortion.

The new gynecologist—a woman, very elegant in a tweed suit, with a cigarette holder—was mildly contemptuous. How had Gloria got herself into this predicament in the first place? Now, at three months, it was almost too late.

"What are you going to do now?" she demanded to know, and when Gloria answered that she was going to India, the woman responded with what Gloria would always consider a racist remark: "Well, I don't suppose you'll get pregnant there."

Nonetheless, the procedure commenced. The doctor inserted a large tampon with a wire attached. Gloria was to go home and come back the next day.

The next day, there was an anesthetic, some pills, and somehow, it was over.

"There will be a little bleeding," the gynecologist said. "If there's a lot, let me know."

Gloria stayed in bed for a few days, pretending a back ailment. In spite of the ignorance, in spite of the horror tales, Gloria—like many women who underwent abortions—gave little thought to the physical consequences. Displacing terror with terror, the lesser with the greater—the birth of an unwanted child.

Basically, the abortion technique the gynecologist had used—insertions into the womb—was little different from the dangerous methods women had used for centuries. The conditions, however, were sterile, the evacuation performed hygienically.

And indeed, after a few days, the bleeding stopped. What Gloria would remember, most vividly, was the relief.

"Enormous relief," she would recall. "I used to try to stir up feelings of guilt. I used to think: Now if I had this child, how old would this child be? But I could never muster up one iota of feeling. It was the first time that I took control of my own life, the one time I made a decision totally on my own."

And though she would wish that the first physician, that kindly old man, had spared her those months of agony, she would also remember his words. He had sent her to Harley Street only after extracting a vow.

"You must promise me," he had insisted, "that you will never tell anyone, and you will lead your own life."

And so finally, she was off to India.

She studied there, traveled among the people, wore saris to graceful advantage, lived with a new lover. (In time, she would describe such relationships as a sort of extralegal serial monogamy, with former lovers becoming members of her extended family.)

Instinctively empathetic with the poor and the powerless, all those who could conceivably be viewed as victims of life, she was moved by the poverty she saw in India. She discovered, as she would write, that India's standard of living, "not ours, was the norm for most of the world."

She also learned about—found herself entranced by, as a matter of fact—the Emperor Asoka, who reigned in the second century B.C. Somehow, Gloria, unlike most young women, could perceive this ruler—a man—as a role model.

"He established a rule of law," she would say, "which was the same for everybody. He wrote all the laws on big stone pillars so everybody could see. He was very ecumenical. He didn't make religious wars. He protected animal life as well as human life."

And she returned, after two years, full of what she would describe as "a crusading zeal."

Leo, the cheerful adventurer, met her at the boat in San Francisco.

But what was this? His little girl with a college degree, two years in India, and no money, no rich husband? She was overeducated. Too specialized. What was she going to do to make a living? How impractical, said Leo, who at the moment had not enough cash to ferry them both back to Washington, D.C.

Still, he had an idea. A friend of his, a very important man, was about to market something new and very remarkable. (And if a person said he was important, Leo believed him.)

Now, said Leo, here's what this invention was—aerosol cans! How about *that* as the answer for Gloria? How would she like to be one of the first salespeople for this marvelous new invention!

But Gloria, twenty-four years old, fresh from India and visions of the Emperor Asoka, thought not.

All right then, the amenable Leo was ready with plan number two. Las Vegas! Gloria was lucky, he was sure of it.

And, sure enough, in Nevada, Leo's beloved daughter won about fifteen dollars. Not quite enough money for the trip, but an excellent start.

The next step, Leo explained, would be even more fun. He had been peddling his antiques and jewelry to storekeepers (staying in motels and rooming houses along the way), and now he would take his daughter along with him. They would both pretend that they were very poor and were forced to sell Gloria's rings (thus implying, of course, that the rings were far more valuable than either of them imagined). Gloria would wear the rings on her fingers and then sadly, oh so sadly, take them off and give them up. For cash on the barrelhead!

And, sure enough, Leo's ruse worked. As this attractive, unconventional pair meandered across the country, the trick took in suckers aplenty. The duped retailers thought they were getting a bargain. Gloria, like Leo, thought it a grand adventure.

But if Leo's horizons were severely limited, Gloria's were not.

She headed for New York, tried to get a job as a reporter, and when she failed, co-founded, with Paul Sigmund, a young Princeton professor, a small organization in Cambridge, Massachusetts, called the Independent Research Service, which financed Americans attending world youth festivals largely dominated by the Soviet Union. In 1959, she made her first trip to one of these Communist-run festivals—in

Vienna. The program was modest, only about a dozen people and a jazz band. The idea was to communicate, to reap the benefits of an international youth exchange, international cooperation.

A few years later, after Gloria finally gained a foothold in New York, she attended another such festival, this time in 1962 in Helsinki, along with Clay Felker, whom she had met at *Esquire*. Also attending was Sheila Tobias, a young woman who within the decade would begin the first women's studies course at Cornell University. Sheila would remember that Clay, along with Gloria, worked at the festival on a newspaper that was translated into several languages. As far as Sheila knew, the newspaper—along with the jazz bands and the art shows—was funded by an independent foundation. Only later did she discover that there had been, apparently, "two tracks."

"The CIA," Sheila found, "was interested in spying on the American delegates to find out who in the United States was a Trotskyite or Communist. So we were a front, as it turned out."

Among the students at these festivals, too, were some of the country's fledgling journalists—writers and editors of college newspapers —who filed reports to their readers on the political and cultural activities they attended. Unaware of their secret backing, they were, to an extent, compromised.

How much Gloria knew of this, she would never exactly say. The Independent Research Service was indeed funded by the CIA, as was the soon-to-be-famous National Student Association, but no one thought much about such agencies in those days. Since the Korean War, college boys had been signing up for such mildly cloak-and-dagger operations as the Army Security Agency, learning Russian and Japanese so they could listen to "enemy" radios. The day would come, however, when, the CIA having fallen into deep disgrace, and Gloria herself accused of being one of their agents, she would anger many feminists with her silence.

At the moment, though, such serious political implications were nowhere in the climate of her life.

In 1960, a New York boyfriend introduced her to Harold Hayes, an editor at *Esquire*, and Hayes, in turn, introduced her to Harvey Kurtzman, the creator of *Mad* magazine. Kurtzman was starting a new humor magazine called *Help!*, and for the child of the punster Leo, *Help!* was the perfect place to begin. Gloria delighted her new employer not only by writing funny photo captions, but by her ability to persuade rich and famous men—Sid Caesar, Milton Berle, Jackie Gleason, and the like—to appear on the magazine's cover.

And was she ever gorgeous! Sexy! Her long hair always beautifully brushed, the trademark tinted aviator glasses, the clothes that rode on her perfect body like, as one profile would eventually put it, "a midsummer night's dream!"

Kurtzman would remember that "all the visitors—all the *male* visitors anyhow—would fall for Gloria. She was very effective in personal relationships. I've never seen a woman so effective with the opposite sex. Her femaleness was very obvious in the course of whatever she was doing. Men wanted to go out with her, see her socially."

Kurtzman thought she was a lot like *Playboy's* Hugh Hefner. (Far from a compliment, in Gloria's view.)

"They were both manipulative," he would recall. "Hefner was involved with women in the pursuit of his enterprise, and Gloria was involved with men. Both were very effective in that they got what they wanted, in a business sense. Once I received an award at Harvard, and Gloria picked up a fancy Cadillac from her friend Blair Chotzinoff so we could drive down to Cambridge in style."

Gloria left a lot of broken hearts behind, Kurtzman would remember. "A lot of people were hurt. She was a femme fatale." But, like everyone else in the office, he liked her. "I suppose if she didn't want the guys, she had a perfect right . . ."

In the years to come, reporters would wrench themselves into high-gear clatter trying to describe Gloria's looks, her "splendidly milky and columnar throat," her "chic apotheosis of with-it cool," her flowing hair with "those blond strands that fell over and triangularly framed her lovely cool brow," her even white teeth, high broad cheekbones, "elegant filly legs," "incredible" sexual appeal. And her quiet, agreeable, understanding charm. All manner of powerful men, the rich, the well-born, and the talented, would offer these reporters, unasked, the unabashed confession: "I was in love with Gloria."

In these stories, the men themselves—director Mike Nichols, Olympic track star Rafer Johnson, playwright Herb Sargent, Viking publisher (of Joyce, Bellow, and Steinbeck) Thomas Guinzburg, Kennedy cohort Ted Sorensen—would be described as "dates" or "escorts." Many of them were, however, partners in what were, well, the best way to put it, Gloria would finally decide, was "a series of little marriages." Minus the legality.

Times, of course, were beginning to change. Gloria had moved into a third-floor walkup on West 56th Street with Barbara Nessim, a young painter whom she had met double-dating with her current boyfriend, author Robert Benton (art director of *Esquire*, who had already published several children's books and who, with his friend David Newman, would eventually write the movie *Bonnie and Clyde*).

Barbara created a lovely living and working environment, spectacular white walls with lots of posters. Though seven years younger than Gloria and deeply impressed by what she would call "Gloria's sense of the world" and "powerful leadership capacities," Barbara would claim that she never felt overshadowed. Gloria had only one quality that she envied, one that was both remarkable and rare for a young woman, especially in the early sixties.

In those days, the man in a woman's life was a central figure, if not *the* central figure. A woman who appeared alone at a party, a chic restaurant, or a hotel was treated with condescension, if not outright suspicion.

"You were nothing," Barbara would remember, "unless you had a boyfriend." And yet Gloria—and this was what was so unusual—was never emotionally dependent on a man.

She would listen patiently to the tales of stormy romance that absorbed the energies and dominated the between-us-girls conversations of most young women, and then, as a sort of antidote to that dependency, she would recommend the acerbic Dorothy Parker stories her mother had loved.

But Gloria herself never seemed to be "wounded" by love. Perhaps, Barbara thought, because she chose her men so carefully, or perhaps because so many men were always available to her. Barbara, who regarded herself as "man-addicted," wished she could be so self-contained.

"It wasn't that Gloria wasn't sympathetic," Barbara would remember. "It was just that she never had those feelings. She was beyond that."

Or perhaps there was a certain "emotional remoteness," as a *Newsweek* piece would note years later, at least in the romance department. Gloria's friends, this article would report, "tend to conclude that Steinem does not feel very much moved by, say, a friend's broken romance . . ."

Her friend Liz Smith, who was soon to become the country's premier gossip columnist, for example: "If I told Gloria about a disastrous love affair, she told me about the cultural and social strains that had broken it up. . . . It's like getting a message from Gandhi. . . . Gloria has all the irritating qualities of a saint—she is a rebuke."

She worked hard at her writing. "Like most of us," Kurtzman would recall, "she wanted to get to the top. What was so amazing about Gloria was that she had the self-confidence, the absolute assurance that she would. She wasn't quite sure what the direction would be, but she was certainly interested in political power. We used to play a guessing game in the office as to who she was dating. When she went to Washington, we would wonder if it was Jack Kennedy. She kept dating higher and higher."

As even-tempered as ever, already concerned more with political issues than individual problems, Gloria roomed amicably with Barbara for about six years, introducing her roommate to the galaxy of important people she was meeting. And if, as Didion had complained in her *Mademoiselle* article, the young women in New York were rudderless, without real career ambitions, she had obviously never run up against this pair of roommates. Barbara was convinced that, in their own separate ways, the two of them were making history.

"I didn't know anybody *like* us," Gloria's roommate would remember. "We were most different from anybody I knew. Powerful. Strong. Individual. We each knew we had a place in this world."

In 1962, Gloria wrote her first bylined piece for *Esquire*. She had been taking on small tasks around the office, more often than not diligently researching the articles her boyfriend Bob Benton was writing. Clay Felker, who had noticed both her industry and her intelligence, suggested she write a piece on how the recently available birth control pill was affecting college women.

"The Moral Disarmament of Betty Co-Ed," though an otherwise workaday piece, included this sensitive, if somewhat enigmatic, observation: "The problem is that many girls who depend on the roles of wife and mother for their total identity are being pressured into affairs they can't handle and jobs they pretend to like."

A decade later, Gloria would be a public figure important enough not just to write for *Esquire* but to be written about—"profiled"—in the magazine. That piece, "SHE" by Leonard Levitt, while not exactly a hatchet job, would be sharp-edged (though no more so than the political commentary she herself would then be writing for *New York* magazine). It would describe Gloria as a girl-about-town, "the intellectuals' pinup . . . who advanced in public favor by appealing to powerful men," and it would quote ex-boyfriends like a string of disposable beads. She—and her many friends—would be deeply angered and, in her words, "hurt" by the article.

For the moment, though, with Benton and Newman, *Esquire* was home base, and they all also helped out with editorial ideas at the new magazine *Show*. At the time, *Show* was engaged in heavy competition with a publication Hugh Hefner had launched called *Show Business Illustrated,* and the word around the *Show* office was that Hefner's New York Playboy Club was not the most pleasant place to work.

Who it was who conceived the idea of Gloria's going "undercover" at the Playboy Club would vary with memories. Hardly anyone in the New York publishing world, however, would ever forget that she did.

Gloria spent nearly three weeks as a Playboy Bunny and wrote a clever, entertaining diary of her experience:

"A blue satin band with matching Bunny ears attached was fitted around my head like an enlarged bicycle clip, and a grapefruit-sized hemisphere of white fluff was attached to hooks at the costume's rearmost point. 'Okay, baby,' she [the wardrobe mistress] said, 'put on your high heels and go show Sheralee.' I looked in the mirror. The Bunny image looked back."

The piece was amusing, but it was also an exposé of nasty and degrading job conditions, of stuffing the bosom of a too-tight, electric-blue-and-orange costume with athletic socks, of painful high heels, of a physical that included an internal exam, of heavy-breathing customers, of Bunnies who were supporting children, and, most of all, of wages that averaged far less than the help-wanted ad stated.

"I Was a Playboy Bunny" ran in two parts in the May and June 1963 issues of *Show* and caused a sensation. It was both "sexy" and very much in line with the idealism of the sixties. It made the point that Playboy Bunnies were exploited, though it did *not* make the point that they were exploited because they were women.

"It was interesting," Gloria would say in retrospect, "that I could understand that much and still not make the connection."

Yet one man whom Gloria would often cite as an influence on her thinking did make the connection, and he would distinctly remember discussing it with her that year.

One spring weekend, before the Bunny story was published, at the Hamptons home of some friends, Gloria met the economist and diplomat John Kenneth Galbraith, who was resting there while recovering from a bout with hepatitis contracted during his recent tour as ambassador to India. Galbraith was one of those intellectuals who had swung a well-honed ax at the self-absorbed fifties with his influential, widely read book *The Affluent Society*. As the two of them—the gaunt, towering, Lincolnesque economist and the slender, graceful new writer—basked in the glorious Hamptons sunlight, Gloria described what Galbraith would remember as "her awful experience at the Playboy Club, the insults and abuse that were implicit in that terrible job, those Bunny tails and being the object of repetitive sex slurs of the customers. And the courage of the women who stood up to it—for some of whom it was the only available form of livelihood."

The famous liberal economist was fascinated. He had served as a trustee of Radcliffe College, and he began to talk about his frustrations there, about the minor flak he had raised.

"I had begun to puzzle as to why we had to have a separate 'ghetto' for women," he would remember. "I had raised the matter at a board meeting only to get slapped down, not by the men on the board but by the women! I remember asking: 'Don't we have something more important than the assumption that our students will be housewives and family members?' And one of the women trustees turned on me and said, 'Professor Galbraith, will you tell me what is more important than being a wife and a mother?' "

And then there was the subject of parietal rules. At Radcliffe, women students were required to be indoors—alone, of course—by eleven o'clock. Men had no restrictions at all.

Galbraith had objected, only to be confronted with a peremptory: "Who is going to protect them?"

To which he had replied, " 'There comes a time when a woman should be the protector of her own virtue.' And that," he would recall, "was put down as being possibly obscene!"

All this was the main topic of conversation that day in the Hamptons, a charming meeting, in Galbraith's memory, with a young woman whose terrific good looks had gone a long way toward holding his interest. ("If Gloria says it's otherwise," he would add, "she's wrong.")

Not long afterward, Gloria began dating Tom Guinzburg, who would publish *The Beach Book*. Galbraith had returned to India, and she sent the book to him there with a request that he write the introduction.

An introduction to a beach book? By the country's most famous economist?

But since, as Galbraith would remember well into the eighties, Gloria was "so agreeable, so beautiful, and so motivated by the hardships of those women," he undertook to write:

"Except that I like this book and the girl who put it together, I could seem a most improbable person to write this introduction. Not a dozen times in the last fifty years have I gone to the beach for as much as overnight."

And so it happened that *The Beach Book,* with an introduction by John Kenneth Galbraith, and "I Was a Playboy Bunny" appeared in print in 1963, the same year that saw the assassination of the youngest president in history—John F. Kennedy.

Gloria was interviewed by the talented Nora Ephron in the *New York Post* under the title "Sun Bather." The article noted Gloria's distress at being identified as the girl who exposed the Playboy Bunnies, along with the amused comment, from Ephron: "Now that, in fact, is what Miss Steinem did."

"Much of Gloria's free-lancing," Ephron wrote, "has been, inevitably, articles about women. 'I never read anything about women,'" Gloria had told her, " 'so I went out and read sociology. That situation has been forced upon me—as a magazine writer, you develop what are regarded rightly or wrongly as your specialties.' "

That year of *The Feminine Mystique* and *The Beach Book,* Betty was forty-two years old. Gloria (even though she conceived the need to subtract, then restore, a two-year debit) was twenty-nine. In the sixties—a decade that would barrel its way toward Nirvana with insistent shouts of "Don't trust anyone over thirty!"—youth was the true Excalibur. The difference mattered.

9

WHY
I DESPISE
WOMEN

Perhaps I am not old enough yet to promise that the self-reliant woman is always loved . . . but certainly in my experience it has always been so. Lovers who are free to go when they are restless always come back. . . . The bitter animosity and obscenity of divorce is unknown where individuals have not become Siamese twins. A lover who comes to your bed of his own accord is more likely to sleep with his arms around you all night than a lover who has nowhere else to sleep.

—Germaine Greer, *The Female Eunuch,* 1970

The sexual revolution, more than anything else, was the province of youth, and England, to which Germaine had finally made her escape—from her infuriating mother, from the calm, staid life of Australia—was, in a way, the heart of it.

Germaine arrived there in 1964. She was twenty-five years old and had won a coveted Commonwealth scholarship to the University of Cambridge to take her doctorate in the early comedies of Shakespeare.

In the throes of the rebellion, the country was home to the new "subculture," to the fey and funny fashions, Mary Quant and mod

117

styles, tie-dyes and violets, poetry and experiment; a summer thunderstorm of expression so honeyed and warm it promised to turn the whole planet green forever. Love and satire. Underground presses and *That Was the Week that Was.* Everybody dancing in discotheques, and the pale, skinny model Twiggy, peering great-eyed from magazine covers.

And everywhere, the strange, mystical harmonies, the plaintive strains of the Beatles. Teenage girls in the throes of Beatlemania screamed and swooned at their concerts, gave way, in tumultuous shrieks, to a yearning adolescent energy. Sexual mores were shattering as everyone hummed—or tripped to—"Michelle," "Nowhere Man," "Sgt. Pepper's Lonely Hearts Club Band," the sweet, irresistible tunes of a free, nonconformist eroticism.

To many of her classmates, the coming of Germaine Greer to England, to that "precious stone set in a silver sea," would be unforgettable.

She was six feet tall, with high, rounded cheekbones and the strong, unselfconscious gait of an Olympic runner. She took pride—as she still would, in future years—in imitating speech patterns, a range of accents that would render her listeners teary-eyed with laughter. She was hilarious, totally irreverent, an unabashed show-off, and an absolute original who had already led, in her college years, a thoroughly bohemian existence.

After the convent school, she had gone to the University of Melbourne, where she had acted with small theater groups, written drama criticism, served on the aboriginal scholarships committee. And—though she was not yet a great "something," as she had imagined at the convent she would have to be to have lovers—she had taken one, anyhow. A skeptical, free-thought Libertarian, a member of a socially resistant, independent sect in Sydney.

"I was infinitely attracted to the Libertarians," Germaine would remember. They were, she was certain, exactly the sort of free-spirited people she had always been looking for. One of their tenets, in fact, of which Germaine would speak proudly in the future, was the unconventional notion that women had the right to control their reproductive destinies. And among their activities was raising money for abortions.

Life with this anarchic group, however, was actually very strict; in a way, quite difficult for the spirited, affectionate Germaine.

"You could not be possessive about your sexual partner without coming under a good deal of contempt," she would remember. "You couldn't even hold down a job without having your credentials questioned, and you certainly couldn't go on to get a higher degree at a university. You had to just resign yourself to having no social status, to being a sort of grub in the woodwork of the state."

To avoid becoming "pawns of the state," most of the Libertarians made their livings by gambling on the horses, but Germaine displayed no predilection for that particular sport. After teaching at a girls' school for a while, she concluded that she was really an academic by nature. She went back to school, to the University of Sydney this time, to study with a professor who cared less for her lightning Libertarian-style intuitions ("the confidence," she would remember, "they gave me in my version of the facts") than for the reasons behind them.

"He used to try to discipline me, to keep me earthbound," Germaine would remember. " 'Now, Germaine,' he would say, 'that won't do. You can't make that leap there. You'll have to go back and start again.' "

Finding a reason for what you thought would always seem, to Germaine, "a somewhat factitious pursuit," but she became, in her own words, "quite good at it." So good, in fact, that she earned her masters in English with first-class honors.

And from there, that precious scholarship.

The little girl who had stood at Port Melbourne watching the ships, who had always been sure she would leave Australia, had won her ticket.

And not just to England, but to Cambridge University. Not only a luxury of ideas and scholarship, but, for Germaine, a gift of appreciation, even thunderous applause.

Jaunty, commandingly forthright, she was regarded as a thoroughly alluring presence, both on and off the stage. Aside from her studies, her taste for contemporary thought drew a coterie of rebellious, avant-garde artists, not only the "Angry Young Men" of that generation, but the witty satirists who would soon regale audiences in *Beyond the Fringe* and *Monty Python*.

"She's a remarkable woman," the playwright and classmate David Hare would tell a reporter years later. "The courage she needed to be bohemian in the nineteen-fifties!

"She acted," he would add gratefully, "as if I were a plausible person."

Strikingly dramatic, Germaine was soon cast as the recruiting sergeant in Cambridge's Footlights production of *Oh, What a Lovely War,* which Hare directed. And just as she successfully completed her Ph.D., she was also acclaimed the Cantabrigian "Actress of the Year."

And then, all at once, it seemed, it was over. From the creative stimulation—and the applause—of Cambridge, Germaine was plunged suddenly into a gray, penurious existence at the lowest level of the academic scale. She was hired as a teacher by Warwick University—paid, as she would put it, "like an office boy," a salary of about 1,100 pounds a year. Her "bed-sitter" flat used nearly every penny she had, leaving barely enough to keep the gas fire lit. The bus that passed by her door hourly headed solely for the university or for the city of Coventry ("a wilderness, a desolate landscape"). She had no money for travel, hardly even to London, which was some ninety miles away, and she might as well have been back in Australia.

"I was really dying," she would remember, "I was just dying."

She was by then twenty-eight years old, exuberant, beautiful, accomplished, yet these were, in her own, never undramatic terms, "the lost years." Cold, wretched, and lonely. Oh, there was, occasionally, a lover. Usually married, inevitably academic. But little else.

"The young academic couples wouldn't touch me with a barge pole," she would recall. "They were much too paranoid and insecure. I didn't know what they were afraid of, or why they were so nasty and unfriendly."

Eventually, though, she would interpret their behavior through her own feminist lens, her own distinctive mix of reason and racy street talk: "The single women in that academic situation were always at a disadvantage. They were regarded with immense suspicion by wives. And the husbands were desperately afraid of the competition, because the unmarried women worked a fucking sight harder than they did. And by continuing the ostracism, of course, they intensified the paradigm because we all worked so hard to just get the hell out of there."

Back then, though, trapped in that "wilderness," Germaine was far less sanguine, less cerebral. Her misery took a psychosomatic route, and she soon found herself in physical pain, in what she would characterize as "neuralgia."

"Every tooth in my head ached until I thought I was going to go mad. I thought I was going to have to tear my head off."

She hated taking drugs, even the prescribed codeine. Since self-pity was anathema, she simply had to do something about it.

What she did, finally, was to travel to London and audition for a television show, a special, wacky, light-hearted program that was just then being mounted by friends of hers from Footlights in Cambridge.

Which was how Cambridge's Actress of the Year, with her doctorate in Shakespeare, came to be seen cavorting for the BBC cameras.

"Nice Time," a television show not unlike America's "Real People," sought out such singular characters as the man with the biggest feet in England. ("They were like great mushrooms!") Or would have Germaine, on camera, reverently beg strangers on Kensington High Street for a kiss . . . or offer them five pounds to climb a lamppost. She cajoled housewives into sliding down banisters, old men into staging a shoot-out at the O.K. Corral in a shopping center.

In short, Germaine had fun.

Her teaching job at Warwick was now compressed into two days a week, and once again her life was full of color. She had maneuvering money and London friends. Jazz musicians, rock performers—the underground scene. She began writing for experimental presses, for serious magazines such as the *Spectator,* even staked herself to a trip to the most exciting place on earth: New York.

What an adrenaline trip that was! "A gas!" Germaine would remember. It was winter and so cold she would swear "the dogs' pee froze before it hit the ground . . . and the snow clattered down like little topazes!" And those Americans! She had thought them so clever about snow, shoveling it out of the way and all. But—how amazing —they just drove all over the melting, soot-covered stuff, sideswiping each other!

She and a girlfriend swung with the hip culture, the music world. She met the Andy Warhol gang at Max's Kansas City and, at a rock concert, the M.C. Five, from Detroit, a band that was "just the newest, hottest thing. They made music that sounded like World War III, but they were really just down-home kids from the Midwest."

"This is Miss Australia of 1956," her friend would say, which Germaine certainly could have done without. Still, she had a lovely affair with the lead singer of the M.C. Five, even if, years later, she couldn't remember his name. ("How awful," she would chide herself, her eyes half amused, half stricken, "when you can't remember their names!")

But she loved them all—the miniskirted activists, the hippies, the swarms of youthful rebels whose convictions stood tall as a glowering sky and faced their elders as a rebuke.

"The people I liked best, quite frankly, were the ones who were working their guts out in the peace movement . . . really putting themselves on the line." The ones who had, most of them, begun their protest in the black civil rights movement.

Under Lyndon Johnson, as the battles in Vietnam—and against the draft—escalated, the civil rights rebellion had moved to (or merged with) antiwar issues and, with them, "Make Love Not War," the euphoric sweep of the hippies. The psychedelic highs of mescaline and LSD, the sweet, thick odors of marijuana and incense, flowers twined through flowing hair, stuck flagrantly in the barrels of rifles. Young men with beards, girls in Victorian gowns, began to throng by the thousands to the Haight-Ashbury district of San Francisco. By 1967, twenty thousand flower children—poet Allen Ginsberg, drug guru Timothy Leary, the Hell's Angels among them—would be singing and dancing at the Gathering of the Tribes in Golden Gate Park, the "World's First Human Be-In."

Unbeknownst to Germaine, however—or, for that matter, to most Americans—an odd discontent had begun to seethe *within* this apparently united, loving, and generous exterior. It was stirring in activist pockets in the South, on a few college campuses, beyond the view of the daily press or the television cameras, and it would not reach the eyes and ears of the American public—let alone a visitor from abroad —for several years. Hidden in the bustling centers of student rebellion, where by now "Black Power" and "separatism" had begun to sting and anger and teach, it was felt by young women in the groups that were now described as the New Left.

Across the country, the New Left organizations were centers for a freshly minted, highly rhetorical politics. At their meetings, young men, both black and white, unquestionably committed to their causes, delivered a spectacular form of high-voltage intellectual display. In dozens of small underground presses, hundreds of bulletins, pamphlets, papers, these male leaders held forth on political theory. In hundreds of conferences, they exercised their pyrotechnical verbal skills, and it was at one such conference that a flip dictat by the civil rights movement's most glamorous leader would soon sear itself into legend.

"The only position for women in SNCC," pronounced Stokely Carmichael, the leader of the Student Nonviolent Coordinating Committee, "is prone."

Which, in a way, said it all. If you were a female in this otherwise dedicated, spiritual, idealistically egalitarian community, you knew what you were there for. In addition to sex, that is. For the most part, the "chicks" who had traveled to Mississippi and Alabama, at a good deal of personal risk, did the housework, the clerical duties—in short, the "shitwork" of the civil rights movement. And then, as the white male leaders began to apply their radicalism to *themselves* rather than blacks, the "chicks" schlepped the garbage of the movement's offshoots as well, the myriad new uprisings—the Berkeley Free Speech Movement, booming new organizations such as the Students for a Democratic Society.

"Girls Say Yes to Guys Who Say No."

It was the most famous slogan of the draft resistance.

Years later, in *Personal Politics,* writer Sara Evans would quote one male leader to the effect that "women made peanut butter, waited on tables, cleaned up, got laid. That was their role."

Courage might burn in the heart, but if you happened to be female, you were still—and once again—"auxiliary," peripheral. You could not, after all, be drafted. You could not burn your draft card.

According to most accounts, the "women's issue" was first raised, with utmost caution, in a memo to SNCC in 1965. The memo, written by Mary King and Casey Hayden (the wife of activist leader Tom Hayden, who would later marry Jane Fonda), described, in standard New Left rhetoric, a "common-law caste system" that, "at its worst, uses and exploits women." The memo would be published the next year as a two-part article, "Sex and Caste," in a pamphlet called *Liberation,* but the women would be laughed at and thrown out of the SDS convention when they went so far as to demand a plank on the subject.

Yet everyone knew—though they managed not to talk about it— that among the heroes of the civil rights movement were many women. Rosa Parks, who started it all by refusing a seat in the back of the bus, Ruby Doris Smith and Diane Nash, who faced the truncheons and jail cells of southern sheriffs, Kathie Amatniek, who would eventually adopt the name "Kathie Sarachild, child of Sara," Naomi Weisstein, Jo Freeman, Marilyn Salzman Webb, Roxanne Dunbar, Shulamith Firestone, and many more.

Only a few were writers, well connected in the publishing world or savvy about attracting what was just now beginning to be labeled, not "the press," but, in awesome tones, "the media." All, however, were fully familiar with the revolutionary Chinese Communist technique

"Speak Pains to Recall Pains," the theory that talking about one's problems in a group would lead to political solutions. And not long after the memo was written, these women would begin to apply the idea to themselves, to form their own incunabula, their own little workshops, at the hundreds of New Left conferences springing up around the country. They would begin to talk, not about the poor, not about the "Negroes" or the draft, but about their own problems, women's problems as women.

The "rap session," in short, would soon transmogrify into that remarkable tool of the Golden Age of Feminism: "consciousness raising."

Germaine was not aware of any of this on her visit to New York. The delicious idealism and freedom of the sixties was all she saw and heard.

When she returned to London, she continued writing for the underground papers. She wrote lots of experimental pieces, reviews of music, "wild prophecies," and she would recall, in the offhand style she used to describe her most outrageous pranks: "I designed a cock cozy. . . . It was gaily striped. Pink . . . all colors. It was very pretty, actually. My editor posed in it."

She welcomed, naturally, American visitors from the peace movement, from the hip new magazines like *Screw.*

"The underground press," she would remember, "was like the underground railway. It was safe conduct. They knew they could pick up drugs, hang out, find out what was going down and all that."

And Germaine herself would soon attempt to create her own pornographic magazine, the first and sole issue of which, called *Suck,* would be, in fact, a profound disappointment.

"I wanted it to be nonsadistic pornography," she would remember. "I wanted to do an edition which would have cost a fortune . . . where you get a closed parcel, a membrane that you had to break into, and inside were all different things. And depending how you broke into it, what methods you used, you could find out something about yourself. Did you bite it? Did you tear at it? Did you slice it neatly? How did you get in here? It was going to have pages of pure silk, of fine rice paper . . ."

And it would have a democratic editorial policy, in which not only other people, but the editors themselves were shown naked.

"Let's all have our own photographs taken in compromising sexual positions," Germaine would blithely propose to her all-male board.

"That means you guys have got to show your dicks, you know, impressive or otherwise. Little or big, you've got to stand up and be counted. I don't care if it's stiff or lying down or what it's doing."

But then, of course, the question arose of how Germaine herself would pose. She would remember suddenly realizing at that moment that *hers* was the only picture that would be picked up by the tabloids.

The only solution, this uninhibited young woman had quickly decided, was to take a photograph that could appear nowhere.

"It was easy," she would recall. "I just lay on my back on the floor of the studio and put my knees over my head. It was shot from there. So that all you can see is legs, a huge bottom, like a great apple, a cunt, an anus and a face. Can't see the tits, you see, which is what they would have published."

And then—looking back on those wild days—Germaine would also, for just a moment, remember her mother with just a flicker of reluctant admiration. Peggy herself was unconventional, her grown daughter would admit, "not ordinary in the least. . . . Her blind defiance of the laws of decency does strike me as involving a crazy kind of courage."

Back then, though, Germaine's days and nights delivered their own kind of craziness. Not long after her trip to America, in April 1968, outside a London pub, some friends introduced her to a man named Paul du Feu.

She was twenty-nine years old. He was thirty-two and gorgeous. "A hunk." Such a hunk, in fact, that within a few years, Helen Gurley Brown would choose Paul du Feu as the first nude male centerfold of the British *Cosmopolitan*. (Less hirsute than his American centerfold counterpart, the actor Burt Reynolds, Paul, one female reporter would trill, was more like "a Greek god sprung from the sea or some father god's forehead.")

He had longish, straight brown hair streaked with blond, and smooth, heavy muscles; powerful shoulders, a dreamy smile. Born in Wales, the son of a civil servant, he had a degree from Kings College but was attracted to what he called "the lower-class life." He had been so successful building houses that he found himself with what he regarded as "too much money" and quickly got rid of it—about $100,000—playing *chemin de fer*. He was intelligent. And incredibly sexy.

That evening, Germaine and Paul and their friends went inside the pub for drinks. Later, she went to his flat.

The two spent the next three weekends together.

Then they got married.

Germaine, Paul would tell a reporter, had said she was against marriage, but when he asked her, she went along meekly to the Paddington registry office.

"I suspected she wanted to get married, and she was the greatest lady I'd met in a long time. She accepted on the spur of the moment. Of course, it didn't involve fidelity, lifelong or weeklong. It would have been hypocritical to pretend otherwise."

"Listen," Germaine would confess years later. "I'll tell you . . . If you're living amongst academic men and Paul comes into your life . . . Well, it was like drinking a cup of sperm."

The marriage ended three weeks—weekends, actually—after it began.

"That legal paper is an invitation to the rest of the world to start butting in on your relationship," Paul told a reporter. "We started having rows and we were always drinking. For a pacifist, she does a lot of fighting. No, she didn't throw the crockery, she has resources enough in her tongue."

And Germaine: "I'd take the train on weekends down from Warwick and be all worn out and the next morning he'd be up at six full of vigor, asking for his cup of tea. I'd say, 'But dear, I'm asleep, you're up, can't you get your own tea?' "

Yes, they were still friends, but the quicksilver sojourn in the conjugal bedroom proved an important lesson for Germaine.

"I realized, within a week, that I was in serious trouble," she would remember. "It was just like being home again.

"It was just as if I had never run away all that long time ago. Everything I did was wrong. Humiliation seemed to be required all the time; a constant self-abasement . . . and then I began to realize something about it, when there was a man standing between me and the light. I began not to despise other women because I began to see how you could get into that kind of jam."

By then, Germaine had an agent for her writing, a woman who suggested one day that she write an article in honor of the fiftieth anniversary of women's suffrage. The gist of this proposal, as Germaine understood it, was the pompous notion that in spite of suffrage and because of their helpless nature, women had made no impact on politics.

Before Paul, Germaine had always liked men better than women, or at least better than the middle-class variety of women, who seemed to her "absolutely terrible, not worth talking to, untrustworthy, manipulative, blind, cowardly, feeble-minded—intellectually feeble-minded." After her marriage, all that changed.

"I began to realize that if you wanted to get on in this man's world, that was the kind of personality you were supposed to have. . . . And it was only luck that I didn't have it. It wasn't that I chose not to be that way. I just couldn't do it. I always say whatever comes into my head. I can't use language in the way that women traditionally do, which is, you know, what will be the effect if I say this?"

Germaine, in short, was inexorably given to popping off.

As now she did.

"What the hell are you talking about?" she shouted at her agent. "Do you suppose this democracy we live in is real? Have women ever been recognized in the law? Is there any reason why they should emerge as a voting power? How could emancipation fail when it had never happened in the first place?!"

Stunned by the force of her client's tirade, the woman meekly withdrew the suggestion. A few weeks later, though, in another context, the subject surfaced again.

Germaine was lunching with the respected editor Sonny (Ajai Singh) Mehta, who was looking for books for his Paladin list, the first major paperback imprint to give the giant Penguin serious competition. Mehta, who would one day be recruited as editor and president of Alfred A. Knopf in America, and who often befriended struggling writers, had loaned Germaine his apartment a few months earlier.

Actually, he would recall, "I was away traveling and someone had given her the keys to my apartment. She had very little money and she was looking for a place to stay. When I came back . . . here was this very tall person. Everyone had told her that I wouldn't take any money, so she had completely neatened up the place and filed my papers. It took me months to find them."

Germaine, Mehta would remember, was provocative, exciting, intensely curious about everything, and wonderfully entertaining at dinner parties. The two had become friends, and now at lunch, they were discussing ideas and writers who had recently produced articles on interesting subjects when Germaine mentioned, incidentally and somewhat contemptuously, her agent's suggestion.

"It's all based on a wrong concept, this idea that we have been liberated," she remarked disgustedly. "We haven't been liberated because there's no positive concept of female sexuality. There's just this idea of these domestic creatures, whose lives are all in response to other lives and whose posture is always receptive and never innovative, and what women really need is a theory about—"

"That's the book," said Mehta.

"What book? I haven't been talking about a book."

"The one about women, freedom, sexuality, liberty."

Could she think of a title?

"The Female Eunuch," Germaine smartly replied.

"You can sign a contract this afternoon," said Mehta, who expected the book would be, at least, provocative.

Seven hundred and fifty pounds.

It was no fortune, but compared to Warwick . . .

Germaine sat down and typed out a frisky summary.

She would write about "Venus power" and it would "outrage the editress (male or female) of every women's magazine in the country."

The book would be called *The Female Eunuch* or *Why I Despise Women*.

Because, it would explain, women "have accepted a concept of womanness essentially conditioned by the needs of a male society, a society which is changing so rapidly in our time that woman no longer satisfies her mate's or her own desires . . .

"I shall strive to write with the fullness of my femaleness . . . a direct rhetoric aimed at the viscera of womankind, not the babble of bluestockings . . .

"I shall have woman release her last clutch at man, not to have her retreat into some absurd Amazonian society, but to improve female congress with the male, to ally female with male in a way which is not mutually limiting but—but what? I cannot *know*, but 'I have a dream.' "

It was, by then, 1969.

In America, Martin Luther King, Jr., the inventor of that stirring phrase, had been shot. Germaine's dream, the dream of a new feminism, already had been murmuring and scuffling and scratching at the doors of the public consciousness for several years.

1

During World War II, the formative years for those feminists whose voices would soon change the world, many women—like "Rosie the Riveter"—pitched into the war effort. Most surrendered their jobs when the G.I.s returned, but the wartime ideal of the foxholes—Betty Grable— remained.

2

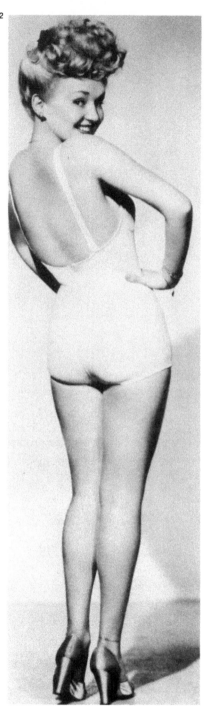

Betty Goldstein (Friedan) graduated from Smith College in 1942. The following year, she turned down a fellowship when the boy she was dating told her he could never win one to match it.

"The Best Years of Our Lives" portrayed the problems of returning servicemen. In this 1946 film, the soldiers' need to feel needed by the women they had left behind created poignant problems for wives and sweethearts.

Gloria Steinem at about 11 years old. Her parents were among the rare couples who divorced and Gloria was forced to care for her painfully ill mother in a run-down house in Toledo, Ohio. One of the little girl's major pleasures was reading.

Television reflected the post war values. The Nelsons—Ozzie, Harriet, and their two boys—were a perfect American family, amusing and uncomplicated, embodying an ideal that seemed to be worth the lives lost in the country's defense.

Kate Millett grew up in St. Paul, Minnesota, the daughter of a conservative, Catholic family. Intellectual exploration was encouraged but not when it ventured into irreverence or sexual variety.

During those years, the woman's role was staunchly *auxiliary*—a helpmate. In the 1952 film *Women's World,* the comportment of each of three wives is a major criterion for her husband's chance at the top job in a company.

At the age of 12, Germaine Greer won a Junior Government Scholarship to a convent in her hometown of Melbourne, Australia. Contrary to standard notions of a cloistered education, the girl's lusty curiosity and imagination were nurtured here.

Marilyn Monroe was the sex symbol of the age and Gloria would eventually write a book that focused sympathetically on the actress's exploitation. Germaine found the strength of an Anna Magnani far more inspirational.

Integrating Little Rock Central High School in the late fifties. For some young women, the civil rights movement was a training ground for the feminist rebellion.

Simone de Beauvoir and her lover Jean Paul Sartre. Many women, especially those who regarded Betty Friedan's views as too conservative, would regard de Beauvoir's book *The Second Sex,* published in the United States in 1953, as the basic text for what would soon be called "the second wave of feminism."

In that decade, Gloria—after graduating from Smith College and after an emotionally traumatic search for an illegal abortion —spent two years on a Chester Bowles Scholarship to India.

By the mid-fifties, the signs of the restlessness to come were revealing themselves in the popular attraction to a few significant rebels. Among them, the actor James Dean and the writers who came to be called "the beat generation."

13

14

In 1962, Helen Gurley Brown published *Sex and the Single Girl,* which advocated far greater sexual freedom for women than had ever been suggested by a mass-appeal book. Most new feminists, however, would reject Brown's philosophy along with her giggly, male-flattering style.

One year later, Betty, a suburban housewife by now and mother of three children, published her ground-breaking polemic, *The Feminine Mystique,* about the psychic disaster caused by the repression of educated women. Most historians would agree that the book launched the Golden Age of Feminism.

In 1963, Gloria went
"undercover" as a Playboy
Bunny and wrote an article
about her experience for *Show*
magazine. Writing the piece,
she later said, had been a
mistake because she was so
frequently identified in
connection with it. (Much
later, she supervised its
transformation into a television
movie.)

That same year, President
John F. Kennedy was
assassinated and, though the
White House reign of this
glamorous family came to an
end, the lovely First Lady,
Jacqueline, continued to exert
a strong influence on the style
and image of the times.

Betty Furness, Betty Friedan and Richard Graham announce the formation of NOW—the National Organization for Women—in 1966. From this inception, men were specifically included.

In 1967, Dr. Kathryn F. Clarenbach of the University of Wisconsin, NOW's first chair of the board, and Betty, its president, announce the fledgling organization's "Bill of Rights for Women," thereby provoking many resignations.

Gloria would often recall "trying to tap dance my way out of Toledo." Here, in 1966, with writer Herb Sargent, she "frugs" at a 1966 fundraiser for New York's Shakespeare in the Park.

Muriel Fox, a pioneer in public relations, and Marlene Sanders, one of the first women reporters on television, were both original members of the fledgling NOW.

Ti-Grace Atkinson and Flo Kennedy march in one of NOW's earliest demonstrations—against gender-separate help-wanted ads at the *New York Times*. Both women resigned from NOW in 1968 in a split that highlighted the powerfully diverse factions that swirled within the movement.

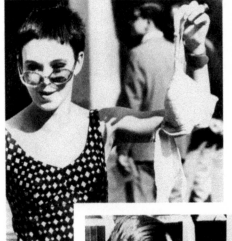

A protester drops a brassiere in the Freedom Trash Can at the Miss America demonstration in Atlantic City in 1968. This action caught the imagination of the American public and gave rise to the epithet "bra burners."

The Miss America protest was an illustration of a far angrier, more expansive revolution than the founders of NOW had envisioned.

Valeria Solanis being booked by police after shooting and wounding artist Andy Warhol. Solanis, an actress and author of the SCUM (Society for Cutting Up Men) Manifesto, was supported by Ti-Grace and Flo.

28

PLAZA'S OAK ROOM BARS WOMEN, AND THAT'S WHAT THE PICKETING IS ALL ABOUT.

We Will Not Be Barred!

It was the birthday of Abraham Lincoln, the Great Emancipator, the day NOW was to launch its nationwide Public Accommodations Week to protest sex discrimination in restaurants, bars and public carriers.

New York was still digging itself out of the worst snowstorm in year. And although the site of the demonstration had been carefully chosen, the timing--it seemed to the coordinators--was awful.

The sit-in and picket were to be directed at the Oak Room at The Plaza--a hotel of such international reknown that its exterior can remain unblemished by anything so unnecessary as a name. (A discreet "P" only stands out in bas relief on the building's 19th century facade.) The Oak Room has outlawed women during the lunch hours for the last 60 years.

The symbol of America's 'Grand Hotel,' which new feminist could resist a

This report of NOW's Oak Room invasion, written by Dolores Alexander, appeared in the organization's 1969 winter/spring newsletter and noted the headwaiter's warning that "the men-only policy would be strictly enforced."

That same year, authors Jimmy Breslin and Norman Mailer ran as co-candidates for Mayor of New York. Gloria, whom Mailer credited with suggesting the idea in the first place, offered her apartment and advice.

Susan Brownmiller, who would later write *Against Our Will: Men, Women and Rape,* was the architect of a protest in which, on March 18, 1970, hundreds of women stormed the office of John Mack Carter, the male editor of the *Ladies' Home Journal.* (Below) The siege lasted for nine hours, until Carter agreed to publish a supplement written by the feminists. "Never Underestimate the Power of a Woman" was (and is) the magazine's slogan.

(Opposite, top and inset) One month after the *Journal* sit-in, nine women stormed the offices of Grove Press, protesting the publishing company's "sexist editorial policy." Robin Morgan, who, at this demonstration was dubbed "the Little General," lights a cigarette. (Center, right) Robin as a child actress—Dagmar in *I Remember Mama.*
Police handling of the Grove Press group was traumatic for Ti-Grace Atkinson, (bottom, right), but Flo Kennedy, their attorney, (bottom, left) would soon be out on the hustings, drawing attention by wit ("Very few jobs actually require either a penis or a vagina") and costume.

31

32

33

34

35

36

(Left) Barbara Seaman testified at the 1970 Senate hearings on the safety of the birth control pill. She recommended that men use condoms, noting that if slide-off was a problem, condoms should be manufactured in sizes, like women's brassieres. Here she displays another option—the cervical cap.

(Right) Tiny, blonde whiz kid Letty Cottin Pogrebin was author of a somewhat less-than-liberated book called *How to Make It in a Man's World* when she discovered and was captivated by the new feminism. She would soon join forces with Gloria and Bella Abzug.

(Left) Betty speaking at a glittering East Hampton, Long Island, fundraiser for her upcoming nationwide march. She fought a losing battle with a broken drawstring on *The Dress,* purchased especially for the event.

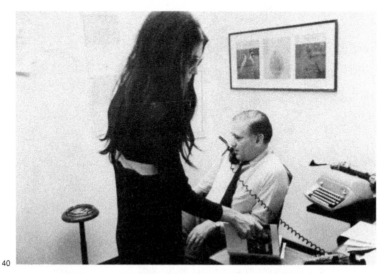

Gloria was one of the founding editors of Clay Felker's powerful *New York* magazine and by then an influential political columnist and member of "the beautiful people."

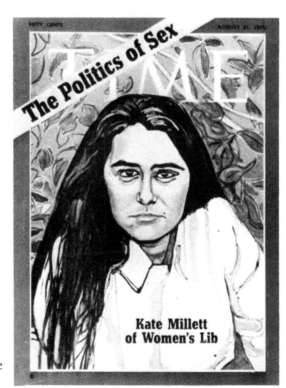

Kate Millett on the cover of *Time*. After the publication of her book *Sexual Politics,* Kate, along with her many other feminists, was shocked to find that *Time* used her portrait on its cover to represent the entire women's movement.

Pre-march. "This is our hour of history. We're going to take it."

Gloria acts as MC.

Betty, at a federal building in lower Manhattan, tries to get someone to open the door.

August 26, 1970: The fiftieth anniversary of the granting of women's suffrage in America. Fifth Avenue, New York: The historic Women's March for Equality. A turn-t beyond anyone's wildest dreams.

After Kate is publicly vilified, many feminists, including Gloria, rally to her defense at the "Kate is Great" press conference on December 17, 1970.

March 11, 1971, Catholic University, Washington, D.C.: Conservative Catholic magazine editor Patricia Buckley Bozell, sister of columnist William F. Buckley and Senator James C. Buckley, strikes out at Ti-Grace Atkinson for her attack on the Catholic Church.

49

The lesbian issue proves extremely disruptive at the second annual March for Equality. NOW leader Jacqueline Ceballos offers to get down on her knees and beg for unity.

The publication of *The Female Eunuch* launched Germaine Greer as a feminist oracle. Here she hams it up for British photographers, proving that she can—if she cares to—play pinup.

This magazine cover was no surprise. Even *New York* editor Clay Felker knew it was coming.

Kate continued to speak in behalf of feminism, but events were taking a toll on her psyche.

Jill Johnston staged a surprise play-within-a-play during the Theatre of Ideas debate at Town Hall billed as "A Dialogue of Women's Liberation."

A distinguished audience packed the hall to watch America's brilliant, macho author Norman Mailer tangle with the amazing Germaine. Many regarded the debate as a watershed in the women's movement, but Germaine called it "Town Bloody Hall" and *Esquire* summed up the whole thing with this cover.

54

55

Gloria, Bella Abzug, Shirley Chisholm, and Betty were photographed at
the formation of the National Women's Political Caucus in July 1971.
When President Richard Nixon asked what this photograph looked like,
his secretary of state answered, "A burlesque."

In her book *The Gender Gap,* Bella Abzug recalls instigating the Caucus,
but this notation was scribbled by Betty Friedan at a plenary meeting
several months earlier.

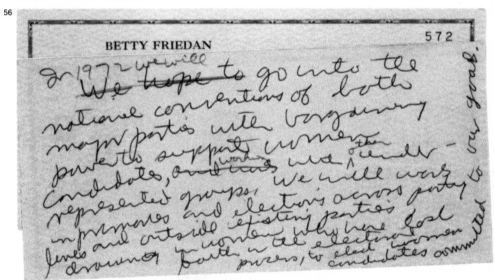

56

The first cover of *Ms.* magazine, which appeared as an insert in *New York* magazine in December 1971. (Right) The actress Jane Fonda, who had learned about the new feminism while doing research for her film *Klute,* here broadcasting antiwar pleas from North Vietnam. In 1972, Bella Abzug, who was popular with such Hollywood stars as Liz Taylor and Shirley MacLaine, was elected to Congress.

At the 1972 Democratic Convention in Miami Beach, the women's movement was the new gang in town.

There was a "conspiracy," Betty insisted, between Steinem and Abzug.

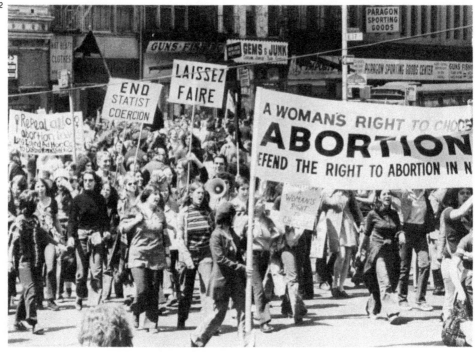

On January 22, 1973, the Supreme Court ruled (in *Roe v. Wade*) that a woman's right to an abortion in the first trimester of pregnancy was a matter between herself and her doctor.

Two who lent platform and voice to the women's movement joined forces in politics and marriage: television host Phil Donahue and actress Marlo Thomas.

64

After disputes with the original publisher (Elizabeth Forsling Harris), Gloria brought Patricia Carbine to *Ms*.

65

Few feminists noticed Phyllis Schlafly when she began her battle against the Equal Rights Amendment in the early seventies, but she would soon prove a formidable opponent.

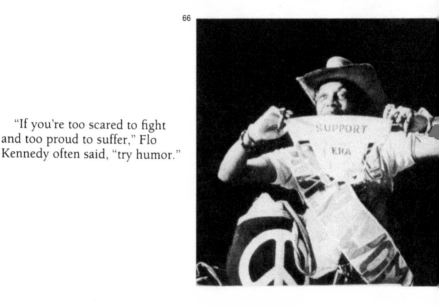

66

"If you're too scared to fight and too proud to suffer," Flo Kennedy often said, "try humor."

67

In the early seventies, most Americans—Ti-Grace Atkinson included— turned their attention to the "dirty tricks" in the White House.

68

Three First Ladies attend the
Houston convention in 1977. Betty
reluctantly—"for unity's sake"—finally
supports the lesbians.

69

The next year, *An Unmarried Woman*
appears. The film was one of the first of
many to be infused with a distinct new
feminist sensibility.

70

71

72

73

The ERA failed, but by the eighties the
world had begun to change. Women broke
into hundreds of all-male strongholds—
from religion to sports to construction to
politics to outer space.

The feminist oracles drifted apart, grew
older, went on with their separate lives—
writing, editing, speaking, fundraising.
(Kate is photographed here at the opening
of an exhibition of her drawings, Gloria
with luncheon companion Jackie Kennedy
Onassis, Germaine and Betty speaking at
the UN.) (73, 77–79)

77

79

80

81

82

10

NOTES ON
A PAPER NAPKIN

*It is a mystery, the whole thing—why it happened,
how it started. What gave any of us the courage to
make that leap?*

—Betty Friedan, *It Changed My Life*, 1977

For the first few years after *The Feminine Mystique* was published, Betty took her lumps. From men who feared that the house would be empty with Mama gone off to "fulfill" herself. From women shocked by the dreadful notion that they had, perhaps, taken the wrong road, wasted the best years of their lives. From call-ins to radio programs who demanded that the "destroyer of womanhood" be taken off the air.

She took those punches and gave back better. The now-famous Betty Friedan, who no longer called herself by the dreaded name "housewife," swept right through the thick-tongued rage of those "scared men," as she called them, the objections of those "dreary, dreary martyred women."

She reveled in her new pursuit.

"I'm nasty, I'm bitchy, I get mad, but by God I'm absorbed in what I'm doing," she told reporters.

She could even deal with the "Aunt Toms." (A later epithet would be "Queen Bees.") These were the rare women who, for one reason or another, had hooked into glamorous jobs and jealously guarded their superiority with the old bootstrap claim: "I did it. So can anybody else." The corollary being, of course, that anyone who complained about it was, ipso facto, a "loser."

At one meeting, packed with successful communications women, ad executives, and the like, Betty aimed a well-placed kick at the feeding trough: television advertising. No woman, she told them in her most gravelly and accusatory tone, gets "an orgasm from shining the kitchen floor."

"What next?" hooted one of these executives. "Daughter of *Feminine Mystique*?" And so on.

Yet nearly every time Betty spoke, she sensed—sometimes just in the intense, fascinated eyes of a few, sometimes in what they confided to her afterward—a kindling affirmation, a rock-bottom *yes*. From Marlene Sanders, that good-looking television reporter, for instance, who seemed so interested in the subject. From the svelte public relations executive Muriel Fox, who had even written her a note after the meeting: "If you ever decide to start an NAACP for women, count me in."

But Betty was no civil rights leader. She was no Roy Wilkins, certainly no Stokely Carmichael or Bobby Seale. She was a writer, not a politician, and what really mattered, she was convinced, was her next book.

She was going to write about the patterns of women's lives, which is why, as she traveled round the country making her speeches, she asked questions as well.

It was slow going, though. Unlike Betty's first, wondrous discovery, no epiphany had yet shaken her soul. No patterns, no secret messages. Just stories, difficulties, unquantifiable problems.

In Washington, D.C., for instance. What the devil was going on there? The city should have been, according to the bright signals beaming from the nation's capital, the beacon of the new president's "Great Society," illuminating a new life for women. Congress had finally passed Helen Gahagan Douglas's long-languishing Equal Pay Act. Kennedy's commission on women, chaired by the formidable Eleanor Roosevelt, had recommended the establishment of new federal and state commissions to help them. "Meet the Press" journalist May Craig and those intrepid leaders Congresswoman Martha Griffiths and Senator Margaret Chase Smith, with the help of Lady Bird Johnson and the black civil rights lawyer Pauli Murray, had pulled off a real coup with the equal employment section of the Civil Rights Act (Title VII). They had managed, with the most dogged politicking, to get the word "sex" added to the act's provision against "race" discrimination.

And so what if that little skirmish had provided congressmen with the laugh riot of the year.

Far from hiding their merriment in those fabled and cloistered cloakrooms, America's elected representatives had nearly burst their britches right on the floor of the House.

Whoo-ee! Now *men* can be Playboy Bunnies! Harrumph! The "Bunny Law"! Ha! "Can she pitch for the Mets?"

So what! Because there it was. The law of the land.

But pretty much useless, Betty soon discovered.

Catherine East, who was executive secretary of the new women's commission and who, unlike many of the highly placed women in Washington, thought neither Betty nor her book was overblown and obsessive, laid it out for her in precise terms, injury by injury.

The so-called "protective" labor laws *protected* women right out of jobs, out of any advancement. (You couldn't work more than eight hours a day, which effectively *protected* you out of most supervisory posts. You could only *lift* a few pounds—unless, of course, it was your own backbreaking typewriter.) Alice Paul and the National Woman's Party had locked horns with the Labor Department over that one for years, and both the unions and the department were still rigidly committed to that "protection."

And the marvelous new Civil Rights Act was marvelous, all right. On the surface, that is. Underneath was another matter.

The truth was that the sex discrimination provision was not going to be *enforced.* The Equal Employment Opportunity Commission (EEOC), which had been set up to monitor the act, had absolutely no intention of pulling a string on that ball of yarn.

And there was nothing "equal" about employment if, throughout the country, want ads read "male" or "female" (meaning, of course, that all the good jobs were kept for the men; qualified or not, you couldn't even *apply* for them). To advertise for "white" or "Negro" would be a no-no, but sex? Forget it! The great wisdom of the EEOC had decreed that American women couldn't care less.

Betty had already heard lots of this from other women. She had heard it from women whose new federal appointments were mere show, little more than flower arranging. One woman, she would later write, "closed the door of her office and told me, in tones of the bitterest frustration, that she'd been sitting here for six months, and no one had given her anything to do but study the department phone book." She had heard it from Dorothy Haener of the United Auto Workers, from Pauli Murray, whom Betty had called after reading about a speech Pauli made suggesting that women might have to march on Washington to assure equal job opportunities.

And she had heard it from Richard Graham, who, besides Aileen Hernandez, was the only member of the EEOC sympathetic to women.

But why didn't *somebody* do something about it? The unions, or one of those mammoth women's organizations like the League of Women Voters?

Because, she was told, it was one thing to work on women's issues, as they had for years. It was another to risk getting themselves labeled *feminist*. That was as good as calling yourself a nut or a wacko, losing your support entirely.

Dick Graham had cautiously shut the door to his office before telling Betty that, Civil Rights Act or no, the EEOC wasn't going to do a thing for women unless they had a pressure group like the blacks. An NAACP for women. (And there was that idea again.)

These issues were dangerous, especially for people with government jobs. Catherine East was sure she would be either fired or "reassigned" if anyone in the Labor Department heard that she was plotting such a thing.

"*You*, Betty, have got to do it," she insisted. "*You* are independent. *You* have no job at stake. *You* are a woman with national visibility, the only one who can start a national civil rights organization outside the government."

It was, Betty would write, a moment of dread, of "existential dread."

Why were they laying it on *her*? She was no organization lady. She had no patience for nitpicking stately procedures, for *Roberts' Rules of Order,* for caucusing and recaucusing and listening to every last thought on everybody's mind.

"I'm an author," she told Catherine and her friends. "I'm not an organization person. I don't even *like* organizations."

But since she hadn't said no outright, the "underground," as Betty had taken to calling her informants, kept after her. Knowing full well, however, that there was a bristling hostility to the "radical" Betty Friedan in certain high quarters of government, to protect their jobs they met with Betty at out-of-the-way places, small restaurants or the Jefferson Hotel, where Betty often stayed. (Catherine was not, apparently, quite careful enough. She later learned of a high-level request to have her "reassigned.")

One night, in Betty's hotel room, they told her about a conference of state women's commissions that was coming up in June of that year—1966.

"Okay," said Betty reluctantly, "get me invited to that. Maybe we can get something started there." Maybe, in other words, those state commission women would do it.

Catherine East agreed to try, though she was also convinced that any request she made for Betty's presence would get turned down. But as long as they happened to be sitting there in that hotel room, they made some lists of possible movers and shakers anyway. Lists of the enlightened. The independent. The underground.

Catherine's first worry, as it happened, proved groundless. Whether by slip or intention, no one nixed Betty's invitation to the conference.

And now, of course, Betty could see for herself. She could watch Lady Bird Johnson pour tea for the white-gloved women in the Rose Garden and LBJ lumber in to bestow his most seductive Texas smile, to tell them what a grand job they'd done and how great it was that they could all go home now to their volunteer efforts for the poor. She could also witness the pure window-dressing, the powerlessness of those highly touted women's commissions.

At the same time, the plan was that she would sort of *recruit,* send out feelers. To that underground list.

Betty agreed, and after the last afternoon session of the conference (and a grand reception at the State Department), she invited the women on the list to her hotel room.

About twenty-five women filed into Betty Friedan's thoroughly ordinary little room at about ten o'clock that legendary night, or so many of them seem to remember. Maybe there were fewer. Or more. Women, still spiffed up after the reception, wearing their high heels and neat dark suits, sitting on the floor, peering at each other over the bed; women, like hundreds of others across the nation, who had been making those small inroads for years, doing the agonizing scut work on women's issues. Some had been working on labor problems, on easing the protective laws. Some—no, it seemed as if *everyone* there that night was furious that the EEOC would not deal with the basic injustice of gender-based want ads, as well as the scuttlebutt that everybody's good friend, Dick Graham, was about to be dropped.

You couldn't tell *exactly* who was who or what they were saying. Couldn't hear it all *exactly*. But many would remember their shock at the appearance there of Dr. Kay Clarenbach, the tall, dignified Wisconsin women's leader. That list they had so carefully written had been designed to avoid spies from the hostile government agencies, the Labor Department, for instance. Kay Clarenbach, they were sure, had close ties to that agency. But Betty, impressed by a speech on discrimination Kay had given, had simply invited her.

"I was very naive," Betty would admit. "Then, I trusted anyone who dared to speak out."

And, sure enough, very soon after they were settled there, Kay's down-the-line announcement was heard:

"We'll have to draft resolutions on those two subjects and get them passed tomorrow."

Resolutions!

"They'll never allow it," someone from the underground ventured.

And then Betty gave it her best. She tried to explain the point of the meeting, tried to tell Kay what Betty herself now understood—how impossible it was, how nothing could happen, nothing be accomplished if they tried to work within government. How they needed an organization with no ties to anyone.

"We need an NAACP for women," somebody cautiously added. A group that could—like the civil rights protestors—march and sit in and *attract the attention of the media.*

To which Kay replied, with her ineffable calm: "We *have* the machinery. We *have* the commissions. We can pass those resolutions through the normal channels."

And from another quarter came the flip comment: "*Another* women's organization! Do we need yet *another* women's organization?"

Betty looked around to find a woman sitting on the floor, leaning against the wall, a woman she barely recognized. The expansive Dr. Clarenbach, unaware of what was brewing, had brought some of her Wisconsin cronies along. Among them, the bright-eyed, jocular Nancy Knaak, a University of Wisconsin dean, who, quite obviously, had her doubts about this whole thing. Including Betty herself.

Dr. Knaak harbored a memory of Betty's causing a near insurrection at a meeting of women deans, not for expressing her ideas, but for standing at the podium with photos of her kids and rambling on and on about them. Or so, at least, Nancy remembered it. She was far from awed by Betty, and she was among the first of her detractors.

Unlike Nancy, hundreds of women were inspired by Betty Friedan, and in the years to come, there would be hundreds more. They would see in her the dynamic, insightful, and visionary leader who could probe a woman's psyche and, with her raspy voice, fire it up. Those dark eyes could come alive, suddenly, with a profound—almost loving—energy. She could thrill. She could, as one follower put it, "make you understand things you couldn't understand and make you want to do something about it."

But she was also erratic and sometimes distracted. Or careless. Not just about the way she looked, but about what she said and how she said it. For those who loved her, it was an endearing quality. But for others . . .

All Nancy Knaak could see in this would-be leader was a distinctly unattractive woman in outlandish clothes, wearing a flowing, brightly colored cape when everybody else was wearing navy-blue tailored suits, an incoherent speaker who, Nancy was convinced, was "not all there."

And now Nancy was asking questions about whether or not they had explored all the channels—and who were *they*, anyhow, to speak for all the women in America? Who elected *them*?

"Who invited *you*?" Betty snapped. And, within seconds, the full tempest erupted.

"Get out! Get out!" she shouted. "This is my room and my liquor and you're perfectly free to say anything you please, but you're not going to use my room and drink my liquor while you're doing it!"

And off she stormed, into the bathroom. *Click* went the lock and—how long was it? Nancy, determined to stand her ground, timed fifteen minutes before Betty emerged.

The meeting was adjourned finally with the cool-headed Kay Clarenbach designated to pass those hopeless resolutions.

And that was that, thought Betty. The end of it all.

And yet, as history would show, it wasn't.

The next morning, as the women breakfasted in their hotels, it was clear that something was in the air. Something had been percolating all night. That wild notion of an activist pressure group was alive again, and by lunchtime, it boiled over. Kay Clarenbach had spent the whole morning traipsing from bigwig to bigwig—both male and female—and back around the circle again. The Wisconsin leader was shocked. It was true, she told them. What Betty and some of the others had said last night was true. They could not, in fact, pass those resolutions! They were, all of them, strong, sensible women with years of political service, and their commissions had no power whatsoever!

Time was running out. The conference would end with the upcoming luncheon meeting, and they would all go home.

"We'll have to get together at lunch," someone said.

Their only chance, in short, to actually get something moving was to huddle together while the final, official meeting was in progress.

Were there only eight women, or were there more? One round table or two? It would be hard to remember. They were seated in the enormous ballroom of the Washington Hilton Hotel, directly beneath a dais inexplicably loaded with enough government VIPs to run a small country—including all those who had given Kay the runaround. And the entire time, smack under the noses of these official bigwigs, and through the grinding drone of political speeches, these unlikely insurgents, in stockings, high heels, and proper suits, whispered and plotted and wrote notes to each other. About getting organized to take action, about reaching the grass roots, about *rights*.

Every now and again, one of them rose and sidled over to another table to spread the word. Soon, the great ballroom was buzzing with the rumor that *something* was happening there.

Somebody at the table volunteered Kay Clarenbach as temporary chair of the *something*, which made one important figure in the underground—Mary Eastwood of the Justice Department—extremely suspicious. Were they bypassing Betty to play pattycake with the government and the "protective" unions? Nancy Knaak, on the other hand, would be sure that she had heard the whole idea from *Kay*—not Betty—in the first place and that, furthermore, nothing at all could possibly happen without Kay's prestige and organizational skills.

"We need a name, a good acronym," somebody said.

"Do we want men in this or just women?"

"Men *and* women," came a strong reply. "In partnership. To help further women's rights. Not *of* women. It has to be *for* women."

"And we need a statement of purpose. And a treasury."

"Put your money where your mouth is!" So saying, labor leader Catherine Conroy, who had seen many a great idea die aborning, threw five dollars on the table.

All the women anted up, and as the curious from around the room stopped by to inquire, the cadre of rebels hit them up as well.

Some of the pioneers at that table would recall writing notes, or that Betty, for a few rare moments, had been silent, that she was scribbling on her paper cocktail napkin. They would remember that the disheveled head rose, finally, and that she thrust one napkin, then another into the nearest outstretched hand.

"How about this?" she said. "Or this?"

Everybody, it seemed, approved. For the moment, at least, the name that Betty had scratched on the napkin would serve. And indeed, perhaps it wasn't, in retrospect, quite so histrionic, quite so grandiose as they had thought when the lively New Yorker with the incendiary eyes rose and proclaimed, in such auspicious tones, that this was a *historic occasion* and where was the photographer?

Because Kay Clarenbach, at least, would distinctly remember reading the words on those crumpled napkins:

". . . to take the actions needed to bring women into the mainstream of American society, now, full equality for women, in fully equal partnership with men.

"NOW. The National Organization for Women."

By 1984, it would be powerful enough to pressure a presidential candidate into choosing a female candidate for vice-president on his ticket. On that day, June 29, 1966, it had a treasury of $135.

NOW. Action now!

It was nearly a year since the memo on women had been written to SDS, since the women who wrote it had been jeered right out of a national conference, but no one—outside the inner circles of the student movement—had any hint that any women's rebellion was brewing *there*. Oh, everyone knew about the "youthquake." About the "love-ins and be-ins," the great "Satisfaction" of the Rolling Stones. And whether you indulged or not, you surely knew about "grass" and "pot" and "tokes," about Timothy Leary's seductive appeal to "turn on, tune in, drop out." About the "counterculture."

A different theater entirely. An invitation to join NOW was not a ticket to ride in a Yellow Submarine; it was a deep bow to your status as an accomplished professional. Far from intending to *counter* culture, the women of NOW proposed to *join* it, to join the "mainstream" as full and equal members.

Even before leaving for home that day in June, they had fired off telegrams to the recalcitrant EEOC, and all that summer, Betty, Kay, all of them, rushed out to gather important and worthwhile members.

Betty had moved her family to an apartment in the cavernous Dakota on West 72nd Street in New York City (the same apartment building where the Beatles' John Lennon was later to live and die). After a summer of recruiting, she gathered top-flight communications experts—television's Betty Furness and Marlene Sanders, public relations executive Muriel Fox—for a powwow on "image."

The time, they knew, was right. Women out there were beginning to stir, to move the courts to reconsider restrictive laws—laws that held that a woman couldn't serve on state juries, dispose of her property without her husband's consent, enter bars, restaurants, or hotels unescorted—dozens of injustices that most of them had always simply taken for granted. The presidents of Sarah Lawrence and Radcliffe colleges had even voiced, publicly, the idea that the women of the nation might desire *both* careers and families.

And yes, the communications experts agreed, the twenty-eight-member board they had assembled was superb. All these labor leaders, college professors, executives, deans, ministers, black and white, about 10 percent of them male, could not have been better chosen. Important people. Attractive, respectable, prosperous. The last thing in the world you wanted was an image of a sad-sack group of disgruntled women who needed either a man or a job.

On November 21, 1966, Betty called a press conference at her apartment and carefully presented a thoroughly "feminine" image. She held forth from her curlicued Victorian loveseat, wearing a ruffled, tomato-red blouse, the lacy frills at her wrists dancing in the air as she waved and gestured with her arms.

NOW was not a club for women, she told the reporters. "It is a civil rights organization. Discrimination against women in this modern world is as evil and wasteful as any other form of discrimination."

At the same time, Muriel Fox sent out press releases announcing the official formation of NOW with three hundred high-credentialed members. The stories that followed were thought to be, though they were not, in fact, the first press notice of the new organization. Earlier that summer, the Milwaukee *Sentinel* had reported its birth, listing Kay Clarenbach as temporary "chairman" and noting Betty only at the end of a long roll of charter members. And perhaps this story simply reflected certain early loyalties, especially in the Midwest, where Kay's stability and prestige far outweighed what some of the women had assessed as Betty's New York, media-oriented flamboyance.

Muriel's official release announced Betty as president, Kay Claren-bach as chairman [sic] of the board, Aileen Hernandez and Richard Graham as vice-presidents, and Caroline Davis (director of the women's department of the United Auto Workers) as secretary/treasurer.

Within hours of official formation, Kay was blasted into motion by the inimitable, audacious Friedan style. Betty had an idea a minute and wanted them executed yesterday.

"We gotta do *this!*" Betty would order over the phone. "And *that!*" Whereupon the efficient Kay would have to figure out how to do it.

Betty, Kay believed, thought of her as a slow-witted midwesterner; Kay, for her part, regarded Peoria-born Betty as a fast-talking New Yorker, and it was a year before they worked together congenially. Somehow though, across the country, members like Catherine Conroy suddenly found themselves responding to Kay's call: "Betty insists that . . ." "We have to move on . . ." Letters. Notices. Minutes. Phone calls.

Many of the women—Betty and Kay certainly included—gave their entire working days to the cause. They spent their own money as well, which would force them, in time, to curtail their efforts. At the moment, though, the fledgling group was firing full blast.

First off, NOW petitioned the EEOC on the subjects of those male/female help-wanted ads that corralled women into low-paying jobs, as well as the forced retirement of airline stewardesses if they married or reached their early thirties. In December, a handful of NOW members picketed regional EEOC offices in a few cities across the country and dumped symbolic red tape. Early in 1967, Betty threatened to *sue* the government in full view of tipped-off TV camera crews and called this peppy little display by a few committed souls a "national demonstration." In the congressional hearings that followed, Congresswoman Martha Griffiths told airline executives: "If you are trying to run a whorehouse in the sky, then get a license."

Later that spring, NOW formed task forces on marriage and divorce, women in sports, employment, textbooks, television. Small groups of women worked tirelessly, setting up speakers bureaus, analyzing legislation, bombarding government agencies with letters and phone calls, traveling to Washington or state capitals to present their arguments. That fall, they began to meet and plan and campaign against the "barefoot and pregnant in the kitchen" images of women on television. Letters were sent to the president, and face-to-face interviews were held with EEOC commissioners. And, though two decades hence these women would be criticized for failing to address this issue, lobbies were indeed organized for child-care centers.

Often, in their picketing and demonstrating, the women were jeered mercilessly. Sometimes, the battles involved lawsuits that dragged on, like *Bleak House,* for years.

The fight to remove "male" and "female" from help-wanted ads was one such misery. After those early months of pressure, the EEOC did rule in NOW's favor, only to face a lawsuit from the American Newspaper Publishers Association, which claimed that the issue had been raised by a "minuscule group of no consequence." Newspapers argued that such a rule would "confuse" the reader and that they would lose money in this disturbing change of format. A few cartoons appeared in their columns showing women marching on restrooms marked "MEN."

"She laughed when I asked her if she would look for her next job under Help Wanted Male" was a typical jibe as the influential publishing forces warned against "unisex."

The *New York Times* was adamant. Betty and a group of women met with its executives again and again, with no results. The powerful men were "absolutely unbending," Jean Faust, the first president of the New York NOW chapter, reported in her notes to the new group, "one in particular growing more and more agitated. At one point, he said, 'If you were a man—' The lawyer jumped in . . . to soothe things down."

The women began to picket, at first outside the *Times* building itself, dressed in old-fashioned clothes with a husband-and-wife team carrying placards. His read: "I got my job through the *New York Times*"; hers: "I didn't." But the press coverage that lively picketing garnered could not, of course, continue forever. More than a year later, the women were still doggedly trying to raise the issue.

"A Death Watch at ANPA," a NOW memo reported. "Picketers wear veils and black arm bands and march around a coffin representing Title VII.

"ANPA ignores us; so do the newspapers; ditto TV."

Meanwhile, Betty raced around the country, scattering chapters of NOW like sunflower seeds. ("Okay, *you're* the president of the Syracuse chapter.")

Not that the job was difficult. A low, sparking brushfire was spreading out there, and all the members were getting more phone calls than they could answer: "How do I join? What can I do?"

Union organizer Catherine Conroy, for one, was amazed. Long used to soliciting, teaching, urging, she suddenly found eager joiners calling *her.*

On November 18, 1967, Betty presented a Bill of Rights at the second annual convention of NOW. She demanded paid maternity leave, tax deductions for child care, educational aid, job training, access to contraception. She insisted on passage of the ERA, that constitutional amendment languishing since the twenties: "Equality of rights under the law shall not be denied by the United States or any state on account of sex." And she delivered the bombshell: legalization of abortion.

Sure enough, many members resigned. Some over the ERA and more over the abortion issue.

A few had already dropped by the wayside simply because of Betty's imperious manner, her impatient growl of orders. As Muriel Fox would remember: "Sometimes I thought that my main role was to keep Betty from killing people and people from killing *her.*"

Nearly everyone would remember the sudden thunder, the unpredictable roar that could spew from that turbulent center. Betty would come into the middle of a meeting, and suddenly, bosom heaving, arms waving, jumping up and down on her impatient little legs, she would insist, over and over, at the top of her lungs, that you were doing it all *wrong!*

"She would just start yelling," *Newsday* journalist Dolores Alexander would remember. "If she didn't approve of what we were saying or doing, her voice would rise and she'd start talking a mile a minute, abusing people. Everything was an issue for Betty. The way a meeting was run, the way a press conference was run, any plans you might be forming. She'd yell, 'No, no, no, you can't do it this way, it's gotta be done *this* way.' *Her* way. And God help us if we didn't do it that way."

But under certain circumstances—and this Bill of Rights meeting was one of them—Betty could conciliate, unify. And she was deeply admired, both for her courage and for her unflagging commitment to certain issues. Abortion, for instance. Well into the eighties, Dolores would remember with great respect her leader's unequivocal stand for legalizing abortion at that difficult early conference.

Neither Dolores nor any outside member of the press was present at certain caucuses held prior to the formal meeting, however. If they had been, they would have discovered a far more *politic* leader than they imagined. Betty was, in truth, a reluctant convert, not, certainly, to the legalizing of abortion itself, but to its advocacy by NOW.

"Betty was, at that juncture, very much on the side of the women who dropped out over abortion," board member Alice Rossi would recall. "She wanted NOW to have a restricted range of platform issues. Economic, employment issues, not those that got into the private side of life. Her first priority was for NOW to become as big an organization as possible, and she was afraid that abortion would narrow the base of appeal. It was only after it became clear, in the caucusing, that the spin-off group against it would be small, that the overwhelming majority would vote to support the plank—it was only then that Betty went along. It took a couple of years for her to swallow hard and say, yes, we can sustain this and still grow."

Once committed, though, she was fearless.

We'll use every tactic available, Betty told reporters, and that won't exclude the possibility of a mass march on Washington.

Barely a year had passed since the black riots in Watts, a year since Martin Luther King led the march from Selma to Montgomery. Medgar Evers and Malcolm X had been shot. The most unpopular war in American history was in full bloody cry, and antiwar demonstrations were everywhere.

And now *women* were going to march? A scared government began to respond. The EEOC held public hearings. Johnson signed an order prohibiting sex descrimination in the federal government and its contractors, and another one removing the restrictions against women attaining any military rank higher than colonel. (Prohibition against male/female help-wanted ads and stewardesses' forced resignations took a little longer, but they, too, would eventually follow.)

And all along, the demonstrations continued. ("But why," one tired soul was quoted in a memo, "always in the dead of winter?") The sweat-labor organizational work poured out of Kay's Wisconsin office while what pop and dazzle could be generated flashed from the country's media center: New York.

There Betty's dynamism was reaching a growing number of women. A few were reluctant to join, to expose themselves to the calumnious label "feminist," but most were pleased to be included, to meet the other women, not for a sorority conclave, a coffee klatch, but, as men had been doing for years, on the basis of accomplishment and the prospect of action. Dolores Alexander, for example, sick of having male editors pit one "girl reporter" against another for the few available "women's stories," was thrilled to be part of what she quickly recognized as history in the making, and she was delighted, at the very first meeting of the New York chapter of NOW, to meet such intelligent and successful professional women as Muriel Fox and the Barnard College lecturer Kate Millett.

Kate, already active in the civil rights and peace movements, had joined New York NOW the minute she heard of it. That "hobbyhorse," as her classmates had called it, that obsession of hers with women's status, had turned out, to her delight, to be other people's too. Smart people. Accomplished people.

"The best minds," as she would one day describe one of these new feminist gatherings, "of my generation."

She was chosen to chair the education committee, a fine spot, it seemed to the founding members, for the pretty, solid-bodied young academic with the white Irish skin, the dark brown hair pulled back severely into a bun. Kate was witty, sometimes frighteningly, cuttingly so, some thought to the point of insolence. But she was soft-spoken and smiling, and she threw herself into nearly every demonstration, every picket line NOW proposed.

Kate was, by then, a "downtown" artist, and in New York, "downtown"—the Village and environs—was the home base, the refuge of the rebels. "Uptown," where corporate headquarters were housed in gleaming steel skyscrapers, was "establishment" territory. For many budding playwrights, artists, and activists, it was a mark of social concern and artistic honor not to set foot above 14th Street for months on end.

Kate was at home there. Except for the two years she had spent in Japan, studying painting and sculpture, she had been living in a rented loft in the Bowery for nearly ten years, scraping out a joyous if meager existence, doing small jobs, lecturing at Barnard College, hanging out with other struggling artists. She chose this way of life in spite of the fact that she had earned first-class honors at Oxford.

Biographical data on Kate Millett, printed as late as 1971, would report that her wealthy aunt had sent her to Oxford after her graduation from the University of Minnesota because of her "increasingly apparent tendency to flout convention." The real reason, of course, was that Kate was in love with a woman, a fact of which her co-workers at NOW—"uptown" women for the most part—were completely unaware.

Homosexuality in the repressive fifties had been a dangerous threat to the rigid defense system the country had hammered up around home and hearth. But even the sexual liberation of the sixties, even the publication of Masters and Johnson's *Human Sexual Response,* had barely dented attitudes in this area. The exuberant paeans to "letting it all hang out" and "doing your own thing" had managed somehow to completely skirt the subject of homosexuality, and the taboo still hung heavy and ominous as the word of God. Even when the musical *Hair* freed the emotions of Broadway audiences, delighted them with the new glories and boundless love of the "Age of Aquarius," it offered not a whisper of "the love that dared not speak its name." Television viewers may have suspected the outrageous, pixyish Truman Capote, the delight of talk show hosts, of sexual proclivities other than the heterosexual norm, but Capote himself would not yet be so daring as to admit to them in public.

The environment for the homosexual was still forbidding. Except, of course, in certain circles. Among them was the richly tolerant world of lower Manhattan.

The scholarly Kate had, in fact, enjoyed Oxford, living well on Aunt Christina's allowance, skiing the Alps, dashing about Europe in her own car. When, as a trained academic, the first in her family to achieve such honors, she had rebelliously headed for the Bowery and the life of the downtown artist, her mother and the Millett aunts were appalled. But the Kate who had been so proud of the hard-earned cash of her adolescence was now independent—and not to be deterred.

In 1961, she had managed to ship out to Japan on a freighter, and there had met the charming and talented sculptor Fumio Yoshimura, who became her lover and, in 1965, when he was threatened with deportation from the United States, her husband. For years, Kate had been faithful, but eventually, there were women lovers as well—a lusty, sensual life full of adorations, jealousies, wrenching and glorious passions that she would eventually describe in profuse detail, but a life which was, at the moment, well concealed.

From the NOW members and, of course, from the press.

For there was, as yet, no reason for it to be otherwise. NOW trudged forward on the issues, actions, Betty's Bill of Rights. Private matters—what went on in one's bedroom—were, to them, hardly the point.

Yet the sexual revolution was surely not to be ignored, nor were "personalities," the celebrity journalism that would soon produce *People* magazine. Reporters were learning to truck out intriguing or glamorous figures to lend face and voice to otherwise dry ideas, and they would thereby, inevitably, create "stars."

Whether by design or error, the Golden Age of Feminism would have its celebrities as well. Ready or not, for better or for worse, new voices with new and remarkable ideas would be heard.

The "stars" were about to come out.

PART III

11

THE NEXT
GREAT MOMENT
IN HISTORY
IS THEIRS

Now the largest minority group is getting angry.
Women are tired of working for everyone's liberation
except their own.

—Joreen, *Sisterhood Is Powerful: An Anthology of Writings*
from the Women's Liberation Movement, 1970

In early fall of 1968, even before the crisp turn of the leaves, a new, remarkable turn came in the fame and fortune of the women's movement, a moment that changed the world's view of this rebellion—and therefore perhaps the rebellion itself—forever.

It happened on September 7 and danced across nearly every television screen in the country.

Betty, in her autobiographical book *It Changed My Life*, would mention the event only in passing, as having occurred *after* NOW's Oak Room demonstration. Simply a mistake, perhaps. Or perhaps not. Getting there first was, clearly, a point of pride, and Betty's cliffhanging Plaza invasion would not take place until February 1969, five months later.

This great splash—the Miss America protest—was such an attention grabber that it garnered, in the *New York Times* alone (though in hundreds of other papers around the world as well), ten times the

149

space allotted to the actual winner of the immensely popular beauty contest.

The demonstration was engineered, primarily, by Robin Morgan, a former child star best known for her role as Dagmar in CBS's hit series "I Remember Mama." As a college student, Morgan had been active in the New Left, and suffered, as she soon would write, from male put-downs, from those all-too-frequent moments on the barricades when some leader of the Students for a Democratic Society would ask for "chicks to volunteer for cooking duty."

Robin and her New York contingent were offended by the Miss America Pageant, which, they protested, touted a doll-like ideal of what men wanted women to be—inoffensive, bland, mindlessly wholesome, and apolitical. And they were not alone in their indignation. That spring, in Seattle, Washington, a group of women had mounted a small but fiery demonstration against the degradation implicit in such beauty contests.

The Seattle skirmish, however, had been a protest from afar. Robin's had all the elements of a major spectacle. It would be a face-to-face confrontation. . . .

In Atlantic City, New Jersey, America's beloved, ballyhooed pageant of pretty girls, clothed and half-clothed, was covered from beginning to end by network television. Given its fairy-tale quality, it was a national favorite, the only program, presidential candidate Richard Nixon announced, that he and his wife had allowed their children— Tricia and Julie—to stay up late to watch.

About two hundred women had answered the angry, mimeographed flyer "No More Miss America," and sure enough, at about three o'clock in the afternoon, the TV cameras caught them, marching down the boardwalk, singing and shouting:

"Atlantic City is a town with class. They raise your morals and they judge your ass!"

All you could see on the screen was a crowd of women, some waving their arms, some laughing, some holding up placards.

"No More Beauty Standards—Everyone Is Beautiful."

"Welcome to the Miss America Cattle Auction."

"I Am a Woman—Not a Toy, a Pet or a Mascot."

"Girls Crowned—Boys Killed," read one placard protesting the Vietnam War.

"Miss America Is Alive and Angry—in Harlem," read another, a pointed reference to the fact that no black woman had yet appeared in this national contest.

And there were others, too, though you didn't see them on your television screen: "Miss America Sells It"; "Miss America Goes Down." What you *did* see was a random parade of women in jeans and miniskirts, braless under T-shirts, long hair blowing wild in the ocean breeze.

It was all a bit confusing. Now they were tossing objects into a round receptacle marked "Freedom Trash Can," and though you couldn't quite make out what the objects were, the flood of press reports (in spite of the flier's warning that only female reporters would be recognized) would soon clarify.

Dishcloths, girdles, false eyelashes, copies of *Playboy, Vogue, Cosmopolitan, Ladies' Home Journal,* and, yes, bras.

"Freedom for women!" they shouted as they tossed, and the "Freedom Trash Can" was soon brimming with the everyday symbols of the contemporary woman's housebound, stereotyped role.

The scene was far from orderly. From behind the police barricades, set up on either side of the boardwalk, rough-voiced hecklers jeered: "If you got married, you wouldn't have time for all this!" "Lesbians!" "Screwy, frustrated women!" "Do you play around with monkeys or men?"

A former contestant emerged from the crowd with a sign: "There's only one thing wrong with Miss America—she's beautiful." Then another placard, the inevitably divisive "Jealousy will get you nowhere."

But on the women marched, tall ones, short ones, fat and thin, old and young—but mostly young—shouting about the degrading, mindless "boob-girlie" symbol of Miss America, singing songs that at times rivaled the pageant itself for tastelessness:

Ain't she sweet?
Makin' profit off her meat.
Beauty sells, she's told
So she's out pluggin' it.
Ain't she sweet?

They were indeed young. And suddenly—empowered. As Robin Morgan would write: "We all felt, well, *grown up . . .* we were doing this one for *ourselves,* not for our men . . . getting to do those things the men never let us do, like talking to the press or dealing with the mayor's office. We fought a lot and laughed a lot and felt very extremely nervous."

They auctioned off an eight-foot-high wooden puppet, a great-bosomed Miss America dummy resplendent in spangles. They trotted out a live sheep with a big bow strapped to its tail, draped it with a banner, and crowned *it* Miss America.

By 8:30, as the pageant proper began, a few of the protestors, holding precious tickets, entered the convention hall, followed watchfully by a contingent of policewomen, troopers, and plainclothesmen. About two hours later, as an odd, putrid smell wafted uncomfortably through the hall, police promptly arrested the one who was spraying the place with butric acid from a Toni hair spray bottle. A stink bomb.

At midnight, the Nixons presumably, along with much of America, were rewarded with the coronation of eighteen-year-old Judith Ann Ford, Miss Illinois, as Miss America, and the losers, as usual, smiled lovingly.

Flashbulbs popped. Television cameras moved in. The pretty, teary-eyed woman in the long evening gown began to speak, when suddenly shouts burst out in the hall.

"Down with Miss America!"

"Freedom!"

Then it all came clear.

A great, white bedsheet floated slowly down from the balcony, the cameras wheeled around, and there (undoubtedly for the first time) most of America saw on that wavy banner, a *t* and an *i* hidden in the folds but the message still unmistakable:

"WOMEN'S LIBERATION."

And so millions now learned about the women's movement.

Like it, of course, or not.

The perpetrators were immediately hauled off by the cops, and the black civil rights lawyer Flo Kennedy hustled to the central police station to do battle for bail. It was, she would later write, "the best fun I can imagine anyone wanting to have on any single day of her life."

Nobody, of course, had actually *burned* her bra, though the "Freedom Trash Can" was undoubtedly what gave rise to that calumny. And that reporter's error, Flo would decide, was all to their advantage: "It made us look tougher and smarter than we were."

"The only real concern was attention," Frank Deford would observe in a reverential book about the Miss America Pageant, "and the Libs slaughtered the Pageant at this game. . . .

"To the Women's Liberation Movement," he added, "the skirmish at Convention Hall is roughly analogous to the Boston Tea Party."

A call to revolution, he meant, a revolution, it now appeared, that was taking a different turn, aiming far wider than Betty's (and NOW's) basically civil rights agenda, at what scholars and poets had been tangling with for centuries. Truth. Beauty. Sex. Love and morality. The great mysteries of life. In essence, what is woman?

This change in pitch, this reach for the high notes, had all begun quietly enough.

Early in 1968—with the light snows of January—came a hint in the press that NOW was not the only game in town. That month, just after the Vietnam Tet offensive, a coalition of women's peace groups called the Jeanette Rankin Brigade appeared among the dozens of antiwar demonstrations in Washington. A newly formed group calling itself the New York Radical Women staged a torchlight parade billed as "The Burial of Traditional Womanhood"—which really had nothing to do with the war.

Or did it?

The leaflets of this avowedly "radical" group of women implied that the war and women's issues were part and parcel of the same thing, that the policies and problems of America began at *home*, that to turn the country around, even to stop the war, women had first to raise their "consciousness," to *recognize* their own oppression. They wrote —and this may have been the first notice of a slogan soon to activate thousands across the country, said to have been coined by the imaginative young radical Kathie Amatniek: "Sisterhood Is Powerful."

Just a hint, perhaps, but there it was.

By spring, the bright and bizarre sounds of youthful rebellion were everywhere, and most Americans began to regard all this noise (or sweet music, depending on one's politics) as something more than "just blowin' in the wind." The voices of the young and disaffected, the dreamer, the activist, the ragtag poets and the priests, were not merely naive and quixotic. Collectively, they were a momentous force at the highest level, shatteringly powerful, or so it appeared.

In the last days of March, a Gallup poll revealed that 49 percent of

Americans agreed with the antiwar demonstrators: America should not be in Vietnam. And then, a few days later, in a shocking announcement, President Lyndon Johnson told the world that he would not run for reelection.

The rollicking, creative, morally indignant, anti-establishment young had actually brought down a president of the United States (or so it seemed). For the counterculture rebels, for youth in general, the sense of empowerment was stunning, inspirational.

That spring, at about the same time that *Soul on Ice*, Eldridge Cleaver's clarion call to black revolution, and *Armies of the Night*, Norman Mailer's grandiloquent antiwar plea, were pouring into mass-market bookstores, a slender newsletter called "Voice of the Women's Liberation Movement" was published in Chicago. Written by a group of New Left women, it was barely noticed by the public. Such a plethora of ideas and slogans and images was popping in the air that what was probably the first use—in print, at any rate—of the term "women's liberation" was swallowed in the rainbow sky of crazily colored balloons. Of attacks on "the system," "the power structure," "the establishment."

On March 10, however, as the peace candidate Eugene McCarthy was edging toward the Democratic nomination, the *New York Times Magazine,* with a circulation of over 1,500,000, ran an article by Martha Weinman Lear entitled, with a bow to the suffragists, "The Second Feminist Wave." And to Freud: "What do these women *want?*"

The term "women's liberation" had not yet reached the alert ears of the *New York Times,* but Lear's piece was a full-scale recognition of the fact that those picket lines outside the *Times* building on 43rd Street, the demonstrations against TV's ubiquitous soapsuds on Madison Avenue, were not just isolated events. There was enough action, enough emotion, enough felt injustice out there to generate—and let the country beware—a *women's movement.*

The Lear article quoted Betty, of course, most tellingly on the subject of the EEOC chairman's reference to "girls": "I said, 'Mr. Chairman, I would hope you're interviewing *women.*' It's like calling a fifty-year-old Negro 'boy.' "

But also Kate Millett: "By the time a girl is ready for medical school, she doesn't want to go any more. She never really had a choice. She's been conditioned to her role ever since she got the doll to play with, and her brother got the gun."

154

And the piece did venture, if somewhat gingerly, beyond the sober issues of NOW—child-care centers, maternity benefits, equal employment—and into what Lear described as more "militant" views.

More personal, that is. More complicated and far reaching. Women who objected to being treated merely as "sex objects," for example, or believed in "profound social revolution"—the movement's "intellectual hip," Lear wrote, "the female version of Black Power."

Most striking of all was the attention and space lavished on the woman the piece described glowingly as "the militant's *haute* thinker," the tall, glamorous Ti-Grace Atkinson, at that moment the president of New York NOW.

"Miss Atkinson is twenty-nine," wrote Lear, "unmarried, good-looking (in the *Times,* she has been described as 'softly sexy,' which is not *necessarily* a compliment to a feminist)."

Her name, as Ti-Grace would later tell reporters, was Cajun for Little Grace, her family was an old southern one, conservative and influential. She had been married for a short time but was now single. She wrote reviews for art magazines and was working for her doctorate in analytic philosophy (as she still would be, well into the eighties) at Columbia. She had been practically hand-picked for her NOW position by Betty Friedan, who thought the willowy blonde's patrician carriage, her purring, seductive voice, would be perfect for coaxing money, much needed for the new organization, out of wealthy Westchester and Long Island matrons.

Nothing, however, could have been further from Ti-Grace's purposes, and many members would remember their shock at discovering the immense gulf that separated Ti-Grace's soft-spoken, ladylike demeanor from the explosive revolution she espoused, much of it quoted in this article.

"The institution of marriage," Ti-Grace had told Lear, "has the same effect as the institution of slavery had. It separates people in the same category, disperses them, keeps them from identifying as a class. The masses of slaves didn't recognize their condition, either. To say that a woman is really 'happy' with her home and kids is as irrelevant as saying that the blacks were 'happy being taken care of by Ol' Massa'. . . . I think it's time for us to go on the offensive."

Atkinson, the piece went on to explain, believed that the nuclear family should be abolished and that children should be raised communally.

155

Marriage as slavery, communal child raising, class warfare! All this was quite beyond the mainstream focus of NOW.

From an editorial standpoint, however, the *Times* was on the money. In those tumultuous years, the media pursued every new "lifestyle," every new social trend, with the passion of the hunt. And it had absorbed, as well, a corollary interest—the lucrative lessons of celebrity journalism, the cult of personality that would seem, by the eighties, familiar as a rock beat.

Beginning with outrageous stories about movie stars in a magazine of the fifties called *Confidential,* celebrity journalism had been painted into a high art by the Kennedy campaign blitz. Dozens of photos of the candidate's beautiful wife and appealing children had run in all the magazines, most especially *Life* and *Look,* charming the country out of its socks, and, not incidentally, translating into political and financial power. ("I do believe," Jackie Kennedy was supposed to have remarked to her husband's media experts, "that you would have me pose nude in a bathtub if it would help get Jack elected.") Magazines that, back in the early sixties, had alternated covers (Liz and Dick this month; Jack and Jackie the next) were by now absorbed in a quest for not what, but *who,* would sell out on the newsstands.

Faces, names—the newest, the hottest, the latest. So surely it behooved a reporter to truck out intriguing or glamorous figures to lend face and voice to otherwise unpalatable ideas. Not just Betty Friedan and company protesting "help wanted—male" and "help wanted—female" ads or the plight of stewardesses. Not just the dry stuff of discrimination in employment.

Something new, different, exciting. Something—or someone—sexy. A star.

Ti-Grace Atkinson was a star. Charismatic. Almost hypnotic. The pale blaze of the woman! The ice castles of her theory!

Soon, the media passion for stars would make a pack of trouble in the movement. Differences would arise, of course, on philosophic grounds, but none would seem—would, in fact, *be*—so virulent as those that involved the media.

Already, there was a ruffling and snuffling in NOW. Jean Faust, who had preceded Ti-Grace as president of the New York chapter, was particularly annoyed.

"The media," she would remember, "lost interest in you if you were married. If I said that women needed a better self-image, they'd ignore it. If Ti-Grace said, 'Women should commit suicide,' they grabbed it."

Yet the *Times* article surely did help put the movement on the map. You couldn't help noticing, though, that it also changed the composition of those relatively decorous NOW meetings, meetings that were sometimes held in cramped local schoolrooms but often in elegant townhouses, or in Muriel Fox's big apartment on East 83rd Street (which she eventually sold to actor Frank Langella). Now, nearly overwhelming the spit-and-polish businesswomen, those outstanding "winners" in their crisp Chanel-style suits and pearls, came a thundering flood of younger women, some of them with pale, makeupless faces, ragged, tie-dyed blue jeans and streaming hair, some who were living the new, permissive, communal life-style, but most young housewives from the Upper West Side and the Village who had not, for all sorts of reasons, sex discrimination not the least of them, won *their* impressive roles outside the home.

"They were angrier, much more hurt than we were," Muriel would remember.

And Ti-Grace, she was sure, was the magnet.

Not that anyone in NOW objected to the rush. Far from it.

The movement needed bodies, and these younger women were, as Betty liked to put it, "the troops." They seemed to be, in other words, and for the moment, trainable, controllable.

On June 3, however, something happened that was beyond *anybody's* control. The swirling orbits of the counterculture and the women's movement—in NOW, at any rate—accidentally crossed in a bizarre and violent explosion. Just three days before the assassination of Bobby Kennedy, a counterculture actress/writer named Valeria Solanis, a woman who called herself a feminist, shot artist Andy Warhol in the stomach.

The story blazed across the front pages of New York's two daily tabloids and most of the world. Feminists in Europe—still silent, for the most part, far behind the Americans—were fascinated. Warhol was well known internationally for such gestures as painting everything silver, including his hi-fi set and the hair on his head, for satirizing cultural decadence by translating Brillo pads, Campbell soup cans, photos of Marilyn Monroe into Pop Art (and money). Lately, he had been making "underground" films, mostly about sex and sin, mostly populated by a coterie of stunning if strangely expressionless young women known by such names as Viva, International Velvet, Nico, Ultra Violet, Ingrid Superstar, and, in the movie *I, a Man,* Valeria Solanis herself.

It was a "mad, mad world with a lot of mad people in it," as Ultra Violet observed.

According to police accounts, Valeria Solanis had barged into Warhol's sixth-floor studio on Union Square late in the afternoon, wearing a yellow blouse, tan pants, and a brown jacket, and, without a word to anyone, fired a barrage of bullets.

"Valeria, don't do it! No! No!" Andy yelled before collapsing on the floor.

Three hours later, while Warhol was undergoing the five-hour surgery that would save his life, Solanis handed a traffic cop a .22 revolver and a .32 automatic and confessed: "The police are looking for me. I am a flower child. He had too much control over my life."

Which, in Ti-Grace's view, was a sharply accurate assessment.

"I knew how horribly exploitive Warhol was," she would remember. "He paid Valeria just twenty-five dollars for her work in the film." And Valeria, according to Ti-Grace, couldn't pay her rent at the Chelsea Hotel, where she was living, and had been put out on the street.

Ti-Grace also quickly discovered that Solanis, a University of Maryland graduate, had written a twenty-one-page feminist tract entitled, perhaps (or perhaps not) with a touch of tongue-in-cheek, "The SCUM [Society for Cutting Up Men] Manifesto."

The opening salvo of the manifesto read:

"Life in this society being, at best, an utter bore and no aspect of society being at all relevant to women, there remains to civic-minded, responsible, thrill-seeking females only to overthrow the government, eliminate the money system, institute complete automation and"—in retrospect, this ominous addition—"destroy the male sex."

The details of how to accomplish this (through "sabotage") followed, along with a scattering of four-letter words.

"Women, in other words, don't have penis envy; men have pussy envy. . . . The male, because of his obsession to compensate for not being female combined with his inability to relate and to feel compassion, has made of the world a shitpile. . . . SCUM will kill all men who are not in the Men's Auxiliary of SCUM."

No, a friend of Valeria's told reporters, Solanis was not a lesbian, the character she had played in the Warhol film. She was a "man-hater."

Enter the publisher of the frequently pornographic Olympia Press, Maurice Girodias, who had paid Valeria $500 for the rights to the

SCUM manifesto, "the only thing," according to Ti-Grace, "that Valeria had." Girodias had then sold the movie rights to Warhol, and years later, Ti-Grace would still stick loyally to this tale of injustice.

"Girodias was infamous for finding people on their uppers, down and out," she would explain. "He would pay them $500 for their work and own it completely.

"Valeria couldn't believe it was legal but she found out it was. She was powerless. In the power of all these guys. When she couldn't get it [the manifesto] back any other way, she was going to scare him [Warhol] into not doing the movie."

(Friends of Warhol would report the reverse, however—that Andy had enraged Valeria by *refusing* to make the movie.)

Warhol survived the shooting, to have photographs of his stomach scars taken by Richard Avedon. Solanis, charged with attempted murder, was sent to Matteawan State Hospital for the Criminally Insane.

But Ti-Grace (who had already championed the cause of a young female student expelled from Columbia for the still-scandalous behavior of living off campus with her boyfriend) believed in defending women in trouble. She visited Valeria at Matteawan and ran off copies of the SCUM manifesto on the mimeograph machine in the Columbia philosophy department. She supported Solanis openly, and the press, entranced for the moment with their long-legged, blond philosopher, began printing her comments. Among them—in the *New York Times* —Ti-Grace's proclamation was headlined "Valeria Solanis a Heroine to Feminists."

Within NOW, as the shock waves registered, the New York president began to catch flak.

On June 17, at an emergency meeting, the consensus, according to the recorded notes, was "TG has badly damaged NOW. . . . She should resign to make it clear she was not acting for NOW. . . ."

And: "TG refuses to resign; wants a week to 'think it over.' "

"I told Ti-Grace," *Newsday* reporter Dolores Alexander would remember, "that since she had no standing in the community except as president of NOW, she had to be careful of what she said. But it was impossible . . . frustrating. We'd have these long meetings, come to a consensus, finally, of what to tell the press, and then Ti-Grace would go out and say something entirely different, whatever she wanted to."

Such as: "The oppression *of* women *by* men is the source of *all* the corrupt values throughout the world."

Or: "By God, you'd better learn it [the vaginal orgasm], lady, especially if you're with a liberal man; you'd better learn to shuffle, nigger, because if you don't, you won't get the job."

Always a marvelous vision—in low-cut necklines or a soft, fluffy fox coat—Ti-Grace could rap out slang while she posed, at the same time, with elegant, mathematical precision, many of the vatic notions that would spark discussions—and divisions—well into the eighties: reform or revolution; women as equal to, different from, or enemies of men; women as a "class" or "caste."

She would eventually weave an intricate caste analysis in her book *Amazon Odyssey*, but even now, that fall, as the objections from the founding members swirled around her, she began to hold forth more forcefully for a true and complete revolution of women. Resolutely, she painted a classless utopia—to be constructed right there in New York NOW—in which there would be no leaders at all. No bosses.

Such a revolution would require, of course, an entirely different organizational structure. The others, the ones everyone had always known, had been set up *by* men and for the benefit *of* men. Ti-Grace proposed instead an entirely new set of bylaws, a complex nonhierarchical organization with no "leaders," a revolving chair to be chosen by drawing lots from a system of pools.

Some members of NOW were intrigued. Among them was Flo Kennedy, who even her detractors would admit was *sui generis*.

Tall, skinny, self-deprecating (the beauty parlor, in her vocabulary, was the "ugly shop"), the fifty-two-year-old Flo, a longtime civil rights lawyer, generally appeared in one of her amusingly arranged and attention-getting costumes—a Mexican hat and beads, a helmet and an empty gun holster, a turban and a slogan-covered T-shirt. In her cowboy hat and cowboy boots and wild T-shirts and chains and symbols draped over her copious bosom. With her ubiquitous shopping bag crammed with clippings and leaflets. And her mouth. Oh, what a mouth! Flo, as she was likely to put it, didn't take *no shit* from *nobody*. She growled and guffawed and turned everything upside down and inside out. Married once, she had no great love for that institution and saw no reason why Ti-Grace shouldn't wield the ax. Right now and right on!

Born black and poor in Kansas City, Missouri, Flo and her four sisters had absorbed unforgettable lessons in not taking "guff." Their

Daddy Wiley was a Pullman porter, a waiter, then finally owner of his own taxicab. When the Ku Klux Klan tried to put the family out of their home, Wiley appeared on the front porch with a shotgun and the announcement: "Now the first foot that hits that step belongs to the man I shoot." And when the school principal threatened Flo with a strapping, Daddy and his gun blockaded that move as well. No one, but no one, was going to strike the Kennedy girls.

"My mama always told us we were precious," Flo would remember, "so we believed it. Also, we were always nice to each other. Nobody could understand that." All five of the youngsters were, according to Flo, crackerjack students (if high-spirited and mischievous), and their scholastic ability was part of what made them "special."

Of course, in Mama Zella's view—and inextricably Flo's as well—being special meant *looking* smashing as well. To that end, a lot of hair straightening went on, and a lot of value judgments were applied on the subject of lighter and therefore "prettier" skin, straighter and therefore "prettier" noses. (Flo was convinced early that she was far from pretty.) Zella cut out patterns from magazines and sewed lots of dresses for her daughters—pink-and-white gingham with flared skirts or black sateen, each with a different colored binding. And since the girls loved all the attention the colorful clothes brought them, they had not a moment's hesitation about flaunting them.

Once during that rosily remembered childhood, however, Flo experienced an emotional charge of a higher voltage by far than even dressing up could deliver. It was the incomparable kick of a flamboyant dramatic gesture as social protest.

As Flo would tell the story, Zella was at work in the home of a woman who was "quite preoccupied with dirt." One day, Zella's employer approached her with a list of complaints—not unheard of, certainly, but this time, added to her normal harangue, was the accusation of theft. To be accused of stealing was beyond Zella's endurance. In a tantrum of rage, the young domestic removed every article of her clothing, down to her sanitary napkin. Then, her anger still unspent, the outraged Zella pulled off that last soiled item and shook it in her employer's shocked face.

Flo adored the story.

In one simple, economical, utterly theatrical gesture, Mama had said it all.

As Flo soon would as well, for remarkably early, her mind was geared to protest. In the mid-forties, while she was attending the night extension division of Columbia University, she wrote a school paper entitled "The Case Against Marriage." Marriage, she held, was something society had set up to further its own purposes, and glorifying the institution militated against full equality for women. In a second paper, "A Comparative Study: Accentuating the Similarities of the Societal Position of Women and Negroes," she observed that "a returned serviceman may be especially upset to find his job occupied by a woman or Negro."

Two decades later, the mobilizing concept of "woman as nigger" would surface again, along with the outrageous, magnetic style with which Flo Kennedy would regale college students across the country.

"Listen, honey," she would warm up some "round-eye." Then she'd lay it on, let loose a torrent that would make you wonder how you could possibly have been so *naive*.

Sex: "Most people are not taught . . . that the two o'clock orgasm leads to the three o'clock feeding."

Sports: "A jockocracy."

Hippies: "Dropouts" with "slumlord uncles."

Cooking: "Women's work until it pays thirty-five thousand a year, then a man with a blazer becomes the cook on TV."

Jobs: "There are very few jobs that actually require a penis or a vagina."

Rape: "Silence is collaboration and rape without struggle . . . is just a bad screw."

Research: "You always have those who—when the shit is hitting the fan real hard—get busy measuring the size of the turds to make sure you don't overstate the oppression."

"I'm just a loud-mouthed, middle-aged colored lady," Flo would confess real easy-like, and audiences everywhere would love her. Especially on college campuses. Soon, she would even make money at this speechifying, grossing, she would figure proudly, about $60,000 a year. (Poverty, Flo figured, never cured the impoverished.)

"You see, the establishment comes around and gives you bridge mix," which, the irreverent Flo would quip, thus enlivening many a bored reporter's notes, "is chocolate-covered bullshit that the establishment hands out saying, 'Here is your candy. Don't bite it.' And the reason they don't want you to bite it is that if you bit past the chocolate you'd get in touch with the bullshit."

The "bullshit," in Flo's view, also included the courts and the law, for, after putting herself through law school, she had spent many frustrating years battling for the rights of black jazz musicians and civil rights rebels—Billie Holliday, Charlie Parker, and H. Rap Brown among them.

Zapping the enemy with theatrical gestures, such as picketing ad agencies ("Is there a bigot in your market basket?" "Jim Crow lives on Madison Avenue"), would be, to Zella's daughter, far more satisfying. As well as, by then, as an early member of NOW, romping outside the Colgate-Palmolive building on Park Avenue in a demonstration against the ubiquitous television images of women wedded to housework. A toilet bowl (part of a sculpture supplied by Kate Millett) into which they poured various Colgate products would gratify them all with substantial press attention.

"That's my whole thing, you see," Flo would explain. "I'm ruthless and I go to the media." There to apply pressure, as she put it, "in the testicular area."

"The media" by now meant, most especially, television, which in the 1960s had proved its ability not just to entertain, but to convey what was actually going on in the world and to influence the thinking of millions. In 1968 alone, it had already brought to Americans, to their dens and family rooms, against a backdrop of beer, potato chips, and playpens, enough news to shatter their worlds forever. The Vietnam War, the assassinations of Martin Luther King, Jr., and Bobby Kennedy, and the violence erupting around the country—the Columbia student takeover, the burning of draft files, the conviction of the beloved Dr. Spock for counseling draft evaders, the Democratic Convention in Chicago beset with riots, billy clubs, police clashes.

So if Ti-Grace wanted to tell the media that marriage was slavery, Flo thought, let her. "If you're oppressed, you're supposed to be pissed and you're supposed to show it on any and all occasions." Flo thought marriage was "a crock of shit" anyhow, the surprise you get "when you're looking for the pot of gold at the end of the rainbow.

"See, any time our establishment tries to get you to do something, you can be sure it's not in your interest. And so the minute you hear all these love songs—see, religion and love songs are always available to peasants—you know it cannot be politically to your advantage. It's like a landmine, see, with lilies planted over it."

Flo the Mouth. Professional she might be—like so many of the early members of NOW—but "mainstream" she was not. Some whiff of that mainstream brand of caution in NOW had already set her revolutionary nostrils aquiver.

"When I said something about the war," she would write, "how women ought to oppose it—Betty Friedan and Muriel Fox went bonkers. . . . They thought I was crazy."

And when, at Ti-Grace's request, Flo took on the Solanis case, she received the following telegram from Betty:

"Desist immediately from linking the National Organization for Women in any way with the case of Valeria Solanis. Miss Solanis's motives in the Warhol case are entirely irrelevant to NOW's goals of full equality for women in truly equal partnership with men."

Flo simply could not bear Betty Friedan, and years later she would have no hesitation about labeling the founder of NOW with such blatant zingers as "pig bitch." She would remember, angrily, Ti-Grace in tears because Betty had yelled at her.

Well, nearly *everybody* would remember some tears.

In spite of them, though, the business of NOW went on, and that fall, the image-conscious members in New York still had Ti-Grace to deal with.

Granted, one of the basic problems was that women had always been *led*, but this sheeplike behavior pattern should not be perpetuated in the women's movement. NOW, however, was dedicated to helping women get *into* positions of power, not to eliminating the so-called "power structure" altogether. This would be chaos! And Dolores Alexander, for one, was convinced that eschewing "leaders" was simply a ploy to give Ti-Grace the power to continue to speak to the press when and if she wished. Studying Ti-Grace's organizational charts with a friend one night, Dolores threw up her hands in despair.

"Pools, pools," she wisecracked. "Everybody into the pool! Sure they don't want any leaders. Just so Ti-Grace can be the leader and Kate can be the leader!"

So it happened that the October 17, 1968, meeting of New York NOW—calm as silk on the surface—was seething beneath. Most of the original members and their allies had been summoned. A coup was brewing.

Ti-Grace demanded an amendment in the bylaws that would eliminate all leadership positions, and then the voting process commenced.

No, they would not do away with officers or terms of office. No, they would not do away with official committees, or with a clear designation of responsibility. No, they would not go the route of the newly forming radical groups, of collectivism and anonymity. Slowly, methodically, Ti-Grace was voted down on each point until it was finally clear that she had been completely defeated.

Seeing all that, her lovely pale cheeks flaming with anger, Ti-Grace (who was Flo's idea of a woman truly willing to *risk*) fell silent. The next day, she issued a statement of resignation to the press, noting "irreconcilable ideological conflicts" between the young and the old, between those who "want women to have the opportunity to be oppressors, too, and those who want to destroy oppression itself."

New York NOW would remain as it was, with the underpinnings, at least, of standard establishment structure. The coolly determined Ti-Grace Atkinson, taking with her the irrepressible Flo Kennedy and —at least for several months—the acerbic, fluent academic Kate Millett, would never be seen again at the New York NOW meetings.

Like Flo, Kate, too, thought Ti-Grace was a marvel, perhaps the "finest mind" of all of them. And Kate was also beginning to wonder if hierarchies, leaders, bosses, were not, in fact, the folly of the male world, and if the core of all of humanity's suffering, the wars and the famines, was not indeed the rule of men.

The young education director of New York NOW, growing increasingly pacifist, had taken to wearing dark glasses to faculty meetings and interrupting debates over student antiwar demonstrations with heartfelt harangues about the slaughter in Vietnam. Her stubborn support for the students was not, apparently, appreciated by the faculty. In December, two days before Christmas, she was fired.

For days, Kate shed angry, bitter tears. Then, in a white heat of inspiration, she began work on what she decided would be her doctoral thesis. She had written for NOW a saucy critique of women's education—especially teaching and nursing and home economics courses—and she had received, for her pains, a long warning from Jean Faust:

"We must not seem intellectually arrogant. . . . We must not give the impression that we scorn such careers and the women who choose them. . . . Does your comment need to be so sarcastic? Is there a better approach? . . . Please leave out the down-with-the-government-and-capitalistic-society here."

A friend had sent Kate's work to Betty Prashker, then an editor at Doubleday, who had told her that though Doubleday couldn't publish the critique, she would like to see whatever else Kate wrote. Maybe, Kate thought, she would send her the first few chapters of her thesis.

She would write about what she had thought, no, what she had *known*, really, all her life. That the pain and suffering on earth, particularly of women, was caused by the arbitrary, birthright rule of men. She would trace in its most profound and revealing form that pervasive, insidious, coercive authority which permeated every home and every stratum of society. Through the actual writings of the oppressors themselves, she would expose "the patriarchy."

Meanwhile, she joined Ti-Grace, who after her defeat in New York NOW had formed, with Flo Kennedy (and with grand, revolutionary fervor), "The October 17 Movement," later called the Feminists.

Even earlier, other small groups of young women, identifying themselves as "radicals," had been popping up as well, especially in the big cities. In many of these groups it was a given, just as it had been in the student movement, that if you got the social theory down, the analysis (*why* had all this happened to women; *how?*), everything else would eventually follow. But what a wicked hunt that was! The answers hid like rattlesnakes nearly everywhere, in the dense underbrush of denigrating attitudes so deeply ingrained in the male-dominated culture that even these young women themselves had, unknowingly, absorbed them.

"Women who grasp the male point of view more than momentarily," Ti-Grace would soon announce in a speech at Juniata College in Pennsylvania, "are not feminists." And on a local New York television program, driving that point home: "Women must commit suicide." (Before they could rise again, free of male influences.)

If women were indeed oppressed, the oppressors must be men, and therefore no more than one-third of the Feminists' members could be married. Furthermore, in the Feminists, as promised, there was no leader, no hierarchy.

Yet somehow, to the public at large, and eventually to the rank-and-file Feminists as well, it didn't look that way.

By then, in local press accounts, you were beginning to catch the choppy shortcut "women's lib," or occasionally "libbers" or "libbies." Not that a stampeding horde careened down out of the hills or anything like that, or even that most American women thought these "far-out" protestors had anything much to do with *them*. Still, the televised sights and sounds of police beating up students at the Democratic National Convention in Chicago had created a certain amount of sympathy for radical youth, and by the late months of 1969, while *Alice's Restaurant* and *Midnight Cowboy* were playing in movie theaters, hundreds of curious folks wanted to hear from Flo and Ti-

Grace . . . on campuses, at church organizations, on TV talk shows. Each, in her own special way, had style. Each was a "presence."

Tall, blond Ti-Grace, always a fetching sight, had taken to wearing round, blue-tinted, professorial glasses. She spoke often—and engagingly—to the press.

She had cut herself off from men, she told one reporter (though she "found the conclusion as difficult to support as others do"), thus leading the reporter herself to suggest that the life of a feminist revolutionary must be lonely and frightening.

Ti-Grace did not disagree.

"Most women reject the feminist philosophy because they are afraid. They are afraid that if they reject marriage and men—the same way the southern slaves rejected slavery—they will be treated like enemies by those who still endorse the institution."

Women should openly identify with prostitutes, she would explain in her lofty, transcendent manner. ("Whenever Ti-Grace called to tell you something," the journalist Susan Brownmiller would remember, "she began with 'I, Ti-Grace Atkinson . . .'.")

"My impression is that the prostitute is the only honest woman left in America," Ti-Grace told a reporter, "because they charge for their services, rather than submitting to a marriage contract which forces them to work for life without pay." For every woman arrested for prostitution, four men should be arrested for obscenity.

At least prostitutes got a price, she would add. Not that the price they demanded was high enough. Their price, in Ti-Grace's view, should be revolution.

"We have to go to the streets with them. We need street fighters."

By 1969, that singularly explosive year, there was a bewildering array of radical groups to choose from, though none, perhaps, so severely demanding (or so short-lived, as it would turn out) as the Feminists.

In New York, the Redstockings, the name a play on "bluestocking," the derogatory term for intellectual women, was formed by writers Shulamith Firestone and Ellen Willis. New York Radical Women, New York Radical Feminists, WITCH (on the theory that witches were the original resistance fighters against women's oppression). In Boston, the socialist Bread and Roses and Cell 16, which included among its most vocal members Abby Aldrich Rockefeller, daughter of

David Rockefeller of the Chase Manhattan Bank. Word was sifting out of Seattle and San Francisco of more diverse groups, more early actions, and in New York, unsure (though sometimes sounding *very* sure) of exactly the "right" direction, some of the rebels began shifting alliances, moving from one group to another. By the end of the year, one reporter would have—somehow—come up with a count of thirty-five groups in the San Francisco Bay Area, thirty in Chicago, twenty-five in Boston, a scattering across the continent from Florida to Canada, but fifty in New York alone—the cutting edge, a micro-cosm, as some would later see it, of the movement as a whole.

Most of these groups theorized, one way or another, from the class exploitation dialectic of Karl Marx or the revolutionary teachings of Mao Tse-tung and Frantz Fanon. Almost all of these young women credited the person they considered the true mother of the Golden Age of Feminism—not Betty Friedan, but Simone de Beauvoir.

Simone de Beauvoir's *The Second Sex* was first published in France in 1949. This complex book, an exploration of the female condition through de Beauvoir's enormous range of learning in the arts and humanities, contained the seeds of nearly every protest ever expressed by women's liberation. She, too, attacked Freud and his notion that "anatomy" was "destiny," and she offered a thorough examination of women's social role as the "other" sex, of the "submission" intrinsic to marriage and its correlation with prostitution, of the entrapment of beauty, the "hypocrisy" of criminalizing abortion, a woman's need for "agreeable sexual adventures." And though de Beauvoir did not directly express feminism as class warfare, she, like most European intellectuals, had no intention of abandoning one for the other. And yet . . .

"Men have always kept in their hands all concrete powers," she had written; "since the earliest days of the patriarchate they have thought it best to keep women in a state of dependence."

From these radical groups would spring amplifications of that con-cept, the "position papers" of women's liberation, often printed on cheap, colored stock or run off on university mimeograph machines, a prolific harvest of rhetoric that would soon leave the essays of the male New Left in the high, dry fields of memorabilia.

There were articles on the enslavement of beauty, the temptation of becoming a beautiful "object"; admonitions against shaving your legs or under your arms; polemics on the politics of housework; essays on sexist language and—what would turn out to be especially prophetic—on the use of the term "lesbian" to condemn any woman who acted independently.

But none, perhaps, was more central than "The Redstocking Manifesto" hammered out in the summer of 1969—the ground-breaking "pro-woman" line:

"We are exploited as sex objects, breeders, domestic servants and cheap labor. We are considered inferior beings whose only purpose is to enhance men's lives. . . .

"We reject the idea that women consent to or are to blame for their own oppression. Women's submission is not the result of brainwashing, stupidity or mental illness but of continual, daily pressure from men. We do not need to change ourselves, but to change men. . . . We take the woman's side in everything."

It was an answer to the view of women—common in every walk of life—as bitchy, catty, unable to get along with one another, as well as, of course, the derogatory equation of "unhappy" with "neurotic." The "pro-woman" line held that criticism of women—even any one woman—was a case of "blaming the victim."

Some would see this concept as an impossible, unnatural demand for some sort of Patient Griselda–like sisterhood, leading, inevitably, to hypocrisy. Others would see it as the impetus for what would come to appear as an unhealthy focus on women as victims. Still others, however, would regard the pro-woman line as a check on unbridled (and male-induced) competitiveness between women, and the basis for the explosion in feminist thinking and writing throughout the next decade.

Already, this exciting stuff was pouring out of the scruffy little underground papers, the new magazines: *Aphra; Majority Report; Liberation, Inc.; Women*—most of it attacking assumptions about the nature of woman.

In *Notes from the First Year*, Anne Koedt wrote the soon-to-be-classic "The Myth of the Vaginal Orgasm":

"Frigidity has generally been defined by men as the failure of women to have vaginal orgasms. Actually, the vagina is not a highly sensitive area and is not physiologically constructed to achieve orgasm. . . . Women have thus been defined sexually in terms of what pleases men . . . an orgasm which in fact does not exist. . . . We must begin to demand that if a certain sexual position or technique now defined as 'standard' is not mutually conducive to orgasm, then it should no longer be defined as standard."

·Ti-Grace wrote about women as the first political class, of the need to completely destroy sex roles; about her concept of "metaphysical cannibalism" (men, searching for potency, subsume women's energy in the process) and romantic love as a soporific, blinding women to their oppression.

Marge Piercy wrote "The Grand Coolie Damn," an eloquent plea for unity. (This, too, certainly took a different tack from NOW's goal of joining the "mainstream.") "Women must shed their passivity and act," Piercy wrote, but especially *against* "careerism and competition."

Psychologist Naomi Weisstein's " 'Kinder, Küche, Kirche' as Scientific Law: Psychology Constructs the Female" was a powerful attack not only on Freudianism but on the prejudice of the entire field of psychology itself, its focus on unproved "innate" traits.

At the same time that the writers were writing, a growing number of women in government, unions, education, law—NOW members as well as those in other formal organizations, new and old—were battling discriminatory regulations in every walk of life. This was the "scut work" of the movement, the hard, unglamorous, day-to-day work, the picketing in freezing weather when nary a reporter showed, the organizing that led that year to 7,500 charges of sex discrimination filed with the EEOC. Some of these accomplished, behind-the-scene toilers believed—with good reason—that theirs was the work that was effective and they would never quite forgive the press for focusing on the flash and dazzle, the "theater" of it all instead, from those jazzy, insistent little episodes of the WITCH street theater group "hexing" Wall Street to Ti-Grace and the Feminists picketing the New York City marriage license bureau, claiming that marriage enslaved women.

Yet this was also the year that a few more male magazine and newspaper editors, admitting that something important was going on out there that a man might not quite understand, assigned articles on the movement to women whose names would soon be listed among those of America's finest journalists: Sara Davidson, Gloria Steinem, Julie Baumgold, Vivian Gornick.

From these pieces, America caught a glimpse of this strange and remarkable rebellion. Some women, we discovered, were taking lessons in karate! Julie Baumgold, in *New York,* had an amused and ambivalent take on *that:*

"Witness the Liberated Women: Her feet are swords. Her body is a weapon (it has to be; she is a revolutionary). She doesn't need to use

170

her sex to get what she wants from men. She knows karate." These women, Baumgold continued, "carry their babies tied around their necks, or papoose style. It keeps the hands free for hammer blows and elbows to the guts of men with ideas."

Not exactly a winning image for the local garden club. But neither was the notion that some women were urging others to leave their husbands and children and to avoid pregnancy. Or that leaving one's legs and underarms unshaven was a political statement of independence, that Rapunzel's golden locks were now *de trop* but, on the legs, the natural growth. ("Oh, my God," one rebel was caught moaning, "I'll die for the revolution but don't ask me not to shave my legs!")

Women exploited as sex objects. What had emerged at the first Miss America protest had, in some covens, hardened into party line.

Ti-Grace Atkinson was quoted in a karate chop at marriage, not just as slavery, but as state-licensed rape: "The more I understand what's going on with men, the less I miss male companionship and sex. Men *brag* about domination, conquest, trickery, exploitation. . . . Male chauvinism comes out in waves—every gesture, every word."

And now, from these articles, Americans began grappling with "male chauvinism," that odd locution. And "machismo," "sexism." Thousands of women began to scrutinize not just their bosses or the local garage mechanic, but the men they lived with, for telltale signs of that oppressive constellation of attitudes.

At the same time, however, the country also began to learn a few of the facts that lay behind what the press now took to calling "hard-core" women's liberation groups:

Fact: Only 1 percent of the nation's engineers were women, only 3 percent of its lawyers, 7 percent of its doctors. One-fifth of employed female college graduates were clerks, factory workers, and cooks.

Fact: Women earned little more than half of what men earned, and the gap was widening. Ten years after graduating from law school, men earned 200 percent more than women. Yet most working women were working, not for fun, but because they needed the money.

Fact: The number of women in elected positions had dropped drastically in the past ten years. They were almost nonexistent in government—except as political "auxiliaries."

Fact: College faculties consisted of less than one-quarter women, far fewer than there had been as far back as 1879.

Fact: Women performed the housekeeping tasks of industry. They were for the most part secretaries, not executives; nurses, not doctors;

researchers, not writers; bookkeepers, not accountants or merchants; and almost never decision makers.

Fact: Under American law (based on English common law), "the husband and wife are one and that one is the husband." In many states, a wife's income and property were under the husband's total control, and the rape of a wife by a husband was perfectly legal.

Fact: Nowhere in the Ten Commandments was it written that only women, and not men, would be required to choose between family and career.

Vivian Gornick, in the *Village Voice,* cut to the bone of it, giving respectful notice to the radical wing. The new women's movement paralleled the black movement, she wrote, most especially in what could be termed the " 'nigger mentality,' the terrible inertia of spirit that accompanies the perhaps irrational but deeply felt conviction that no matter what one does, one is going to end up a thirty-five-year-old busboy." (Not exactly the way Flo Kennedy had put it back in the forties, but close.)

Gornick told a moving story of her own paralyzing anxiety, the internal conflicts that had drained her energy and retarded her capacity for concentration, and which were only resolved when she was forced, by circumstances, out into the world. The anxiety was caused, she wrote, by the constant implication that women were "all victims of some biological deficiency, that some vital ingredient had been deleted."

She attacked the idea that only the male of the species (the "accidentally dominant white male") needed real work else he might "shrivel up and die."

"This assertion," Gornick wrote, "is, quite simply, a lie. Nothing more, nothing less. A lie."

And the prophetic title of this piece in the *Village Voice* was "Women's Liberation: The Next Great Moment in History Is Theirs."

12

THE CHICKENS
AND THE FOX

*Certainly I knew that what all women's magazines
were giving to women to read was largely illusion,
fantasy and too often cruel deception . . .*

—Shana Alexander, 1975

And now, as Susan Brownmiller would remember, "Everything began
happening so fast."

Susan, a small-boned, delicately featured woman in her mid-thirties, was a respected, established journalist. She had worked at both
ABC- and NBC-TV, had written profiles for the *New York Times Magazine* on Eugene McCarthy and Consolidated Edison's chief executive
officer, Charles Luce. And on a subject close to her heart—Congresswoman Shirley Chisholm.

In 1968, Chisholm was elected to Congress—the first black woman
in history—and Susan's devotion to the black civil rights movement
had been long-standing.

In the early sixties, not long out of Cornell, and not far from her
birthplace in Brooklyn, Susan had joined the Congress of Racial
Equality (CORE) and the first civil rights picket line in Manhattan.
She had even formed her own picket line, marching in front of the
segregated Woolworth's store near Bloomingdale's every Saturday for
a year, and had worked for the East Harlem Reform Democrats. In

1964, on vacation from *Newsweek* (where, like nearly every other female writer, including the talented Nora Ephron, she was consigned to the research department), she had gone to Mississippi.

It was Freedom Summer, that infamous year when civil rights workers James Chaney, Andrew Goodman, and Michael Schwerner were beaten with chains and shot to death. The South was a dangerous place for young activists. For Susan, as for hundreds of other young people of moral spirit who poured out of churches and liberal arts colleges, it meant risking one's life.

"We Shall Overcome."

The brave power of the song thrilled the heart, and when, the summer over, Susan returned north, one of her employers had startled her with the question: "What do you plan to do with your life?"

"Nobody had ever asked me that before," Susan would remember, and when she found herself answering "I'm going to work for the civil rights movement," she had quit what she saw as a meaningless job at *Newsweek* and made plans to go back to Mississippi, this time without a time limit. Before leaving, however, Susan read *The Feminine Mystique.*

"I hadn't intended to read it," she would remember, "because I thought it would be all about how to be mysteriously feminine."

Not that *feminism* (which some would regard as the opposite concept) was much of a recommendation, either. To Susan, as to many young educated activists steeped in Marx, Fanon, and Marcuse, feminism had certain bourgeois overtones. And Friedan's book was indeed, in Susan's view, directed mainly at middle-class housewives. As Betty herself had written, the problem was not to be felt by "women preoccupied with desperate . . . hunger, poverty or illness." And yet, reading *The Feminine Mystique,* Susan would remember, "I began to think, who the hell was I? Wasn't I one of these women, too? Wasn't I a woman with fantasies, who wanted to be an actress? [Which she actually had been, for a few years, Off Broadway.] Who wanted to write plays, work in politics? And where was I putting all this? Wasn't it possible that I had harbored—all through my life—the feeling that, being a woman, to have these ambitions was *wrong?*"

Nonetheless, as planned, Susan packed her jeans and her drawstring blouses and traveled south. Exhilarated by the sense of purpose she had found in Mississippi and prepared, like so many of her friends, to give her life for "the movement" (which meant, in those days, civil rights, New Left), Susan reported to the black organizer in charge.

"I keep asking for volunteers," the annoyed civil rights leader sniffed, "and they keep sending me white women."

After a few months, stung and angered by Black Power separatism, deeply disillusioned, Susan had gone back up north. She returned to New York and worked at ABC-TV for several years. Then—it was in 1967, perhaps, though she would never be sure of the exact date—a friend mentioned what seemed, to Susan, to be very strange meetings. They were held, for lack of a permanent place, at the New York office of the Southern Conference Education Fund (SCEF). They were very much like New Left rap sessions, but with an important difference.

"Susan, you won't believe this," her friend said, "but they're really talking about women."

And—just as the black separatists had excluded whites, thus teaching them a bitter lesson—only women were permitted to attend.

"You're right," Susan told her friend. "I don't believe it."

Radical-left politicos rapping about American women? Bourgeois women? The ultimate "useless parasites"?

But one night, with the utmost skepticism, Susan stopped by the SCEF office.

Sure enough, there were women there. Only women. They were doing something they called, not rapping, but "consciousness raising."

And Susan listened as, one by one, going around the room, the women focused, not on topics connected to class or race discrimination, but on the most personal issues—those that were known, felt, agonized over by them as *women.*

Love, marriage, sex, childrearing, work . . .

There were tentative voices and angry ones, confessions of fear and betrayal, all of them revealing, sooner or later, the injustice they had felt, the experience of that injustice which—without realizing it—they shared with one another. And the result of it all. The conflicted, battered self-images. The enervation, confusion, depression.

"It was absolutely amazing," Susan would remember. "They were talking about things that we had never dared say out loud."

When you think about having a baby, do you think about wanting a boy or a girl? Have you ever felt that men have pressured you into sexual relationships? Have you ever lied about orgasm? What work would you most like to do, and what has stopped you?

175

Such groups soon would pollinate the country, from small university towns in Iowa to larger cities like Seattle, from fishing villages in Maine to prairie towns in Nebraska. In small pockets across the land, women would hear about those "consciousness-raising" sessions, would come together in small groups, and pose the questions: "Did you choose to stay single or marry?" "How do you feel about sexual commitment and fidelity?" "Have you ever wanted to have more than one sex relationship at a time?" Each one would then relate specific incidents in her life and, finally, that "testimony" would be analyzed. If you couldn't find a "CR group" already in existence, you formed one yourself.

"Libchick" meetings, the New Left men scoffed—until, that is, the rebellions (and divorces) began at home.

From these groups, new words and phrases would swarm into popular American culture like aroused bees. Terms such as "sexism," "male chauvinist pig" ("pig" from students' denunciation of cops); phrases like "anatomy is not destiny" (from Simone de Beauvoir's refutation of Freud) and "the personal is the political."

The personal is the political meant, of course, not politicizing one's neurosis, which occasionally did seem to be the case, but that personal testimony would lead to real political change.

"I was pregnant," one woman was saying that first evening, as Susan listened intently, "and I had an abortion."

One abortion! Susan thought with a surge of emotion. I've had *three!*

"Suddenly," she would remember feeling, "it was just something I did. It was something a lot of women had done, and it wasn't our fault."

And Susan would remember the tears flooding her eyes as, for the first time, she stood up to testify . . .

About standing outside a clinic in Havana, where she had gone to observe the Castro revolution, and screaming, "You have to help me!" About waking up afterward with the words on her lips: "I could have died and nobody would have known," and hemorrhaging most of the way back to New York.

About her second abortion, when she could no longer go to Cuba, about trying to secure the services of that underground hero of the day, Dr. Robert Douglas Spenser, of Ashland, Pennsylvania.

If there was a ray of light in any of this, as many grateful women would report, it shone from Dr. Spenser.

176

His office, they would remember, was spotless. The physician, along with his nurses and counselors, treated the women who came to him for abortions with respect and dignity. Each woman was given a room of her own, and the procedure was quick, painless, and cost $100 or less. There was instruction on when and what to eat, what to expect. And on birth-control methods, the first hint, to many, of how to control their own bodies, their own sexuality. Under Dr. Spenser's care, the women avoided the emotional and physical scars so common with illegal abortions.

But Susan was too late for Dr. Spenser. The doctor had been caught and could no longer practice. After scouring the abortion underground, recoiling from such potentially dangerous techniques as saline and "packing," she finally flew to Puerto Rico, to a clinic run by a local physician.

The clinic, she would recall, housed a legitimate gynecological practice for the poor, and the abortions, illegal in Puerto Rico as well, were performed secretly. When Susan—a middle-class woman from the United States—arrived with her suitcase, the doctor was horrified.

"I won't do this," he insisted. "You'll get me into trouble. I'll go to jail."

"You must!" Susan had cried. "I'm not going back to New York."

"How much money do you have?" he asked. She had brought $300, the amount she had heard was the standard price.

It wasn't enough, the man said, but by then, she would remember, "I was sobbing, so he gave in."

And reliving those desperate moments now, in her newly discovered CR group, Susan cried again:

"I've never told anyone," she said. "Not even my best friend who is sitting here this very moment . . ."

Danger and shame, magnified and intensified by the secrecy.

For Susan, for Gloria, for so many of the young women whose voices would soon be heard—if not by every TV viewer in the country, then certainly by an expanding cadre of women—the illegal abortions of the fifties and sixties had been risky, searing experiences. Even after Masters and Johnson, the blossoming sexual revolution, the Beatles and the Age of Aquarius, the word "abortion" itself was still inflammatory—even, to much of the country, appalling. On those rare occasions when television saw fit to approach the subject, the women involved were invariably cast in deep shadow, in faceless silhouette. And in 1969, radical women's groups, the Redstockings in particular, began to hold "speak-outs" solely on that subject.

These "speak-outs" were seldom—if ever—covered by the press, and many women, attending for the first time, had no idea what to expect.

Barbara Seaman was the wife of a successful Manhattan psychiatrist, the mother of three children. She lived in a spacious apartment on West End Avenue; she was co-author, with her husband, of a women's magazine column and, like many middle-class women, she was not ready to publicly identify herself with feminism. Betty Friedan, however, had taken the young writer under her wing in big-sisterly fashion and Barbara admired the feminist author immensely.

"If Betty asked me to come to an event," Barbara would remember, "I would always go."

That year, one of the events was an abortion speak-out at the Judson Memorial Church.

Barbara should be one of the backup speakers, Betty told her. She could represent the women's magazines and maybe give some statistics on abortion . . . something like that. Typically, Barbara would recall, Betty was winging it, huffing along, maneuvering on the spot. "We'll decide what we'll talk about when we get there."

Barbara, of course, was happy to oblige, and at the church, in the back of the room before the meeting started, the talkative, prosperous psychiatrist's wife launched into an animated personal discussion with a poor black woman from the Harlem Consumers Council. Barbara had undergone an abortion when she was a student at Oberlin, she told the woman. Properly paid for by her resourceful, educated young lover, it had been, though emotionally traumatic, perfectly safe. The black woman's experience, she soon heard, had been horrible and life threatening.

Betty had been listening, in repose for a few minutes, the heavy lids of her eyes lowered. Then, suddenly, she jumped in.

"You've *got* to talk about that!" she insisted. "You've got to show the comparison between your experiences. It's essential!"

And Barbara, of course, could not refuse.

Up on the stage then, as the meeting got under way, she found herself giving the thirty or forty women in the audience not impersonal data at all, but the entire story of her abortion. Somehow, it all poured out. How she had heard of the doctor from a friend, how the boy she loved, still a teenager himself, had managed to come up with "the absolute fortune, the incredible sum of five hundred dollars," how she had gone through the entire operation in a kind of trance, how the boy had brought her home afterward, where she had lain on the couch and told her mother that she was having menstrual cramps. And then how, wracked with confusion and fear, she had run away from the boy, married someone else, and had never—to that date— seen him again.

"I don't think I noticed the cameras," Barbara would remember. "Or if I did, I didn't know whose they were. There were always cameras around in those days, somebody in the movement recording for the archives or some local reporter whose film would never actually be broadcast."

She saw herself on the television screen the next night. The local TV producers had found Barbara Seaman's upper-middle-class story far and away the most newsworthy, and the story of her abortion, in step-by-step detail, was broadcast throughout the evening and even the next morning. Over and over.

Every New York friend and acquaintance, it seemed, had seen it. Everyone knew the details. "Aren't you afraid you'll lose your job?" they asked. "Don't you think your husband is going to be very upset?" "How does your mother-in-law feel about it?" And, of course, "Did your children see it?"

One of them had indeed seen it all.

"Mommy," Barbara's little girl asked, "what's an abortion?"

The personal led to the political. Both NOW and the Redstockings soon were badgering the New York State Legislature to change the abortion laws. The assembly's outright rejection of a mild reform bill had already infuriated many women, Flo Kennedy among them.

"We ought to go out and murder a state legislator every time a woman dies from an illegal abortion," she snapped.

And then she sued. Along with her good friend Diane Schulder and two other lawyers, Nancy Stearns and Carol Lefcourt.

At the hearings, expert witnesses—prize-winning author Grace Paley, journalist Claudia Dreifus, and Susan Brownmiller—told the stories of their abortions, and Flo and Diane wrote about the hearings in a book called *Abortion Rap*.

New York State would pass a liberalized abortion law a year later (following Hawaii and Alaska), but since, even then, a federal change would be nowhere in sight, Flo would keep on pressing.

"Nobody with any brains would arrange to have children," she would quip. "Apart from the fact that they hurt when they come out and maybe you'll lose your waistline, they're expensive and they shit all over." ("We must not let our rage go without expression," was her theory. "If you're too scared to fight and too proud to suffer, try humor.")

Of course, at the same time that Flo and Betty and so many other feminists were fighting for abortion rights, something else was happening, *had been* happening, in fact, in that very personal area of sex and reproduction, for nearly a decade.

The contraceptive pill.

The pill—and the pill alone—was the entire cause of the women's revolution. All else, if not fluff, stemmed directly from that technological advance.

Or so some social analysts would contend.

This nearly foolproof method of birth control, they would argue, had suddenly thrust women into an equal position with men. It had given them independence. With the pill, women no longer had to concern themselves with last-minute devices or depend on men's willingness to use condoms. Suddenly freed of the fear of unwanted pregnancies, they could indulge in sex at whim, pretty much as men had always done. Since, according to this view, freedom and confidence in the bedroom inevitably translated to the world at large, expectations rose and, with them, the demands for equal treatment everywhere.

To many, in short, the pill was the ultimate feminist boon.

By the late sixties, 8 million American women (12 to 15 million throughout the world) were taking it.

And yet there was clearly something a bit more complicated in the contents of that little round plastic case that suddenly appeared in thousands of homes, as Gloria had discovered on her first writing assignment. In a number of ways, it was rife with ironies. Some people even had serious questions about its safety, and, in 1969, Barbara Seaman addressed that subject in a frightening book called *The Doctors' Case Against the Pill.*

Originally conceived as a magazine article for the *Ladies' Home Journal*, Barbara's book was assigned by managing editor Peter Wyden, and the subject was so hot by then that, years later, editor Bob Stein of *McCall's* would accuse Wyden of stealing the idea when he left to go to the *Journal*. In 1967, both magazines had published articles on the pill, and though the *Journal* hit first, with the coverline "The Terrible Trouble with the Birth Control Pills," *McCall's* followed with a report that drew the opposite conclusion.

At the heart of this steamy journalistic competition were two elements, the first being the current rage for consumerism, which had begun a few years earlier with Ralph Nader's *Unsafe at Any Speed*.

Women's magazine editors, hustling onto that speeding bandwagon, had been questioning whether *everything* that was handed to the public (that is, the female consumer) by the great forces of the capitalist free market was *always* perfect. Maybe even the *doctor* wasn't *always* right, especially in the area of women's health, which was, in fact, the second element. "Health," some editors called it; others—more cynical, perhaps—called it "sex."

For all the growing tumult, the feminist movement had been pretty much ignored by the glossy, high-circulation women's magazines. American women, the male editors were convinced, had little interest in such disturbing and "esoteric" issues. The surefire magazine "mix" was still, invariably, celebrity stories, romantic fiction, and comforting advice on home, children, and love life. In the newly permissive atmosphere of the late sixties, however, love—if handled with just the right degree of "scientific" insinuation and justified under the rubric of health—could also mean sex, the best seller of all.

"We were always looking for stories involving people's sex lives," Peter Wyden would remember.

"Anything involving sex and the reproductive tract sells magazines," Dick Kaplan, another *Journal* editor, would agree. "Women's tract, that is. After all, there's no such thing as a gynecologist for men. You never see a story on the care of the penis, on smegma. Women pay more attention—to their vaginas, their clitorises, menstruation, pre-menstruation, tumors, hysterectomies, polyps, endometriosis. They're constantly aware of it, monitoring, watching, spending a lot of money on it."

Women's health, therefore, spelled a bonanza for these high-circulation magazines. Two birds with one stone. Consumerism plus sex.

Barbara had written a sidebar on sterilization for the *Journal's* "Terrible Trouble" story, and when Peter Wyden suggested that she write a book about the pill for his new publishing firm, she accepted the offer.

The Doctors' Case Against the Pill, published in the spring of 1969, reached women far beyond the boundaries of the feminist movement. Barbara's research had convinced her that the pill was extremely dangerous, and not long after she sounded that warning, she was credited by the Library of Congress as the first person to raise women's health as a national issue.

In January 1970, Barbara testified at a Senate subcommittee hearing on the pill, and women from a new magazine called *Off Our Backs* protested, on the Senate steps, that women were being used as "guinea pigs." The pill was extremely dangerous to women's health, Barbara told the senators, and it would be a good idea if men returned to using condoms. If "slide-off" was a problem, she added mischievously, maybe they should be manufactured in sizes—A, B, and C, like women's bras.

The practice of medicine being as much art as science—a matter, often, of balancing risks—not everyone agreed. Some NOW women —Jean Faust among them—wrote letters to Congress pointing out that the pill was a great aid to women, and Barbara's book was mercilessly dissected in the *New York Times.* It was "disorganized, scatterbrained," Christopher Lehmann-Haupt wrote, "and could easily be stuffed back into the magazine article it must certainly have grown out of.

"Mrs. Seaman gathers up quotations from doctors near and far and flings them at us with such gay abandon that one's credulity grows numb. She wrings our hearts with tales of sad deaths and bereft children without ever calculating total percentages. Her idea of a chapter on a particular pill-associated disease is a shopping list of quotes and anecdotes. . . . The book contains almost nothing of solid substance."

The fairness of Barbara's reportage was not, however, the heart of the issue. The issue was the cavalier, sometimes dangerous treatment women had been receiving from their doctors and the drug companies, and the pill was simply one facet. How carefully had it been tested? (Its composition, in fact, would be altered.) Were women dying of its side effects because doctors didn't know who was and who wasn't at risk? Or because they didn't monitor their patients carefully after prescribing it? The complexities of the problem, the pill's risk-benefit ratio, would be argued well into the eighties, when 56 million women would be on it, but Barbara had issued a warning call. Women across the country responded, and this first alarm coincided very closely with the incipient and powerful offshoot of women's liberation soon to be known as "the women's health movement."

All over America, many women who had no connection with or even interest in the new feminist uprising were already beginning to question the quality of their medical treatment. In Western society, physicians (only about 7 percent of whom were women) had been encouraged to harbor certain God-like delusions for decades and though both male and female patients may have suffered from them, the full force of patronizing attitudes fell on women. For too many doctors, it was a given that most women were neurotic complainers, that their illnesses were psychosomatic until proved otherwise, that they were best treated with pats on the head, placebos, or drugs—most recently, some of the new psychotropic variety.

The reaction was inevitable, and in 1969 twelve women who, along with many new allies, would come to be known as the Boston Women's Health Book Collective gathered in a Boston church basement to exchange the names of doctors and information about health care. They would soon publish *Our Bodies, Ourselves,* one of the most widely read books in America, and many other women's health books would follow.

By January 1971, in fact—at least partly in the interest of health—some women would be looking in places they hadn't looked before.

"Cunt is beautiful," Germaine would write in *Suck.* "Squat over a mirror or lie on your back with your legs apart and the sun shining in. . . . Learn it. Study its expressions. Keep it soft, warm, clean. . . . Give it your own loving names, not . . . pussy, twat, box, or the epithets of hate, like gash, slit, crack. . . . What we need is a genuinely descriptive terminology." Barbara, who was already at work on a new book about female sexuality, would also strongly recommend self-examinations, and the Los Angeles Self-Help Clinic, founded by two mothers of six children, soon would teach women how to see what their gynecologists saw, with the help of a two-dollar plastic speculum and a mirror: "That tiny slit is called the external os," they would explain. "It is the entrance to the uterus. Surrounding it is the cervix, that section of the uterus that extends into the vagina."

And self-examination would become, in some quarters (including one memorable NOW conference in Los Angeles), a naively solemn philosophical exercise. Less amusing was the talk of, and some instruction in, self-induced abortion by means of menstrual extraction, which for a variety of reasons (some of them valid) also made the medical establishment nervous.

Meanwhile, in the late sixties, while Barbara was writing *The Doctors' Case Against the Pill*, Susan Brownmiller was publishing major articles on a variety of subjects in *Esquire*, the *Village Voice*, and the *New York Times Magazine*. By then she had been living with the journalist Kevin Cooney for several years, and with his encouragement, her writing career had blossomed. She had also joined the New York Radical Feminists, which concentrated mostly on consciousness raising, and Media Women, a diverse new group of both working and would-be journalists. The meetings were often wildly fragmented politically, and ideas skittered in the air like flushed birds, only to be shot down ten or fifteen minutes later. Theoretical analysis was always important and, Susan would remember, "some of the women were better at it than others. They were the leaders, the stars."

None of them, certainly, listened to her very much—bourgeois journalist that she was.

Until, that is, one cold winter evening when, to Susan's delight, she hit one raw and universal nerve.

She had suggested it in an offhand way. She was a respected writer, after all, not given to incivility to major publishing institutions. Yet the thought had crossed her mind.

"How about a sit-in at the *Ladies' Home Journal?*"

The *Journal?*

Suddenly, everybody—all those radical theorists who had practically ignored Susan up till now—was all ears. Suddenly, everybody was listening to *her*, Susan, and, just for the moment, maybe it didn't matter that she wasn't totally entranced with "overthrowing the system" or tended to shy away from the current shibboleth that all work was "exploitation." It didn't even matter that she was such a success in the thoroughly suspect world of mass media, that she had actually held (and enjoyed) well-paying jobs with network television. What mattered was this terrific idea. Those three little words. *Ladies' Home Journal.*

With its 6.9 million readers, its glossy, glamorous ads, its luxe

184

spread of impossibly gorgeous stars, gourmet concoctions, relentlessly uplifting advice. The very epitome of—the name itself practically interchangeable with—slick women's magazine.

Obviously, as Betty Friedan had pointed out years ago, the *Journal* degraded women, sold them saccharine passivity and a panacea of products with an editorial skill and circulation range that were breathtaking. But not only did Betty still occasionally write for the *Journal* herself, her howl of derision hadn't changed those editorial policies one jot. To the *Journal,* the only *real* woman was still a housewife, her sole purpose in life exemplified in the enduring column "Can This Marriage Be Saved?" Supposedly a vehicle for women, it was run (like most of the mass women's magazines) by men—such as Peter Wyden, who was known to them less as a crusader for women's health than for his widely circulated wisecracks: "The Bungalow Journal," he had once said, was "just us ladies in our big, flowered hats." And there was the horror tale that Wyden had dropped a manuscript on Gloria Steinem's desk (when she was working there on a short-lived New York section) with the admonition, "Here, make believe you're a woman and tell me what you think of this."

The *Journal* was an intriguing target for those reasons alone. Yet there was another as well. In those days, if you scratched almost any one of these new, urban feminists, her blood would run inky blue. Most of them held bachelor's degrees in liberal arts, which translated to high expectations and no jobs. With this ambiguous credential, just about the only thing you could imagine doing, the only "career," the only hope of progressing beyond the file cabinet or the typing pool, was some form or other of "writing." So many of them being hopeful but unpublished, they hid in their hearts the wound of thwarted ambition—and among those, inevitably, were a number whose efforts had arrived at the offices of the women's magazines, only to make it as far as the slush pile and depart with the standard polite rejection slip.

Not that you wanted to write that treacly stuff. Not if you could help it!

The women's magazines, however, paid thousands of dollars for a story. Their writers could actually *support themselves.*

So . . . hey, wait a minute! What was it that Susan Brownmiller just said?

A real sit-in–style demonstration against . . . oh, Jesus, the *Ladies' Home Journal!*

Within seconds, Susan had allies everywhere. Within minutes, it was clear that the former Off Broadway actress was headed for a new and unwritten role. General Brownmiller, front and center.

Susan didn't mind one bit.

Dozens of women flocked to her strategy meetings. Redstocking women, Feminists, Radical Feminists, everybody brimming with ideas.

Maybe some of them should occupy editor-in-chief John Mack Carter's office while others took over the *Journal* "test kitchen."

Gales of laughter. Giddy revenge.

"How about the presses in Dayton?" somebody said. "Can we get a group to stop them?"

"Listen," Susan warned, "we don't have the forces for that. We only have enough to walk in . . . to stay overnight if we have to."

"How about Mace? Should we carry Mace?"

And what about that important rule, begun way back at the Miss America demonstration, that only women reporters should be allowed?

Well, they would certainly try . . .

But how about some truly workable suggestions, so it wouldn't look as if you were just a bunch of angry women. A fact sheet. A list of article ideas. Instead of "Can This Marriage Be Saved?" and "Zsa Zsa Gabor's Bed," articles on "How to Get an Abortion," "How and Why Women Are Kept Apart," "How to Get a Divorce," "Developments in Day Care," "What Our Detergents Do to the Rivers and Streams."

It should be a lightning strike, Susan insisted. They would march into the *Journal* offices unannounced, "occupy" the space, and conduct a filibuster—letting it go on and on and on until that Kentucky-smooth charmer John Mack Carter could not ignore the depth of their anger and what it was about.

Through all these meetings, for three long months, Susan held tight to her command. The *LHJ* sit-in was, to her mind, truly effective political action, and she was determined not to let any disorganized whirlpool, no matter how creative, swamp it. Everything—her sense of drama, of news, her experience with the media—rang true. Especially the news peg. She could imagine the headlines, or the announcer on the six o'clock news: *Women* invade the *Ladies' Home Journal.*

"It was," Susan would remember, "a real good 'man bites dog.' "

Meanwhile, she was also hard at work on an article, about the movement itself, for the *New York Times Magazine.* The *Times* had phoned her with the assignment, the editors convinced that this strange new uprising, this new feminism, had something to do with the ominous and violent radical underground, of groups such as the revolutionary Weathermen.

They were not, as it happened, *completely* off the track. On March 6, 1970, the Weathermen accidentally detonated a bomb in a Greenwich Village apartment, killing two of their people. Shortly thereafter, twenty-three-year-old Jane Alpert was arrested, along with her lover, for bombing military and war-related corporate buildings, only to jump bail and disappear into the fugitive underground, her camouflage—bleached hair, makeup, tortoise-shell glasses—engineered by the feminist Robin Morgan.

In January of that year, in New York, Morgan and the women's staff of the underground paper *Rat* had ousted the male publishers and produced their own "all-women" issue. Robin, the architect of the Miss America demonstration and creator of WITCH, had been a member of the New Left, and closely connected to its more violent spin-offs, such as the Weathermen, for several years. Her article "Goodbye to All That," which appeared in the special one-time women's issue of *Rat,* hailed the "Weather Sisters" while it skewered the high-rolling bravado of the brothers. "Free Our Sisters!" Robin wrote, tolling among the revolutionary heroines the names that would be associated forever with the violent underground: Bernadine Dohrn, Jane Alpert, Kathleen Cleaver, Valeria Solanis . . . and her own.

"Let it all hang out," Robin wrote. "Let it seem bitchy, catty, dykey, frustrated, crazy, Solanesque, nutty, frigid, ridiculous, bitter, embarrassing, man-hating, libelous, pure, unfair, envious, intuitive, lowdown, stupid, petty, liberating. *We are the women that men have warned us about.*"

Susan admired Robin Morgan, but knew nothing of her connection with Jane Alpert. Furthermore, since that first day in consciousness raising, Susan, the committed political activist, had fallen completely in love with radical feminism.

"I felt that this was the movement that I had been waiting for all my life," she would remember. "I felt that they were really on to something, and I wanted to be a part of it."

She had, therefore, no intention of forging a public link between the feminist movement and the bomb-wielding underground, and she had quickly set about disabusing the *Times* editors of that connection. No, she could not, as they had suggested, begin her article with the story of Jane Alpert. What she would write instead was an inside view of it all—as a journalist, yes, but also, frankly and openly, as a *member*.

What Susan delivered to the *New York Times* was a sensitive recounting of a consciousness-raising session and a precise, entirely empathetic etching of the various radical groups. She praised Betty Friedan but also included the offhand—but from then on oft-quoted —remark that the radicals considered Betty to be "hopelessly bourgeois."

"Well, look," Susan would explain years later, "those kids had gone to an early meeting at Betty's apartment and there was a *black maid!* Their mothers may have had maids, but they never did. They were deeply offended by this."

Furthermore, Susan was convinced, it was the radicals, not Betty, who started a mass movement. She would remember, in fact, writing a letter to Betty in the earliest days of NOW offering to join, and receiving in return a polite rejection from a NOW official. NOW, Susan had been told, was to be "a lobbying committee of no more than 100 women."

Noticeably absent, therefore, from Susan's article in the *Times* was the conviction of many NOW members that the "radical fringe" was scaring off the majority of American women.

Instead, on March 15, 1970, splashed across the page in great black letters was that phrase first heard at the antiwar rally in 1968: " 'Sisterhood Is Powerful,' " followed by "a member of the Women's Liberation Movement explains what it's all about."

Naturally, Susan expected at least a cheer from the troops, a couple of pats on the back for helping to spread the word. Strangely, none was forthcoming, but she was too excited, too intent on the mission at hand, to give it much thought.

"Sisterhood Is Powerful" appeared three days before the *Ladies' Home Journal* crusade. The next day, along with Sandie North, who had worked at the *Journal,* Susan scouted the premises, including editor-in-chief John Mack Carter's corner office. She picked up the posters—large cover mockups splashed with the logo *Women's Liberated Journal*—and Xeroxed the twenty-six pages of fact sheets, proposals, demands. By Day One of her carefully planned countdown, she was ready.

March 18, 1970, 8:45 A.M. Cloudy, gray, overcast. Temperature just over freezing, scattered snow.

About seventy-five women converge on St. Peter's Lutheran Church at East 54th Street in Manhattan, across the street from the *Journal.* Susan is at the center of the group. Her dark hair is smoothly coiffed and she is wearing, for the occasion, an expensive, gray, sleeveless dress, designer simplicity, Jackie Kennedy style—appropriate, she has decided, for her destination. Now she motions the women toward the glass skyscraper, the home of the *Journal,* at 641 Lexington Avenue.

Immediately, one faction, from the Redstockings, refuses to cross the street.

"They were scared," Susan would remember. "They wouldn't even go into the lobby."

"You're going to get arrested!" they yell at Susan.

Susan ignores them. John Mack Carter, she is convinced, would never be so foolish as to call the cops on *women* entering a *women's* magazine. Stepping smartly at the head of the line, she proceeds across the street, through the lobby, and into the elevators. Seconds later, the lifts disgorge the women into the vestibule and, with Susan in command, a news photographer hopping backward as he snaps pictures, the troops veer to the left, down the corridor, and . . .

"Wait a second," Susan mutters. "This is wrong. This is wrong!"

Carter's office, it turns out, is down the long hall to the *right.* Susan, under her breath, curses her terrible sense of direction and gives orders to retreat. Which, in disorder, they do.

But then—hurrah!—they march forward again, along with the photographer. Three abreast. Down the corridor where the secretaries sit like a row of bunnies on the edge of a forest, heads popping up one at a time. Startled, these conscientious toilers stare at the marching women. A wild assortment. From the stylish Susan (who, one editor was certain, had just had her hair done at Elizabeth Arden) to the sloppiest, most defiantly unkempt hippie. Women of all sizes and shapes, in pants and dresses and sweaters and shirts, some carrying posters labeled *Women's Liberated Journal.* Constricted into the narrow hall, this strange and motley army flows like a flood-rushed river, streaming, unchecked.

Meanwhile, in the sumptuous office at the far end, with its self-consciously masculine decor, dark blue and brown, its shuttered windows, the Arrow-shirt-handsome, curly-haired editor of the *Journal* is waiting. Carter has already poured himself a cup of black, chicory-laced coffee from a gleaming silver service, coffee that is brewed for him every morning in the *Journal* kitchen by female elves. He is sitting behind his polished mahogany desk in the far corner of the room with a few members of his staff. He is—he thinks—ready. He has been tipped off by a reporter. What he expects, however (and is actually looking forward to), is a small delegation of "ladies," a few women whom he can—as always—easily and totally charm. If the media were alerted, Carter figures, all the better. Terrific publicity for his magazine.

"We had been laughing about it," Dick Kaplan would remember. "We joked about what would happen when the chickens got into the fox's lair. Of course, there *was* a bit of uncertainty. We read the newspapers and we knew something was going on out there."

And now, in fact, Carter does hear a distinctly unladylike rumbling down the hall. Before he can move or utter a word, however, a thundering horde of women bursts into his office. A crunching crush of absolutely furious faces. They crowd in through the door until there is no more room and then climb onto the windowsills, plunk down on the couches, the thickly carpeted floor. Suddenly, Carter is surrounded.

The welcoming smile freezes on his handsome face. He utters not a word.

With no further ado, Susan, in her most dramatically magisterial voice, begins the thoroughly prepared recitation:

"We demand . . ." Carter's resignation and a woman editor-in-chief in his place, an all-female staff, free day-care centers for employee children, elimination of ads that degrade or exploit women, of the focus on a life-style in which there is no alternative to marriage and the family, of articles tied to advertising, of back-to-the-home romance ficton and . . . now hear this! . . . one issue of the magazine edited entirely by members of the women's liberation movement.

Carter still does not speak.

As his staff sees it, the set of their editor-in-chief's mouth, his controlled glare, the slight twitch of a muscle in his jaw, his very silence signify a refusal to be provoked, a solid and impenetrable defense.

And now others begin showering him with reproaches.

190

"Why hasn't the magazine mentioned how many women die every year from butchery at abortion mills?"

"Your magazine won't save my marriage. It'll ruin it!"

"My mother was browbeaten by your magazine all her life!"

"Well, Mr. Carter," says Marlene Sanders, who has arrived with full ABC crew and now shoves the microphone up to the editor's face, "what do you have to say about that?"

As Susan would remember it, Cool-Hand John at that moment could not speak a word.

"I really felt sorry for him," she would remember.

Finally, however, Carter told Sanders that he would not negotiate under siege. Then, very quickly, he lapsed back into silence, leaving Lenore Hershey, the *Journal's* one senior female editor, to speak— and screech—for him. The matronly Hershey, wearing a large, dark mushroom hat, had a cold, and she punctuated her objections with sniffs into a soggy handkerchief.

As writer Claudia Dreifus would report, "Lenore Hershey, who looks very much like the Hollywood stereotype of an aged fifty sub-urban clubwoman ('Girls, our speaker today at the Larchmont Garden Club is Mr. Whortley Toad, the world-famous author of Horticulture and Your Health!'), and who has super-connected connections with the Johnson and Nixon administrations, was constantly spewing forth with periodic shrieks at the feminists. Surveying the group, Mrs. Hershey asked, 'Are any of you girls *working???*' There was a tone in her voice suggesting that everyone in the room was quite, quite un-employable. To the question of day-care nurseries for *Journal* employ-ees: 'You girls can't love your children so little that you would leave them in a stranger's care!' To our request for more intelligent maga-zine content: 'How many of you girls here are married?' Sister Lenore firmly assumed that in addition to being unemployable, we invaders were horribly unmarriable."

By mid-morning, at least two hundred more women had arrived: Ti-Grace Atkinson and her Feminists, the important movement the-orist Shulamith Firestone, Lucy Komisar, who wrote articles for such prestigious publications as the *New Republic.* Carter moved out from behind the desk to sit atop it, one foot firmly on the floor, the other dangling in a sort of studied relaxation. Sometimes he tossed a large silver paperclip from one hand to the other. Sometimes he just crossed his arms and glared. Once he announced—and then again and again as the hours of occupation dragged on: "I will not turn over editorial control of this magazine and I will not negotiate under siege."

And so it went. Eventually, sandwiches and coffee were sent for and paper cups and napkins began to litter the office. Susan read the demands four or five times in a voice as determined and calm as Carter's.

Others in the room, however, were far from calm. They argued, cajoled, screamed, plastered the walls and pictures with printed slogans. Four-letter words flew, shocking the *Journal* staff to the core. Not all of these women, after all, were rebellious counterculture hippies. Some were adults, respected writers in fact! Susan herself; Sandie North, the former *Journal* editor! Carter at one point recognized Sandie (the "spy," in the *Journal's* view of it), who then came forward, sat at her former boss's feet, and announced, "I'm one of them now."

By afternoon, nothing had moved off square one, and Ti-Grace's Feminists, along with other even more radical women, were growing impatient. Let's up the ante, somebody yelled. "Let's overturn the file cabinets. Show 'em we're serious."

Susan moved in quickly to discourage that move. She was having trouble with some important members of her own group as well.

"You shouldn't be talking to the press," one of them howled at her. "I'm your leader in the Radical Feminists. I should be talking to the press!"

"Some of these women," Susan would remember, "were trying to out-radical each other."

Sensing that danger, she gripped tighter on the reins of control.

"We'll end up in jail," she warned, and a friend, a law school student, added: "We'll have to spend the night there."

"Oh, listen," somebody murmured, "I have to be home for dinner." And: "Yeah, I've got a class tonight."

Which cooled things for a few minutes until—suddenly—someone else shouted: "We've had enough of this. Get him off the desk!"

And with that Shulamith Firestone lunged at Carter.

At almost precisely the same moment, another young woman, obviously skilled in karate, thrust an arm forward and caught Shulamith as she flew, shifting her momentum in a great, graceful arc and landing her—without having touched a hair on Carter's head—on the other side of the desk.

More chaos. More shouting. Somewhere in the midst of it, one heavyset woman sprawled across the desk, whisked a cigar from a silver box, and lit up.

"Carter," she sneered, "you are a male chauvinist pig."

Then somebody threatened to throw Carter out the window.

"We can do it!" came a yell. "He's small."

"Sisters, sisters!" Susan raised her arms in a gentling, protective gesture. "This is not the way!"

"You see," Ti-Grace leveled ominously at Carter, "if you don't deal with them [meaning Susan's peaceful contingent], you get us."

And so the siege continued for hours. Eleven full hours, the press reported. Carter and Dick Kaplan, the other male editor present, neither ate nor visited the bathroom for the duration. (Kaplan would remember growing increasingly gassy, actually entertaining the thought that he might, unwittingly, clear the place out without so much as a word.)

All the while, demonstrators milled around in the hall, explaining their position to the staff, calling strategy meetings, press conferences. One group invaded another editor's office and began rifling through the desk drawers. Another bunch wandered into the fashion department—just, Kaplan was sure, to look at the clothes: "But of course they couldn't say so. I mean, what's Susan wearing to the barricades? Is Sandie wearing her Calvin Klein?"

At one point, the *Journal's* public relations honcho called Pinkerton to request "someone unobtrusive, who can blend in." A black cop, in full police regalia, showed up, and Carter sent him back. He certainly didn't blend in, not only because of his uniform but because—as the *Journal* editors gleefully one-upped—there was not one visibly black woman in the activist pack.

Carter continued to handle the press in his inimitably cool manner, but eventually, he seemed to soften toward the demonstrators.

"They have a point," he admitted, "but they can't have my job."

Slowly, as the hours dragged on, one by one or in little groups, the protestors began to leave. And. finally, as the sky outside the fifth-floor office darkened, Carter agreed to publish a feminist supplement, with a $10,000 fee to be paid to the writers. The exhausted cast—dwindled by then to a cadre of thirty or so—straggled out, their success recorded on television screens around the country. It had been, Carter conceded, "one of the most interesting days of my career."

"Our Mother," he added ruefully, "who art in heaven . . ."

Each side, in their own view of it, had won the day.

"It was John's shining hour," chortled a *Journal* editor. ("And a tribute to his kidneys," quipped Kaplan.)

We *got* our supplement, crowed the countdown crew.

For the *Journal*, lots of free publicity. For feminism, perfect timing. That same month, several magazines, including *Newsweek*, the *Atlantic Monthly*, and *Mademoiselle*, published extensive, thoughtful, almost *respectful* pieces on the movement.

Of course, editing that *LHJ* supplement—"The New Feminism"— proved to be something of a problem, since five separate women's groups—writing by committee—were designated to supply five separate stories.

"I had a hard time," Susan would remember, "convincing some of them that you didn't need to have 'racist,' 'imperialist,' and 'oppressor' all in one sentence."

Nora Ephron helped her and so did the writer Sally Kempton, but the process, Susan found, was a grueling, bitterly fought ordeal. The factions could not agree on what to write or even how to spend the money. Years of bitter disappointments steamed into a hothouse of friction. A committee of women *Journal* editors was supposed to make the final cuts, but those demonstrators who understood the editing process wanted the capable Dick Kaplan instead. "Some sisters," Kaplan sniffed, taking on the job only after the committee of *Journal* women agreed to sign off it.

The whole thing, to Kaplan's mind, was somewhat ironic since he had lunched with Gloria Steinem several months earlier with the specific purpose of asking her to write a long piece on this exact subject—"The New Feminism."

Kaplan had asked Gloria to write the piece for several reasons. The *Journal* had published some of Betty Friedan's work a few years before, so that, he thought, was old news. And, like most men, he was knocked out by Gloria's movie star glamour, her youth, and the growing clout of her name. (She had just written, on assignment from *Look* magazine, a piece on the possibility of a woman president in 1976.) Editor and prospective writer lunched, Kaplan would remember, at the Chateau Richelieu:

"I'll never forget Gloria sailing across the room to the table. She was wearing thigh-high boots and lots of dangling gold chains and necklaces. Heads turned. The only other time I've ever seen that was when Jackie Kennedy walked into the Four Seasons and some men actually stood up.

"Gloria looked like a Barbie doll, a department store mannequin, which made it absolutely amazing when she actually talked. She had that quality—also like Jackie Kennedy—of focusing on you completely. It was incredibly flattering."

Kaplan didn't have much fun at the lunch, though.

"Gloria was so *serious*," he would remember. "She was ready with a million references, quotes—like a schoolteacher—but they all had a message attached. Something political. Either antiwar, anti-Nixon, feminism, *something*. She wouldn't just say that she had seen a fascinating movie so we could discuss it on its own terms. There was always a cause attached. Whatever I said, she had another source for me. On feminism, for example, it was Gunnar Myrdal on the parallel between women and blacks. On the grape pickers, it was somebody else. It was like chess. From position to position."

But the most important reason Dick Kaplan asked Gloria to write the piece on the new feminism, in his memory of it, was that Gloria —unlike Susan or some of the other established journalists—was not a member of women's liberation. Sympathetic though Gloria might be, the article she would write, he figured, would be popular fare, "not one of those long, unendurable harangues all those women's lib people were shoveling out."

But Gloria had turned Kaplan down. She was too busy, she told him, negotiating for a television interview show in Canada. She suggested he try several other writers—perhaps Nora Ephron or Lucy Komisar.

Kaplan lost interest after that, however, and he had never got round to following up the assignment.

Now, here was "The New Feminism," for about the same price he had offered Gloria!

The eight-page supplement appeared in the August issue, the committee-written prose clumping heavily across coarse, blue, pulp-stock pages. Still, whatever its literary merits, the supplement's ideas and hard data on discrimination were far afield from the cheery, reassuring fare that ordinarily confronted nearly seven million *Journal* readers.

For most of its readers, the *Journal*, like other women's magazines, was a sort of guide for women; if not exactly a bible, certainly a trusted source of direction and understanding. For these alarming feminist notions to appear in the subscribers' *own magazine* gave them a powerful new credence. It suggested that those "crackpot" women marching in the streets might not be so crazy after all. They might be, in fact, just *women*. Like the *Journal* readers themselves.

There, in the pages of the "Bungalow Journal," slapped down in the racks at the A&P, in mailboxes from Altoona, Pennsylvania, to Sacramento, California, was the insidious proposition that there was more to be said about women's condition than their own trusted magazine had been telling them. That, in fact, all was *not* peach nectar heaven for women, and that their problems might *not* be solved by cultivating a more cheerful attitude or creating yet another Jell-O surprise for hubby and kids. Furthermore—and to top it off—the section supplied precise instructions on how to form your own consciousness-raising group, as well as the names and addresses of dozens of women's liberation groups across the country.

One small step for woman, as astronaut Neil Armstrong did *not* say the previous summer.

One giant leap, in fact, for womankind.

Susan, who had been covering the space shots for ABC-TV, could not have been more pleased.

As for that other matter, her sister activists' total disregard for her "Sisterhood Is Powerful" article in the *Times,* her careful explication of the movement, so what!

For the moment, Susan forgot all about it.

13

WHO IS
THE ENEMY?

We've seen that letting any representative of the male establishment—man or woman—in to report on our meetings is as smart as it would be for black power men to invite Lester Maddox to their caucus.

—quoted in "Reporting the Movement" by Sandie North,
Atlantic Monthly, Special Edition, March 3, 1970

The *Ladies' Home Journal* sit-in had been, by all counts, a great success, but not every demonstration would end in total victory.

"Nine Feminists Are Busted at Sexy Publishing House," read the headline in the *New York Post* on April 13, 1970, less than a month later.

According to this account, the nine women had broken into the office of Grove Press and barricaded themselves behind the door. At about 2 P.M. they were arrested and charged with a variety of offenses, including "resisting arrest, criminal trespass, disorderly conduct and malicious mischief."

Among the Grove protestors were Ti-Grace Atkinson and Robin Morgan, who claimed to have been fired from the firm while engaged in union organizing. The women told the *Post* that the pornographic tilt of the publishing house, which distributed the film *I Am Curious (Yellow)*, victimized women. Grove, they insisted, should pay reparations, finance a fund to meet the needs of women who had been raped or assaulted, and provide a bail fund for prostitutes.

It was the first public notice of feminists declaring pornography an enemy. It was also one of the few times they were kept in jail overnight.

The women had been told, at first, that they would be arraigned at 5 P.M.; their bail would be set and, once posted, they would be released. They soon found, however, that the district attorney had increased the charges against them, and all that night they were moved from police precinct to police precinct, from detention pen to detention pen, their lawyers—Flo Kennedy and Emily Goodman—unable to find them.

According to a moving recollection of the evening written later by Barbara Kevles, who was one of the protestors, the women were ordered to sit in a five-foot-square cell, cramped "butt to butt," and the scene was, from the very beginning, frightening.

"They've got the fucking fantasy they always wanted—nine women in a cage," Kevles heard one of the women complain.

Instances of police hostility to protestors had been in the news for several years. Stories of brutal treatment of jailed students—in the Columbia University "bust"—had circulated for months, and that night in jail was, for Ti-Grace at least, traumatic. That night, she would later insist, changed her forever.

At about 2:30 A.M. in a cold cellblock, the cops began a search for narcotics.

"Remove your sweater."

The order, according to Barbara Kevles, came from a police matron.

"My long hair catches in the zipper," Kevles would write. "A moment longer and I hand over my navy wool for inspection. I didn't know. I didn't know it would be like this.

" 'The blouse, take it off.' I do and expose my braless torso to the corridor spotlights and the matron's stare. Every curve, every crevice of my breasts, visible.

" 'Hold up your arms.' Goose pimples spring to my skin. I ask for my blouse back. She gives it to me.

" 'Hey, T.G. [Ti-Grace],' I shout, buttoning the red buttons, slowly, trying to deflate what I really feel, 'I've liberated my chest.' "

And then: " 'Take off your underpants.' I balk, can I keep my skirt on? The matron hangs on to her ritual, it's procedure. I beg hard. 'All right, keep your skirt on.' I lower my pants modestly and put them on the table. 'Hold your skirt up,' she commands. No choice . . . I raise my skirt. 'Higher.' The hem of the flowered print blindfolds my eyes. I cannot see the matron. To her, I am a headless pair of legs and ringlets of black genital hair. Her stare, much too long. I swallow and swallow again, not to cry. 'Turn, turn now and squat.' My head twists again for one last look of 'please, not this . . .' 'Squat,' she repeats, as I face the sterile, friendless cellblock in her power. My skirt tucked in my fingers, I plié, bare from the waist down, buttocks exposed like two tiny, smooth-skinned melons in the food market."

It was the much-feared strip search, with its corollary procedure designed to force the vaginal muscles open so that anything secreted there would drop out.

Ti-Grace—unfortunately, as it turned out—had simply refused.

"I just couldn't," she would remember years later. "I just couldn't do it." Nor could she—even after more than a decade had passed— tell the story in other than tremulous, hazy bits and pieces.

Confronted with the demand that she strip and squat, she had broken down, begun to cry. (From down the corridor, Kevles heard her sobbing, "like the shriek of a siren.")

"They took me to another cell," Ti-Grace would remember. "They stretched my arms wide above my head and shackled my wrists high up on the bars."

And as she was pinned there, spread-eagled and crying, the police matron stripped off Ti-Grace's sweater, pants, underclothes, shoes— everything.

Furthermore, in Ti-Grace's memory of it, a male cop gave the order, then stood by and watched.

Whether or not that policeman was actually present and this painful assault actually occurred, there is no question of its effect on Ti-Grace. Kevles found her in the corridor afterward, "sobbing and gasping between sobs for quick breaths. . . .

"Her wet face hangs hidden in the military blue sweater, between her shoulders," Kevles would write, "only her blond hair protrudes. . . . 'Ti-Grace, come on . . . ,' chiding as I might a terrified child, attending to her because her pain is greater than mine. She is shaking, convulsively."

Down the long corridor, over and over, the women called to Ti-Grace, asked if she was all right. They heard only, finally, from a distance: "Nearly."

Nearly, but not quite. There were aftereffects, for Ti-Grace would insist many years later, "nothing, in that position, could have dropped out. It was pure punishment." And to Ti-Grace, the punitive force became all of society.

"I was plunged onto a whole different level of understanding of the State," she would remember. "I learned that it was my enemy and that there was no way to change anything peacefully . . . that it was just a game. All that 'mainstream' was just people deceiving themselves. I'd been told this before but I just didn't hear it in my gut."

As so many of the young radicals saw it, the "grays," the complexities of society, had disappeared. The secret American bombings had led to a coup d'etat in Cambodia, and their president was claiming that it served the national interest. The "establishment," the "system," seemed to them, quite simply, villainy, and writing about that night in jail, Kevles, too, would make that leap.

"As the air climbs my squatting cheeks," she would write, "I feel . . . the *system* has made me degrade myself, the ultimate humiliation."

Unlike Kevles, however, Ti-Grace would also claim that there had been no support from her sister activists.

"It was hard to separate my personal hurt from . . . well, people behaving like it was all part of sexual liberation. As if it [the strip and squat] would only bother somebody because they were hung up . . .

"It was impossible to have illusions anymore. What damaged me was that I just understood profoundly how little substance there was to what women were saying about change. Were they willing to go wherever they had to go to get that change? Well, the answer was no.

"I didn't want to be part of this culture anymore. All of a sudden I felt part of an outlaw culture. To be myself, to be human, that was going to be the price, like an initiation rite."

And so the leader of the Feminists began searching for other, different radical groups, finding a bond with people who hated the police, knowing instantly, as she would put it, "some piece of what that was about."

The first group that drew Ti-Grace's attention was the Black Liberation Army. The next was the Italian-American Civil Rights League, and it was through this group that she met Joe Colombo, the man she fell in love with.

Colombo was both a leader of the League and a suspected Mafia leader. His son had been arrested by the FBI, and the father was picketing on the sidewalk outside FBI headquarters in New York nearly every day, soon with Ti-Grace at his side.

"Sure, it was Mafiosi," she would agree later, "but the Mafiosi didn't frighten me. They hated the police as much as I did."

As for her sudden and loyal appearances there: "Some of these guys got the idea that all feminists were stand-up women and real tough. 'Don't trust the average feminist,' I said. It would be a disaster."

Ti-Grace was impressed ("Do you have any idea how hard it is to get a demonstration going *every day?*") and moved ("People *loved* Joe"). But Colombo had a wife and even, Ti-Grace had heard, a mistress, so she was also nervous and, she would claim, wary.

"It was such a break for me. It took so much courage. I would explain, talk to him about Che Guevara and Mao, give him books. It was funny in a way. I expected him to be an instant radical feminist. We had this 'Freedom for Women' button and he used to wear this button around and nobody even smiled!"

Soon—and for years afterward—rumors about Ti-Grace's Mafia lover would buzz in feminist circles. And she would not—quite— deny them.

"It was intense, yes," she would say. "Very intense. But it was mainly a matter of being around each other, communicating without communicating, all ostensibly about politics . . . standing next to each other, playful back and forth, pushing, grabbing my hand, pulling me forward . . . but most of all, his waiting for me places, wanting me to come places . . . just to see me."

To Ti-Grace, Joe Colombo and his supporters were the *real* revolutionaries.

"Sister Joe Colombo," she would soon be calling him as, throughout the following year, the outspoken Ti-Grace, a popular attraction on the lecture circuit, continued to joust not with windmills but with, threateningly, the world's most powerful institutions.

The Roman Catholic Church, she said, oppressed the poor by its accumulation of wealth and oppressed women in particular by exercising total control over their reproductive rights.

"I, Ti-Grace Atkinson, in the name of all women, most especially the deceased victims of the accused, charge the Catholic Church . . . with murder in the first degree, premeditated and willful.

". . . with conspiracy to imprison and enslave women . . . into marriage and the family.

". . . with forcing many . . . into prostitution.

". . . with inciting rape . . . by degrading and sadistic propaganda . . .

"In the name of all women, I charge the Catholic Church with constituting, by its very existence, an obscenity on the face of the earth . . .

"Motherfuckers! . . . The struggle between the liberation of women and the Catholic Church is a struggle to the death. So be it!"

That lecture was presented on March 11, 1971, at Catholic University in Washington, D.C., where the president of the university had tried—and failed—to have Ti-Grace barred from speaking. The students had secured a court order to allow her to appear, to explain—as she already had done at Notre Dame—why the Church was "the greatest organized crime ring the world's ever seen," as well as to challenge "the virginity of the Blessed Mother." Both were, of course, irreverent and inflammatory notions, even at a time when such new images of religion were surfacing as Broadway's *Godspell* and *Jesus Christ Superstar.*

As usual, Ti-Grace dressed simply for her speech. A pair of dark trousers, a white blouse, a classic cardigan sweater, and her round, dark glasses. Also, as usual, her reasoning was complex. It had to do with the supernatural impregnation of the Blessed Mother, which had forced Mary, in Ti-Grace's view, to bear the responsibility and sorrow of her supernatural child alone, more than she would have if he had been conceived naturally. The Virgin Mary, as Ti-Grace put it, in her own catchy amalgam of theory and street talk, had been "knocked up."

Patricia Buckley Bozell, forty-eight-year-old sister of columnist William F. Buckley, Jr., and Senator James L. Buckley—an editor, with her husband, of a conservative Catholic magazine—was sitting in the well-filled auditorium at the time, her hair neatly styled, classic coat smartly tailored. A mother of ten, and a quick-tempered redhead, she was lifted from her seat by the sound of that reference to the Virgin Mother.

"I can't let her say that!" Pat Bozell shouted, as she leaped to her feet and raced through the auditorium to the platform. Without a word, she swung at Ti-Grace with her right hand, which grazed the microphone. Ti-Grace threw up her left arm, which caught Pat's wrist. Four or five men immediately scrambled up behind the attacker, pulled her away, and hustled her out the door of the hall.

Then, as Pat Buckley Bozell knelt on the sidewalk outside, praying, Ti-Grace quietly commented on the "hysteria" and "desperation" she had seen in the woman's face. The violent reaction had occurred, she would later explain, because it was "the first time in two thousand years that a woman had stood up to the Church."

"I'm only sorry I missed," Pat told a reporter quite cheerfully the next day.

"Frankly, I didn't even recognize some of the expressions. From the titters in the audience, I assume there were other things said, but I'm just not up on the obscenity of 1971.

"I think I did what God would have wanted me to do."

Which was, it seemed, to land a haymaker on the delicate, heart-shaped jaw of Ti-Grace Atkinson.

And then, to add to Ti-Grace's troubles, on June 29, 1971, Joe Colombo, the man she loved and admired, was shot. The newspapers described Colombo as the "forty-eight-year-old reputed chief of a Brooklyn Mafia family," under whose "shrewd leadership the family prospered as never before—expanding such rackets as loansharking, hijacking, gambling, extortion, business infiltration and pier piracy."

According to press accounts, Colombo arrived at Columbus Circle at 11:30 A.M. for a mass rally—the second—of the Italian-American Civil Rights League, the organization he had founded. In his attaché case was his prepared speech and a loaded revolver. As he strode toward the speaker's platform, amid thousands of spectators and heavy police security, he was shot in the back of the head.

As Ti-Grace would recall, she was still at home in her apartment when it happened. Her relationship with Joe had grown "so intense" that she had considered staying away from the rally, but when a friend of Joe's called, urging her to come, she acquiesced.

"I left the apartment that morning, then realized I hadn't set my watch. I went back inside, turned on the radio to listen for the time report, and heard the announcer:

" 'Joe Colombo has just been shot three times. He's in critical condition.' All I remember was being alone in my bedroom, hearing the radio, my body arching back, and just screaming, screaming, screaming. I couldn't believe it."

She rushed to the hospital, where she found Colombo still alive, but—as he would be until he died seven years later—in a state the doctors described as "semi-comatose." She was not, nor would she ever be, allowed to see Joe. Instead, she would remember, she sat in the visitors' quarters with his friends, and waited.

"I learned more about the Mafia," she would remember, "and how to play pinochle," and she would keep this vigil—to the distress of her friends—for many months.

Later that summer, Ti-Grace appeared—wearing black pajamas, like the Vietcong—at a panel on violence in the women's movement. She unfurled an enormous, gruesome, shocking photograph—a blowup of the fallen Colombo. He was lying on his back on the stretcher, eyes closed, blood streaming from his nose and mouth.

There were gasps in the crowd, and barely audible over the murmurs, the sound of Ti-Grace's anger.

"*That,*" she hissed, "is violence. . . .

"I am dedicating my remarks tonight . . . to Sister Joseph Colombo. I am referring to America's latest superstar, gangster, criminal. . . . If my meaning escapes you, consider that recent song hit, 'Jesus Christ, Superstar'. . .

"This STRANGE and BEAUTIFUL and REVOLUTIONARY FOOL and 'criminal'—Joseph Colombo—wore a 'Freedom for Women' button in front of the press and the FBI, and nobody dared laugh."

Some weeks later, Ti-Grace told a reporter that she found the Mafia "morally refreshing": "It's the oldest resistance unit in the world—seven centuries of resistance. The value system of the Italian-American community is Mafiosi, and we have a lot to learn from it."

She did not check with NOW officials before she said this, and the press would report a "familiar refrain" heard in some quarters of the movement.

"Maybe she's right. The thing about Ti-Grace, she's always two years ahead of everybody else."

At what was becoming, perhaps, the most confusing task of all—identifying the enemy.

But then, "women's lib" had been a hot topic of conversation at cocktail parties for at least a year. Not that the majority (of men, at any rate) believed that women were actually discriminated against. Not *really.* Less benign were the accusations—from families and friends—that those weird libbers were either "dykes," a sudden eruption of sick, frustrated bitches, or just plain laughable. The press, male reporters for the most part, still leaned toward the laughable, making sly jabs at what they usually treated as the latest ephemeral wrinkle on the protest scene. In New York, the *Daily News* account of a meeting at Betty's, for instance, quoted the "ladies":

" 'We have just begun to discuss strategy,' one of them hinted ominously, bringing visions of thousands of teenagers and matrons, their miniskirts and granny gowns swirling about them, marching on some bastion of male supremacy—maybe a YMCA locker room."

This wasn't very funny to NOW members who had been out on the barricades, picketing and demonstrating through freezing snow and slush and rain for three years. Not funny when, during a talk show commercial break, David Susskind sweetly cajoled his feminist guests: "You're very attractive ladies. You can always depend on men to get you anything you want. What do you want to do this for? If you were unattractive, I could understand it."

And why was it always necessary to schedule an opposing view—a contented housewife, for instance—on every program? Why, Jean Faust wanted to know, did reporters focus on the Redstockings' noisy disruption of legislative abortion hearings when she'd just given them a calm, reasoned interview two minutes earlier?

"The media was trying to make the country think that only sick and neurotic women were interested in the movement," Jean believed. "They wanted to say it's just a few crazy women, that you other women needn't worry about anything because no sane, attractive women who like men are involved in this movement."

The media . . . that amorphous mass of journalists, editors, writers, producers who always—or so it seemed in those days—got it wrong. Always covered the wrong events, focused on the wrong people. Created "stars" and denied the grass-roots character of the movement. Credited someone as an officer of a group when she wasn't even a member. Used "bra burning" as a major symbol when no one ever burned her bra. Inevitably, they would miss the entire point, the issues. Try submitting a major ten-page proposal for a state constitutional change to these media dolts, some activists moaned, and the press would totally ignore it. But let some deranged soul scream obscenities and they'd cover it as "women's lib."

Worse, being preponderantly male, they would snicker and exercise their wit (mainly sexual innuendo) at the expense of the issues, headlining a story on the feminist movement with "Women Are Revolting."

Worse yet, they'd make trouble. If you were suing the airlines because they fired every stewardess over thirty-two years old, some reporter would inevitably round up an innocent beauty in hotpants and the obliging quote: "I prefer to be a pussycat." Agree to speak on a television talk show and the host would pack the audience with raucous teenagers, wildly applauding the notion of woman as naturally passive and dependent. Or give you two minutes to speak, then laughingly turn the show over to some male joker huffing, "That was no lady, that was my wife," or a panel of guests proclaiming that the chip-by-chip erosion of the male's superior liberties leads to the decline of civilization.

Here was Barry Farber pitting a NOW member against a man who claimed that American women were not only parasitic but didn't bathe enough. Or against two hostile females who insisted that women control all the money. Even the "Today" show—staging a debate in which the "opposing" guest proudly represented the "feminine" role of the loving wife and blissful volunteer.

Perhaps seasoned politicians might have shrugged off these slop buckets of ridicule, or manipulated—to greater advantage—the flirtatious media interest. Few of the new feminists were, however, seasoned politicians. Especially the young radicals. Having been kept so long from the male world of work and validation, their options narrowed and restricted, they, like so many women of all ages, felt painfully insecure, suspicious, and far from confident of their own judgment.

The process of consciousness raising itself produced a certain vulnerability. Suddenly you were opening up, confessing to each other, trusting one another with this enormous explosion of fear and rage. The last thing in the world you needed was a hostile, mocking observer from the press.

"I don't want to be used as an object by *Life* magazine," one WITCH member barked at a reporter over the phone, while in the background another shouted: "Don't apologize, just hang up."

The ubiquitous, fire-breathing mouth known as the media . . . Like the fire itself, it could be bad, but it could also be good, especially since some of these women, of course, actually *were* the media. Print journalists like Vivian Gornick, Sally Kempton, Lucy Komisar, Susan Brownmiller knew how to handle a story and how to find the right press outlet. Anxious to get the movement's issues to the people, they pushed from the inside.

Sometimes, however, even these professionals ran into trouble—in the most unexpected places. Among the embattled was one of those rarest of creatures, a female television reporter.

Marlene Sanders, a founding member of NOW, was an on-camera correspondent at ABC at a time when the number of such reporters could be counted on your fingers. (There were no female news anchors then, and Barbara Walters would not host the "Today" show until 1974.) Marlene's sculptured good looks, her terrific smile, her clean, snappy delivery of the news were a warming, if infrequent sight on TV screens.

Behind the scenes, however, Marlene had been doing battle with subtle discrimination within the network on a day-to-day basis. And she had been trying—as best she could—to explain the legitimacy of women's protests to all manner of male bosses and co-reporters.

"They didn't really get it," she would remember. "They kept asking questions like, 'Are we supposed to stop lighting women's cigarettes? Or opening car doors?' "

And what did she mean, women had no power? They had power in the home, didn't they? What was more important than that?

All of which added impetus to Marlene's conviction that it was time for some *serious* coverage of the emerging movement. With that in mind, in the late fall of 1969, she set out to cover for ABC News what was billed as the Congress to Unite Women.

"Right off the bat," she would remember, "there were some highly unusual demands from the women in charge."

The meeting was closed to the press, and though, yes, Marlene herself was a woman, she was also working for the "male establishment" and therefore probably was "co-opted." All sorts of rigamarole, all sorts of preliminary negotiations ensued, and Marlene was finally permitted to attend only if she agreed to certain rules.

"I was not to film anyone except the speakers without their permission," she would remember. "None of the usual free-floating reaction shots were allowed."

Finally, after agreeing to everything the Congress officials asked, Marlene arrived at the opening session in the large auditorium of a high school in Manhattan, on November 21, with full camera crew. (The crew was all male, of course; women were totally excluded from TV's technical arena, and it would be 1976 before Marlene could pull together a female crew.)

Sanders found the place jammed. "At least five hundred women, most of them in their twenties. They were all in jeans and no makeup."

Marlene, no Brooks Brothers conservative, had actually caused a stir at ABC offices—risked her job, in fact—by wearing the first pantsuit, but in the midst of this crowd, in her working clothes and camera-ready makeup, she was very noticeable. She sensed hostility but proceeded, nonetheless, to set up near the stage and begin filming the reading of manifestos, a vote passed overwhelmingly for twenty-four-hour child care, and lively, provocative skits, including, about halfway through, the most theatrical of all:

Up on the stage, about a dozen women from one of the radical Boston groups formed a semicircle. All but one had short hair. The sole long-haired woman—the respected movement theorist Roxanne Dunbar—walked to the center. One of the short-haired women followed and raised a pair of scissors. From the crowd, which understood immediately what she planned to do, came moans, gasps.

"Clip!"

A long strand of hair fell to the floor.

"Oh, don't!" someone in the audience yelled.

Clip, clip, clip, the scissors snapped on relentlessly until, finally, clumps of brown hair littered the stage, and the unblinking, stoical Dunbar faced the audience, minus her crowning glory.

Marlene would not remember any explanation for the ritual, but a few months later, the first issue of a small magazine called *No More Fun and Games* would urge women to dress plainly, to drop their husband's or father's name—thus Kathie Amatniek became Kathie Sarachild—to live alone and not have sexual relations with the "enemy," and, yes, to chop their hair short because it was long only for male pleasure, not their own.

After the haircutting, there seemed to be pressure for everyone to submit to the ritual. Rumblings could be heard, a few shaky objections percolating. The beautiful actress Anselma Dell'Olio stood up with tears in her eyes, her long chestnut hair flowing like velvet over her shoulders. Her hair, she explained tremulously, was essential to her career, her means of surviving. No, she would not cut it off. And the moment passed.

"It was all on film," Marlene would remember, "the haircutting and all. It was a great record, great symbolism."

Conscientiously, quietly, the ABC reporter had also moved up and down the first few rows, gathering the stipulated signed consent slips before she turned the lights and cameras on these spectators for re-action shots. (Maybe, she would speculate years later, people in the back of the room hadn't seen her collect those signatures.)

Several hours later, after all the skits were over, Marlene and her crew moved out of the auditorium and into the lobby. They filmed a few interviews and then—close to midnight—as they began to pack up, they discovered that one whole roll of film, a half hour's worth, was missing.

"I thought we must have left it back in the auditorium," Marlene would remember, "so we all went back in—the whole ABC team—and began searching. Under the seats. Behind the curtain. I couldn't imagine where the hell it was. How could we lose something the size of two city phone books?"

For a full thirty minutes or so, they hunted and groped, Marlene growing more and more frantic. The crowd was filing out, totally ignoring her distress and her crew's frenzied rummaging.

"I was swearing by then," Marlene would remember. " 'What pains in the ass. . . . Here I want to tell the story . . .' "

Finally, someone took pity. Marlene should stop looking, one woman said, because she was not going to find it. The film had been stolen.

"Some friends you've got here." This, immediately, from Sanders's crew.

From Marlene, a stream of under-the-breath cusswords and a quick grab for some of the women she had negotiated with: "God damn it! You didn't live up to our agreement!"

Frustrated and furious, the TV reporter quizzed, argued, scrapped, and demanded the film.

Finally, she gave up. "I didn't even go back to the office. I was too tired and too embarrassed. I took a cab home and tried to figure out what I would say at the office the next day."

Where, soon enough, the teasing began, quick on the heels of Marlene's careful explanations of the "legitimacy" of the new move-ment.

She would remember her mumbles, her attempts to make light of it all, to insist that this group was a "fringe" bunch, but . . . "To the pros at ABC, these people—and therefore the movement—looked like complete nuts." And she did not tell her professional colleagues, of course, what she learned a few days later.

That the film had been delivered, all right. To the bottom of the Hudson River!

The culprit, according to many who were there, was the novelist Rita Mae Brown, and though the Congress was, in the view of most of the radicals, an enormously successful gathering, a bonding of hundreds of women, Marlene was inconsolable. (As was Betty Friedan, who had set it up in the first place but did not attend.)

"I hated the fact that the movement could be represented by these women . . . women like this," Marlene would later say.

" 'Not *everybody* in the movement,' I told the guys at ABC, 'is rational,' " a statement that could be made, surely, about the composition of any social uprising.

But the Second Congress to Unite Women, held about six months later, proved to be treacherous ground for yet another journalist—Susan Brownmiller.

On May 1, 1970, a lovely, sunny day in Manhattan, Susan, the *Journal* sit-in behind her, was sailing on to other matters—at the moment, an assignment from *Newsday* to review a play by the feminist Myrna Lamb. Feminist theater was a brand-new happening, sometimes using grotesque props such as huge, pasted-on breasts to parody sex roles and attack "sexual exploitation."

Once before, in the *Village Voice,* Susan had reviewed—unfavorably—one of Lamb's plays, and the flak ("How can you do this to a sister?") had been more than she bargained for. Now, as she faced her portable typewriter in her fifth-floor Greenwich Village apartment, she struggled for the right tone. The new play was, in her opinion, no better than the last.

"It was just," Susan would remember, "god-awful theater."

Which is what, according to the most basic standards of journalistic integrity, she should have—and normally *would have*—written.

But for the first time (and, Susan would always insist, the *last*), a higher priority loomed. Susan fudged. As she sat at her desk in the corner of the living room, she was forcing herself to hammer out a critique of a sister's work that was far kinder than she believed it deserved. Meanwhile, too, she was missing a meeting she was very anxious to attend.

At that same moment, at a junior high school only a few blocks away, hundreds of women were gathering for the Second Congress to Unite Women.

The First Congress had careened off center on a path so far afield from Betty Friedan's vision of a "mainstream" and a "partnership with men" that Betty and most NOW officials were pointedly ignoring this one. Susan, however, successful "establishment" writer though she was, regarded the wild, off-the-wall energy of the disreputable, ragtag young radicals as a wellspring of ideas, the life breath of the movement.

"Nothing would have happened with the feminist cause," she would insist, "if those kids hadn't used their rebellious anger and made loud noises." Without that, and the techniques learned in the civil rights and peace movements—the struggle of theorizing, the nerve and imagination to create events—no "movement," Susan believed, would have actually occurred. And indeed, dashing over during a writing break, she caught an original skit performed by a group of self-professed lesbians. Wearing lavender T-shirts, they accused the crowd in that packed auditorium of practicing sexism by ignoring lesbian needs.

Remarkable, Susan thought, but hadn't they seized on that "lavender" idea from her own "Sisterhood Is Powerful" piece in the *Times?* That article no one had mentioned? That strange brush-off that Susan herself had ignored?

"A lavender herring," Susan had called the lesbian issue in that piece.

Amusing, she thought, as she watched the performance for a few minutes. Then she ducked back out the door and rushed home to work.

She would have to miss Bella's speech—which was too bad. Susan was proud to have helped out this meeting by recruiting Abzug, the charismatic Bronx lawyer with the ubiquitous broad-brimmed hat. Bella had a large and devoted following among the liberal left contingent, especially since her 1961 Women's Strike for Peace, and she was revving up for her U.S. congressional race that fall. Still, for Bella, this meeting was a first. The lively, flamboyant politician had never before delivered a specifically feminist address to a specifically feminist audience. Bella's fiftieth birthday was coming up that summer; Susan had convinced her to announce that milestone at the Congress to Unite Women, and she figured Bella's speech would be a rouser.

Finally, on Sunday, the third day of the Congress, Susan put the finishing touches on her gentle, generous review, phoned it in, and then, still in her work jeans, rushed eagerly back to the school. Her spirits could not have been higher. Once again, she had used the so-called "establishment press" to say a good word for the movement, and Bella's speech, she'd been told, had drawn thunderous applause. Now, at last, Susan could watch—perhaps join in—the political action she loved.

By then the auditorium seemed restless. Dozens of women were milling around the hall, magnetized first by one group, then another, politicking in the aisles and behind the seats. Susan had no time to sort out the players, to make sense of the scene, when—within seconds, it seemed—she was surrounded. There at her elbow were several member of her CR group.

"They were agitated," she would remember. "They were all chattering at once."

"Oh, boy," one of them said, "are you in for something!"

"What are you talking about?" Susan half shouted over the din, and she would remember "getting the idea—sort of—that a paper had been, still *was*, circulating around the room."

But what was so dire about that? This was a political meeting. There were *bound* to be resolutions.

Then, through the babble of voices, she heard more clearly.

"It's a proclamation, Susan. And it's against *you!*"

"What?!"

Suddenly, she was alert, and she heard her own voice boom back at them.

"What? *What did you say?*"

"They have a resolution against you and they're going to bring it up. You just be quiet!"

"Quiet?" Susan shouted. "What do you mean be quiet!"

"Just let it ride, Susan. Lay low."

Impossible. Of course, it was impossible.

"I didn't really believe what they said," Susan would remember. Still, she had felt herself flush.

Stunned, baffled, still lacking any real sense of what had been and what was likely to be going on, Susan slid into a seat near the middle of the auditorium where, sure enough, she could see that *something,* some piece of paper, was indeed being passed round in that sea of women. And some people were indeed signing it.

And then the storm arrived.

A small group of women rose quietly from their seats near the front of the auditorium. There were eight of them, all in their twenties, younger than Susan by about ten years. She recognized several of them from the earliest meetings.

They seemed to be leaning together, holding on to each other for support. Their faces were tight and tense and, suddenly, for Susan, there was the awful, inescapable flash of reality.

The adrenaline began to pump. Her arms and legs began to tremble. There was no time, then, to reflect on the conflicts, the tensions she knew lay beneath the skin of the movement. Her CR friends had been right.

"We condemn Susan Brownmiller . . ."

The entire auditorium—hundreds and hundreds of women—fell silent.

The voice was strained, squeaky with fear, but unmistakably resolute.

"We condemn Susan Brownmiller and Lucy Komisar for trying to climb to fame on the back of the women's movement . . ."

Crash! The cannon boomed out from the center of the hall.

"That's *my name,* sister!" Susan howled, the report of her outrage crackling through the auditorium. "Who the hell are you to say that?"

Shouts. Catcalls. Boos. Hisses. Pro. Con. Which side were they shouting for? In the ruckus, Susan couldn't tell.

Rita Mae Brown, wearing a heavily encrusted male military outfit —like a costume for *The Nutcracker,* Susan thought—leaped onto the stage. They were *all* writers, she shouted. *All* leaders! No one of them could presume to speak for them all . . .

As Susan had done, presumably, in her *Times* piece, the article that everyone, she thought, had simply not noticed.

Now, amid shouts of "Point of order!" and the pounding of the gavel, a cauldron of anger roared to the surface. The fury of the powerless. Barred from the community of work, taught from childhood that you were less than your brothers, denied the tools—credit, mortgages—in a society that operated on money, denied the male's outlets in the world of sports, now suddenly, very suddenly, you were sprung from this prison of isolation by your *own* movement. The power of numbers. Shoulder by shoulder, testing your courage. No longer willing to be "led" or "explained" by men or anyone, not by leaders and not by "stars."

In those little cell meetings, lifetimes of perceptions had been ripped away, especially for the younger ones. And if all those perceptions had been false, force-fed by the white male establishment world, *anything* was possible. Maybe you were a Marxist! Maybe you were a lesbian! Whatever you were, you were a hundred, a thousand, a million times better than the world—and your own ego—had allowed you to imagine. You could write. You could organize. You could think. And you would not be pushed back by someone else climbing up!

Quickly, of course, that "climbing up" was given a name.

It was "elitism."

Susan was guilty of *elitism.* (And the Congress, on the other hand, was guilty of what Flo Kennedy would soon label "horizontal hostility.")

All this was clear, of course, unless you happened to be the focus of the explosion. As Susan was, sitting there.

She was aware, even then, that her attackers were *seriously* trying to work out important ideological notions, yet as she listened to the proclamation drone on, her body continued to shake with anger and humiliation.

"I do remember that some NOW women interrupted to object," Susan would recall. "They said that they were appalled at the thrust of this attack."

But the group of eight continued.

Susan and Lucy had betrayed the movement by writing articles for the establishment press. Susan in the *New York Times,* Lucy in the *Saturday Review.* No woman should ever sign her name to a feminist article or book. All expressions about the movement should be approved by the movement.

And on and on.

"The proclamation," Susan would recall, "seemed to take forever." A great rolling drumbeat of sins while the audience listened.

Eventually—though Susan would never remember how long it took—the resolution was brought to a vote. And, since compassion —or reason—in the long run prevailed, defeated.

The meeting ended and Susan left, finally, alone.

"No one," she would remember, "had apologized. No one *said a word.*"

She trudged home, cooked dinner, and told her boyfriend about it.

"Kevin understood," Susan would remember. "He gave me a Vonnegut short story to read. It was a sort of Orwellian piece about a society after the revolution where everyone was being equalized. The dancers who were too graceful were forced to wear weights on their legs and the smart people had to wear a headset that scrambled their brains. . . ."

Yet crazy as it was—nutty, bizarre—she would endure, Susan concluded. This movement was *that* important.

In the months to come, in fact, she even capitulated to that "elitist" notion.

"I felt terrible when offers came from magazines to write about the movement. I absolutely couldn't do it. It was getting very unclear what I wanted to say. I didn't want to antagonize, to lose my place in the movement. I really didn't."

Nobody in the outside world had much of an idea what had happened at this Second Congress. This time, the press had been totally locked out. Two years later, though—and a century measured in mood change—Sara Davidson would write about it for *Esquire*.

"Members of women's groups were afraid that their ideas would be distorted by the press," Davidson wrote, that "they would be labeled dykes and lunatics and then isolated and picked off through the media's process of star-making." Many writers had stopped writing altogether, and there had been, one writer told Davidson, "mass freak-outs all over the place."

It was an age for freak-outs. The day after the Congress, four Kent State students protesting the Vietnam War were shot and killed by the Ohio National Guard. That same Monday, Jane Alpert admitted to conspiring with the Weathermen to bomb "military and war-related corporate buildings," and seventy-five thousand antiwar demonstrators would soon converge on the White House.

"There is something every woman wears around her neck on a thin chain of fear—an amulet of madness," Robin Morgan wrote in "Goodbye to All That." "For each of us there exists somewhere a moment of insult so intense that she will reach up and rip the amulet off, even if the chain tears at the flesh of her neck."

A minefield. Both inside and out. Whose ego would be up to it?

Susan went back to her CR group where, she would remember gratefully, the idea for her powerful best-selling book, *Against Our Will: Men, Women and Rape,* was hatched. Even then, women asked her accusingly why she had to sign the book with her own name, why she hadn't credited the movement as a whole.

"It was very difficult to survive," Susan would remember. "People used to say that the only person who could get up and say something and not be shouted down was a black lesbian single mother on welfare.

"It was interesting, though. The person who did survive, who was not susceptible to the troops somehow, who didn't have to be, was Gloria."

14

WITH·
LEGS LIKE THOSE . . .

*A change of consciousness must precede a new and
enlarged understanding of our society, just as it has in
the case of our young people, who first "changed their
heads". . .*

—Charles A. Reich, *The Greening of America*, 1970

"That's it, that's her, that's who. The world's most beautiful byline,
the sweet belle of success, the queen of the slicks and the sweetheart
of the slickers . . ."

Harvey Aronson, a reporter from Toledo who had journeyed to
New York to write a profile of the hometown "career girl" made good,
had described Gloria this way just two years after her Playboy Bunny
article.

By then, Gloria had so captured the New York scene that she was
appearing in magazines as a fashion leader, and for this interview she
was photographed in a glamorous Donald Brooks dress—a splashy
modern print—reclining, in her apartment on West 56th Street, on a
zebra-striped throw. Her hair was a shiny, shoulder-length dark cap,
not yet, as it would be in a few years, streaked blond, long and
flowing.

Aronson was quite obviously dazzled. He listed Gloria's beaus—

217

Theodore Sorensen, Mike Nichols, Herb Sargent, Paul Desmond, and remarked on the expensive Cartier watch sent to her by an admirer.

What impressed Aronson most, however, what seemed to puzzle him, in fact, was that Gloria commanded $3,000 per magazine article and would earn about $30,000 that year as a free-lance magazine writer.

"Why Gloria Steinem?" he asked in his story. "Why not a hundred other girls who come to New York with pretty faces and fresh type-writers?"

To which Gloria had confidently replied: "Well, the wife of the late humorist George Ade once said, 'Lots of people could write as well as my husband does—but my husband does.'"

Thirty thousand dollars was a substantial sum for a free-lance writer, especially in 1965, and Gloria would eventually earn much more. Well into the eighties, however, as she herself would admit, she never saved any of it, or planned for her future. Fortunately, her friends would later report, there was usually some devoted male at hand to manage those incidentals.

"The interesting thing about Gloria is that she can do anything," her friend Letty Cottin Pogrebin would one day report, "except the things that all the rest of us can do, like figure out how to use the postage machine or understand that you have to pay your taxes by April 15th. She's not good at it. She's always in arrears with the government and in a lot of trouble. She doesn't pay bills and she doesn't understand how to keep subscriptions going. She's not a detail person; she's a big thought person, which is a lovely thing to be able to do. There's usually some man around to take care of that stuff. I don't think she's ever had to figure out her budget for three days. . . .

"The psychology," as Letty would put it, "is just different."

Gloria's lack of domesticity, for instance, her willingness to allow someone else to redo her home, would be as baffling to Letty as her empty refrigerator was to reporters. She received lots of expensive presents, Letty would remember. "But she took them for granted. She never noticed if something . . . a needlepoint pillow, say, took some-body a year to make."

Gloria, as her hometown reporter concluded, was not just one of those "hundred other girls." She was something else. Something *un-usual*.

"Just sitting in a restaurant, Gloria 'looks like somebody.' Not necessarily a writer, but somebody. . . . She has a five-foot-seven, one-hundred-twenty-pound figure of the sort that shows to great advantage getting out of taxicabs. . . . Her wide, long-lashed brown eyes focus on the interviewer and make him think that he never had a better steak nor saw a prettier tablecloth—and man, but he feels alive and what is he supposed to be asking her about anyway?

"The point here is that Gloria, in the words of a woman who knows and likes her, 'has the power to cloud men's minds.' "

And Gloria was happy, she told Aronson, because " 'I'm doing what I want to do . . . writing is the only kind of work that when I'm doing it, I don't feel like doing something else.' " Several years later, however, looking back on those days, Gloria would see her writing career in a different light.

The Playboy Bunny article in *Show* had been a mistake, she would insist. She hated being introduced as "the girl who wrote [it]"—and furthermore, it had brought her the wrong sort of assignments.

Marvin Barrett, *Show*'s managing editor at the time, would disagree.

"If Gloria had wanted to write the definitive work on Pakistan," he would insist, "she could have. She wanted to be a success and she used the prominence she got from that one article. If it hadn't been for the Playboy Bunny story, who would she have become? With it, she was a package, a real human being with real plausibility, one of those incongruous things the human race loves."

After that exposé was published in *Show* in 1963, Gloria had been deluged with assignments, especially from the high-paying women's magazines. There were profiles of James Baldwin, Barbra Streisand, Paul Newman, fashion stories on Rudi Gernreich, lighthearted pieces (that target of the protesters, the *Ladies' Home Journal* article on Zsa Zsa Gabor's bed, in fact, had been Gloria's).

Gloria would recall her own life in those free-lancing days not as happy, as she had told Aronson, but as "schizophrenic . . . working on one thing and caring about another." Her American Express card (a rarity for a woman in those days) had been repossessed when she charged the expenses of the Poor People's March, the protest of Cesar Chavez and California's migrant grape pickers.

As for the stories she was writing, they were, as she would come to describe them, traditional "girl writer assignments."

"I would think, Well, it is the *New York Times,* and find myself writing on something I didn't care about." (Textured stockings, in this case.) "The good gray *Times* also had a high incidence of editors who asked you go to a hotel with them in the afternoon, or, failing that, to mail their letters for them on the way out. . . .

"It wasn't until *New York* magazine was founded in 1968, and I became one of its contributing editors and political columnists, that my work as a writer and my own interests began to combine."

Politics was what truly interested Gloria, and with the founding of *New York,* Clay Felker gave her the chance to write about it—in a biweekly column called "City Politic." Always distinctly leftist, the column caused a minor sensation when Gloria caught Pat Nixon, the wife of the presidential candidate, off guard and printed the cranky and embarrassing results.

" 'I never had time to think about things like that—who I wanted to be or who I admired or to have ideas,' " Pat had let slip to Gloria. " 'I had to work . . . I'm not like all of you . . . all those people who had it easy.' "

Gloria's column did not prevent the election of Richard Milhous Nixon, of course, but in New York, her position was becoming a powerful one. At least one politician, New York liberal congressman Richard Ottinger (though not liberal enough, in Gloria's view), would attribute his defeat to the criticism in "City Politic."

Clay was pleased with his choice of columnist. Unlike some male editors, he never differentiated between the sexes in his allocation of assignments. Sheila Tobias, who was also writing for *New York,* would remember Clay as "the most pro-feminist, absolutely nonsexist man, one who did everything to help women journalists." He had worked with Gloria both at *Esquire* and on an aborted TV show similar in format to *That Was the Week that Was.* A few years earlier, in fact, when Felker left *Esquire,* Gloria—through her connection with Viking's Tom Guinzburg, whom she was dating at the time—had secured a job for Clay with the publishing house.

"I was in love with Gloria," Clay would confess years later, but he would deny the rumors that he had been having an affair with her.

"I had to protect myself in the clinches there," he would explain. "I knew Gloria would break my heart so I never let her do it. I looked at this trail of broken men and I just knew what could happen. Nobody wants to go through that kind of pain."

And Gloria didn't marry because, she would eventually explain to a reporter: "Well, what I would do is play the classic woman's role, that is, subordinate my time and work to a man and then resent it. Whether a husband asked me to or not, I would still sacrifice in his favor. And eventually I would come to dislike both myself and him. The relationship would be doomed from the beginning."

And in another instance: "Marriage is like a door slamming in my head. That's only because the role of 'wife' is so inhuman and unattractive to me. Marriage makes you legally half a person, and what man wants to live with half a person?"

Well into the eighties, Gloria would remain unmarried, even though, until then, at least, most of her lovers did want to tie that knot.

"I must have chosen men who wanted . . . I mean, it must have been my doing," she would speculate, thinking back. "But I thought if I did it, it would be all over." And then, quickly switching the personal pronoun, as she so often would, to either the global "we" or "you": "If you think that's the only way you can change your life then marriage becomes like death. It's the only choice you have so you keep putting it off."

Once, Gloria would recall, she had gone so far as to get a marriage license and rings, even to make a plan for her lover to buy a suit and herself a wedding dress.

"We got up through the suit . . . I never bought the dress. Finally, I got a little note in the mail that said my marriage license had expired.

"It wasn't that I thought out why, it's just that I ran away. I don't know if I would have been strong enough to get married and survive. I don't know. But I would always disappear at a certain point."

She would disappear, in Clay Felker's view, because she was afraid of personal commitment. Years later, the man who was Gloria's editor and, in many ways, her mentor in those days, would ponder the enigma of Gloria Steinem and attempt—quite carefully—to explain.

"Gloria is a complicated person," Clay would venture. "She's intellectually committed, politically committed, but not personally. And that seems strange except that probably the motivation for all of those things is the same. She probably felt that her father let her down and let down her mother. She felt cheated, misused by a man."

And while apologizing for his "amateur psychology," Clay would add: "Particularly identifying with her mother . . . and at the same time loving her father . . . that causes confusion."

Yet Clay would also recall with admiration Gloria's creativity, her wealth of ideas for the new magazine—among them, a popular column called "The Passionate Shopper."

"Gloria was funny and fun to be with, and I trusted her because she thoroughly understood what I was trying to do."

A sterling compliment since *New York,* the much-admired and sophisticated vehicle that launched the glittering, juicy meld of literary technique and reportage known as the New Journalism, was a spectacularly salable expression of one man's idiosyncratic and demanding taste. Or style. Or perhaps fashion, which, in those days, at its most visible, was the "Beautiful People," whose currency was not simply cash in the bank, but social concern, what New Journalist Tom Wolfe described, in a hilarious satire, as "radical chic."

Gloria's name was frequently listed among the Beautiful People, and she was in such demand at social occasions that actress Julie Andrews confessed to a reporter that if she wasn't herself, she would like to be Gloria. As *Time* magazine said in its press section:

"One of the best dates to take to a New York party these days—or, failing such luck, one of the most arresting names to drop—is Gloria Steinem. Writers, politicians, editors, publishers and tuned-in businessmen are all intensely curious about her . . . a trim, undeniably female, blonde-streaked brunette who has been described as the 'thinking man's Jean Shrimpton'. . . with legs worthy of her miniskirts . . . and a brain that keeps things lively without getting tricky."

Gloria—who often appeared on the arm of black Olympic track champion Rafer Johnson—was always an intriguing addition to any party, frequently appearing in her signature outfit: scoop-necked leotard top, raspberry-colored jeans, and tinted aviator glasses. Not only was she lovely and amusing, but, through Gloria, busy politicians, business moguls, etc., could learn—painlessly—the inside story of the social uprisings of the sixties.

Gloria was in her mid-thirties by then, but her politics were tightly wedded to the youth rebellion—not only antiwar, but Black Power—and the welfare movement.

"The thing about Gloria," as Clay would remember, "was that she didn't *look* like a revolutionary. She looked like a beautiful Ivy League girl." Who could articulate the causes she believed in—Black Power separatism, Cesar Chavez and his grape pickers—with disarming, persuasive charm.

"I try to charm everybody," she told a reporter frankly, "man, woman, and dog."

For Felker, all this was bankable. And promotable.

"With legs like those," he once joked, "that girl ought to be a writer."

Besides being a feminist (albeit, as many would note, a snobbish one), Felker had a special talent for creating stars. Not film stars, but writers, which was something of a new twist in the magazine game. Actors and actresses, of course, had always been star material, and to a lesser degree, television and radio commentators as well. Print journalists, however, had been—until then—practically incognito. Even the eloquent writers who graced the pages of *Esquire* were, more often than not, familiar names from the covers of books long before they drew readers to the pages of the magazine.

Felker, on the other hand, promoted his weekly's journalists, especially on television.

"We had somebody doing public relations at the magazine," he would remember, "calling up the television networks and getting them on."

So, of course, for Gloria, there were TV appearances, forays that were never easy.

"I had canceled out at the last minute so often that a few shows banned me as a guest," she would eventually write.

And though she would soon become one of the most popular and eventually highly paid performers on the lecture circuit, speaking in public was even worse.

"Though I wasn't shy about bearding lions on a den-by-den basis, the very idea of speaking to a group, much less before a big audience, was enough to make my heart pound and my mouth go dry. The few times I tried it, I became obsessed with getting to the end of each sentence without swallowing, and then obsessed for days afterward with what I should have said."

Nonetheless, she negotiated, successfully, for that television interview series in Canada, gained experience interviewing Prime Minister Pierre Trudeau, actor James Earl Jones, and Congressman Adam Clayton Powell.

And she was, on television, a marvelous sight.

Long, tapered fingers brilliant with stylishly pastel lacquer, a soft, quiet manner, an expression that often seemed to hide, like a cautious, plumed bird, behind a center-parted curtain of smooth hair. A certain—and enduring—mysteriousness, just a shade less regal, perhaps, but not altogether dissimilar to the apparently reticent charisma of the endlessly fascinating Jackie Kennedy. The ideal girl, Dick Cavett called Gloria. Beautiful and brainy. And when, in the summer of 1969, the first men would land on the moon, Gloria would be on screen, side by side with Walter Cronkite. Instead of speeding into the heavens, she would quietly insist, America should be searching for a solution to its problems on earth. "Politico-saintly," *Time* would soon call her.

But TV appearances or no, Gloria's main job—her professional role—was still print journalism and in her columns for *New York,* she gave voice, and legitimacy, to the churning rebellions of the sixties.

Among these rebellions, of course, was the women's movement, which had been popping into press reports for several years. In the early months of 1969, at a New Left "counterinaugural" of Richard Nixon in Washington, D.C., women using the term "male chauvinism" were booed off the stage amid shouts of "All she needs is a good screw." A few days later, in Chicago, a women's lib group protested the firing of a feminist female professor. They objected as well to college advisers who recommended that female students marry instead of continuing their education, teachers who disparaged women, and the restrictive dormitory rules for women. In San Francisco, demonstrations were mounted—"Here Comes the Bribe"—against the "commercial exploitation" of the Bridal Fair. Iowa college students staged a "nude-in" aimed at *Playboy*'s demeaning attitude toward women. Both NOW and the Redstockings were demanding repeal of the New York State abortion laws, and even Governor Nelson Rockefeller of New York admitted that labor laws that were supposed to "protect" women actually protected men's jobs instead.

"It was the biggest story of the decade," Gloria's colleague Sheila Tobias would remember, and in January of that year, she asked Gloria to attend a women's conference Sheila had set up at Cornell University. "I figured we needed somebody like Gloria because of her skills with the media. She was exactly my age and she seemed to belong where I belonged."

The Cornell conference, it would turn out, was the model for what many would believe was the lifeblood of the Golden Age of Feminism—"women's studies" courses—and Gloria, who did not attend, would often mention, years later, that she regretted her absence.

Gloria did, however, observe that demonstration at the Oak Room of the Plaza Hotel the following month—that fateful day in February 1969 when Betty and her NOW colleagues sat down where they were not welcome.

Jean Faust would remember appearing with Gloria on a television talk show at about that same time, and afterward urging her to join NOW.

"Gloria felt it was narrow to be a feminist," Jean would recall. "She said she preferred to be a humanist.

"I could understand her point," Jean would reflect. "But, well, she and Barbara Walters were alike in this, I think she had an obsession with men in power. She was always talking about how women were attracted to them. She didn't want to identify with women who were asking for things. It was too humiliating. For a woman with such a drive for success, it was an embarrassment."

The Oak Room sit-in being, Jean thought, a case in point.

"Gloria thought it was embarrassing," Jean would remember. " 'Oh, I couldn't do that,' she told me."

When asked—and she often would be—Gloria would always say that she had been "radicalized" (Redstockings' definition: "engaging with basic truth") at one of that group's abortion hearings. She attended a "speak-out," she would recall, sometime in 1969, in a church basement in Greenwich Village, where she saw and heard dozens of women cast off the protection of anonymity, face the crowd, and tell the unvarnished truth. She did not stand up to reveal her own abortion at the meeting, but, she would recall, "I felt free to talk about it for the first time."

Unlike fellow journalist Susan Brownmiller, however, Gloria did not join a women's liberation group. She remained an observer, though she eventually did write a column about the movement.

"After Black Power, Women's Liberation" appeared in the April 7, 1969, issue of *New York,* and it was as sympathetic to women's liberation as Gloria's earlier columns had been to the various sixties rebellions.

But the women's liberation movement, as Gloria described it, consisted solely and entirely of the radical groups. NOW—the organization that would one day be synonymous, for much of the American public, with the women's movement—was, in her view, an entirely separate movement, older and middle class.

"The women behind the women's liberation movement, and influenced by it," she wrote, "usually turn out to be white, serious, well-educated girls, the same sort who have labored hard in what is loosely known as the Movement, from the Southern sit-ins of nine years ago to the current attacks on the military-industrial-educational complex. . . .

"If the WLM can feel solidarity with the hated middle class," she predicted, "and vice versa, then an alliance with the second mass movement [Betty Friedan's NOW] . . . should be no problem."

Among the beliefs of women's liberation, Gloria noted in the article —and this may well have been the first time this notion appeared in a major publication—was the total rejection of alimony.

"What do women want?" Gloria wrote.

And then answered: "The above events are in no way connected to the Bloomingdale-centered, ask-not-what-I-can-do-for-myself-ask-what-my-husband-can-do-for-me ladies of Manhattan, who are said by sociologists to be 'liberated.' Nor do the house-bound matriarchs of Queens and the Bronx get much satisfaction out of reading about feminist escapades. On the contrary, the whole thing alienates them by being a) radical and b) young."

And: "Having one's traditional role questioned is not a very comfortable experience; perhaps especially for women, who have been able to remain children, and to benefit from work they did not and could not do."

"After Black Power" concluded with a suggestion that men should "just keep repeating key phrases like, 'No more guilt, No more alimony, Fewer boring women, Fewer bitchy women, No more tyrants with all human ambition confined to the home, No more 'Jewish mothers' transferring ambition to children, No more women trying to be masculine because it's a Man's World'. . . (and maybe one more round of 'No more alimony') until the acrimony has stopped."

But though the article did mention the enormous gap between men's and women's wages, it did not confront the question of how, if women were paid so little, they would fare after a divorce without money from their ex-husbands. Or if, in fact, they were "benefiting from work they did not or could not do," how years of child care and housework fit into a just or fair exchange.

In those years, however, the "hated middle class" had been shunted —for so many and for the moment—into the wings. Different, and indelible, battle lines had been drawn in America, and even Richard Nixon admitted to a "generation gap." On one side, the peace lovers

226

of Woodstock, the burners of draft cards, the wearers of peace neck-laces; on the other, the cops, the "pigs," the ubiquitous sign "America: Love It or Leave It," the voice, supposedly, of the "silent majority."

Gloria would not include "After Black Power" in her 1983 collec-tion *Outrageous Acts and Everyday Rebellions* because, she would write, "it would seem about as new as the air we breathe." Yet the article won a Penney-Missouri Journalism Award, and because of it, within a few months, she would come to be viewed in some quarters as a spokeswoman for the burgeoning feminist movement.

That spring, however, far more interesting—to Gloria and most of New York's hip intelligentsia—was the fact that one of America's greatest novelists, party-goers, peace activists, and angry young men about town was revving up to run for mayor of New York City. Norman Mailer, the country's number one, full-fledged literary celeb-rity, was going to head that ticket, and along with him, Gloria's colleague, *New York* columnist Jimmy Breslin. Not only was this Glo-ria's milieu but, according to Mailer, it was Gloria herself who had first suggested to him that he run for the office.

Soon Mailer's campaign committee was meeting in Gloria's newly acquired, three-room apartment on East 73rd Street, the heart of Manhattan's chic Silk Stocking district. This time (there would be other incarnations) the apartment was decorated by her friend the lion-maned socialite Baby Jane Holzer. The front room was gaily stuffed with couches, chairs, and pillows in reds, oranges, yellows, pinks, and purples, with a staircase leading up to a hidden sleeping balcony with a canopied bed.

The back room, with a battered desk, served as a study. Posters of Che Guevara and Cesar Chavez hung on the walls, along with a photograph of Bobby Kennedy, warmly inscribed by his widow, Ethel. The kitchen was both minuscule and empty. Gloria seldom if ever cooked, and there were those who wondered if she ever ate.

Flo Kennedy, valued for her trusted relationship with the Black Panthers, was on hand, and Gloria raised money for the campaign.

In *Managing Mailer,* journalist Joe Flaherty would credit Gloria with "a voice that doesn't want to go home again, so, like Daisy's, it reflects the sound of money." And he would snipe at "her social work among the rich," her supply of "lovely gold diggers to arrange parties and fundraisers."

But Gloria *did* raise money, as so often she would in the future. In her growing circle of highly placed acquaintances, her powers of persuasion would be legendary. They were not yet used, however, in behalf of feminism, although by the summer of that year, President Nixon signed an order prohibiting sex discrimination in federal employment and suggested that birth control information be available to all women. By September, Sheila Tobias's "women's studies" idea having taken root, some universities were beginning to add courses. And then, in October, the National Democratic Women's Club in Washington, alerted by Gloria's "After Black Power" piece in *New York,* invited her to speak to them about women's liberation.

Clay came along and, glancing at Gloria prior to this speech—one of her very first—he saw her legs trembling uncontrollably. Furthermore, he would remember, his send-off was less than helpful.

"Gloria is the best thing that has happened to women's rights since the exploding corset," Clay announced to this highly credentialed, hard-working political audience.

When shock, dismay, and muttering arose, Felker struggled to recover: "I love Gloria," he said. "I want to marry her."

"It was awful," Clay would remember, "but Gloria was so nervous she didn't hear me."

By the early spring of 1970, many of Gloria's lesser known colleagues were battling furiously—risking their jobs, in fact—for employment equity. Forty-six women at *Newsweek,* most of them researchers, filed a complaint with the EEOC, charging discrimination against women in editorial jobs. Soon afterward, women at Time, Inc., filed charges against all four of the corporation's magazines: *Time, Life, Fortune,* and *Sports Illustrated.*

The movement—both NOW and the radical groups—was in full, noisy cry. *Notes from the Second Year* was published, and it included over 100 pages of theoretical papers and personal statements. Representative Patsy Mink demanded that women's rights be considered at a priority meeting of the Democratic National Committee. Informational and meeting centers for women activists were opening in cities and on college campuses across the country. The *Washington Post* sent guidelines to its staff stipulating that descriptive words for women such as "blonde divorcée" be eschewed unless the same words could also be used for men, and the American Civil Liberties Union included the defense of women's rights in its policy.

In May, the graduating class of Vassar, which included for the first time in history a sprinkling of male students, chose a commencement speaker they admired as a peace activist, a campaigner for Adlai Stevenson, the Kennedys, and the migrant grape workers—the successful, glamorous writer they had seen on TV talk shows.

They chose Gloria, and there, in the outdoor theater in Poughkeepsie, New York, she delivered the first of what would be many, many commencement speeches.

Nervously clutching the lectern, Gloria put on her large, lavender-tinted glasses and read: "In my experience, commencement speakers are gray-haired, respected creatures, heavy with experience of power in the world and with establishment honors . . ."

Hardly a description of the speaker the students saw before them. Far closer to their own experience, Gloria focused on civil rights and Vietnam, only mentioning women's liberation as part of—not separate from—that context.

"The movement that some call 'feminist' but should more accurately be called humanist; a movement that is an integral part of rescuing this country from its old, expensive patterns of elitism, racism, and violence.

"Our first problem is not to learn, but to unlearn. . . . The process currently called 'consciousness changing' by academics, and 'turning your head around' or 'getting yourself together' by people in the streets—this is a process primarily of unlearning, of clearing some of the old assumptions out of our heads and letting a fresh breeze blow through.

"Patriotism means obedience; Age means wisdom; Woman means submission; Black means inferior: these are preconceptions embedded so deeply in our thinking that we honestly may not know that they are there."

She seemed, to so many in the audience, to have accomplished a miracle. She was part of the "establishment" world—enormously successful in it, in fact—without giving up any of the important principles that endeared her to the counterculture. Furthermore, just as Clay had observed, Gloria had a natural, Ivy League air about her, much like any one of them. She was, in short, the person almost every young woman on every eastern college campus very much wanted to be.

That year, in *The Greening of America,* academician Charles A. Reich had described the youth movement as the most idealistic, anti-materialistic, magnificently selfless of revolutions. It was a "great moment in history," he wrote, "the rebirth of a future, the rebirth of people in a sterile land." It was something called "Consciousness III."

Caroline Bird, the author of the recently published *Born Female, or the High Cost of Keeping Women Down,* attended the ceremony at Vassar. Gloria, she wrote, represented "Consciousness III." She was "something new, an authentic culture heroine."

But she was still, as far as the women's movement was concerned, a sympathetic observer.

Not yet down in those feminist trenches.

". . . Gloria Steinem, a contributing editor of *New York* magazine, whose journalistic curiosity ranges from show business to Democratic politics. Miss Steinem admits to being not only a critical observer but a concerned advocate of the feminist revolt."

This was how *Time* credited Gloria's essay in its August 31, 1970, issue, an issue which would, in fact, precipitate searing trauma for another young woman who would soon emerge as a feminist oracle.

Gloria's essay described a "women's lib utopia" and included many of the themes from her "After Black Power."

"No more men who are encouraged to spend a lifetime living with inferiors; with housekeepers, or dependent creatures, who are still children. No more domineering wives, emasculating women, and 'Jewish mothers,' " the last epithet softened this time with "all of whom are simply human beings with all their normal ambition and drive confined to the home."

Added to this piece, too, was a spirited defense of the single woman:

"No more sex arranged on the barter system, with women pretending interest and men never sure whether they are loved for themselves or for the security few women can get any other way. (Married or not, for sexual reasons or social ones, most women still find it second nature to Uncle-Tom.) Single women will have the right to stay single without ridicule, without the attitudes now betrayed by 'spinster' and 'bachelor.' "

Both Gloria's empathy with the young, far-left elements and her ability to weave highly radical notions into a tapestry of soothing phrases were evident in the piece.

"Lesbians or homosexuals," she wrote, "will no longer be denied legally binding marriages. . . ." A bombshell, had it not been followed by the comforting prediction—at least for those who were frightened by it—that the feminist utopia Gloria envisioned would probably "reduce the number of homosexuals and the growing divorce rate."

This utopia would cease encouraging "men to be exploiters and women to be parasites. . . . If Women's Lib wins, perhaps we all do."

"What It Would Be Like If Women Win" was the title of the piece, but "winning," as Kate Millett soon discovered, could mean losing as well.

15

THE NEW
HIGH PRIESTESS

*The lesbian is the rage of all women condensed to
the point of explosion.*

—Radicalesbian position paper, *The Woman-Identified
Woman*, quoted in *Sappho Was a Right-On Woman*, 1972

Sexual Politics.

The title alone was intriguing, promising, as it did, to unravel the
mysteries that lay behind women's anger.

The bedroom, it seemed to say. And power. Two eternally fascinating topics.

Advance copies of the book by Kate Millett (which was, in fact, her
Ph.D. thesis) had been circulating among magazine and newspaper
editors during the spring of 1970. Even a year earlier, Kate's editor,
Betty Prashker at Doubleday, had been deeply impressed. "I felt the
scales drop from my eyes," she would remember. *Sexual Politics* was
the most exciting stuff she had seen in years. This was no dry academic thesis in Prashker's view. Nor was it simply a polemic for
women's rights. It was a remarkably conceived, relentlessly detailed,
scornful, witty, full-blown attack on some of the literary giants of the
century . . . Henry Miller, Norman Mailer, D. H. Lawrence. These legendary male authors, through the aggressive characters and violent

situations they created, Kate contended, had constructed a cultural scaffold on which to display and denigrate women.

Spurred on by her editor's enthusiasm, Kate had roared forth in a sustained burst of creativity, working up to eighteen hours a day, the cultural analysis developing into an indictment of thousands of years of "the patriarchy," the rule of men over women. Freud was the arch-villain, romantic love a trap, chivalry a "sporting kind of reparation."

"I was really afraid to write this book so much," Kate would eventually tell a reporter. "I used to go crazy with terror about it."

So wide was its scope, so daring its challenge to literary heroes, surely the wrath of the literary establishment, the male reviewers and media honchos, would descend on her head.

Amazingly, they did not. Quite the contrary. Perhaps it was the force of Kate's argument, her erudition, the sharp penetration of her insights. Or perhaps the ground had been softened by the months and years of dissent—outcries against the war in Vietnam, against the prejudice that seemed to hide in every corner of society. By now protest films—not just *M*A*S*H,* but *Getting Straight, The Strawberry Statement,* even *Myra Breckinridge*—were demanding that everyone, male and female, examine their actions. The best of men were beginning to probe their consciences for symptoms of the callous phenomenon Kate called "male supremacy."

Furthermore, as magazine and newspaper editors were fully aware, the fiftieth anniversary of women's suffrage was coming up that summer, perfect timing for full-scale pieces on the women's movement, this still relatively new blossom on the protest scene. *Sexual Politics* was a fresh—and obvious—approach.

Which is how it happened, in those early months of 1970, that the quiet peace of the Bowery loft where Kate lived and worked with her sculptor husband, Fumio, was suddenly shattered. Reporters began plodding past the abandoned warehouses of the Bowery, gingerly navigating round the bums and winos slumped against broken wire fences and beat-up garbage cans, insistently pressing the buzzer outside the peeling gray building. Kate, in her dashiki and sandals, her hair streaming over her shoulders, would clump down the three flights of stairs to let them in and then lead them up again, where they peered around with little sighs of surprise. At the sprawling living room with its flowering plants and old wicker chairs and bookcases, at Fumio's airy paper-and-bamboo sculptures swaying like hanging flowers from the ceiling, at Kate's own whimsical furniture sculpture (chairs with legs in human shape, a piano with fists poised over the keyboard), at this haven for private gatherings of artists and avant-garde writers, where wine and laughter had once lasted late into the night.

Now the phone began to ring incessantly, uptown journalists begging for a chance to talk to the nervy iconoclast Kate Millett. Now TV camera lights bounced off the wood floor, their black wires snaking round the sculpture, blowing the fuses. Fumio, his sculpture better known by far than Kate's, was practically ignored.

"Fumio, I love you," one reporter overheard Kate say as she raced down the stairs to an appointment. "I'm sorry I never see you anymore."

Full of the fun of it, Kate offered herself as a lively subject for interviews. She let loose a blizzard of words, sometimes the expletives that spoke for the counterculture, sometimes exaggerations for dramatic effect—the legacy of witty chatter from her days at the Millett dinner table.

"I wrote it bang, bang, bang. Like wow! A triple orgasm."

"My mother had a college degree and do you know what she was offered for her first job? Demonstrating potato peelers."

"You go around feeling neurotic and then, Christ, you find out that you're not alone."

Yes, of course, she belonged to a full range of women's liberation groups, from NOW to the Radicalesbians.

"You don't want me to print that, surely?" asked one sympathetic reporter.

No?

In Fort Lauderdale, college girls were dancing on tables in wet T-shirt contests. *Oh Calcutta!*—with its joyously stark-naked actors expressing youthful defiance—had been playing to full houses (in spite of scathing reviews) for months. And everybody, it seemed, was sleeping with everybody.

"Sure," Kate would remember telling the reporter, "print that if you don't print anything else."

And Kate's membership in the Radicalesbians was indeed included in articles in both the *New York Times* and the *New York Post*. It was listed as one more organizational membership, the *Post* assuring that her alliance with the group was only "a blunt defiance of a culture that makes labels."

All this attention, of course, was heady stuff for the obscure, thirty-five-year-old academic who had spent most of the last decade or so hanging out with impoverished artists, saving pennies, teaching—in the last few years at Barnard—to stay alive. Corporate media power, image making, television and magazine journalists were a world apart. Kate didn't even own a television set, and, aside from a few quotes, a few back-page stories on her sculpture, no reporters had paid much mind before to the soft-spoken—if often arch—little English instructor. By now Kate had given up on Ti-Grace's Feminists. ("They didn't seem to get much done," she would remember.) She had returned to NOW, and if she had been known at all, it was simply in that role— the education director of New York NOW.

Sexual Politics had changed all that.

All Kate could think of was how proud her mother must be. Helen Millett, who valued literacy above all, could see her daughter's book stacked high and bold in the front windows of the St. Paul bookstores, her talent extolled in all the magazines. She could read the amazing review of "SexPol," as Kate had taken to calling her book, in the *New York Times*. Amazing because, in a most unusual move, critic Christopher Lehmann-Haupt actually had written *two* reviews that ran consecutively.

In the first, he went so far as to suggest that because of Kate's book, "all vestiges of male chauvinism ought by rights to melt and drip away like so much fat in the flame of a blowtorch," and to speculate openly about his own guilt, "the particular brand of guilt that, as Millett herself points out, all oppressors feel toward the people they oppress."

In the second, while taking note of a certain nagging "distrust," a sense that between its lines the "book itself is too masculine, itself a denial of femininity," he nonetheless concluded with the ultimate praise: "But it will be a long time before I forget the book."

And now, on top of that, here was a *Time* editor calling Kate, asking questions for a review of "SexPol" that the magazine planned to include in its major story about the movement.

Naturally, Kate was full of enthusiasm, even sharing her ideas for the magazine's cover. It was no great service to the movement to use just one person, Kate told the editor, but if they intended that, "it should be Betty Friedan.

"Look," she burbled on, "it would be a great idea to put a crowd of women on the cover since that really is the feeling of the movement."

She'd be glad to help. Of course she would. She even knew, she said, "some photographers who have great shots."

Which was the last Kate heard from *Time* until August.

"I didn't see it," she would remember, "until it was on the cover and all over the world." Until . . .

Swack!—the magazine hit the newsstands, the supermarkets, the drugstores everywhere.

But my God, what had they done?

Kate was horrified, shocked nearly speechless.

This was the big issue that she (along with nearly every other feminist she knew) was counting on to carry the message of the movement to women all over the country, to every literate person on earth. But there on the cover was not the grand, mass photo of joyously united women Kate had expected. Not even a picture of Betty Friedan (as legitimate a "leader," Kate thought, as any one woman could be). There on the cover of *Time,* in thick brush strokes of crashing color, was, instead, an artist's rendering of *her*—Kate Millett —with a smoking, biblical rage in her dark eyes, a deathless fury that could have pulverized the temple of the Philistines into dust.

Talk about your media stars! About elitism!

"Until this year, with the publication of a remarkable book called *Sexual Politics,*" the article announced, "the movement had no coherent theory to buttress its intuitive passions, no ideologue to provide chapter and verse for its assault on patriarchy."

No ideologue?

Kate had been sitting in the audience at the Second Congress. She had heard the proclamation against Susan Brownmiller and Lucy Komisar. And she had understood the point perfectly.

They were *all* supposed to be theorists, *all* leaders, *all* perfectly capable of analyzing and understanding what had happened in their own lives.

And yet, suddenly, there *she* was—Kate Millett, the new "high priestess," the "Mao Tse-tung of Women's Liberation," as *Time* called her.

No glowing reviews, not even that extraordinary critique in the *New York Times,* could make up for what Kate knew was coming.

Years later, many women would look back with regret on this Age of Agony, this battlefield of petty jealousies, would dismiss their attacks on their more talented "sisters" such as Kate and Susan Brownmiller as merely the growing pains of a new movement. But Susan would remember that bitterness, the shock of realizing "that there were people who wished that I'd never write anything else again."

236

And the testy, sensitive Kate had no crystal ball with which to peer into a more sanguine future.

Which was, perhaps, just as well, for if she had, it would have revealed far greater personal trauma in the months to come.

That summer, the assault was minor—a buzz of angry phone calls pricking her ears and her psyche. Why had she signed her book? Why had she played the game? Why had she let the media loft her into "stardom" to the detriment of everyone else? Within minutes of *Time's* appearance on the kiosks of New York, the wrath of all manner of feminists descended on Kate's head.

She hadn't known, Kate pleaded with friends and acquaintances over and over, often through tears, always within the tight, panicky time limits of what was now suddenly a whirlwind of interviews and lecture appearances. She had no idea that the media would anoint her the "high priestess" or the "Karl Marx of the women's movement"—no idea, really, that one publication after another would print those damned out-of-context quotes about her family: "We were constantly reminded that we weren't sons . . . that we were mistakes."

Or once, with her pretty sister Mary (who had changed her name to Mallory) present at an interview: "I was smart and ugly, and you were dumb and beautiful. I did the being-a-good-girl-in-school act because they had convinced me I was so ugly I couldn't make it any other way. I did my shuffling that way."

Or, "All my life, guys said I was neurotic. I didn't accept my femininity . . ."

And indeed, for all Kate's absolute, no-holds-barred assurance, her conviction not only of the righteousness of her cause, but the dead-on accuracy of her attack on the male power structure, she had been naive. Years later, the *Time* editors involved would be hard-pressed to remember how that cover decision was made, but chances are good that Kate's suggestion for a mass photo had been shrugged off without a second thought.

Kate had never worked inside the offices of a mass magazine or newspaper, had no notion of the well-paid expertise in cleverly transmitting ideas through one face, not unfocused hordes of them, through one magnetic image that would grasp the attention of potential buyers as they rushed past newsstands on their way to work. The *Time* cover provided the ultimate hook, the practically guaranteed double-take—Kate-to-reader, reader-to-Kate—the infallible snap/catch of eye contact.

The isolated, quiet academic, the protected downtown artist, had foreseen none of it.

But how could her friends ever believe that?

Dependent, as so many were, on the affection of her new companions in battle, she shivered in their disapproval, fought off what was for her a near paralyzing emotional chill, the one thing she could least afford. Because no matter what was happening to Kate personally, she passionately believed that she was honor bound to continue as an activist, to speak to any group that asked for her.

"I took it very seriously," she would remember, "the business of explaining the women's movement to people at large."

To fail to appear at a scheduled engagement was to fail what was paramount in her life: The Movement. The protected St. Paul teenager who had risked rebellion against the authority of her own Catholic Church had become a woman with a driving mission of another kind.

And now in the once jolly studio in the Bowery, the phone rang even more insistently, sending Fumio to search for refuge elsewhere. Kate, meanwhile, flew from meeting to meeting, campus to campus in her attempts to "explain" the movement, to carry the message. Off to describe to the acolytes how society, being ruled by men, was a "patriarchy," how the brainwashing began in the family, how it encouraged conformity, how male power was enforced through the man's position as head of the household, how it influenced every female child's perception of herself and what she could do, how Freud's conception of women as damaged or castrated males had helped to prop up the patriarchal hold on women's lives.

And, most important, how the patriarchy that had ruled the world for so many centuries was directly responsible, not only for all power imbalance, for the domination of one human being over another, but for the slaughter then raging in Southeast Asia, and for all the wars that had afflicted humanity since the dawn of time.

Unlike the feminist Virginia Woolf before her, Kate did not merely *suggest* that male hegemony might be the major cause of war. Kate was sure. Always sure . . . a quality that would lose her several potential admirers in the years to come. Editor/writer Michael Korda, who would eventually edit one of Kate's books, would note her "glorious certainty" with an epigram: "If Kate Millett had a shoe store, she would have all the shoes in her own size."

But, in a news sense, perhaps, *Time* had been right. Perhaps Kate

Millett, not Betty Friedan—with her circumscribed, democratic, individualistic claims for feminism—more precisely illustrated the latest, hottest wave, the movement that would demand as its philosophical province not just the arena of women's rights but the entire history of the world. And how much more fascinating than the day-to-day progress—the caucuses and protests against television commercials, the demands for day-care facilities—was Kate's topic: sexuality. One reviewer had even suggested that she had concealed what was essentially pornographic content under a blanket of documentation.

And what could Kate do about any of this?

She could and did, rebelliously, dispense with the teacherish, conventional bun at the back of her head. Her hair would flow down over her shoulders, in spite of her mother's opinions on the matter in *Time*: "Kate's missing the boat if she appears on the 'Mike Douglas Show' without her hair washed."

If she made any money on the book, she told a reporter, "I'll only keep enough to live—and after being poor all my life it doesn't take me much to live. The rest I'll give to the movement—it's my whole life now."

And she could keep talking.

Faithfully, Kate the devout believer, Kate the conscientious academic, would lecture. Anywhere, anytime anybody asked.

Ironically, though, as the weeks of Kate's lectures wore on, despite her unwavering belief that the women's movement was the most important force for social change on the planet earth, this media-ordained "high priestess" found herself chafing at the demands of this role. At each new lecture, she was obliged to go over what she had just said the day, or the hour, before. The repetition, the mouthing of rhetoric, had begun to pall—and with this insidious gray fog of boredom came doubts.

"If I am bored," she would write, "am I a traitor?"

Perhaps Kate was feeling the resistance in the wind, the defiance of women across the country whose concerns were quite different from hers.

Perhaps it was the fear—always trailing her—of her friends' disapproval. Or perhaps, as she would see it in retrospect, the doubts came from within. Who was she to be speaking for the movement? What right did she have to voice the innermost thoughts of millions of women?

"I began to feel foolish, a silly figure, a propped-up factotum," she would remember.

Often as she mounted yet another lectern, looked out at yet another sea of expectant faces, she thought of Betty Friedan, wished she were more like her, more the orator, the politician. Instead, feeling isolated and unbearably lonely, Kate began to dream. Even to work fitfully at more artistic endeavors. A film about the movement, an autobiographical book . . .

The latter, *Flying*, as it would finally emerge from the scraps of paper scribbled in airport waiting rooms, would not be structured in the conventional prose of "SexPol," but in a sort of stream of consciousness, what Kate liked to call her "run-of-the-mouth Americanese," her "own voice."

These new works were the hope and emotional sustenance for Kate, but as she droned on, at meeting after meeting, something—was it the artist, the innovator in her?—howled and sometimes struck out in frustration . . .

At Bryn Mawr College for her lecture series, the hall was packed with students—until Kate speared them with a reading list. Here, you really want to understand? Cut your teeth on this. (The Bryn Mawr audience diminished quickly, though many students claimed it was less the mountainous reading list that turned them off than Kate's rhetoric, her ideological drumbeat.)

Fall came to New York and then the sharp, early winter winds of November. An anonymous underground pamphlet appeared, accusing Kate of damaging lesbians on her "media trip." It was provoked, she was sure, by a comment attributed to her in a *Life* magazine article. When questioned about her membership in the Radicalesbians, Kate, according to the magazine, responded: "I'm not into that."

A public confession of homosexuality was certainly not recommended for any aspiring author in 1970. But still, Kate would be absolutely positive that she had never said such a thing to the *Life* reporter.

But then . . .

It was a typically hectic evening. Kate had met with the wives of Democratic congressmen in Washington, D.C., then flown back to New York to find that she was scheduled uptown at a meeting at

Columbia University. By now feminist seminars and meetings were proliferating on college campuses. The women's studies program at San Diego State University already provided ten different courses, and the first women's law course was offered by the University of Pennsylvania. Across the country, colleges and universities had appointed task forces to study sex discrimination.

The Columbia meeting, however, was extracurricular—a joint gathering of gay liberation and women's liberation groups. The topic of discussion—a popular one that year—was sexual liberation, and Kate had been asked to address, in academic, descriptive terms, the subject of bisexuality.

Bisexuality was an innocuous topic, its "natural" basis a well-accepted tenet in academic psychology. And Kate planned to deliver a fairly standard moderator's speech, sandwiched, as she was, between a representative of the still mostly underground homosexual community and someone who would express the feminist point of view.

She was almost late. She rushed through the great iron Delacorte gates with their towering statues, their fleur-de-lis crowns, and the brass inscription "May all who enter here find welcome and peace." The leaves had long vanished from the well-tended bushes in the campus courtyard, and only the damp chill of a rainy November evening greeted Kate. She heaved open the heavy black door of MacMillan Hall and hurried into the auditorium.

Inside, the lovely theater with its curved rows of seats was packed, nearly overflowing. People wedged back into the balcony. Was there an ominous, quivering sort of volatility in the room? Tired, rushed, Kate barely noticed.

Looking back on it years later, when she could bear to, she would think that the nightmare really began then, that she should have known.

"They're going to zap us tonight," a friend whispered as Kate climbed up onto the graceful stage, past the long red velvet curtains, took her place at the speaker's table, and gazed out at mostly female faces. Some of the women were still bundled in their thick sweaters, their scarves and boots.

Hecklers here in this lovely theater? she thought wearily. Well, she was used to them by now, used to defending her position. And furthermore, compared to the other two speakers, both of whom had "rights" issues to propound, her talk would occupy a thoroughly middle stance.

Soon she could make out a few familiar faces in the audience—old colleagues, members of a variety of the new groups, some from fringe factions of the women's movement. She spoke, when her turn came, in a weary voice, though practiced and smooth, her tone colored by a light touch of the cultured accent she had acquired at Oxford. Afterward, as usual, there were questions from the floor.

Only a few queries were posed before it happened.

Someone shouted a question.

Not to one of the advocacy speakers, as one might have expected, but directly to her, Kate Millett. Astonished to hear her own name echo through the hall, Kate anxiously leaned forward, searched for the face to connect to the voice. Amazing that so many were out on a night like this!

Kate finally located her questioner, even vaguely recognized the woman. Teresa Juarez, a member of the Radicalesbians. What was she asking?

The woman repeated Kate's name in a voice harsh as the winter winds, a blizzard of pent-up anger. This was no ordinary academic inquiry!

"Bisexuality, as we all know . . ." The woman chiseled the words. "Bisexuality is a cop-out!"

Silence. The audience in the theater suddenly hushed, waiting.

Kate froze, the awareness slowly dawning, the realization of what that audience was waiting for, why the faces were staring at her so intently. Thoughts whirled crazily, uselessly, in her head. But she knew what the woman wanted. Perhaps, in some hidden realm of her subconscious, Kate had actually been waiting for this terrible moment.

The woman, and so many (how many?) others, was demanding something from the famous Kate Millett. At this moment. Publicly. And that something was decidedly not the sober, academic discussion of sexuality she had just delivered, the ostensible purpose of this meeting within the august halls of Columbia University. It was something else entirely.

And then it came. Venomously.

"Are you a lesbian?"

Silence.

"Say it. Are you?"

Kate knew she would have to answer. Something.

In the years that followed, Kate would insist again and again that she had never denied being a lesbian, that within her own circles, within the openly lesbian Daughters of Bilitis, for instance, she had spoken about it several times—often, as she was sure was the case, when reporters were present.

She was, in fact, living a bisexual life, was very much in love with her husband, Fumio, she would always insist. In 1970, however, when most homosexuals were still very much in the closet, the term "bisexuality" was often used as a smoke screen, a way to distance oneself from the stigma of being what would soon be known as "gay." But in using that term—even if it actually applied—these "bisexuals" seemed to condone the public's disdain for homosexuality in general. It was a sad and hurtful business, inevitably resulting in explosions of resentment at the nearest target. Like the now famous Kate. Noticeable. Privileged. Crowned. She had been photographed in *Life* kissing Fumio just as if she were an ordinary, conventional, happy housewife!

"Are you a lesbian? Say it!"

At that awful moment, Kate Millett could not have imagined what the ugly consequences of her answer would be.

She knew that most everyone in the women's movement was nervous about accusations of lesbianism. Many feminists—Betty and Susan Brownmiller among them—feared that the taint of homosexuality could destroy whatever progress had been made. And if she, Kate, now heralded far and wide as the new leader, was to make a public "confession" of lesbianism . . .

But somehow, in some part of her, Kate felt that she *had* to answer. She would later insist that the question carried with it an unspoken claim from the lesbians she knew had worked so hard for the cause. She *had* to answer honestly. Or perhaps she truly wanted to answer. As she would later write in *Flying*: "I hear them not breathe. That word in public, the word I waited half a lifetime to hear. Finally I am accused."

And with what she felt was the last strength she had, she answered.

"Yes, I am a lesbian."

And there it was.

At barely past dawn the next morning, the doorbell rang. Kate climbed down the stairs to find a young woman outside. A *Time* reporter.

243

"Did you say at Columbia last night that you were a bisexual?" the woman asked. She had been there, it seemed, in the audience.

"No," replied Kate. "I said I was a lesbian."

"Well," said the reporter, "I'm from *Time* magazine."

Numbly, Kate led the journalist upstairs to the loft. In her hand, Kate noticed, was a tape recorder.

Now the question was repeated. "Is that true?" The tape recorder was running. "Is that correct?"

Kate slipped into the next room, frantically dialed the numbers of several NOW officials. Maybe they could tell her what to say to this *Time* reporter, how to handle it.

No answers anywhere. The reporter waiting. Kate returned, saw the young woman's finger flip on the recorder.

"Now once again, was that correct?"

"Yes," Kate said.

Yes, of course she had said she was a lesbian. Of course it was correct. And of course she knew—without precisely knowing how or why—there was risk in her answer.

But when the reporter asked the question again, and yet again, she answered.

Yes. Yes. Yes.

And so, finally, the aggressive young journalist climbed back down the long flights of stairs, out into the early morning light of the Bowery, and thence to the great media power center uptown.

The incident was, clearly, one of the earliest signs of a feminist paradox: A female journalist, following the bent of the achievement-oriented feminism pioneered by NOW, pursues what she regards as the crux of an important story. She can now assure her editors that the "high priestess," the major theorist of a burgeoning social movement, had made a potentially damaging statement. Conscientiously, using a tape recorder, she had verified her facts.

In career terms, the reporter's curiosity was legitimate. Given the public's now insatiable hunger for personal detail, along with the view of homosexuality as depravity and/or mental illness, it was a scoop. After all, Kate and the new young radicals had extended their claims far beyond such issues as job discrimination or the confinement of the homemaker, what would one day be described as "liberal feminism." They had adventured into universal questions of male dominance, love, and sex—and, in particular, how women felt about men.

Reading Kate's book, her own professor had told *Time,* was "like sitting with your testicles in a nutcracker."

Inevitably then, some editors regarded as relevant the fact that their "Mao Tse-tung of Women's Liberation" chose women as sexual partners.

Well into the eighties, long recovered from the tumultuous events that followed the reporter's visit, Kate would adhere tenaciously to her contempt for the media as the "great exploiter of American life." That damp fall morning in 1970, however, the "exploitation" of Kate Millett was still ahead of her.

What would *Time* do with her interview? Would they print it? How? When?

Kate phoned some of the women, including Ivy Bottini, then president of New York NOW, to alert them, at least, to what she had done.

And she called her older sister, Sally, pleaded with her to explain to their mother, to prepare, as best she could, the conservative, lady-like Helen for whatever might come of this. And Kate would recall, in *Flying,* that Sally responded:

" 'There it goes down the tube for the rest of us. I warned you. It's too hot to confuse with the women's movement.'

" 'I'm not Women's Lib, Sally, just one woman in it who happens also to be a queer.'

" 'I've got every sympathy for homosexuals, but middle America simply can't take this sort of thing.'

" 'Sally, I did what I thought was right.' "

Early in December, it hit. *Time's* December 14 issue offered readers "A Second Look" at women's lib. It did not mention the hard, day-to-day advances that had been made that year—that women employees at the Little, Brown publishing company had won agreement on equal hiring, training, and promotion; that for the first time since 1948, the Equal Rights Amendment was forced out of committee and onto the floor of the House of Representatives by Representative Martha Griffiths; that the Labor Department reversed its stand on the ERA, publicly announcing its support; that the Department of Health, Education and Welfare told its field personnel to include sex discrimination guidelines in all its contract negotiations. Or that a Superior

Court in the state of Washington agreed to allow a married woman to reinstate her maiden name.

Instead, *Time* presented an acidulous sampling of nearly every opposing diatribe (and there were plenty to choose from) that had appeared in the press in the past few months.

From anthropologist Lionel Tiger, author of *Men in Groups,* the scornful suggestion that feminists had chosen not to recognize that there was such a thing as biology.

From writer Helen Lawrenson, among whose contributions to belle-lettres was the essay "Latins Are Lousy Lovers," the claim that feminists could not think clearly.

From writer Janet Malcolm, soon to be known as a perceptive apologist for psychoanalysis, the accusation that the women were condescending toward and would sacrifice the needs of children.

And by far the most extensive, an attack by the famous critic Irving Howe on *Sexual Politics* and on Kate herself. Howe ripped into the book as "a farrago of blunders, distortions, vulgarities and plain nonsense." Kate was guilty of "historical reductionism . . . crude simplification . . . middle-class parochialism . . . sexual monism . . . methodological sloppiness . . . arrogant ultimatism . . . comic ignorance."

Dead center on the page was a grotesque and ludicrous drawing of a grim, balloon-breasted woman idiotically attired in leather sandals and a lacy, infantile pinafore that rode a foot above her knees. She was waving aloft in one ridiculously militant, upstretched arm a formidably capacious brassiere.

A vicious caricature of Kate?

So it appeared.

With it, the story angle provided by the enterprising *Time* reporter. It was not at the top of the piece, but halfway down. Chummy. Confidential. Off-handed. As if to say, it doesn't really matter much to us, folks, but just thought you'd like to know:

"Ironically, Kate Millett herself contributed to the growing skepticism about the movement by acknowledging at a recent meeting that she is bisexual."

Kate read those words, knew that her mother was reading them. And her aristocratic St. Paul family who so guarded their privacy that they scrupulously avoided allowing their names to appear in the newspaper. And the neighbors. Now, of course, along with the rest of the world.

"I had 'come out,'" she would remember, "in ninety-seven languages."

The whole town of St. Paul would now read about Helen's daughter. The pariah, the deviate!

Kate, who just six months ago had made her virtuous mother so proud . . .

It was clear to most everyone who saw Kate Millett that bitter December that she was in a state of extreme agitation.

No one knows quite why *Time* had avoided using the word "lesbian." Timidity? A misguided sense of chivalry?

For years Kate would return to that question and to the subject of *Time's* motivation like a homing pigeon. *Time* had used her, she would believe, "as a club to beat the movement," and the magazine had attacked *Sexual Politics* because they regarded it as "too powerful a statement of something which they no longer wanted to hear anything about.

"I had told them the truth," she would say more than a decade later, "but they printed it as if it were a lie. The media is governed by fashion at the lowest level and big corporate money interests at the highest. The women's movement began for them as entertainment, but then it became serious. It began to make economic demands. Maybe you'll have to pay women equal pay, the whole clerical level of Bell Telephone, for instance. Here was a minority group, a pressure group, and they were getting someplace. So it became necessary to downplay, to do a number on me that week."

A "number" that included the most enraging comment of all:

"The disclosure," said the article, "is bound to discredit her as a spokeswoman for her cause, cast further doubt on her theories and reinforce the views of those skeptics who routinely dismiss all liberationists as lesbians."

To some feminists, many of them wives and mothers, these were the words that reached beyond the pale. There was a swell of sympathy for Kate, of course, but beyond that was the distinct sense that they were all somehow very vulnerable.

The emergency meeting followed swiftly. It was held in NOW member Dolores Alexander's apartment at 33 West 93rd Street, in the brownstone building where Betty Friedan also lived. But Betty was not present at the session.

"I guess we all knew," Dolores would recall, "where Betty stood on the lesbian issue."

Conflict was a standard feature of many NOW meetings, but some who attended this conclave remember it as more stormy, more unsettling than any other. Not that there was any question of supporting Kate. All those who gathered there—about twenty-five in all—were affronted and angered by the *Time* article. There in Dolores's comfortable living room, with its exposed brick walls and glowing fireplace, was a painful awareness of the nasty threat—not quite verbalized—that the *Time* coverage had exposed. How, after all, did you prove that you were *not* a homosexual? To these women, only a very few of them admitted lesbians, there was the clear sense that anyone's work, anything you wrote or said, could be discredited by an accusation of "lesbianism."

Angry denunciations began to fly before coats were off or seats taken. Much murkier, of course, was the question of what to do about the whole thing. Lesbianism as an issue had never before surfaced in any earlier phase of feminism. Never, certainly, in public. Never before had the media assumed a mandate to investigate private lives with as much energy as was applied in the pursuit of hard news. Never, in short, had so much personal data been revealed to so many.

"We've got to make a statement in support of Kate."

"No, not Kate alone. That won't work with these bastards. God damned if we should descend to their level. We've got to stand for the women's movement."

"We should denounce *Time*."

"But the whole point is the gay movement."

And so it went until Kate was dispatched up the gracefully curved, floating wrought-iron staircase, up to the bedroom to work on a message that included it all, that—after four hours of wrangling and a few last-minute changes hammered out by the emergency corps— was ready for the press. They would announce a news conference, and they would call in all allies. And never mind now if these allies were also media "stars."

"This is the real test of sisterhood," as Ivy Bottini, president of New York NOW, put it. "We've got to stand behind Kate."

But a few days later, before the scheduled press conference could be held, the issue hit the front pages in living color, and the color was lavender.

It happened in New York on Saturday, December 12, at a march held in freezing sleet in support of abortion and child-care centers. It had been called by a new group, the Women's Strike Coalition, organized by Betty Friedan. Betty, Gloria, Flo Kennedy, and Kate were slated to speak, and they had just climbed up on the flatbed truck parked in front of Gracie Mansion, the mayor's residence, when a speckling of pale purple—like pointillist dabs of paint—began to glow here and there in the crowd. Some women—no one was sure how many—were wearing and distributing lavender armbands to the entire crowd. They were also handing out leaflets explaining why "we're ALL wearing lavender lesbian armbands today."

"It is not one woman's sexual experience that is under attack," the leaflet said. "It is the freedom *of all women* to openly state values that fundamentally challenge the basic structure of patriarchy. If they succeed in scaring us with words like 'dyke' or 'lesbian' or 'bisexual,' they'll have won. AGAIN. They'll have divided us. AGAIN. Sexism will have triumphed. AGAIN. . . . They can call us all lesbians until such time as there is no stigma attached to women loving women. SISTERHOOD *IS* POWERFUL!!!"

Ivy handed Betty Friedan an armband, then watched her carefully as Betty's deep-brown eyes gazed at the flimsy lavender cloth in her hand. Ivy saw her thoughtfully consider the symbol—its implications —and then make her decision.

Betty let the piece of purple cloth fall through her fingers to the floor of the flatbed truck.

To Ivy, who had helped engineer the lavender display and who would go on to play an active role in gay rights, this was the turning point, the moment when the women's movement took on a life of its own, moved beyond Betty Friedan's "civil rights" structure, leaving the creator of NOW—respected, admired, feared, and sometimes hated—behind. Ivy and many other women would come to feel that Betty's approach had dealt only with "symptoms," that only those willing to explore the significance of "women loving women" would come to grips with the underlying causes of women's oppression.

Well into the eighties, when the women's movement on many college campuses would be dominated by lesbians, many other women would disagree. In Muriel Fox's view, for instance, such statements of solidarity, "political lesbianism," as it would be called, damaged the image of the movement.

"Sexual politics is highly dangerous and diversionary," Betty had already declared in the magazine *Social Policy,* "and may even provide good soil for fascist, demogogic appeals based on hatred . . . *we cannot permit the image of women to be developed by the homosexual.*"

At the moment, Betty did more than let that "lavender herring" drop. This coalition—*her coalition*—had never asked her permission to make that pro-lesbian statement.

Immediately, she phoned the offices of the coalition and resigned. If they ever used her name again, she informed them in no uncertain terms, she would sue. She hauled Kate into the nearest bar and told her, in much the same tone Kate's sister Sally had used: You blew it.

Less than a week later, on December 18, came the "Kate Is Great" press conference.

The Washington Square Methodist Church, downtown on West 4th Street, was crowded with reporters. Banners and posters decorated the walls. "Kate Is Great." "We Stand Together as Women, Regardless of Sexual Preference." "Is the Statue of Liberty a Lesbian, Too?"

Kate sat at a table in the front of the church with about fifty supporters behind her.

In the group were, according to the *New York Times*, feminist "leaders: Gloria Steinem, the journalist; Ruth Simpson, president of the New York chapter of Daughters of Bilitis; Florynce Kennedy, a lawyer; Sally Kempton and Susan Brownmiller, journalists and members of New York Radical Feminists; and Ivy Bottini, Dolores Alexander, and Ti-Grace Atkinson of NOW."

Many would remember that Gloria, her glamorous, streaked-blond hair flowing over her shoulders, sat directly beside Kate and held her hand. Gloria's essay for *Time*—which insisted on the links between women and homosexuals—had appeared in the same issue that carried Kate on its cover. Now Gloria's Playboy Bunny good looks went a long way toward conveying one clear message to reporters. If a woman so distinctly female, so attractive to and attracted by men, could not be co-opted, induced to turn against her sisters in order to win favor with the male establishment, these women might indeed be a force to be reckoned with.

In a trembling voice, Kate read her statement:

"Women's liberation and homosexual liberation are both struggling towards a common goal: a society free from defining and categorizing people by virtue of gender and/or sexual preference. 'Lesbian' is a label used as a psychic weapon to keep women locked into their male-defined 'feminine role.' The essence of that role is that a woman is defined in terms of her relationship to men. A woman is called a lesbian when she functions autonomously. Women's autonomy is what women's liberation is all about."

Bella Abzug sent a message of support. So did Aileen Hernandez, who had just been elected the new president of NOW, and writer Caroline Bird. Betty, the *Times* noted, did not attend. "Leaders said they had tried to contact her, but that she was 'out of town.' "

Kate, tormented, emotionally fragile—leaning on the shoulders of her sisters—was deeply warmed.

In January, however, Kate's father died, adding grief to her already threatening emotional load. (And she would blame the media—which had, in some stories, characterized Jim Millett as an alcoholic—for hastening his death.) She was famous, but "being thrown into fame was," she would later say, "enormously confusing for me." The financial rewards were substantial (though the sales of *Sexual Politics* began to drop—because of the *Time* attack, her editor thought), and Kate was, as she would write in *Flying:* "Shamefully, pointlessly rich. I could live three years on my royalties."

She plunked down $31,600 for a seven-acre farm in the rolling hills outside Poughkeepsie, New York, and rushed off to friends in England, desperately trying to escape the public exposure and what had become a deteriorating relationship with Fumio. She worked there on the film about the women's movement and on her book.

In New York, meanwhile, as the local chapter of NOW panicked and purged in its struggle with the lesbian issue, on the national level the problem was—for the moment—quietly solved. "Asking women to disguise their identities so they will not 'embarrass' the group," a resolution proclaimed, "is an intolerable form of oppression, like asking black women to join us in white face." Lesbianism was indeed a "legitimate concern of feminism."

Not too little, but for Kate Millett, too late.

In the years that immediately followed, she threw herself into a variety of human rights causes, in Berkeley, mostly, where she taught for a short period at the University of California. Her fervor—the obsessiveness of it—soon began to alarm her conservative St. Paul family.

One evening, Kate would remember, she was attempting to show her film to some students when the projector broke. Nervously, to cover the silence, she chattered to the audience. She was often nervous these days. She talked a lot, and perhaps it was that—the chatter, the emotional exhaustion, the fame, the money, the threatening loss of a woman she loved, of Fumio . . .

Years later, Kate's recollection of what happened would be edgy, disjointed.

She had been working to free the Trinidadian civil rights activist Michael Malik, she would explain. Her sister Sally had arrived in California . . .

" 'We're worried about you,' is what Sally said. Actually the family was worried that I spent a lot of money and that I was doing it for this black man. All very well but we mustn't go too far . . ."

Kate *must* see someone, the family decided.

"Sally told me a fairy tale. 'You're freaked out because you're working so hard on that case,' she said. 'Look, kid, you need to see a psychiatrist.' "

A psychiatrist?

Well, now, Kate didn't think very highly of *them*. She would always know more about the truth than they did.

"All they can do," she would insist years later, "well, it's like trying to know an elephant by feeling the back end, tail, tusks, trunk. . . . One always selects what one tells them . . ."

At the time, though, she was unconcerned.

" 'This is just my sister,' I thought. 'I can outsmart her.' "

And so, amenably enough, Kate drove in her grand and wonderful Dodge convertible to the address she was given. Where, suddenly, an enormous iron gate slammed shut and locked behind her. It was the Oakland, California, mental institution. There were police, someone took her car keys, and soon there would be Thorazine.

"That's what they do to people," Kate would remember. "You make your little civil liberties speech, ask what it is, say you're not taking it . . .

"What they'll do is put you in solitary, tie you upside down, and give you a shot in the ass. Well, who wants to go through that since you're going to get it anyway? You might as well swallow it mixed with the orange juice."

After ten or twelve days, Kate would remember, only by waiving certain rights was she allowed to transfer to another institution. She would go, she had thought, freely.

" 'I think I'll go in my own fine car,' I told them. 'My friends will drive me.'

"But no, they began to twist my arm.

" 'Oh, my God,' I said, 'don't do this!' Then they beat me to the floor of the parking lot . . . big guys . . . and then I was trussed upside down on a stretcher."

Whereupon the suffering Kate, who had been anxious in small spaces for years—a claustrophobe—spent one horrible night in solitary.

"Then Mother got me to go to St. Paul. The doctor persuaded her to commit me. I was committed about three hours when the lawyers showed up.

"It was a wonderful trial, though. It established a precedent, so no one can be committed to a mental institution without a trial." Her husband, Fumio, she would remember, being "utterly bewildered" by the process, having "no knowledge of American bullshit psychiatry," left her soon afterward.

Fumio did indeed leave, but the procedure—less dramatic than Kate remembered—was merely a hearing with a court-appointed attorney and psychiatrist, too low a step in the judicial process to affect any future litigation, forgotten even by the judge who presided. It was reported in the *St. Paul Pioneer-Dispatch,* under the headline "Author Commitment Papers Withdrawn":

"A petition for commitment against Kate Millett, a leader of the national women's liberation movement, was brought against the native St. Paul woman last week in Ramsey County probate court by her mother and two cousins, but was withdrawn this week upon stipulation of voluntary psychiatric treatment."

Kate, this report noted, had been staying with her mother, and "the agreement between attorneys for Miss Millett and attorneys for the family include that she leave Minnesota and go to her farm in New York, where she is to be assisted by unnamed persons in New York who have been contacted by the attorneys.

" 'She will have the right to select her own psychological and medical help in an atmosphere she considers conducive to assistance from professional colleagues whose opinions she believes she can respect and rely upon,' the stipulation agreement says."

Many years later, when Kate talked about all this she would indeed be safely at her farm. Here, hidden behind the trees on what was now eighty acres of Kate's hilly land, would be three buildings, each of them painted, like a child's dream, a different color—lavender, white, and a brilliant cobalt blue. In summers, Kate would run a women's art colony here, and after a hard day's work planting Christmas trees, the women would swim naked in the pond. Kate would cook simple but delicious country dinners for such distinguished visitors as Doris Lessing and Simone de Beauvoir. She would speak about her conviction that America was headed toward a fascist state.

Yet there would be, before this, six attempts at suicide.

16

THE FEMME FATALE
OF A
NOVELIST'S DREAMS

O beauty, are you not enough?
Why am I crying after love?

—Sara Teasdale, "Spring Night," in
A Little Treasury of Modern Poetry, 1946

Not long after the publication of *Sexual Politics*, a voice would be heard in the land that was so exuberantly heterosexual, such a glowing tribute to straightforward, spontaneous female sexuality that its owner was promptly labeled "everybody's favorite feminist."

The voice was Germaine Greer's, and her book, *The Female Eunuch*, could not be interpreted, by any stretch of the imagination, as a lesbian complaint. Furthermore, it was written in a style that shattered any notion that the heart of this women's rebellion might be grim and austere, narrow or coldly analytic. To thousands of women across America—who were definitely not, as Betty had put it, "anti-man," who took great pleasure in their sensual lives, whether with husbands, boyfriends, or children, through literature or domesticity —the lush phrases of this ringing opus came as both inspiration and relief. Militant as Germaine was, and angry, she also spoke to the souls of millions of women who were as devoted to Eros and art as to climbing the rungs of the employment ladder.

"The struggle which is not joyous is the wrong struggle," she wrote.

"I'm sick of the masquerade. I'm sick of pretending eternal youth. I'm sick of belying my own intelligence, my own will, my own sex. I'm sick of peering at the world through false eyelashes, so everything I see is mixed with a shadow of bought hairs, of weighting my head with a dead mane, unable to move my neck freely, terrified of rain, of wind, of dancing too vigorously in case I sweat into my lacquered curls. I'm sick of the powder room . . . I refuse to be a female impersonator. I am a woman, not a castrate."

In England, where *The Female Eunuch* was first published in 1970, the book had sold out its printing of a few thousand copies within a week, and the fact that the thirty-one-year-old Australian emigrant was not a "castrate" was made abundantly clear to television viewers across that country. Visions of the robust Shakespearean scholar-cum-TV-cutup, with her high, rounded cheekbones and her great mop of wavy dark hair, were soon flashing across the screen almost as often as shots of Prime Minister Edward Heath or pictures of the embattled British troops in Northern Ireland. She looks like Greta Garbo, burbled one reporter. A combination of Vanessa Redgrave and Anna Magnani, raved another.

Ah, Magnani! Many years later, Germaine would still remember the impact of that earthy actress, the colorful contrast she seemed to present to pallid, restricted images of women.

"I was used to Doris Day and all that kind of crap," Germaine would recall, "and I'd think, 'Christ, is this what being a woman is? I don't think I can do it!' Then I came across Anna Magnani and realized that there's something else . . . something heavy and dark and strong and female that can kill and that can save."

Six feet tall and certainly strong and female, Germaine, this casually déshabillé Amazon beauty, not only could exhort British women to resist the systemic pressures that bored away at their powers, sexual and otherwise, but she actually materialized on the TV screens in their kitchens and parlors as the restless, glamorous embodiment of what she preached. The Greer persona—the light from those gray-green eyes that splashed onto the screen like a mountain waterfall, the stylishly disheveled shag haircut, the merry, quick laugh, the sparkling, easy discourse—caught the attention of nearly every "telly" watcher in England.

Sometimes Germaine sported a Che Guevara military look—but with a neckline cut down to *there*. Sometimes, the slinky, funky designs of Britain's rock culture. Often, she was interviewed in her flat, lounging casually on her couch, her live-in lover, the manager of a rock group, nearby. This young man could not read her books, she told a British reporter slyly, "But I'm sure he's looked at every page for quite a long time." And then, with that dash of frankness which always warmed her style: "I don't feel like some girls who feel they have to sleep with their intellectual equals. If I did I would be scurrying around in a state of sexual frenzy."

But that amenable fellow, hanging cool in the background, was a profound shock to most telly watchers. A lover? In public? Only one word fit that sort of behavior. *Prostitute!* Even as late as 1970, most British women—perhaps even more than their American counterparts—still presented self-portraits of the utmost propriety, still scrupulously colored over any signs of their own sexual desires or career ambitions. So many had remained stolidly centered on post–World War II values of duty, on hearth and home, thrift, preservation, service to others. Not only was England's feminist movement several years behind the United States, but there were other boundaries as well.

In England, life and living arrangements—even in the universities —were still gender separate, and proper womanhood implied, of course, "saving" oneself for marriage. The standards of the earlier, postwar culture were embedded, like a maze of underground walls, in the psyches of nearly every adult—from executive to street cleaner, from office worker to housewife. Unconscious feelings were tightly bundled in those earlier restraints, in spite of such films as *I Am Curious (Yellow)* and *Darling.*

Into this brewing tension, without a moment's backward glance, strode Germaine Greer and *The Female Eunuch,* strewing a remarkable mix, a rhythm of expression that drew from Shakespeare and the great English literary tradition, spattered like a Day-Glo rainbow with the four-letter words of the sixties youth revolution. There was nothing soft, nothing timid, surely nothing properly "feminine" (that is, self-effacing) about this feminist's prose.

Or her philosophy:

"To refuse hobbles and deformity and take possession of your body and glory in its power, accepting its own laws of loveliness. To have something to desire, something to make, something to achieve, and at last something genuine to give."

Boldly spray-painted with: "Women who fancy that they manipulate the world by pussy power . . . are fools."

Laced as it was with Germaine's childhood fury at female guile, flirtation, and manipulation, *The Female Eunuch* echoed with a Rousseauesque reverence for the natural being. Unlike that anti-female philosopher, however, Germaine's idyllic "noble savage" included *women*, most especially the sort she had discovered during her teenage exile to the farm in the midlands of Australia. Lovingly, she quoted one "lusty wench" from a seventeenth-century ballad; provocatively, she prescribed a whopping dose of pornography as an antidote for romantic trash.

Seductive, voluptuous, gracefully erudite, and immediately intriguing, *The Female Eunuch* quickly sold to an American publisher—McGraw-Hill—for $63,000. Sally Kempton, in the *New York Times Book Review*, described it as "art," and the name Germaine Greer was immediately launched into the stratosphere of American feminism.

Like the Americans, Germaine voiced her outrage—in this case, at the male prerogatives to energy, "resource, application, initiative, ambition, desire, motive," at women's enforced fear of freedom, their abandonment of autonomy. At the same time, though, the tilt of her polemic—as male reviewers on both sides of the Atlantic gleefully pointed out—was not scornful of men. Her soaring fountain of energy, unmistakably erotic, was also affectionately, almost caressingly heterosexual.

"Many men are almost as afraid of abandonment, of failing as husbands as their wives are . . ."

"Men are tired of having all the responsibility for sex; it is time they were relieved of it . . ."

"The cunt must come into its own."

The new feminism, according to Germaine, should be directly linked to the vital if still repressed female libido. Not to lesbianism, not to the pompous and "dull" ministrations of the sex clinics of Masters and Johnson, the brouhaha over clitoral orgasms, not even to what the author, back in those days, regarded as Betty Friedan's altogether too conservative association of sex with motherhood. Women should hold out, Germaine wrote, not just for orgasm (certainly not just the clitoral variety) "but for ecstasy." Not the standard "low agitation, cool-out monogamy" of the isolated nuclear family with its "lecherous wife-swapping," but the freedom of independent lovers "always restless to come back." Not women's loathing of the female sexual organs ("No woman wants to find out that she has a twat like a horse-collar . . . ") but the vagina as a "Temple of Venus."

"I only wish," wrote the critic Christopher Lehmann-Haupt, "that the timing of the publication of this book had been such that it could have caught the lightning that struck *Sexual Politics.*"

The lightning was, of course, American media attention, for it was many months after Kate's book had appeared that American reporters came hustling across the Atlantic in search of the newly acclaimed Germaine. *Life* magazine ferreted her out at Warwick University, where she had continued to teach her classes, and found her dressed in a long buckskin shirt, clogs, bangles, and beads. Warwick's "most popular lecturer," *Life* proclaimed, headlining her sartorial view: "I don't go for that whole pants and battledress routine. It just puts men off."

Far from distracting, Germaine's imaginative costumes invariably enhanced her rowdy erudition, not just in the classroom or in front of the TV cameras, but soon, as a sort of feminist standard-bearer, in the halls of staid, conservative British academia. One woman on the faculty of Goldsmith College would report a confrontation in which the male establishment had been lined up like soldiers in the front row of the lecture hall, fully expecting to demolish this free-and-easy, frowzy, undisciplined feminist. Germaine had surprised them. Eschewing baubles, beads, and miniskirt, she had arrived at the college in a fine suit, an unassailably ladylike vision. Instead of pretty songs and revolutionary slogans, Germaine had parried each academic thrust with logic, carefully researched historical data, and a delivery nearly as precise as it was creative. She had staged, as was her wont, a coup.

Still, for Germaine, English audiences were a known quantity. Less comfortable by far were the performances ahead of her. A major book tour was planned by her American publisher, appearances across the United States, and here, on ground already scorched by Betty Friedan and Kate Millett as well as, by then, several other accomplished feminist writers, precious little shock value was in the offing.

Shulamith Firestone's *The Dialectic of Sex,* for instance, was a deadly serious, driving, impatient assault on the "tyranny" of the biological family. It reasoned from a Marxist paradigm and demanded that childbearing be taken over by technology. "Pregnancy," Firestone wrote, "is barbaric."

(People *read* those books, Betty would wail, though *The Feminine Mystique* would by then have sold 1,500,000 copies in paperback.)

Sisterhood Is Powerful, edited by Robin Morgan, was a fiery collection of essays, poems, and manifestos, some of them already well known in the inner circles of radical feminism; others, personal outpourings from diverse women, from Ph.D.s to schoolgirls. Whether amusing, bitter, silly, or hard-headed—and they ran the gamut— each revealed an anguish caused by sexist attitudes.

All this being a bit too much for such "neutral" observers as columnist Pete Hamill.

"Women's Liberation has been the greatest thing to hit the media (and especially that area that specializes in *schlock*) since Jackie Kennedy . . . ," Hamill wrote, "and the people signing the book contracts are all self-described as members of the Movement. Take the money and blame the one who pays."

Which in itself wouldn't have mattered much, except that there was more. Much more. As male commentators began to back off in confusion, the most vehement voices were women's.

"You might have to go back to the Children's Crusade . . . ," wrote Helen Lawrenson in *Esquire,* "to find as unfortunate and fatuous an attempt at manipulated hysteria as the Women's Liberation movement." "Phony," "ludicrous," "vicious"—the movement, she continued, was a "hair-raising emotional orgy of hatred.

"These are not normal women. I think they are freaks . . . incapable of coming to terms with their own natures as females . . . neurotic, inadequate women . . . appallingly selfish . . .

"Besides," this extremely successful writer lectured the insurgents, "has it ever dawned on you that whatever equality women get is given to them by men?"

Mrs. Spiro Agnew, the vice-president's wife, announced that she would "object" if her daughter joined a women's liberation group. Anthropologist Margaret Mead deplored the "utter nonsense" and, in *Commentary,* Arlene Croce protested that the new feminism was "not a liberation movement at all but an attempt to mobilize vengeance." After ripping both Firestone and Morgan, Croce characterized Kate:

"If you were to say to Miss Millett, 'Jack fell down and broke his crown and Jill came tumbling *after*,' she would say, 'A clear case of sexual politics' and carefully note the double significance of the word 'crown.' "

Feminism, scolded Croce, was something that should be "outgrown."

"At twenty it's useful and fulfilling . . . at thirty (and over), it's indulgent and wasteful and, at the present moment in history, not a little crazy. . . . As a set of ideas, Women's Lib is about as creative and inspiring as a set of Tinker Toys . . . its adherents a bunch . . . of ugly women screaming at each other on television."

All this in the America Germaine was about to face in her new role as feminist standard-bearer, a country where, as she very well knew, the feminists themselves, having waged battle for more than half a decade, might easily regard her book as merely a crowd pleaser. All this *plus*—as she discovered even before she departed—Norman Mailer.

The invitation was delivered to Germaine in England. A full-scale debate, she was told, was in the works at New York's Town Hall under the auspices of the prestigious Theatre of Ideas. Four leading feminists had been chosen to participate in a panel discussion that Mailer would moderate. Germaine, who, as she had proclaimed in *The Female Eunuch,* was "sick of pretending that some fatuous male's self-important pronouncements are the objects of my undivided attention," was to be one of these important voices of feminism.

But Norman Mailer was not, of course, simply one of those "fatuous" males. He was, conceivably, America's greatest novelist, the major talent of the age, and since his *Armies of the Night,* even an antiwar hero to Germaine's beloved "peaceniks."

Kate Millett had devoted more than twenty-five pages in *Sexual Politics* to excoriating this priapic, best-selling writer. He was "a prisoner of the virility cult," she had written, a man who had "fallen in love with violence as a personal and sexual style," whose strategy was "fucking to win." His book *An American Dream* was "an exercise in how to kill your wife and be happy ever after." As well as: "Little wonder that Mailer's sexual journalism read like the sporting news grafted onto a series of war dispatches."

Unlike Kate, however, Germaine thoroughly admired Mailer's writing. Her appreciation of his expansive, virile talent, his poeticized sense of the romantic, of the mysteriousness of women could not, for her, be completely subsumed in feminist theory.

"It's absolutely philistine," she told the *New York Times,* "not to recognize what a great book *An American Dream* is." Kate, she added, had "misidentified the enemy."

So yes, of course, she would appear at Town Hall. If nothing else, the invitation was an extraordinary recognition for a new writer, and before she embarked for New York, with all the verve and concentration so much a part of her nature, Germaine began to study, to warm up.

"I was in training," she would write . . . reading and rereading *The Prisoner of Sex*, Mailer's long, brilliantly graphic essay in *Harper's*, which punched and jabbed and generally tormented the youthful corpus of women's liberation.

Midge Decter, writer and editor at *Harper's,* had put Mailer up to that work.

Decter, married to the conservative intellectual editor of *Commentary*, Norman Podhoretz, was no friend of women's lib—or, at any rate, of its new voices. She signed up Mailer for a response to the movement, and the ensuing diatribe not only took up the whole of one month's magazine, but turned out to be the largest-selling issue in the history of *Harper's*.

In *The Prisoner of Sex,* the title an unmentioned bow to Kate's metaphor, Mailer portrayed himself not only as ambushed but "chewed half to death by a squadron of enraged Amazons, an honor guard of revolutionary (if we could only see them) vaginas." And never mind that Gloria had been the one who asked him to run for mayor of New York. Mailer took on the gals with the roar of a hell-of-a-place-to-be-wounded beast.

He culled from the current writing only the most provocative and inflammatory:

"Women, in other words, don't have penis envy. Men have pussy envy" (from Valeria Solanis's SCUM manifesto).

"I no longer need a man . . . no longer see myself through men's eyes" (from *Off Our Backs*).

"The existence of the clitoral orgasm threatens men because it suggests that they are not necessary for a woman's pleasure. Case can be made for the extinction of the male organ" (from Anne Koedt's "The Myth of the Vaginal Orgasm").

Then, hell-for-leather, in his most gorgeous, rolling prose, this powerful writer lit into all of it, noting, along the way, that Bella Abzug had "a voice which could have boiled the fat off a taxicab driver's neck."

Mailer was, of course, polite to Gloria, but he took a mean and skillful scalpel to Kate. She was not, he noted sarcastically, "a future leader of millions for nothing."

The land of Millett, wrote Mailer, "was a foul and dreary place to cross, a stingy country whose treacherous inhabitants . . . jeered at difficulties which were often the heart of the matter. . . . Bile and bubbles of intellectual flatulence coursed in the river, and the bloody ground steamed with the limbs of every amputated quote. Everywhere were signs that men were guilty and women must win."

Kate was "an honor student in some occult school of thuggee (now open to the ladies via the pressures of Women's Liberation . . .)." She wrote like a "gossip columnist," her style suggested to him "a night-school lawyer who sips Metrecal to keep his figure, and thereby is so full of isolated proteins, factory vitamins, reconstituted cyclamates and artificial flavors that one has to pore over the passages like a business contract."

And on and on, until Kate, the writer, emerged as the literary criminal of the age.

Now, it seemed, Mailer intended to go for a second match—this one face-to-face. Kate surely was in no shape for such an encounter.

Germaine, on the other hand . . .

Thoroughly educated, quick with a quip, as the formidable William F. Buckley would soon discover in a debate before the Cambridge Union in England, Germaine was able to match wits and discourse at the highest levels, in or out of academia.

Yet she *was* nervous. Perceiving herself more as gadfly than ideologue, certainly not a leader of the important American women's movement, she worried about her reception. Furthermore, as she would soon discover, many New York feminists were flatly refusing the invitation to appear at Town Hall with Norman Mailer. Kate turned it down, of course, but so did Gloria Steinem. (She would join Norman on a less confrontational panel several months later.) Robin Morgan, according to Germaine's subsequent account in *Esquire,* "said she would come if she could shoot Mailer, citing the particulars of her license to possess a firearm. . . ."

As a matter of fact, the organizers of the debate—Shirley Broughton, author Elizabeth Hardwick, and editor Bob Silvers—were hard put to keep the panel from cracking at the seams. From the day Broughton began planning—more than six months ahead—one or another prospective panelist began backing out, under pressure, as she would describe it, "from the women's libbers." She would even be forced to reprint a flier when a featured speaker suddenly changed her mind.

"I kept telling those party-line women," Broughton would remember, " 'If Norman is such a male chauvinist pig, why don't you come and show him up?' "

Because, of course, since Norman was the moderator, he was bound to run the show. And after what he had done to Kate in *The Prisoner of Sex,* to the entire movement, in fact, why should they cooperate? Why should they open themselves to attack?

Mailer was a formidable foe—the only clearly intelligent male who had seen fit to openly challenge the new feminists. And he himself had spawned this drama, writing, in reference to feminism, that "the themes of his life had gathered here." Furthermore, to judge by his novels, as well as his life, Norman Mailer not only adored women, he was fiercely determined to tame them.

Germaine, however, was hardly the sort to retreat in the face of challenge:

"Imagine my consternation," she would write in *Esquire,* "when the New York women asked me to boycott the whole shindig." Not only would notice of the Town Hall event be printed in the ad for *The Female Eunuch,* but shining brightly in his by-now-famous diatribe was Mailer's praise for *her* book. Germaine would vehemently deny that his literary kudos had influenced her decision, but still, the aroused "Prisoner of Sex" had found *The Female Eunuch* so much to his liking, so completely worthy of his favor, that when he left off, for a page or two, railing against Kate, he had tossed a sweetheart rose at the feet of the remarkable Germaine.

"A wind in this prose," he had written seductively, "whistled up the kilts of male conceit," a sentiment which gave rise, very quickly, to an altogether delicious international rumor that Germaine did absolutely nothing to quell. Mailer obviously admired Germaine, and this cultured, witty foreigner, this femme fatale of a novelist's dreams, America's literati soon heard by the grapevine, had a bit of a yen for our Norman, too.

"She wished to meet Norman and go to bed with him," co-panelist Diana Trilling would later report in *We Must March, My Darlings.*

To fuck him, Jill Johnston would announce in *Lesbian Nation,* for as Germaine herself had told the *New York Times*:

"Norman Mailer is his own worst enemy, and if you don't catch him in a defensive position, he'll admit it. I'd really like to help that man."

And, on another occasion: ". . . to carry him off like a wounded child across the wasted world. . . ."

Thus the stage for Town Hall was set, plot and subplot to wind through the heart of the script. More than a decade later, Norman Mailer would publish a novel called *Ancient Evenings*, in which the hero fought bitterly to maintain control of a harem. Now, in reality, he would enter the female cage—alone.

"Step right up, ladies and gentlemen. See and hear the brilliant, macho novelist Norman Mailer, the avowed 'Prisoner of Sex,' rassle with—among others of the female persuasion—the six-foot-tall, gorgeous, witty, *tres chic* and specially imported revolutionary Germaine Greer."

It would be a night to remember—the first tantalizing meeting of that fantasy couple, sexy symbols of a violent, rebellious, idea-dense decade.

No one could quite imagine what would happen.

17

A
HUNDRED
TROMBONES

A person's not free if their freedom has to be "given."
Who are you to "give" me freedom?

—Erica Jong, *Fear of Flying*, 1973

While Germaine was still writing *The Female Eunuch,* and Kate *Sexual Politics,* while so many women were working on feminist projects, Betty Friedan had been racing from town to town, speech to speech, meeting to meeting. Maybe, some of her friends thought, Betty kept her life in such a frenzy (maybe she had even written *The Feminine Mystique*) just to avoid the problems in her marriage.

The truth was that Betty had been thinking about divorce for quite a while. The "physicality" of the marriage, as some of her friends would put it, was no secret. Just who threw what at whom was debatable. Technically, of course—though the term was yet to have a place in the public lexicon—Betty Friedan was a battered wife. And perhaps, too, Carl was a battered husband.

Yet in a way, or so Betty would see it in retrospect, Carl was actually *more* loving after her book came out.

Well, sometimes.

At other times, more violent.

"Carl was so threatened," she would remember. "My success was

266

threatening to him somehow. I would start to be friends with writers and he would suddenly develop an aversion to writers. . . ."

In the years to come, Betty would generally avoid two subjects of major importance to many women in the movement: pornography and rape, the entire area of physical violence, in fact. Some feminists —Susan Brownmiller among them—would suspect that her reluctance on these subjects was connected to the violence in her own life.

Betty's view was, as usual, more psychoanalytic. "I think there are always two people involved," she would explain. "If you don't have enough confidence to claim your own rage and stand up on your own feet, and you can't bear the fact that you feel this way, then what you do is—unconsciously—you provoke the rage in him. Then you have the black eye, then you feel justified in having the rage."

"It's complicated," she would add.

By 1969, however, that complication, that emotional tango, was threatening to slip into the public arena. There was that tricky moment at the Oak Room of the Plaza Hotel, when Betty needed makeup to cover her black eye. And other times, on television programs, when she feared that the bruises might show.

She wanted to end that destructive scene, but how would it look if the president of NOW—the most visible leader of the women's movement—got a divorce? Would people blame the movement? (Many, in fact, would. Life, at least in the suburbs, still seemed, fixedly, two-by-two.)

At bottom, however, the real trap, the toughest prison of all, was Betty's own monstrous—"pathological," she would call it—fear. Still. In spite of all the activity, the friends, the enemies, the tumult, she was still terrified of being alone.

"I was taking a lot of guff," she would remember. "And I used to think, 'What a phony I am, what a *worm*, a masochist.' On the one hand, I clung. On the other, I had to get out to save my life."

And so, that spring, Betty made another one of those personal pacts she had been making since childhood.

She had been invited to lecture in Zurich, and unlike the children of the affluent fifties, Betty Friedan from Peoria was not wise in the ways of the seasoned traveler. She had been a suburban housewife, raised three kids, and knew what *that* was about. She had stripped the molding and painted the walls and knew what *that* was about. But she had no idea how to get around, or what to say and do, in Europe.

So the pact she made was this:

"If I could go to the lecture, then travel to Rome and Paris, if I could survive staying by myself in a hotel and having dinner by myself and walking around and going into museums . . . If I could do it, then I could get a divorce.

"And I did it."

She traipsed around Paris all by herself, and the loneliness didn't kill her. Then she came home and she told her husband.

"Carl used to threaten divorce to get me to do things he wanted me to do," she would recall, "so when I came back I said, 'Okay we *will*. Get your things out of here. I'm going to the Philharmonic, and when I come back, I want them out.'

"He was surprised and I don't think he believed me. My strength had gotten too much for both of us."

But, she would also add: "I sat through the concert with tears streaming down my face."

And on May 14, 1969, Betty and Carl Friedan obtained a Mexican divorce.

"The loneliness," she would admit, "was never as bad as I thought it would be."

Later that year, however, the pots and pans and sugar bowls that had flown at home would come clanging and clamoring into the press.

"Betty has a great need to be independent on the surface," Carl would tell a reporter. "What she is actually is a very dependent little girl. And she keeps fighting that."

Betty: "He hated my success and he would throw my schedules, my notes, all over the house."

Carl: "She hates men. Let's face it, they all do—all those activists in the women's lib movement. I've seen 'em traipse through my living room."

B: "There are men I love and men who love me. . . . Man is not the enemy."

C: "I just didn't take her crap anymore."

B: "A man who is strong enough to be gentle will be strong enough to march with the woman who is leaving behind her ruffles and her rage."

C: "That's straight crap. A strong man cannot stay married to this type of woman. Betty never washed a hundred dishes during twenty years of marriage."

B: "I've done my share. He got away with murder because our

attitudes were different then. I never even thought of asking him to help."

She would ask him to help, however, with child support. Carl was to pay $100 a week toward support of the couple's three children. In 1972, he would petition Family Court for a reduction to $25. Married to a model by then (though later divorced), Carl would claim that Betty's ability to earn money was "practically unlimited."

"This is not the case of a starving mother and child," he would tell the judge. "She is a world-famous woman with an income of $40,000 a year."

Carl would lose that case, and a few years later Betty would successfully sue and receive from him $13,300 in back payments.

"It wasn't alimony," she would insist, raising once again that thorny point in the feminist argument.

Meanwhile, Betty ignored—as best she could—the press reports, and went on with the business of NOW, hammering away, at every opportunity, at that "partnership with men."

Nobody—least of all men—could know, of course, quite *how* it would all happen, or predict the force of the tornado.

The most cunning protested that women were the most powerful creatures on earth *right now*—males being their slaves, wrapped around little fingers, etc.

Others seemed only to hear the sound and fury of women's voices. Many—even those who tried—didn't quite understand.

Had they insulted women in some way? Wives? Girlfriends? Did it have something to do with . . . *sex?* Or were these women, now let's get right down to it, really after their jobs?

Snide remarks about Betty crackled over the caviar canapés and the onion dip alike, from big-city penthouses to the paneled family rooms of suburban split-levels. About Betty's looks, her prominent nose, her "abrasive" manner, her "missing" husband.

Nonetheless, the message was spreading.

Major religious institutions, the United Presbyterian Church among them, appointed task forces to study sex discrimination. Female high school students were suing to take shop classes, and a feminist radio program was on the air.

Betty and NOW charged that NASA discriminated against women, gaining, for that effrontery, the clever headline: "Space? NOW

Women Ask to Go There Too." She flew to Chicago to help form the National Association for Repeal of Abortion Laws, and early in 1970 she argued vehemently against the appointment of Judge G. Harrold Carswell to the Supreme Court.

Carswell had approved an employer's right to refuse to hire a woman (though not a man) with preschool-age children, and Betty's testimony before the Senate Judiciary Committee marked the first time that such a nomination had been challenged on the basis of a record of sex discrimination.

"Over 25 percent of mothers with children under six are in the labor force," Betty wrote in a letter to President Nixon. "Eighty-five percent of them work for economic reasons. Over half a million are widowed, divorced or separated. Their incomes are vitally necessary to the support of those children."

And, while she was at it, she threw the senators a curve—the possibility of a woman on the Supreme Court. *That* wild idea, which the senators regarded, of course, as just another silly women's joke, would become a reality a decade later. Still, Carswell's nomination was blocked.

Meanwhile, Betty was preparing for the moment when she would have to step down from the presidency of NOW.

She had held that post, battling for her cause, for four years, the organization's constitutional limit. Like all NOW leaders (except for a few staff members), she had been paying her own expenses, transportation and the like, and her personal costs were escalating into the thousands of dollars. She was divorced, the book she had planned to write was late (nonexistent, as it turned out), and she was worried about money.

Also, the proposed new president of NOW, Aileen Hernandez, was black.

"Well," Betty would confess years later, "you know what *that* guilt trip was like. . ."

Indeed, that year, no issue could have been more sensitive. Two Black Panthers had been shot dead in Chicago, two unarmed black prisoners had been killed at Soledad, and black radical Angela Davis would soon be on trial for murder. Daniel Moynihan's "benign neglect" memorandum to the president—"We may need a period in which Negro progress continues and racial rhetoric fades"—drew howls of liberal protest. Racism, as many saw it, was a far greater concern than sexism. Black men were fighting and dying in Vietnam in numbers far beyond any fair representation, and many black women had little patience with the idea of a white housewife from Larchmont in the role of "oppressed victim." What, after all, was to guarantee that newly "liberated" white women wouldn't use their advantage for the same age-old class privilege? Nor had the press overlooked the embarrassingly low numbers of black women in NOW, or for that matter in the entire women's movement.

So, for a bunch of reasons, Betty was stepping down.

Not that anybody really knew for sure why Betty did or didn't do *anything*. Why, for example, she so tirelessly courted Bella Abzug, the feisty Bronx lawyer who was running for Congress. Or Gloria Steinem. Betty seldom discussed her decisions with her colleagues beforehand. Sometimes, they seemed to erupt from some deep, steaming well inside her.

No one really *knew*, for example, why she was suddenly so disenchanted with Dolores Alexander, the woman who had put so many of Betty's ideas into action. Dolores was a sensible, professional type, certainly not one to promote what Betty had now taken to calling the "pseudoradical copout, which talks about test-tube babies, eliminating men and the one-sex society."

Dolores had become executive secretary of NOW, a paid position. She and Betty had recently traveled to Los Angeles together, where, Dolores would remember, she didn't think much of the way Betty was ordering people around.

"You can't do that, Betty," Dolores would remember objecting. "These people are working for nothing."

When they were in San Francisco, Dolores would also recall, Betty didn't like the looks of things. The women who were running that chapter, she told Dolores, looked "dykey."

Did Betty think Dolores was too sympathetic to lesbians, top NOW officials wondered. And was Betty's skittishness on that subject simply Peoria-bred naivete—or foreboding?

Whatever the reason, that winter Betty exploded over the subject of Dolores. If the executive committee of NOW did not oust its executive secretary immediately, she threatened ominously, well, by God, she would call a press conference and announce to the world that NOW was being taken over by lesbians!

Worried and nervous, the NOW leadership—Kay Clarenbach and Muriel Fox among them—powwowed on the spot, putting through a conference phone call that spanned half the country. They pleaded with Betty for hours. Dolores, at their behest, had left a job at *Newsday* that paid over $10,000 a year for one that brought little over half that much at NOW. And she was *effective.*

But Betty argued, bellowed into the phone (as was often her wont), and, eventually, Muriel would remember, "she wore us all down." And though, even many years later, Betty would still refuse to discuss this particular incident, she would publicly air her belief that there had been a conspiracy, that the CIA and FBI, acting as *agents provocateurs,* had encouraged an attempt by lesbians to take over NOW, that she had been informed, in fact, that to facilitate this takeover, a lesbian had been assigned to seduce *her.*

The NOW officials, hard put to remember what Betty's stated reasons were, would recall only that, at the time, her distress had run too deep to ignore, like some jagged earth fault threatening to crack the whole thing open. If Betty wouldn't—or couldn't—work with her executive secretary, nothing would hold.

And so, with no more ado, Dolores—who had worked with Betty all those years—was out.

Traumatized, the ex-journalist went home to try to piece her life together. The idea of a lesbian relationship, she would remember, "hadn't even entered my mind."

Within two years, however, Dolores would indeed find solace in the lesbian world she had been accused of inhabiting.

In late March of 1970, at the third annual NOW convention at the O'Hare Inn outside Chicago, Aileen Hernandez, the new president of NOW, was installed and a special high-level post created for its unpredictable founder.

Betty's outgoing speech trumpeted on for at least two hours. Fidel Castro, friends kidded her, couldn't have done it better.

"Our sisterhood," Betty exhorted the two hundred members gathered there, "is powerful. The awesome political power of 53 percent of the population. . . . The rage women have so long taken out on themselves, on their own bodies, and covertly on their husbands and children, is exploding now. . . . In this era of recession . . . there is bound to be more resistance than we have yet encountered. We are going to have to show that we mean it. . . . There is an urgency in this moment . . ."

And the divine afflatus roared on, only to wind down, at last, with the rousing cry: "I have led you into history. I leave you now—to make new history."

An ambiguous note, perhaps, but behind it, glowing like a phosphorescent bead in those crashing waves of rhetoric, had been Betty's surprise move.

She was not, apparently, about to relinquish the making of history *quite* so quickly.

In that same speech—and later on a Chicago radio station—the once-lonely little girl from Peoria staked her claim. In a sudden move that took the NOW leadership completely by surprise, Betty wired out a great rousing rallying call to *"every American woman."* On August 26, 1970, she proclaimed, on the fiftieth anniversary of women's suffrage in America, there would be a nationwide, twenty-four-hour "women's strike for equality."

It would be "an instant revolution against sexual oppression" and it would take place in *every city in the nation.*

"It is our responsibility to history, to ourselves, to all who will come after us . . ." she alerted the country.

"I therefore propose . . . that the women who are doing menial chores in the offices as secretaries put the covers on their typewriters and close their notebooks and the telephone operators unplug their switchboards, the waitresses stop waiting, cleaning women stop cleaning and everyone who is doing a job for which a man would be paid more . . . stop.

"When it begins to get dark, instead of cooking dinner or making love, we will assemble, and we will carry candles symbolic of the flame of that passionate journey down through history—relit anew in every city . . .

"Women will occupy for the night the political decision-making arena and sacrifice a night of love to make the political meaning clear . . ."

The NOW women, of course, were stunned.

Who was going to pull this thing together? Who the hell was going to do all the work?

By then, political bombast was thundering out of Washington as Richard Nixon sought to calm the country's outrage over his secret bombing of Cambodia, and the press was screaming about a "credibility gap." Nearly every paper in the country was *bound* to carry some notice of this grandiloquent speech of Betty's, this call for a *nationwide* strike of women. What if they couldn't carry it off?

273

Talk about your "credibility gap," they muttered as they fanned out, that spring, to pass the word.

By summer, Betty was commanding her forces from the Hamptons, from her "commune," as she liked to call her rented summer home.

Five people "communed" there that summer—Betty and her ten-year-old daughter, Emily, two men friends, and Betty Rollin, who would soon write *First You Cry*, the moving account of her breast cancer. In the next few years, there would be more. More people and more holidays, different houses out there in the sweet, salt air of the Long Island coast. Thanksgiving. Christmas. There would be no husband for Betty, no father for Emily or the boys, so instead Betty would create what she wanted so deeply. Family.

"A funny little family," Betty Rollin would recall, along with domestic scenes that were etched in her memory:

> *Early one Sunday morning in a big old white frame house in the Hamptons. A bedroom door slowly opens. Out pads a small, plump, full-bosomed, distinctly female creature in an athletic suit—an early version of the ubiquitous "sweats" of the eighties. Through the hall . . . thump, thump, thump . . . and then down a long flight of stairs into a large kitchen. The tousled head of this five foot, two inch apparition is quite large in proportion to the body, and it is hung low.*
>
> *"I was bad," it announces to the assembled group of eminent writers, philosophers, sociologists.*

This is Betty Friedan. The visionary. The power. The leader of the new women's movement.

She tied one on last night, but, of course, so did they all. The kids may be shredding their jeans with pinking shears to make cutoffs, singing along to Bob Dylan records, tippling in Boone's Farm Apple Wine and grass, but Mommy and Daddy are still laying into highballs, vodka martinis, and scotch on the rocks. This is the well-over-thirty group, those "establishment" types, according to the slogan of the day, you're not supposed to "trust."

In this intellectually high-powered bunch, the dinner table conversation is, of course, lofty, although, in truth, subjects such as dialectical materialism give way very quickly to: "Whose turn is it to do the dishes? Who did them last?"

"I did *so!*" Betty yells, and everybody jumps into the act, shushing, shouting, but *caring,* loving each other, Rollin would remember, especially loving the adorable, pulled-together Emily, whose contribution, more often than not, is a plaintive "Oh, Mom. . . ."

Unlike her daughter, Mom is not pulled together. Mom is a scattered, inspired frazzle of passion, analysis, schemes. Always thinking. Or talking. Or thinking and talking at the same time. Mom is now planning the greatest demonstration for women's rights in the history of the world, or so she imagines, the strike that will prove, as she has confidently proclaimed, "our revolution" as "a fact." She is doing all this without an address book, scribbling numbers on every available surface. Shreds of paper, matchbook covers. Searching for them, she rummages around by the wall telephone in the kitchen, growing more and more frustrated, angrier and angrier.

Betty Rollin, meanwhile, often sits at the dining-room table working on her article for *Look* magazine that makes a case against motherhood. (It's a wrong-headed idea, Friedan has said, but she respects Rollin and never discourages her from writing it.)

And Rollin, overhearing the mounting disorder in the kitchen, the huffing and puffing, the tempest brewing, calls out in exasperation:

"Look, Betty, they have these *books!* They are *alphabetical.* You write people's *names* in them, and then you write their *telephone numbers* and you put in their *addresses!*"

"Yeah, I know, I know," Betty mutters, and then finally—Eureka! —comes upon the number she needs and forges ahead, shouting into the phone—capital letters, as usual, italics—knocking herself out to sign up marchers.

Phoning people is the extent of Betty's kitchen duty. Anything else has proved disastrous.

If Betty went out to do the shopping, she would inevitably return with the major ingredient of the meal—the meat, for instance—missing. If she cleaned the table, she'd push and push with one finger, carefully wrapped in a rag or towel, until something of a minor artwork emerged. ("Fingerpainting," Rollin would call it.) She would begin setting the table, thinking, talking aloud to anyone who was there, plotting some grand scheme, put down a knife and fork, and then either not find the napkins or go off to answer the phone and forget what she had been doing.

Impossible!

"But it was clear to us all," Betty Rollin would remember, "that

275

what Betty was doing sprang from her heart. She had seen the light and she was following it. And she was special."

Not so special, perhaps, when the booze hit the bloodstream and the Friedan temper ran so high that she would yell at someone who didn't deserve it.

"I was naughty," she would say on those mornings after, and she would be forgiven. ("A person would have to be made of stone," in Rollin's view, "not to melt at the sight of a contrite Betty.")

Then the passionate phoning and planning would begin once more.

A gala fund-raising party was now on the agenda. It would be held in early August at the Hamptons estate of Ethel Scull, wealthy wife of the taxicab magnate. Betty and her NOW colleagues rounded up a dazzling array of influential co-hostesses: among them, Gloria Vanderbilt Cooper and the glamorous political columnist Gloria Steinem.

So now Betty needed a dress.

Betty Rollin took over the task of shopping with her, and therefore, Rollin would always insist, the catastrophe that was soon to follow was entirely *her* fault.

"I don't know what I had in mind," she would remember guiltily. "I think I wanted Betty to look feminine."

If only because, perhaps, hostile remarks were still spitting off the presses. Harriet Van Horne, for one, called Betty "she of the feminine mystique and the unfeminine technique" and coined the label "Women's Frustration Movement."

The gossip was lethal, and you heard it everywhere. "That Betty Friedan is a dyke!"

"I mean," Rollin would insist, "how naive can you be?"

It was true, of course, that Betty was no Mary Tyler Moore, no traditional beauty, but everyone who knew her—Rollin included—also knew how much Betty adored men, knew that she was, in fact, an unabashed flirt, often irritating female acquaintances with her attention to the opposite sex. And there were lovers, too, men whom, Betty herself would one day confess, she had loved "not wisely but too well."

It did not follow from this, however, that Betty was either focused on or skillful with her appearance. Her mind, it seemed, was elsewhere. And Rollin worried.

"So many of the women at the party would be fashionably dressed," she would remember thinking. "Gloria Steinem, for instance. Nobody had to tell *her* what to wear!" (And indeed, Gloria would appear in a backless, Indian-style dress, looking as cool as one of Ethel Scull's deftly articulated sculptures.)

Betty, on the other hand, "needed help."

And so that week before the party, under Rollin's concerned supervision, Betty bought *The Dress.*

"It was pretty," Betty Rollin would remember. Red with white polka dots. Ankle length. Puffed sleeves. With a scoop-neck, plunging neckline that showed off Betty's generous chest.

So far so good. And on August 9, they all set out for the party at the stunning Scull estate.

It was a starkly green spread, manicured gardens dotted with sculptures, but immediately, there were certain inconveniences. The house, with its famed art collection, was off limits, and only one bathroom was available.

Furthermore, some of the guests (including Gloria Vanderbilt) didn't show, reportedly because their husbands had forbidden it, had even torn up the invitations. One important speaker disappeared. She wasn't a women's liberationist after all, she told Charlotte Curtis, then the *New York Times's* society reporter, particularly if it had anything to do with "bra burning." Many guests thought that women's liberation had mainly to do with unfettered (and, inevitably, sexy) garb. Body stockings, for instance, were "fashionably liberated." And one local resident, noting that it was her first feminist party, said she was waiting for something to happen.

And something, of course, *did.*

From a microphone at the side of the pool, Betty drummed up support for the strike and fought the "radical chic" image.

"It is time to finish the unfinished revolution of American women. . . . This party is a great event . . . a *political* event and not just a fashionable event to get women into the paper!"

Shouts, bravas, boos. In the midst of which, all of a sudden, a young woman stripped off her jeans and jumped into the swimming pool—a response, as some saw it, to the closing of the bathrooms. Not only was the young woman braless, as Curtis subsequently reported, but, when she surfaced, she yanked off her shirt and floated around the pool on her back.

Jill Johnston—a *Village Voice* columnist who had by then publicly proclaimed her lesbianism—was the half-naked swimmer, and the sharp ears of the *Times* reporter immediately caught Betty muttering:

"One of the biggest enemies of this movement . . ."

But, of course, that was the least of it.

There was something worse.

Unknown to the author of *The Feminine Mystique* even as she held forth at the microphone, something in *The Dress* had given way.

She spilled out of it.

Bountifully.

Unreservedly.

And everybody talked . . .

Pictures of Betty with her bosom almost completely exposed appeared in the papers the next day. Which would lead, very soon, to an outcry from the young radicals. Betty, one of them would complain to reporters, had a "star complex." She was purposely seductive.

After the party, Betty began spending more and more time in the city, making more and more phone calls, sending out thousands of circulars.

She held meetings—fractious, noisy conclaves, it turned out—at her apartment on West 93rd Street, at meeting rooms around the city, and then, finally, at the strike headquarters on Lexington Avenue.

Where Trotskyites shrieked that Betty was too middle class, middle-class women blurted that the radicals were "crazies," and Betty once found herself shouting over the din: "Isn't anybody here interested in child care?"

She raced around drumming up support. Up to Boston to preach with feminist theologian Mary Daly, down to lower Manhattan to confer with Bella Abzug, to a press conference to spearhead a boycott against advertising that depicted women as "playthings, inferior or frivolous"—Silva Thin cigarettes, Ivory Liquid dishwashing soap, the new-on-the-scene Pristine vaginal deodorant, and, well, okay, even her friend Helen Gurley Brown's *Cosmopolitan* magazine. Galloping, galloping. Always aware, though, that her own vision of a women's revolution—*she* herself—was on the line.

For as nearly everyone admitted, the real leadership (along with the purse strings, meager as they were) was hers. The enormous, nationwide strike, its spearhead scheduled for the exact same thoroughfare the suffragists had marched fifty years ago, was "Betty's baby."

Including the problems.

Should she, for instance, have called it a "strike"?

Most women, she and her colleagues soon realized, wouldn't have the nerve to stay away from work. Or—another one of her grand promises—to dump their babies on their bosses' laps . . .

And so they decided, after all, to focus on the "march" aspect of the protest and to have it begin *after* working hours.

Then there was her proclamation that women "sacrifice a night of love to make the political meaning clear." Further, that "men have thought of women as sexual objects for too long," and that "every woman must write her own bill of rights. She must present her ultimatum privately to her husband."

Concerned, on second thought, about the antagonistic, anti-male tone of all that, Betty quickly reversed gears. The war, she rushed to reassure, was not to be "fought in the bedroom." (The backtrack hadn't been quite quick enough. Some press notices were already projecting the whole plan as a replay of the women's sex strike in *Lysistrata,* with husbands banned from bed and board.)

And the sensitive, delicate black issue.

Betty sought to smooth the edges, to welcome black women into the movement by starting the march in Harlem, but that notion soon dissolved in the impossible logistics. So the problem—in this age of "sensitivity sessions," of moral outrage—still loomed.

And what if the whole thing dissolved in some freaky, crazy, New Left violence jag? Fights, confrontations, even riots?

Or, perhaps worst of all, what if nobody—or hardly anybody—showed up?

After Betty and her forces had commandeered (or so she had blithely proclaimed) the grandest of New York's boulevards, what if only a few brave souls straggled onto Fifth Avenue or any Main Street across the country? What if, in short, Betty was *wrong,* and American women—secretaries, housewives, salespeople, waitresses—did *not,* in fact, identify with feminism. Or even if, secretly, they *did* sympathize, were too scared to admit it, terrified of the sneers, unwilling to risk the brickbats: "strident," "unfeminine," "ugly," "repressed."

What a field day for the media that would be! "Women's Lib—The Fad Passes." "Women to Libbers: Drop Dead!"

It could flop. Miserably. It could sputter and peter out like some silly home movie, played, to Betty's acute embarrassment, on national TV.

Even with the impressive array of sponsors Betty and her strike force had rounded up. Congresswoman Shirley Chisholm (who had actually announced, blessedly, that she had felt more discrimination as a woman than a black), ex-congresswoman Jeanette Rankin, Congresswoman Bella Abzug, Kate Millett, Gloria Vanderbilt Cooper, "comedienne"—as she was described in the papers—Joan Rivers, Eleanor Holmes Norton, head of the New York City Human Rights Commission, Ronnie Eldridge, special assistant to New York mayor John Lindsay, Beulah Sanders of the National Welfare Rights Organization, Gloria Steinem, Manhattan councilwoman Carol Greitzer, Flo Kennedy. And the amazing variety of groups: NOW, YWCA, New York Radical Feminists, the Redstockings, the Radicalesbians, the National Coalition of American Nuns, the National Welfare Rights Organization, the Older Women's Liberation, Feminists in the Arts, WITCH, Women's Strike for Peace, and Columbia Women's Liberation.

Even with all this support, it could *still* flop! In fact, bets were on that it *would*.

Because they didn't really *have* Fifth Avenue.

The fact was that Betty—after her ripping, cathedral prediction of an outpouring of millions and millions of women—had failed to convince Mayor Lindsay to clear Fifth Avenue for a women's march. They could have one sidewalk only, he had told her, because, after all, 5:30 P.M. was rush hour! Never mind that the suffragists had marched there fifty years ago or that nearly every ethnic group in America paraded down that street on one holiday or another! Lindsay was just not buying the idea of women as an organized group, a voting bloc.

So even if a great number of women did turn out, almost anything could happen. Would the city cops run them off the street with billy clubs? Charge through them with their horses?

"How could we have a gigantic parade down the sidewalk?" Betty worried.

Yet by that summer they had come so far. Dr. Edgar F. Berman, who five months earlier had claimed that women were unfit for high office, had now resigned—under women's attacks—from the Democratic National Committee. The United Federation of Teachers had come out in support of feminist aims, and the secretary of labor had admitted that discrimination against women is "subtle and more pervasive than any other minority [sic] group."

That week, women demonstrated at the Statue of Liberty. They hung banners:

"Women of the World Unite."

"Strike August 26."

Still, as dawn broke on the morning of August 26, the whole grand, impossible dream was up for grabs, in spite of Betty's brave claim to reporters:

"This is our hour of history," she said grimly. "We're going to take it."

Which was why, that morning, as befit the potential leader of millions, Betty just plain refused to think about it.

Instead, she very prudently hied herself to the fancy beauty salon of Vidal Sassoon, emerging at 10 A.M. with her shoulder-length hair curled smoothly, looking very much like, in one reporter's view, "a gray-haired combination of Hermione Gingold and Bette Davis." Her official strike button—a white medical symbol for women with a clenched fist in the center—was pinned on a simple, raspberry-colored dress she had bought in Finland three years before. She hadn't had time to get a new one, but the dress was pretty and—this time—thoroughly secure.

It was sunny and warm. Thank God, at least, for that!

Already, of course, there were nay-sayers. That very morning, the *New York Times* published an article quoting important members of traditional women's groups pasting feminists with such labels as "ridiculous exhibitionists," a "band of wild lesbians," and "Communists." The incoming president of the 23-million-member National Council of Women complained that the movement had no legitimate purpose at all.

"There's no discrimination against women like they say there is," Mrs. Saul Schary decreed. "Women themselves are just self-limiting, it's in their nature and they shouldn't blame it on society or men. . . . [They are] doing it *'pour le sport.'* There's been too much emphasis everywhere on youth and drugs and Black Panthers and these women just said to themselves, 'What can we do to get in the act?'

"And," added this women's leader, "so many of them are just so unattractive. I wonder if they're completely well."

Harriet Van Horne had been at it again, complaining in the *New York Post* that women's libbers were uncombed, untidy, castrating shrews, viragos who regarded "feminine women" as their enemy. This time she even confessed to having shared an elevator with a bunch of them, and composed a rhyme: "I much admire / Your pluck and fire / But must you smell / So *au naturel?*"

No wonder that a reporter might regard Betty's trip to the hairdresser as newsworthy.

"I don't want people to think women's lib girls don't care about how they look," Betty calmly assured him. "We should try to look as pretty as we can."

And then . . . the kickoff.

City Hall Park. Twelve noon. The first of many events around town preceding the climactic march at 5:30 P.M.

A model day-care center graces the corner of the park, as planned, but *where is everyone?* Could this be *it?* Only a couple hundred?

Well, it is still early . . .

Betty marches to the mike, launches into her opening salvo. About free abortion, day care, equality in pay and education—the three major goals of the march.

"Louder! Louder!" come shouts from the audience.

". . . women . . . aware of their power . . ."

"Louder! Louder!"

Oh, my God, the microphone. It's dead! Nobody can hear!

Fix it! Can't you fix this damned—?

But the women around her can't, don't know *how* to fix the mike.

Total despair. From the audience, you can see it on Betty's face. As if the whole thing was finished.

She collapses back against the sound truck, slouches there, leaning on the door.

"The men in this country fight the wars, so what are you women complaining about?" It is a black woman. She has sprung to the dead mike, shouting to the crowd. "You got all the rights you need!"

A reporter, standing nearby and watching Betty at that moment, thought she seemed like a Civil War general, waiting for news of a distant battle, certain of defeat.

Then suddenly, deus ex machina, a small group of men appears. They fiddle with the microphone for a few minutes, adjust this, replug that, and then, with a quick flex of muscle, hoist both it and the plump, glum, blinking little feminist leader clear to the top of the sound truck.

All at once, Betty's face brightens. And when, with appropriate fanfare, one of the men presents her with a proclamation from the deputy mayor, securing the day as Women's Equality Day in New York, the passionate sparkle flies back to her dark eyes.

Now, suddenly, Betty's world is transformed. *Official recognition!* She has got—the march has got—a fighting chance. (Men, as she has insisted, over and over, are not the enemy.)

She rolls out a short but impassioned speech and then turns the platform over to the recruits. The feisty Bella Abzug, who pumps her fist in anger. Gloria Steinem.

Gloria stands in City Hall Park, pretending not to be nervous, ignoring the whistles and hoots from the crowd. Like Lear's Cordelia, her voice is "ever soft, gentle, and low—an excellent thing in a woman."

"Hey, I'd like to liberate *that,*" remarks one man in the audience, and journalist Pete Hamill, who is observing the scene, will report that comment in his column.

Meanwhile, Betty, recharged, trots off to Wall Street, where a group of NOW women are protesting the minuscule sprinkling of women on the Stock Exchange.

1:15 P.M.

Betty promenades into the formerly "men only" dining room of Whyte's Restaurant downtown on Fulton Street. Are the women she is lunching with secretaries? a customer asks.

"That's what I call a male supremacist remark," she shouts, banging the table. "These girls are security analysts!"

Several male patrons bring their menus for Betty to autograph.

"My wife said she was going to get liberated today," one of them offers with a sheepish grin. Betty nods her approval, orders crabmeat and two whiskey sours with fresh lemon juice and no cherry. After lunch, she begins her trek around town to various demonstrations. She travels by public bus. Alone.

2:45 P.M. The Federal Building.

The doors have been shut in the faces of the demonstrators allocated to the Social Security office. Betty bangs on the plate glass, demands a dialogue with the commissioner.

3:30 P.M. The East Side.

Betty joins the protest against supermarket products that degrade women.

And back on the bus. To another event. And another.

By now her feet hurt. Yet everywhere, there is that look—homage, hope—in women's eyes. They wish her luck and she smiles.

"Join us, sisters, join us," she calls.

The afternoon wears on until finally there is no more time.

It is nearly 5:30.

"Our revolution will be a fact . . ."

The bus, mired in midtown traffic, moves in agonizing slow fits and starts. It carries her to a stop near 59th Street, chugs to the curb, and Betty climbs down. She walks a block to Fifth, where they have been told to gather. Wearily she turns the corner.

Then she sees . . .

Not ten. Not a hundred. Not even hundreds . . .

There must be thousands! Thousands clustered in the Grand Army of the Republic Plaza, the bronze statue of General Sherman looming above them. Mostly women, but many brave men as well, waiting, the sun slanting between the skyscrapers, glancing off the windshields of taxicabs, flashing on . . .

Posters. Banners.

"Don't Iron While the Strike Is Hot."

"Only Four Women in the Bronx Earn Over $10,000."

"Pray to God/She Will Help."

Stunning women in Pucci dresses wave these banners. Frizzled, grizzled old-timers, too. Braless kids in bell-bottom jeans, crisp, businesslike office workers, women carrying their babies, blacks, Puerto Ricans, husbands, boyfriends.

A small, deep sigh escapes.

"Marvelous," Betty breathes.

And now she steps to her place at the front of the crowd, reaches for a hand on each side.

Join hands, she calls, and as they do, they begin inching forward, a narrow line slowly and obediently moving along the sidewalk, easing toward 58th Street.

And now 57th.

The cars and buses still roam down the avenue; the mounted police prance at their side. The marchers in front begin to peer behind them, jump up to assess the crowd. The ranks, they begin to see, are swelling. Waves and waves of people are expanding the side of the line, flowing in behind. The march is overrunning the walk, spilling out into the street!

The cops retrench. They have no other choice. They *halt* the traffic!

There is no stopping it now. The march fills the avenue from curb to curb.

Down and down it flows. Past Bergdorf's and Bonwit's. Past Tiffany's and Cartier's. Past the glittering windows of Saks Fifth Avenue and the great globe at Rockefeller Center.

The narrow band has become a great, surging mass, packing the street all the way back to Central Park. It has *taken over!*

Fifth Avenue is ours!

Nine thousand, the *New York Post* would estimate. Twenty thousand (the police). Fifty thousand (the organizers).

To say nothing of spectators along the side, controlled, when necessary, by the cops.

And it is, sometimes, necessary. Not *all* is peaceful. Not *all* are convinced.

Hecklers in front of St. Patrick's Cathedral, calling themselves "MOM—Men Our Masters," hurl themselves toward the marchers, and are duly carted off by the police.

Some men are angry.

"Baby killers!" they shout.

"Frustrated bitches!"

"Cunts!"

They sneer, hoot, threaten the male marchers, and shout at the women: "If your mothers had had abortions, you wouldn't be here today, you baby killers!"

"Such a thing could never take place in Italy," mutters a female Italian journalist. "The men would destroy them."

And from others:

"I don't think taking over Fifth Avenue is a very great thing. They must be divorced. Or single. Or frustrated."

"I favor equal rights, but to carry it to such an extreme!"

"I think women are doing pretty good. We even have our own cigarettes."

"Stupid, ridiculous, a complete waste of time. Why did they have to prove they were better than men?"

"I have all the rights I need."

But there, too, cheering them on, are those who cannot march. Grateful supporters. A woman whose small children are clinging to her hands, a secretary who had promised to work late.

"Right on! Right on!"

What no one can miss, what taps and clicks under each marching foot, is a jazzy rhythm, an emotion few have ever before associated with the women's movement.

Joy.

It sweeps up in the summer sun of Manhattan like the cry of a hundred shiny trombones, the ring and crash of a forest of timpani. Women—all kinds, all classes, all shapes and sizes—have come together here. From distance. From isolation. There is consumerist Betty Furness marching next to a beautician from Queens. There is Helen Gurley Brown of *Cosmopolitan* (bravely, in spite of the censure), Shana Alexander, editor of *McCall's*, next to a suburban housewife with a child on her shoulders. Dick Kaplan of *Ladies' Home Journal*, Gloria Steinem carrying a poster of the My Lai massacre, the legend reading: "The Masculine Mystique."

Other homemade banners pop up. "Don't Cook. Starve a Rat Today." "You Get Paid for Your Brains or Your Legs?" "Up Against the Wall Male Chauvinist Pig Doctors." "Women Strike for Peace and Equality."

"Right on! Right on!"

Until, finally, the great parade reaches Bryant Park and the culmination. Speeches by Kate Millett, Ti-Grace Atkinson, and many others, with Gloria emceeing it all. Betty, drawing the most tumultuous response:

"In the religion of my ancestors, there was a prayer that Jewish men said every morning. They prayed, 'Thank thee, Lord, that I was not born a woman.' Today . . . all women are going to be able to say . . . 'Thank thee, Lord, that I was born a woman, for this day. . . .'

"After tonight, the politics of this nation will never be the same again. . . . There is no way any man, woman, or child can escape the nature of our revolution . . ."

In Boston that day, clerics had turned pulpits over to women. In Chicago, feminists had demonstrated against the "male chauvinism" of *Playboy*. In Syracuse, high school and college women performed satiric skits in front of a "charm school." Joan Rivers had urged women working in TV to break into programs to express support for the strike, and thirteen women had lunched without incident at the Oak Room of the Plaza Hotel.

New York governor Nelson Rockefeller proclaimed August 26 Women's Rights Day. Richard Nixon issued a proclamation noting that women would "surely have" a "wider role to play. . . ."

In San Francisco, Baltimore, Miami, that day, women marched and shattered tea cups, and yes, some few *did* deposit kids on their bosses' laps.

And the press, finally, sobered up.

"Don't joke about women's liberation," cautioned the editorial page of the *Miami Herald.* "Despite the humorous outlook that prevails when the boys talk it over," admitted the *Washington Star,* "the drive for women's equality is a serious political movement that could have a profound effect on American life."

The march had retired the canard about women's libbers being ugly and repressed, wrote Pete Hamill, though not without noting the presence of one expensively dressed lady with "the remnants of what must have been one of the earlier American nose jobs spreading over her face." Still, Hamill, for one, hadn't "seen so many beautiful women in one place in years."

Among them, of course, was Gloria Steinem.

"Most of the men I know are in love with Gloria Steinem," Hamill wrote, "and it isn't difficult to understand why." Adding with *almost* as much exuberance: "Well, the laughing and the snickering are now officially over." What had been "a cocktail party topic, a media fad or a slightly obscene joke" is a movement that is "only beginning."

In Washington, for instance, where Senate hearings on the ERA were slated for September and for which Betty immediately sallied off to lobby.

"From now on," she announced, "our thrust will be political." And then, in an obvious jab at the radical groups, she briskly dismissed what she called their "navel-gazing rap sessions."

"We know our power, we know how many we are, and I almost think we need a new name, instead of 'women's lib.' Something with no anti-man note about it . . ."

18

TOWN
BLOODY HALL

But will you woo this wild-cat?

Why came I hither but to that intent?
Think you a little din can daunt mine ears?
Have I not in my time heard lions roar?
Have I not heard the sea, puff'd up with winds,
Rage like an angry boar chafed with sweat?
Have I not heard great ordnance in the field,
And heaven's artillery thunder in the skies?
Have I not in a pitched battle heard
Loud 'larums, neighing steeds, and trumpets' clang?
And do you tell me of a woman's tongue,
That gives not half so great a blow to hear
As will a chestnut in a farmer's fire?
Tush, tush! fear boys with bugs.

—William Shakespeare, *The Taming of the Shrew*,
Act I, Scene 2

April 30, 1971. You might have thought they were raffling off Nobel Prizes. You hardly needed to see them all packed into Town Hall, steaming with energy, to be struck half dumb by what this feverish, expectant gathering was all about, the devilry of this supercharged, intellectual circus.

The place had been sold out for weeks. All sorts of important folks rushing up the creaky old stairs to Shirley Broughton's studio on West 21st Street to capture for themselves one of these divine and precious tickets. All sorts of people calling other people: "Can you . . . by any chance . . . get me in?" Broughton's little studio, the makeshift ticket office for the nearly impoverished Theatre of Ideas lecture series, had been awash in sudden popularity, everyone practically begging for tickets. And not just the $10 balcony seats or (unbelievably) standing room for $7.50, but the $25 tickets for the main seats downstairs—a staggering sum in view of the fact that the best orchestra seats for a full-scale musical such as *Hair,* still one of the biggest draws on Broadway, would set you back just half of that, literally, $12.50! A movie, *McCabe and Mrs. Miller,* Woody Allen's *Bananas,* Stanley Kubrick's *A Clockwork Orange,* cost only $3. And this "event," this program in Town Hall, was nothing but a debate, "A Dialogue on Women's Liberation," as it was billed, with panelists Germaine Greer, Jacqueline Ceballos of NOW, *Village Voice* columnist Jill Johnston, critic Diana Trilling, and moderator Norman Mailer. In other words, a whole lot of talk, not a show; not really "theater."

Unless, of course, what would be played out that night on the stage —the full panorama of this disputatious movement, in fact—could be seen as some sort of Aristotelian spectacle. A morality tale, perhaps.

To many, it would raise so many ideas, tangle with so many feminist concepts, that it would seem to be a watershed in the women's movement. "It was the night," Mailer would remember, "that turned my hair gray."

Right now, at 8 P.M. in the audience alone, the "names" were historic. Of course, Betty Friedan was there, but so were prize-winning historian Arthur Schlesinger, cartoonist Jules Feiffer, Norman Podhoretz, golden-boy editor of *Commentary* magazine, Susan Sontag, darling of the intelligentsia, Kennedy clan members Jean and Stephen Smith, a bobbing sea of lauded writers—Elizabeth Hardwick, Midge Decter, Gregory Corso, Richard Gilman. Incredibly, the elite literati of New York had driven and walked and roared through the subways to grab their reserved seats in the first rows in order to witness, perhaps even participate in, what they obviously expected to be a high-flying, multicolored, neon spectacle of cerebral daring. Crowded into the balcony tiers behind these luminaries—many of them cozily wrapped in mink—were, well, just about anybody. The committed and the curious, groupie cats, lots of well-dressed young women with long shiny hair, even a few antiwar activists, the by-now-dwindling cadres of the New Left. And in the back rows of the orchestra, a group that many would later describe as "pernicious" or "sinister."

"An extremely hostile, basically lesbian-oriented, very anti-Mailer group," according to the filmmaker D. A. Pennebaker, who, at the behest of Mailer, was recording the entire event.

Meanwhile, the whole place shimmered in klieg light glare as Pennebaker's cameras swarmed through the lobby picking up raucous complaints. ("Women's lib ignores the poor!") The crowd pushed in out of the chilly drizzle on 43rd Street, then edged into the auditorium, aiming at the main event.

Chattering, puffing with anticipation, this great audience waited.

Backstage, more stellar action, more cameras. Were they Pennebaker's? Or television? Were they attached to the British movie company that was filming a feature on Germaine Greer's peregrination through America? (Entitled, as it would turn out, *Germaine Greer versus the United States.*) No one was quite sure. Someone overheard Norman say to Germaine, "You're better looking than I thought." Someone else saw him gallantly hold a book (not his own) aloft for the cameramen.

Five minutes. Ten. The audience began a rhythmic, demanding *clap, clap, clap.* Nearly thirty minutes, until, finally, the curtain parted.

Through it bounced the Prisoner, his round, cherubic head a cap of curls, sideburns frizzing along the outsized Brooklyn boychik ears. The rumpled gray suit and red-striped rep tie properly Harvard, the blue-eyed, mock-serious expression already teasing the intelligence of the audience. He swaggered, as one wag described it, "like an Irish bartender."

Cheers from the restive, pent-up crowd!

And some loud, raucous boos.

Perfect, in Shirley Broughton's view. No one else, she thought, would do here. No one else was so perfect for the part. Who, among the literary establishment, had Mailer's talent for repartee? His personality? His chemistry?

And now, as the rude noises rumbled through the hall, Norman punched the air for order, grew earnest, prepared to evince what he had once described as his "firm, strong-tongued ego."

"Oh, come on now," he urged in an intimate, buddy-buddy tone. "Anyone who read that piece would be aware that I wasn't interested in trying to pull the tail feathers of women's lib. I had come to the conclusion that it was probably the most important single intellectual event of the last few years . . ." (Not the women's movement. His piece in *Harper's*, he surely meant.)

"Whowaw! Whowaw!"

Such braggadocio! Such chutzpah!

"Whowaw, whowaw!"

"At the least . . . at the least," crooned Mailer, allowing just the slice of a smile, seducing the audience.

No doubt about it. The man was a superb performer.

But so was Germaine.

She was nervous here in Mailer territory. "The Female Eunuch," she had told *Time*, with just a touch of pathos, *"c'est moi."*

Yet what inspires a performance more than a sudden, heart-pounding shot of adrenaline?

"My mouth was very dry," she would remember years later. "I was on the balls of my feet the whole time. But you have to be nervous. I mean . . . I'm a performer. If you're not nervous, it doesn't work."

Still, seated at the table with the other panelists, Germaine managed to gaze on the proceedings with what appeared—for all the world—to be total, ineffable calm. A resting tigress, her rich brown mane of hair floating about her face, long, bare arms, and her hands —rings on nearly every finger—balanced, without the slightest visible tremor, on the table. She was wearing an ankle-length sleeveless dress cut in a deep V at the neck. Between her breasts, an enormous pendant caught the klieg lights and shot them out like some priceless gem. (A neat piece of stage costuming. The glittering pendant, actually a women's liberation symbol Flo Kennedy had given her, was made of chrome. The elegant dress cost ten shillings.) Draped over one shoulder was a skinny, flirtatious fox boa, the "mod" quality of which did not impress Germaine's least-devoted co-panelist.

". . . a floozy kind of fox fur," Diana Trilling would recall. "I expected moths to fly out of it."

For most, though, the impression was altogether fetching. Seeing Germaine poised there, you were not surprised, somehow, that Norman, after introducing Jacqui Ceballos, would retire to a seat at the side of the author of *The Female Eunuch,* who, in turn, would smile at the moderator, delivering a sunburst that could melt Cerberus . . .

"NOW is considered the square organization of women's lib, but we are not too square that we still don't frighten many women and men because they are afraid of the whole women's liberation movement," Ceballos began. "Women have a right to work toward governing the society that governs them . . ."

Roars from the audience.

A male voice: "All of humanity!"

And another: "What about men?"

From her seat next to Norman, Germaine blew a kiss.

But Ceballos, dark-haired and neat in a suit edged with gold braid, seemed taken aback.

"That's right, all of humanity," she agreed. "My goodness, the excitement has started already!"

Bravely, the NOW official launched into the problems of underemployment and pay for women, Social Security benefits, perhaps even marriage insurance. The grit, the grub, the hard work, the important legislative issues of the movement.

"There's a woman outside who can't afford to get in," a male voice suddenly bellowed. "She's on welfare and she is thrown out."

"Knock it off," warned Mailer.

"Why don't you give her ten dollars?" someone shouted. And another: "Give her your seat!"

Which, for no recognizable reason, seemed to solve the difficulty for the moment.

Unruly though it was, however, that cry from the audience telegraphed a problem that would plague the new feminist movement for many years. Could feminism appeal across class lines? Could the needs of the welfare mother be melded to the simmering resentments of the Vassar English major? Would—or should—the movement wilt under the claim (to be repeated once again at chic dinner parties in the early eighties) that it was "just a bunch of overprivileged women looking for self-fulfillment?"

But now Ceballos resumed, protesting the image of women on television, the woman who " gets an orgasm when she gets a shiny floor," who is "pretty and deodorized when young, a shrew when she's old"—doing her level best to hang on in the unenviable position, in this particular circus, of first speaker.

Mailer, for one, was unimpressed.

"Is there anything in your program," he growled crankily at the end of Jacqui's speech, "that would give us men the notion that life would not be as profoundly boring as it is today?"

And with that, ringing down the curtain on Ceballos, he went on with the show.

Center ring, Mailer now humbly and graciously pronounced, was "the presence I suspect has done a great deal to fill this house. . . ." He paused, just for a second. "That distinguished, young, and formidable lady writer, Miss Germaine Greer from England."

A warm clatter of applause followed.

Out in that audience, however, as Germaine very well knew, seated barely a few feet from the stage, were the heavyweights—skeptical intellectuals, trained and eager to pounce on any set of ideas.

She stuffed the boa behind her and rose from her seat. Not that the boa mattered. At Germaine's full height, it was merely a wandering vine strewn across the back of a jungle feline.

"I was so tense traversing the space between the chair and the lectern that I tripped over the air," she would write.

But her "trip" was invisible. Head high, the long dark dress undulating around her ankles, she seemed to glide, like some powerful goddess, across the stage, to turn to her supplicants and . . .

"To me . . ." she began.

Her voice did not betray her. Its practiced tone rang out into the hall, the first long run a glissando, clear as new silk.

"To me, the significance of this moment is that I'm having to confront one of the most powerful figures in my own imagination, the being I think most privileged in male elitist society . . . namely, the masculine artist, the pinnacle of the masculine elite."

Ah, Norman!

The corners of the Prisoner's mouth twitched, a smile ventured, retreated.

"I am caught in a basic conflict between inculcated cultural values and my own deep conception of an injustice. Many professional literati ask me in triumphant tones, What happened to Mozart's sister?" (A close relation, some critics would later note, to Virginia Woolf's musings on "Shakespeare's sister.") "Whyever they ask me that question, it cannot cause them"—and now her voice slipped down a register, softened—"as much anguish as it has caused me.

"Because I do not know the *ahns*wer and I must find the *ahns*wer."

Germaine's precise, articulated accent (more British by now than Australian), her broad floating *a*'s, her deep long *e*'s, serenaded, tugged, like a child's hand, at the heartstrings.

Now, however, abandoning that tone of entreaty, she began to toy with the image of the male artist, the sterling representation of whom sat—watching and listening intently—next to her empty seat.

"Perhaps what we expect of the creative artist in our society is more . . . is more a *killer* than a creator, aiming his ego ahead of all. . . . Is it possible that the way of the masculine artist in our society is strewn with the husks of people worn out and dried out by his ego?"

Thus, she confided, "breaking our hearts."

As so many others had done. Freud, for instance, who described the artist's longing "for honor, power, riches, fame and the love of women. . . .

"As an eccentric little girl, who thought it might be worthwhile after all to be a poet, coming across these words for the first time was a severe check." (The blandness of Freud's assumption that the artist is a *man!* Was the proposition reversible?) "Could a *female* artist be driven by the desire for riches, fame and the love of *men? . . .*

"All of a sudden, it was very clear that the female artist's own achievement will *disqualify* her for the love of men, that no woman *yet* had been loved for her poetry!"

Then reaching higher, in wrenching tones:

"And *we* love *men* for their achievements all the time!"

Applause rang through the hall as everyone was drawn in, caught up in the moving, swirling ocean of her sweet, keening complaint:

"What could this be? Can it be a natural order that wastes so much power that it breaks a little girl's heart to pieces?

"We were either low, sloppy creatures or menials . . . or we were goddesses . . . or, worst of all . . ."

And now the bewitching voice grew stiff, as Cambridge's "Actress of the Year" unraveled a dark and plaintive thread of rage:

"We were meant to be *both!* . . . which meant that we broke our hearts trying to keep our aprons clean!"

The roars broke in waves, but, over them, riding high, as if lashed to the mast of a lurching ship, Germaine now sounded the siren . . . low, throbbing, prophetic:

"When the revolution comes, we will do it as those artists did whom Freud understood not at all, the artists who made the Cathedral of Chartres or the mozaics at Byzantium . . ."

294

And then her triumphant finale:

"The artists who had no ego and no name."

The hall erupted, howling, shouting, stamping the floor in approval, but little noting, in their adoration of a superb performance, one of the toughest of feminist conundrums: the voice of a woman (and there would be many more to come) of powerful ego strength extolling the virtues of the denied ego. For just as *The Female Eunuch* would come to be a treasured part of feminist literature, so would the name of Germaine Greer on other books to come.

The question of "name," of personal ambition—which had so inflamed the women at the Second Congress, searing Susan, Kate, and many other talented women—would eventually, inevitably, burn itself out. Even as Germaine tolled this provocative lure in Town Hall, a torrent of books was in the works at the nation's publishers.

The "women's market," the great powers of publishing quickly realized, was wide open to a new and lucrative attack. Women, so long the mainstay (more than 70 percent) consumers of publishers' lists, would also buy, in breathtaking numbers, all manner of feminist analyses. The previous year, *Up the Sandbox*, Anne Roiphe's daring exposure of a feminist imagination, hit the best-seller lists. By the end of the year *Women in a Sexist Society*, by Vivian Gornick and Barbara Moran, *The New Feminism*, by Lucy Komisar, *Man's World, Women's Place*, by Elizabeth Janeway, and the first edition of *Our Bodies, Ourselves*, by the Boston Women's Health Collective, would be stacked high in the bookstores. Women's magazines were beginning to include columns and articles for "working women" and the "women's pages" of newspapers filled solely with engagements and weddings were slowly disappearing. Even such "upscale" magazines as *Harper's* and the *Atlantic Monthly*, magazines not specifically aimed at women, had begun to sense that the steam was fizzing out of the antiwar, civil rights, counterculture scene, and that the only force to replace it, the only still-undiluted emotional energy, was to be found in the new feminism.

Some of which, fired as it was by rage, was indeed bizarre.

Next up to the lectern was Jill Johnston, who the previous summer had shocked the crowd by plunging into the Sculls' swimming pool and paddling around on her back half-naked. Nor could anyone know what this maverick had in mind now. No one was prepared for what was coming next.

Jill's head, with its wispy bangs and granny glasses perched on her nose, barely reached the top of the lectern. She was wearing order-of-the-day jeans and jacket emblazoned with stars and patches, the British flag much in evidence. She brushed back her hair and, grinning blithely, launched into one of her remarkably breathless prose poems:

"I am a woman and therefore a lesbian. All women are lesbians except those that don't know it . . . the way, of course, all men are homosexuals, being, having more sense of their homo, their homoness, their ecce-homoness, their ecce-prince, lord and masterness, the 350 years of Abraham inter-sample. Abraham lived 350 years because the Bible ages are only a succession of sons and fathers and grandfathers . . ."

A breath and the thin, high, tinny-soft voice continued.

"But who are the daughters of Rachel and Ruth and Sarah and Rebecca and the rest? We do not know the daughters, never had any daughters. They only had sons that begot more sons and sons. So we had very little sense from that particular book, of the lineage and ligaments and legacies and identities of mothers and daughters and their daughters and their mothers . . . they had nothing of each other save sons . . ."

At this, Germaine gave a little crooning chuckle and clapped her hands. Mailer looked merely attentive.

"To be equal," Jill resumed, "we have to become who we really are and women we never will be equal women until we love one another woman . . ." Then, neither missing a beat nor pausing for effect, a play within the play:

"Special from the White House!

"The president of the United States announced last night the appointment of a lesbian to his cabinet.

" 'It is nice if you can invite them in, they usually come in without knocking.'

" 'Liberal schmiberal, maybe we should invite her, uh, one of them to dinner.'

" 'One of what, dear?'

" 'Ah well, she *is* a bit odd, isn't she? I mean, you know, how we would feel if a black man was interested in our daughter?'

" 'Arrrggh,' " screamed Jill, comic-book style.

" 'Oh God and she might make a pass at my wife!' "

And on and on she rilled . . .

"Who wants the moon when we can land on Venus, he said. I want your body, he said. You can have it when I'm through with it."

Amid the laughter, Mailer now rose in protest. Johnston had, by then, far exceeded her time limit.

That was enough, the moderator insisted, little realizing that his sober rebuke was at that moment providing a secret cue.

Suddenly, before Mailer's widening blue eyes, another jean-clad woman catapulted onto the stage. She threw herself at Jill and into an arms, legs, feet, hands, tangling, unwieldy embrace.

"Hey, Jill," came a shout from the audience, "what about me?" And with that, a third woman flung her body at the wrassling, stroking, unisex couple, thereby knocking them down on the stage, where all three now proceeded to grapple and grope, to pet thighs and buttocks, to roll about in a mock erotic orgy.

The wily smile faded from Mailer's face. He was up on his feet at the podium, scowling down at the writhing mass of female arms and legs, his face an expression of disgust that seemed to say: What a mess! Was this where the "themes of my life" have gathered?

And then the Prisoner lost his cool:

"Hey, you know," shouted Mailer, "it's great that you paid twenty-five dollars to see three dirty overalls on the floor when you can see lots of cock and cunt for four dollars just down the street!"

Jill ignored Mailer, struggled upright, and, half leaning on the lectern, inches from the moderator's nose, all three women continued sidling and grappling, teasing the Prisoner as they themselves grew more and more ludicrous.

"I just hissed at him, 'Don't touch them!' " Diana Trilling would remember. "If he had laid a hand on one of those women, there would have been a riot."

"Play with the team, Jill," barked Mailer, his dark brows grinding into a thick knot, "or pick up your marbles and get lost."

And then, in extremis, Norman uttered the line that would bring forth chuckles and cheers in parlor reminiscences for months to come.

"Aw, come on, Jill," begged the Prisoner. "Be a lady."

From there on, the evening at Town Hall tacked windward as ideas, many of them basic to new feminist theory, rose and fluttered and fell. Egos of both genders puffed out their sails, as the high literati in the front rows got into the act.

Mailer called first on Betty.

"Be accurate, Betty."

"Norman, I will define accuracy for myself," she snapped, standing up at her seat and looking, in long, dangling earrings, unusually exotic. "I don't need you!"

But then she continued, in her hoarse voice, to deliver one of her longest and most cumbersome of sentences:

"I was wondering if it might possibly even tonight indicate that the world might be much less boring when instead of the monolithic, changeless, eternal face of Eve, who never transcends her biological self . . . we finally reach the beginning point of self-definition which you are reacting to somewhat like your predecessors 100 years ago, who said 'the dog talks,' you know. That a woman should be here talking at all is something you are finding a little hard to take. . . . Perhaps even you might find that less boring in the end."

Betty, of course, was chiseling away at the same issue on which Germaine had waxed lyrical, a raw nerve, in fact, that Mailer had not —as he would soon prove—recognized or understood at all. What did "woman artist" or "lady writer" really mean? Were they denigrating terms?

"I simply don't know what you're talking about," Mailer replied. "Betty, you are just making speeches. You are appealing to the lowest element in this audience. My God, I've been on platforms with women all my life . . ."

So now Susan Sontag struggled with that question as well.

"It is true," she told Norman, "that women, with the best of will, find the way you talk to them patronizing. One of the things is your use of the word 'lady.' "

The handsome, dark-haired, cerebral Sontag was respected not only for her leftist views, but for her radical appreciation of popular art. She put her questions to both Norman and panelist Diana Trilling, noting that they were "obviously apart from the others."

Diana Trilling, rounded and proper, was older than the other women on the panel by a couple of decades. Earlier in the evening, she had taken it upon herself to define two opposing sides of the argument and, with a benign, maternal stance—at least in regard to the curly-haired moderator—to scold the proponents of both of them. Reading carefully from a long, serious speech, she had mentioned that she had long ago put herself on record as considering Mailer the "most important writer of our time," and though he was wrong to oppose contraception, she preferred "even an irresponsibly poeticized biology to the no-biology-at-all of my spirited sisters."

Trilling was not, it seemed, one to mount the scaffolds indiscriminately, even in support of a still-beleaguered new movement for women's rights, and in an evening of high-trapeze showmanship, many would believe, she was miscast (". . .the token straight," she would remember, "the sacrificial lamb of the evening").

"This is what I want to ask Diana," Susan Sontag continued. When you [Mailer, she meant] said, 'Diana Trilling, foremost lady literary critic. . . .' If I were Diana, I wouldn't like to be introduced that way and I would like to know how Diana feels about it. I don't like being called a lady writer, Norman. It seems like gallantry to you, but it doesn't feel right to us. It is a little better to be called a woman writer. I don't know why, but you know words count. We are all writers. We know that."

And then, as if musing to herself: "Well, how about a woman doctor, a woman lawyer? If you were introducing James Baldwin, you wouldn't say our foremost Negro writer. And we certainly wouldn't say a man writer."

It was a touchy subject but one that would eventually prove both seed and branch to a burgeoning forest of feminist inquiry. *Eventually*—though not yet, not while the wounds of exclusion were still fresh—feminists would question whether or not the psychology and value system of women were, in fact, different from (certainly not lesser, perhaps even superior to) those of men. Did women bring more, less, or a different kind of ego to their tasks in the world? Did art or literature reflect gender as well as nationality? (And should the word "gender" itself be clearly distinguished from "sex"?) Was "woman writer" really a pejorative? And was that notion of "women's art" a self-defeating "separatism" or a long and cruelly buried tradition, a powerful, hidden stratum upon stratum of experience?

Mailer, his blue eyes dancing with the thrill of the catch, simply offered mock—and sarcastic—penitence.

"Susan . . . I will never use the word 'lady' again in public."

And Diana answered, somewhat uneasily: "I don't like it . . . but sometimes I think it is like saying 'lady runner' or 'lady high jumper' or something of that kind. . . . And so I permit it on that basis . . ."

"I wished to say that she was the best in kind," Norman persisted, in a confident, pedagogical tone. "Literary criticism is not an activity that women have engaged in as long as men. There are good reasons why there are very few good lady critics around."

But then, for some reason, sensing the nature of the injury, perhaps, the Prisoner—quite transparently—faked.

"Anyway, what you all would have known if you'd had the wit is that I was doing it precisely to put Diana on . . ."

Germaine's hand flew to her mouth, barely concealing her laughter, and the howls of derision from the audience were deafening. Cornered, Mailer parried: "You are all singularly without wit," a reproach that he could not repeat when, a few moments later, Cynthia Ozick took dead aim at the Prisoner's vision of "ovum-as-artistic-creation."

Small, solid, her high soprano voice deceptively childlike, Ozick, whose complex, mystical-theological stories and novels would soon be known throughout the world, wittily limned Norman's role as a "sacerdotal, transcendental priest of sex," his insistence that, at bottom, just as man was born to create great works, women were born to create children.

"I have been fantasizing it for many many years, since [Mailer's book] *Advertisements for Myself*," Cynthia said, ". . . this is my moment to live out a fantasy. Mr. Mailer, in *Advertisements for Myself*, you said, 'A good novelist can do without everything but the remnants of his balls.' For years and years I have been wondering, Mr. Mailer. When you dip your balls in ink, what color ink is it?"

Germaine grasped her elbows and rocked back and forth with laughter. *Everybody,* in fact, laughed so hard that Mailer himself gamely answered:

"If I don't find the answer in a hurry, I think I'm going to have to agree the color is yellow. I will cede the round to you. I don't pretend that I have never written an idiotic or stupid sentence in my life and that is one of them."

Thus the Prisoner, running the gamut of theatrics, alternately humble and arrogant, sober and clowning, gave the audience their money's worth.

"I'm perfectly willing," he popped off at one point, in answer to some gibe. "If you wish me to act as a clown, I will take out my modest little Jewish dick and put it on the table. You can all spit at it and laugh at it and then I will walk away and you will find it was just a dildo I had up there. I hadn't shown you the real thing."

And at another point, in an attempt, it seemed, to come to grips with Johnston's lesbian display:

"A male homosexual must go to a man to feel like a woman; that is, to have something up his anus or in his mouth. . . . Any man who is really a superb lover can be about 90 percent as good to a woman as a lesbian, just doing the things that a lesbian does . . . and then he has all the other stuff. So, the result is that lesbians do have a tough time and I think it accounts in part for that intense detestation they have of men . . ."

Norman glanced at Germaine frequently as he said all this, as if expecting a sympathetic ear. And indeed, in spite of her laughter, Germaine was not especially impressed by Johnston's public orgy ("It certainly did lesbianism a bad turn," she would comment years later) or by the lesbian issue in general ("We hadn't learned how to be *women*, and before we started even thinking about that, we were suddenly presented with a duty to be, as it were, political lesbians"). At the moment, however, she avoided the issue and answered a question from the floor about homosexuality with the explanation:

"By and large, the act of fucking is to the advantage of the one who fucks and the disadvantage of the one who is fucked, male, female, goat, pig, or stone . . . all characterized as female and inferior."

But then, just as he had in *The Prisoner of Sex,* Mailer took a swing at the absent Kate. The whole issue was not, he insisted, "a simple matter of men tyrannizing the women. I mean, my God, if Kate Millett is the one who has done the historical work, which establishes that men control women in a political class system, then we are all doomed." .

Germaine was busily retrieving the fox boa that had fallen down behind her chair when she heard him. She was, in fact, no fan of Kate Millett's work ("bloated," was a description she would use in private). Immediately, however, she rose to avenge:

"No one would be more surprised than Kate to hear that she had been charged with having done this! Every single feminist knows that the analysis that we have to make of society is very intricate and will take a long time . . . it is quite absurd to demand of any woman at this stage that she show you the complete analysis or that she stand convicted of having made it."

"I'm all for that," Mailer shot back, "but I would ask you why then do you women keep saying, without having made the analysis, why do you keep saying that it is entirely the male's fault?"

To which Germaine replied, her "quality of mercy" tone no longer masking her growing irritation:

"I didn't know that *any* women were saying that it was entirely the male's fault."

Which led somehow, by some mysterious route, to a long recitative by Norman Mailer on the subject of violence. It was not at all clear, however, whether this celebrated author was answering an attack on the equation of sex and violence in his writing, the justification of violence in "The White Negro" (in *Advertisements for Myself*), or whether he was defending the fact that he had stabbed his second wife, Adele Morales, a decade earlier:

". . . let me point out to you where the paradox of male and female violence takes place. When a man and a woman have a bitter, furious, violent quarrel, there comes a point, if the man is stronger, as he usually is . . . not always, but usually, when he is either going to hit that woman or not. Now if he hits the woman, he has lost the argument because finally he has blown up the premise of the argument. On the other hand, if a man swears to himself that he will never strike a woman and he is dealing with a woman who has less honor than he does, which believe me, ladies, is conceivable, then that woman will proceed . . ."

And since this brought more howls from the floor:

"You are asking for dialogue. Here it is. . . . I'll teach you and you teach me! Fuck you! You know. I mean I'm not going to sit here and listen to you harridans harangue me and say, 'Yes'm, yes'm.'

Perhaps, by then, Mailer was responding to what the filmmaker D. A. Pennebaker would describe as "that sinister quality . . . as if they're going to get shot going out the door, and it's their last chance to say what they think." (Germaine would remember it less ominously: "the people asking the questions just showing off in front of their drinking buddies.")

"Let me aim the point," Norman continued heatedly. "When a man has sworn he will not strike a woman and the woman knows that and uses that and uses it and uses it, then she comes to a point where she is literally killing that man because the amount of violence being aroused in him is flooding his system and slowly killing him. So she has engaged at that point in an act of violence and murder, even though no blows are exchanged." Still, just as he had throughout the evening, Mailer also maintained his role as the proper host, moving from station to station, pouring water for each of the panelists from a round glass pitcher. Lone and brave though he might have been—in his cave of lionesses—the battles were not solely his.

Diana Trilling, in her long speech, had taken a sharp, critical knife to *The Female Eunuch*. Germaine, in Diana's view, had discarded love, motherhood, the nurturing instinct, even "the pleasures of a developing relation with the same lover. . . .

"For Miss Greer," said Diana, "sex is not sex unless it is *only* sex."

And since, at one point, Germaine had asserted, in answer to a vaguely psychoanalytic question, that she did not resemble her mother, Diana also demanded to know: "If women are not to grow by identification with their mothers, what are they to grow by?"

Germaine, looking pained, shook her head.

"This is very insidious," she responded. "The household that I was dreaming of so witlessly [an extended, non-nuclear household she had recommended in *The Female Eunuch*] . . . I might have known it would be turned into a club to beat me with. . . ." Then, using her turn at the rostrum to defend herself against Diana's accusation that she had misquoted Freud:

"I adopt the same attitude to Freud as you do. I quote him where it suits me and I don't where it doesn't."

Diana looked stunned. "I didn't say that I quote him where it suits me and I don't where it doesn't. I don't misquote him."

"Oh dear!" Germaine leveled coolly, digging out of her bag of tricks a definition of "horizontal hostility" she had just acquired from her new friend Flo Kennedy: "One of the characteristics of oppressed people is that they always fight among themselves."

"What?" asked Diana.

Germaine leaned across Norman to repeat carefully, "One of the characteristics of . . ."

But Trilling hung on.

"I don't feel as oppressed as you do," Diana insisted, "and I am not fighting with you . . . I have a great deal of loyalty to my sex . . . but that doesn't mean that I can be indiscriminate about the positions I subscribe to just because they're put forward by other women."

"The use of the word 'misquote,' " Germaine whipped back, "can hardly be construed as magnanimous."

But Trilling was in no mood for magnanimity. Years later, she would complain that during her opening speech, Germaine had upstaged her by passing notes and whispering to Norman behind her back (which indeed Germaine had), and that Mailer cut off the speech itself ("a ludicrous piece of brown-nosing," in Germaine's view), before she was finished. Norman had treated her badly, Diana would insist. After all, she had defended him when certain members of the audience had accused him of hogging the show.

"He is not! He is not!" she had shouted.

Obviously hurt, Diana would contend that Norman was "terribly taken with her [Germaine]. But you don't desert a friend, sort of slough a friend off, because you're taken with another woman.

"I didn't press him or tell him I was angry, but I must've said something that implied the question 'Did you go to bed with her?' because he managed to tell me that he hadn't. . . . He indicated that he was kind of fearful of her . . ."

Whether or not this was true, Diana had certainly not moved Germaine to sisterly affection either. She was "a person," Germaine would still insist years later, "for whom I feel the most unbounded contempt . . . a lazy old cow. She wore a hat . . . a matron, has-been, Long Island hat!"

And, all along, wove compliments to Mailer, to his "beautiful intention of life enhancement" and splendid "imagination of women in love." Even as Norman strung a daisy chain of compliments to Germaine, for her "exquisite sentiments" and her "absolutely lovely book." Even as he cheered her on after a hostile question from *New York Times* book critic Anatole Broyard, who was, Germaine would write, "strutting and smirking like a popinjay."

"I tried to make my question nonpolemical," Broyard said.

"Balls, you did," was Germaine's reply.

"All right," answered Broyard, "perhaps I didn't succeed. I really don't know what women are asking for. Now, suppose I wanted to give it to them?"

And with that, Germaine let him have it:

"Listen, you may as well relax, because whatever it is they are asking for, honey, it's not you."

"Atta girl, sic 'em," said Norman.

Emotions ran high through this slick, dense rain forest of ideas, passions, and egos. And Mailer was not, in Germaine's memory, *altogether* adoring. She would not forget (nor forgive) his dismissal of some of her views as "diaper Marxism," or a certain skirmish in which he accused her of coming all the way from Australia just to take a "cheap shot."

To which she had angrily replied:

304

"I think it's too serious to do it just so I can defend myself against hecklers at the Town bloody Hall!"

That evening at "Town Bloody Hall," as Pennebaker would call his film, had been, in Germaine's memory years later, completely parochial, the audience entirely on Mailer's side.

"I got some idea of how New Yorkers pull for New Yorkers always," she would complain, only partly amused at the lesson, "and how important they think they are, how they really think of themselves as the American cultural establishment. The most pretentious people I've ever met! It was funny that night, because they were so terribly indulgent of their own. . . . They sort of babied Norman . . . and I thought, 'Oh, God, can the fate of women really depend on anything like this?' "

The fate of women, as a matter of fact, was already undergoing transformation through major "establishment" institutions.

In the spring of 1971, within weeks of "Town Bloody Hall," the U.S. Supreme Court ruled that businesses could not refuse to hire women with small children unless the same rule applied to men. *Time* magazine, after months of secret conclaves, agreed to its female employees' demands, as did major universities. At least one state, New York, ruled that high school girls and boys could compete in noncontact sports.

Nor did the lively protests diminish. At Harvard, women occupied a building for ten days, demanding a women's center and child-care facilities. The Professional Women's Caucus filed a class action suit against all American law schools, and the New York Radical Feminists held a "Speak-out on Rape," that four-letter word so seldom raised in polite company.

The voices of women's liberation were so pervasive by then that Archie Bunker, hero of the brand-new, outrageously raw "All in the Family" comedy show, included "women's libbers" in his never-before-heard-on-TV litany of enemies: "hebes," "spades," "spics," "dumb Polacks," and "Commie crapola."

Germaine Greer's immediate mission, however, was a luncheon at the staid National Press Club in Washington, where she caught her audience mid-mouthful with her views on vaginal deodorants. ("Dealing with the, uh, Problem," as Nora Ephron would soon write.)

Germaine's solution was simple. Rather than spray with chemicals, this Shakespearean scholar advised, women should go without underwear altogether.

And off she flew in the company of a handsome young cab driver, "a corrupt child of my own generation," she would write, "with a white angelic face (marked a little from experiences on the streets and in reform school), who was to become famous on the West Coast as my 'bodyguard.' "

As for Norman:

The following September, the cover of *Esquire* carried a superimposed photo of him as King Kong cradling a tiny Germaine in his arms.

Inside, her account of the evening dismissed the Prisoner as "no stud."

". . . the tragedy of machismo," Germaine wrote, "is that a man is never quite man enough."

PART IV

19

NOBODY'S
MOTHER

> ... the same considerations incite all revolution-
> aries against the figure of the mother; in flouting her,
> they reject the status quo ... impose[d} ... through
> the motherly guardian of laws and customs.
>
> —Simone de Beauvoir, *The Second Sex,* 1953

"Mother Superior to Women's Lib" was the title of a major article in
the *New York Times Magazine* in the fall of 1970. *Mother* ... who,
having given birth to this marvelous, disputatious movement, could
now, supposedly, retire to the sidelines, to a role as loving approver.

It was Betty, of course, and Paul Wilkes, the writer, had followed
her on her peregrinations. From a chapel at Wake Forest University
(her lecture fee duly noted: $750) to the Senate Committee on Nutri-
tion and Human Needs. He lavished praise on her delivery ("like some
great Shakespearean performer") and her passionate commitment:
"So much like Yves Montand in *La Guerre est Fini,* complete with
flashes of oncoming headlights—the monologue of a tormented
leader and the reassuring nods of cell members."

The piece quoted Betty telling a young female student: "Don't get
into the bra-burning, anti-man, politics-of-orgasm school like Ti-
Grace did. Confront the administration, demand the same rights
as the guys, go door to door when Sam Ervin [the North Carolina

senator who opposed the ERA] comes up for election and get him out."

And from many friends, both in and out of the movement, an effusion of loving warmth, tributes to the catholicity of Betty's interests, memories of happy evenings spent talking about everything under the sun *but* feminism, testimonials to Betty's loyalty and concerned friendship, her wonderful kids.

But the title of the piece waved a red flag at the deep ambivalence of young women who were striving for their own identities.

If the women's libbers needed a "mother," many of them told Wilkes, they would, thank you very much, choose their own.

Betty, the writer Sally Kempton proclaimed, "misrepresents the case for feminism by making people believe that reform is the answer. . . . She is not the movement mother; that is Simone de Beauvoir."

And Wilkes had also dug up the dirt.

In Betty's quest to keep the movement alive, he wrote, she had offended "virtually everyone she has worked closely with."

Quoting a vice-president of NOW on what he called a "typical Friedanism":

"Betty wanted to issue a press release so she called me at home to tell me—*tell me,* that is—to get over to her house immediately and do it. She had the typewriters, she had the facilities for reproducing it at hand, and I told her that she could get it done just as easily by herself and that I had something else to do. The tirade that followed was interrupted when I hung up on her. The woman needs to be brought under control. . . . She's a terror to deal with and there is an overpowering ego at work."

Less clear-cut was a comment from Gloria Steinem:

"She has found that love between unequals can never succeed and she has undertaken the immense job of bringing up the status of women so that love can succeed. Hopefully, so that her own emotional needs as a woman can eventually be fulfilled."

("Where does that woman stand?" Betty would ask years later. "I've never been able to figure that out.")

Others—such as Muriel Fox—were puzzled even then, especially when Gloria formed an organization called the Women's Action Alliance, which Muriel would remember mostly as an unpleasant surprise.

"I was deeply disappointed," she would recall, "that Gloria chose to set up another organization that would solicit funds from the very few sources that might conceivably be out there. We knew there were very slim pickings and we were disappointed that Gloria didn't decide to work with NOW rather than setting up a competing group.

"I guess I understood why Gloria was doing it," Muriel would add. "Betty could be difficult. She was horrible to people, in fact . . . treated them very badly, but I believe that part of Betty's resentment and anger was because Gloria set this organization up."

Gloria's explanation, many years later, would simply be this:

"This thing was like wildfire. After my speeches I would get hundreds of letters. Women were asking where to find this; how to do that. We needed a center of information. There was really no place in the country where people could write and find out who in the community could help them start a child-care center, for instance, what organizations were working on which issues. There was NOW, but you had to join. Lots of women don't want to join."

And Gloria began soliciting funds for the Women's Action Alliance, even gave some thought to a newsletter, even held meetings. People always responded to a call from Gloria Steinem, and by the early months of 1971, writers, editors, publishers, all manner of trendsetters, were flocking to her apartment on East 73rd Street.

"John Lennon and Yoko Ono came once," Gloria would recall, adding with a smile: "I think people didn't know what to make of the fact that Yoko brought her husband."

For by now, it was clear—through her speeches and television appearances—that Gloria's, too, was an important voice for feminism.

"People were beginning to say, after some sexist joke, 'Oh, don't tell Gloria Steinem that!' " Muriel would remember. And Muriel, who by then had labored five years for NOW, who had even tried, at the Oak Room protest, to interest this prominent journalist in the cause, would also remember her shock at this sudden connection and thinking to herself: "Gloria Steinem? Who's Gloria Steinem?"

But, she would also recall, "the minute Gloria came on the scene, the media dropped Betty like a hot potato."

Move on! Move on! Betty insisted as she pressed for some political action that would leave behind "those navel-gazing rap sessions." Once more she embarked on powwows with highly placed women. Once more she headed for the telephone, calling both Democrats and Republicans, leaders of Catholic, Protestant, Jewish groups, the PTA, the League of Women Voters, the American Association of University Women, students at local colleges, even the women's auxiliary of the Veterans of Foreign Wars—Betty's America, her Peoria, *sensible women* who didn't, as she would write, "waste time arguing about women's liberation. . . ."

"In 1972, we will go to the national conventions of both major parties with bargaining power to support women candidates working with other underrepresented groups. We will work in primaries and elections across party lines and outside existing parties, drawing in women who were lost in the electoral process, to elect women candidates committed to our goals."

Those words were scrawled across—and up the far side of—one of Betty's personal checks. They were written sometime during the early months of 1971 at a meeting in the home of New York City's former planning commissioner Elinor Guggenheimer. As usual, the impatient Betty had bustled into this gathering minus her paper or notebook, but still . . . jangling those bells, those same bells that were clanging and clashing across the country . . .

Late that spring—just weeks after "Town Bloody Hall"—the U.S. Senate, for the first time in history, appointed girls as pages, and the Explorer Scouts opened its doors to females as well. By summer, there were rallies and celebrations of the fifty-first anniversary of women's suffrage around the country. In Winston-Salem, North Carolina, at the Jos. Schlitz Brewing Company; in Chicago, in Civic Center Plaza; in Stoughton, Wisconsin, the first known high school course on the history of women in America.

In the past year, NOW membership had multiplied from about 30 to 200 chapters, from 3,000 to 10,000 women, and $30 million in back pay had been awarded under the Equal Pay Act (against only $17 million in the six previous years). By fall, nearly 100 colleges were offering at least one course for credit on women, and Billie Jean King had become the first woman athlete to earn more than $100,000 per year.

In response to all this, uneasy men's consciousness-raising groups were springing up in urban centers (along with, though perhaps coincidentally, the new hermaphroditic images of Mick Jagger and David Bowie).

Scattered, opaque, and often incomprehensible though it may have been, the word was out in the land; the winds had shifted and a sense of women's potential—even as a political force—was sweeping through nearly every activist group.

On March 21, 1971, at a meeting of about a hundred women, the formation of the National Women's Political Caucus—the original concept of which, according to its flyer, "came from Betty Friedan, well-known author of *The Feminine Mystique* and a leading feminist thinker and lecturer"—was announced. Betty invited such prominent figures as Shana Alexander, editor of *McCall's,* and Liz Carpenter, former press secretary to Lady Bird Johnson, among many others, to come to her apartment to help plan a national conference. She phoned Representatives Martha Griffiths, Shirley Chisholm, and Bella Abzug, who, according to Betty, "screamed at me over the phone that I had no business invading her turf . . ."

The point being, of course, that Abzug, whom Betty had vigorously supported, was already *in* the real world of national politics. (And, as Bella herself would subsequently claim, had been hatching such a plan all along.)

Bella Abzug had been elected to represent the 19th congressional district in the House of Representatives in November 1970, the same month that the "Mother Superior" article appeared in the *New York Times Magazine.* And Bella's election had been, for many, a milestone.

Over the years, a bare sprinkling of women had been elected to Congress, most of them—unlike *both* Bella and Shirley Chisholm— the wives of husbands who had died in office. And Bella was special as well simply because of her feisty style.

"She stirs up the people who want to kick the backsides of the powerful," one colleague would soon observe. "She appeals to that quality in people in an incredible way."

Nearly everyone in New York had seen the garrulous Bella, at one time or another, on some street corner or subway stop, a chunky, smart-mouthed "balabosta" in a hat like a giant Frisbee, her hand shooting out like a piston: "Hi, I'm Bella!"

"I and the people understand each other," she'd confide in her New York rasp. "The others, they'll be taken care of by history."

"This woman's place is in the House—the House of Representatives," blared Bella's campaign slogan, though she herself never was —never could have been—a one-issue candidate. Mostly she was vehemently, loudly, thumpingly antiwar, an organizer, in the sixties, of the Dump Johnson movement and a vocal supporter of the nuclear test ban treaty. She railed against her enemies in a foghorn voice, yet with a Bronx-bred, sly-fox humor that left 'em, if not roaring, then at least grinning in the aisles.

Tough, blustery, noisy as the traffic, Bella had been married for twenty-six years to stockbroker-cum-novelist Martin Abzug. She had two college-age daughters who were active in her campaign, and a supportive, encouraging mama. She had been editor of the *Law Review* at Columbia Law School and, as a practicing attorney, represented longshoremen, fur-cutters, restaurant workers. A strong civil rights advocate—long before it was fashionable—she had been seven months pregnant when she defended a black man in Mississippi who was accused of raping a white woman.

The gruff New York congresswoman would soon prove a skillful legislator. Already, in her first year in the nation's capital, Bella and Shirley Chisholm had managed to attach a comprehensive child-care act to another, male-sponsored bill. (The bill would be vetoed, however, by President Nixon.) Fighting so zealously for the issues that affected "the little guy" and the minorities, Bella was soon labeled by her enemies as "red" or "Communist," and by headline writers as "Battling Bella" or "Bellicose Bella."

Feminism, for Bella, was just *part* of the humanist, leftist, antiwar story—not the whole shootin' match—and what the papers were now calling "Bellamania" would soon follow. Bella would be photographed with her Hollywood friends Barbra Streisand, Shirley MacLaine, Louise Lasser, Lily Tomlin, and Elizabeth Taylor, and the blurbs would read: "Bella's politics appeal to socially conscious Beautiful People."

For Bella's ambitions, by now, were perfectly plain.

"My election goes beyond this district," she announced. "I think I represent the entire peace movement, the women's movement. I seek to represent women in the entire country."

Specifically, she promised what she called "a new coalition": women, the elderly, the poor, the minorities, workers, and the unemployed. And unlike Betty or Gloria or Germaine or Kate, Bella wasn't a writer. She was a politician.

The National Women's Political Caucus—the instrument designed to focus the women's movement on elective and appointive politics—met at the Statler Hilton Hotel in Washington, D.C., on July 10, 1971, an assemblage that was to many the most important in the history of feminism.

"It was really thrilling," Kay Clarenbach would remember. "A whole new collection of people. There were political women—both Democrats and Republicans—who never thought of themselves as feminists; there were civil libertarians, members of the League of Women Voters, some who wouldn't touch NOW with a ten-foot pole . . . and there was a wonderful representation of women of color."

Among the two hundred to three hundred women, there were factions, of course, and the ever-American grinding of axes . . . not simply between party ideologies, but between the "celebrities" and women with local leadership experience, between the old hands and students who resented taking minor roles. Among the latter were many young women who were deeply committed, not only to the counterculture, but to the growing suspicion that CIA and FBI agents were infiltrating their ranks. (A suspicion that was not unfounded. In 1975, the Rockefeller Commission would report that "Operation CHAOS" had indeed infiltrated the student movement, SNCC, and, along with other groups, the women's liberation movement.)

"It was *de rigueur* for these young people not to give their full names or biographical information," Kay would remember. "As a result, none got nominated to serve on the board, and a gang of them were sitting in the corridor, getting ready to strike or picket or something." Kay, who chaired the Caucus, dispatched Abzug to deal with that, and two full names were finally elicited.

But soon another question arose that would stir in the wings for decades.

Should the Caucus support *any* and *only* women, no matter what their political stand? Such as, for example, Boston's Louise Day Hicks, who was currently waging war against school integration?

Obviously, given the civil rights agenda of the group, no. But where would this policy begin? Where would it end? And what about male candidates who were strong and straight on women's issues?

Even black women struggled with this one. At this Caucus, finally, *their* voices were being heard, and their own experience often being very different from that of whites, long-simmering suspicions of white women surfaced.

"The faces of those white women hovering behind that black girl at the Little Rock school in 1957," Toni Morrison would write in the *New York Times Magazine*, "do not soon leave the retina of the mind. . . . It is a source of amusement even now to black women to listen to feminists talk of liberation while somebody's nice black grandmother

315

shoulders the daily responsibility of childrearing and floor mop-ping . . ."

Already, certain black periodicals had warned that the women's movement could usurp black women's support for their men, who had suffered bitterly from the "white male patriarchy."

Race. Class. Women constituted over 52 percent of the population. How—in this frankly political, factionalized caucus—would they find a way to unite them?

Fannie Lou Hamer, the longtime civil rights leader, rose to an-nounce, as Shirley Chisholm already had done, that she had suffered more discrimination as a woman than as a black. Others—Myrlie Evers, the widow of the slain leader Medgar Evers, among them—insisted that black *men* needed all the support they could get.

Betty, siding with Hamer and Chisholm, once again pressed for her concept of uniting *across* political lines to elect women and focus attention on *women's issues*. Bella, pumping for her leftist coalition, for what Betty would call "the outs," took the more radical line, announcing that it was "certainly not my purpose to replace or sup-plement a white, male, middle-class elite with a white, female, mid-dle-class elite in the positions of power in the nation."

"Our aim should be to humanize society," Gloria agreed with Bella at the plenary session, "by bringing the values of women's culture into it, not simply to put individual women in men's places."

Yet there was something else brewing here, too—something that Kay, among others, had clearly sensed from the opening note of the Caucus.

The philosophical differences between Betty and Bella were slight. At the heart of it all, as many founding members would remember, with a shrug or, at best, an indulgent smile, was a simple question. Would Betty be the voice of this historic caucus? Or Bella? Which one, in short, would speak to the press?

Since Abzug's election, her voice had been heard in behalf of fem-inism across the country. Often, in fact, when Betty was downed by an attack of asthma and had to cancel a speech, Bella filled in. By the time this auspicious convention met, however, all was not well be-tween these two.

"I think I was drafted to chair the Caucus," Kay would remember, "because I could get along with both Betty and Bella. They were both talking about the need for women in politics, but they each had little private gatherings and invited people separately, independently, to their hotel rooms. Each of them thought she was going to be the keynote speaker and kept sending lieutenants to me to ask how she was going to be introduced."

And though Kay believed that she had solved the problem by avoiding the announcement of a keynote speaker entirely and creating instead a nonpartisan panel, this hardly satisfied Betty. Something— or someone—was loosening her hold on the reins of the women's movement, and she was quite clear about how that was happening.

All along, she would later charge, there was "a scheme . . . to organize a coalition of the 'outs'—the poor, blacks, youth, women, and gays." And it was not only Bella whom Betty cited in this plot, but Gloria Steinem as well. Whether or not this was true, at this convention it was clear that Gloria was no longer an observer. She was a force. And that force was aligned not with Betty Friedan, certainly, but with Bella Abzug. Nor was Gloria oblivious to her own importance. "I'm tired of your face, and yours," she said at one point, pointing at both Bella and Betty, "and I'm tired of seeing my own."

One young woman—Letty Cottin Pogrebin, the blond, size-four, ninety-nine-pound whiz kid, recent author of *How to Make It in a Man's World*—knew quick as lightning where she stood in this particular competition. She had come to the convention at Betty's behest, but once she arrived, everything changed.

"Ever since the Playboy Bunny article, I had followed Gloria as an ideal. She was brilliant and everything she wrote had style . . . she lived with style. She was beautiful and spoke beautifully and I admired her always from afar. I wished always that we would meet at a party and I had tried once to have a mutual friend introduce us. I never actually sat down with her and said, 'Listen, I've admired you for nine years. I want to do whatever you do, you know. I want to be you and whatever you believe in, I believe in.' I didn't have a chance to say that. . . . But I always felt that she wasn't into feminism, either. Like me, she was new to it and so . . ."

Letty, who had herself "made it in a man's world" as the supremely talented promoter of such books (*and* their authors) as Helen Gurley Brown's *Sex and the Single Girl* and Jackie Susann's *Valley of the Dolls*, sided with Gloria and Bella.

"I went with my instincts," Letty would remember.

"I think Betty has felt betrayed by me ever since. And I did. I did. She pulled me in and I left her for them."

(Three months after the Caucus, in fact, Gloria and Kate Millett would co-found a short-lived group called Women's Rights, Inc. It would "augment what NOW is doing," Flo Kennedy would inform the press. "It won't necessarily be different.")

"Self-styled radicals," Betty would sniff, and she would eventually level a charge with which some of her colleagues would agree: that the entire machinery of the Caucus had been manipulated by Bella and Gloria. "Maybe political feminism versus political opportunism," a still stormy Betty would write, "or maybe something more sinister," by which she meant, of course, the CIA—Gloria's earlier connection with that CIA-funded organization having surfaced by now in the press.

Yet despite the clashes, the goals that were set in Washington that summer would be solid enough to carry the women's movement through many years.

"To help elect women and also *men* who declare themselves ready to fight for the needs and rights of women and all underrepresented groups . . ."

This guideline along with an absolute prohibition against any who held racist views, a call to support the ERA, to strengthen the EEOC, and to repeal laws "that affect a woman's right to decide her own reproductive and sexual life" were read and approved to deafening cheers and applause. (As were resolutions on more general issues of medical care, housing, withdrawal from the Vietnam War, etc.) The resulting sense of empowerment was immediately celebrated at bars and pubs in the nation's capital, whether or not, of course, all feminists approved, which some radicals definitely did not.

"One more woman in Congress," Robin Morgan publicly warned, "is not going to change the basic lives of women. The National Women's Political Caucus is in the very long run irrelevant. It could in the middle run even be harmful. I have visions of women bleeding to death in the gutters while Betty Friedan has tea in the White House."

That the White House had, in fact, taken note of this gathering was revealed in a report from the *New York Times*. President Nixon, Secretary of State William Rogers, and National Security Adviser Henry Kissinger, it appeared, had discussed the Caucus at Nixon's home in San Clemente, California. Rogers mentioned a newspaper photograph of Bella, Betty, Gloria, and Shirley Chisholm. The "stars of the women's movement," the caption read.

"What did it look like?" Nixon asked.

"Like a burlesque," answered Rogers.

"What's wrong with that?" replied the president, whose views of women's liberation were already apparent in his recent comment: "I wouldn't want to wake up next to a lady pipefitter."

Kissinger seemed especially interested in the presence of Gloria.

"Who's that?" the president asked.

"That's Henry's old girlfriend," Rogers said jokingly, a reference, it seemed, to year-old reports in both *Time* and *Life* linking Steinem and Kissinger romantically, hardly a seemly alliance for a leftist columnist or, for that matter, a budding feminist activist. That spring, the federal government, for the first time in history, had attempted (and failed) to suppress publication of documents on the grounds of national security. Those documents—the Pentagon Papers—revealed a secret history of war decisions, including the fact that Kissinger had been meeting with the Vietnamese Communists since 1969.

In response to the *Times* report, Gloria issued a statement:

"I am not now," she wrote, "and never have been a girlfriend of Henry Kissinger."

20

THE WOMAN
OF THE YEAR

The belief that was once accorded the priest—and
perhaps in lesser measure the schoolmaster—is now
accorded the spokesmen and women of television and
the press.

—John Kenneth Galbraith, *The Anatomy of Power,* 1983

By the early seventies, Gloria was lecturing to many groups, not as a humanist for whom women's rights was just one plank of an overall philosophy, or as a journalist, which the press continued to call her, but as a determined missionary for women's liberation. More often than not, she spoke in tandem with a black woman, at first Dorothy Pitman Hughes, a director of one of New York's new community-controlled schools, who often dressed in colorful, politically expressive African garb; then the sensational Flo, who skewered the "jockocrats, pigocrats, and friends of the fetus."

Just a few months before the convening of the National Women's Political Caucus, Gloria had delivered the commencement address at Smith College, and her subject was the current wave of feminism. This Ivy League school was Gloria's alma mater, of course, but it was also Betty's—and the birthplace of *The Feminine Mystique* as well. For Betty, the choice of Gloria had to have been—at minimum—a disappointment.

"It was as if," Betty's friend Barbara Seaman would recall, "they had asked the prettiest girl instead of the smartest."

At Smith, Gloria delivered an interpretation of history extremely popular, at the moment, in radical feminist groups. Male rule, this concept held, was a recent phenomenon. Originally—for 5,000 years, in fact—women had ruled the world in a gynecocracy. The discovery of the male role in reproduction had led, as Gloria put it, to "the idea of ownership . . . of property and of children, the origin of marriage, which was really locking women up long enough to make sure who the father was . . ."

The implications of such theories were, of course, far more "radical," inherently more antagonistic to men, than Betty's vision of an "equal partnership." Yet Gloria delivered them quietly, with what anger there was behind them in check, in a manner, as one observer would report, "neither abusive nor offensive."

And though Gloria's sympathies were far from "mainstream," that year—and perhaps forever—the impression was often quite the opposite, as Sheila Tobias, the feminist historian and Gloria's friend and colleague at *New York* magazine, would recall.

"There *is* a part of the movement I can readily accept, identify with, and deal with," the president of a prestigious Ivy League university told Sheila. "That is the part of the movement represented by Gloria Steinem, namely, the part that accepts men and wishes to work in partnership with men. But the part of the movement represented by Betty Friedan, namely, hate-male separatism, I find unacceptable."

It was sexism in full flower, in Sheila's view. "Here was a guy so steeped in his own sexism and stereotypes that he couldn't correctly perceive the two forks of the movement. Because at that point, it was Steinem who was taking a far more separatist, radical line."

The reason this normally well-informed man couldn't see it, in Sheila's opinion, "was that Steinem was so good looking. It never dawned on him that a woman with that kind of face and figure would be bitter or resentful of men. Terrific! I thought. It was a marvelous opportunity. They couldn't read the signals and they were totally confused. They wouldn't be able to do battle for a very long time. We had the advantage of surprise."

Furthermore, frightened though Gloria might be of public speaking, her appearances, in many quarters, were drawing wildly enthusiastic responses, her habit of switching the personal pronoun "I" or "me" to "we" or "us" creating an almost irresistible instant intimacy.

"Friends, sisters," she would usually begin, "we're not glamorous creatures who come to you from the outside . . , " all the while looking very glamorous indeed, in her leotard and tight jeans, or sometimes a bright print dress, stylishly mini.

"So many men I know who have two children really have three," she would say. "Many men marry women they wouldn't hire, someone who is pretty and cooks . . . and when one out of three marriages ends in divorce, the man is filled with guilt at having to leave his child in the care of another child . . .

"It's a myth that women somehow need to be mothers; they no more need to be mothers than every person with vocal cords needs to be an opera singer."

At a time when the divorce rate was beginning its historic climb and the birthrate was dropping, when young people were delaying their wedding dates and the number of people living alone was increasing at a rate that would completely change the face of American life, Gloria—single by *choice*—was a dazzling inspiration for that new "life-style," as the media called it.

On August 16, 1971, Gloria was featured on the cover of *Newsweek*, proclaimed by the magazine as the personification of women's liberation.

In this sunny, bright, smiling, outdoorsy photo, she was wearing her super aviator glasses, and her long, streaked-blond hair was tossed by a light breeze. Light-years from the hellfire and damnation image of Kate on *Time's* cover the year before, this photograph was as friendly as Gloria herself, so blooming with health, so glamorous that you could hardly tell this sober, influential news periodical from . . . well, the *Ladies' Home Journal* in the next rack.

"The New Woman" whistled across the top of the magazine, and inside: "A Liberated Woman Despite Beauty, Chic and Success."

"What gets nearly everyone about Steinem as Liberationist," teased the article itself, "Is That She Didn't Have To."

Meaning? . . . Well, it wasn't the sort of thing you came right out and said. Not, certainly, if you were a feminist. Somehow, however, you *knew*. You knew that, unlike the *Time* issue a year before, this cover story would have less to say about the questions of feminism than it would about this larger-than-life beauty photographed in miniskirt and Bunny costume. You knew, too, that this time the reporters had checked carefully into the sexual preference of their subject.

322

Not that, in Gloria's case, you could very well miss it.

Her string of beaux appeared again: Mike Nichols, Rafer Johnson, Herb Sargent, Tom Guinzburg, Paul Desmond, etc., along with comments on this stunning if, at this precise moment, somewhat mystifying phenomenon:

"She doesn't like this idea of being thought of as a sex symbol," *New York Times* editor Charlotte Curtis commented in the piece. "Yet she seems to ask for it in a way—perhaps without realizing it. Last summer at one of the lib meetings, she had on a backless blouse. With a beautiful girl like that, how could the newspapers help but describe her as very feminine, attractive and sexy?"

And Betty was quoted on "the touch of sexism in all the attention Gloria's getting. The fact that Gloria is very pretty and chic is nice for the movement, but if that's all she was it wouldn't have been enough. Fortunately, she's so much more."

"I am not a leader," Gloria continued to insist, but that summer, by consenting to appear on the *Newsweek* cover, she had also consented —as what ambitious young woman would not—to the appointment, the anointment, the coronation as "the movement's most sought-after spokesman [sic]."

McCall's, with its seven-million-plus circulation, soon seconded the motion.

Nineteen seventy-two, the magazine announced in January, was the "Year of the Woman," and instead of the usual model or movie star gracing its cover, *McCall's,* like *Newsweek,* featured a glamorous, smiling photograph of Gloria.

"Why Gloria Steinem?" the magazine asked rhetorically—the same magazine for which Betty was writing her monthly "Betty Friedan's Notebook." Because Gloria "had become a household word. . . . She is the most visible of the activists, although her precise role remains undefined. In bell bottoms and a jersey body shirt, tinted glasses and a lion's mane that reaches below her shoulder blades, she looks like a life-size, counterculture Barbie Doll." A misleading image, the article continued, for "Gloria Steinem is emerging as somebody to be taken very seriously indeed, the women's movement's most persuasive evangelist . . . a latter-day Billy Sunday preaching a new-found feminism."

She was, in this "Year of the Woman," *McCall's* "Woman of the Year."

.   .   .

McCall's, like the other thick, profitable women's magazines, was edited by a man, a skilled specialist in choosing the right face at the right time for the cover. These editorial titans were also adept at gauging their readers' interest, and a few (most notably Sey Chassler at *Redbook*) had already begun running stories that were sympathetic to the movement.

Clearly, there was more to be said on "the woman question," though not, perhaps, in exactly the manner that Friedrich Engels or Elizabeth Cady Stanton or Susan B. Anthony could possibly have imagined. But who—prior to the age of designer jeans, the "medium is the message," and *People* magazine—could have dreamed of the commercial possibilities of EST, Esalen, and the "human potential movement"?

Inevitably, in New York, in 1971, some media genius was bound to wade into the fast-moving rapids of feminism. Not, of course, the modest little ponds of the feminist presses, but the big time, the big bucks, the big slicks of the women's magazines.

As it happened, the genius in question was none other than Gloria's enraptured boss at *New York,* Clay Felker.

"When ideas are ready to be born," Clay would maintain, "a lot of people think about them. I came up with the idea by myself, but maybe Gloria did, too. Gay and Nan Talese [the writer/editor couple] also talked about it." (As, Betty would insist, had *she*—a couple of years before.) "But this particular magazine . . . I organized it myself, put together the elements."

The elements of a slick, commercial feminist magazine, Clay meant. The production *and* the editor, a selection he made not long after he got wind of the *Newsweek* cover story. Gloria did have, Clay would remember, "amazing leadership qualities"—an ability to come into a room full of people with wildly disparate ideas and, somehow, magically, to unite them. But most of all, as he saw it, Gloria "personified the movement. She was appearing on television a lot and I knew that she could get a great deal of publicity for the magazine. She was the obvious choice for editor."

And so the flushed and frenzied planning, pasting, sketching, writing began at the *New York* offices, upstairs in the brownstone on East 63rd Street . . . the dizzying pace, the full-out, giddy esprit of a bold new venture, terra incognita.

The magazine, from Clay's standpoint, was a "one-shot"—a single issue and that would be the end of it. What went into that issue was up to Gloria and her friends. Clay would provide the financing and split the take with them fifty-fifty. If they chose to regard that "one-shot" as a test for something permanent, well, that—and any further financing—was up to them.

Something permanent? Like a monthly magazine? That idea, according to media savants everywhere, would rival the Edsel. Feminism was *one* topic, *one* subject, *one* movement and bound to run out of things to say. No one, the experts insisted, could possibly find enough to write about month after month after month.

Sojourner? Should they name their magazine—one-shot or not—after Sojourner Truth, the freed slave who campaigned for women's suffrage?

"We tried that out on our friends," Gloria would remember, "and they thought it was a travel magazine."

Sisters?

"They thought it was religious."

Well, *what* then?

Amid giggles, silliness, the spillover of exhaustion, Gloria would recall, smiling at the memory: *Bimbos.*

Until finally a term popped up that was buzzing about the movement those days. Someone had stumbled across the word in a 1930s secretarial handbook, authoritatively prescribed therein as the proper form of address if one was unaware of a woman's marital status. (And one that would be, in time, an accepted form of address whether one knew or not.)

Ms.

It became, on the spot, the name of the only feminist mass magazine in history. It would become, like the acronym NOW, a verbal symbol of the women's movement. And though the authoritative *New York Times,* among several other publications, would resist employing that title for more than a decade, succumbing only in 1986, by then, some surveys would show, 30 percent of American women—and most businesses—would be using it. "Ms. Smith" and "Ms. Jones" would be appellations common enough to find their way into standard etiquette books.

In the years to come, *Ms.,* the magazine, would address nearly every concern of the women's movement, from rape to pornography, from abortion and legislation to literature and art. It would be especially sympathetic to the underprivileged and to lesbians. It would not, however, address the burning issue of the scarcity of maids, which, in Gloria's only half-amused recollection, was Felker's idea of the problem. Like most men, Gloria thought, he didn't really *understand.*

"The magazine was going to be all about the lack of maids, because, in Clay's opinion, if you just imported enough maids from Jamaica, you could solve this whole problem."

"I get the feeling," she would write in the very first issue, "that we are speaking Urdu and the men are speaking Pali."

But it wasn't just men who didn't quite *get it.* As thousands of CR sessions had revealed, most women were so inured to their second-class status that they didn't even recognize the insults, even when they rose, like a river, around their necks. Even at *New York,* there was confusion.

"Clay had to explain the magazine three times before any of us understood," Nancy Newhouse would remember.

Eventually, Newhouse would become editor of the *New York Times's* style sections, including the "Hers" column, one of the most prestigious and wide-ranging voices of feminism in the country. But that summer, for that "one-shot," she was a very minor player on the scene.

"Gloria was the star," Nancy would remember. "There was a great stir whenever she came into the editorial room. She always wore a leotard and fitted pants and she had that wonderful hair. We were all in awe and thrilled to have her around."

And while Gloria and Clay checked out the new magazine, at a central island, Nancy made other silent observations, among them that "Clay was obviously in love with Gloria. Maybe there had been a passing affair or something. . . ."

But what really fascinated Clay—or so Nancy surmised—was Gloria's contacts, her ability to get straight through—with one phone call!—to *anyone,* short, perhaps, of the president.

"All the rest of the women writers needed Clay to boost them up," Nancy would recall. "Gloria was at the most heavy hitting level and she was unintimidated by the big male power figures. She had immense symbolic significance and Clay understood that."

And she seemed, in fact, totally unlike any woman Nancy had ever known.

"Gloria was a big personage. She was like a man. She didn't need security, didn't want a spouse. She had no guilt or remorse about sex and she stayed friends with her lovers."

And she was diplomatic, Nancy noticed, yet, at the same time, firm . . . especially when a battle of near implacable wills loomed over the first cover of the new magazine. Clay wanted a photo of a man and woman wrapped together by a long rope, and though both figures were fully clothed, the picture suggested conflict and, more to the point, sex—a combination that was, in short, commercial.

"Gloria thought the picture looked like an ad," Nancy would remember. She insisted instead on a stylized painting of a female figure with eight arms, each of them clasping symbols of a woman's life: frying pan, broom, clock, telephone, etc., an East Indian face with tears running down her cheeks. And while the argument over that cover ground on for three days, Nancy was struck by the fact that Gloria never let the conflict escalate, never lost her temper.

"She never gave Clay a chance to start screaming," Nancy would recall, "not that he'd ever scream at *her*. She had all the women behind her and she simply came back and back." To the Daliesque female juggler, to be introduced in a forty-page insert in *New York*'s December 20, 1971, special year-end double issue, and then, in the following January, as a 128-page "one-shot."

Inside both issues were "Welfare Is a Women's Issue" and "The Black Family and Feminism," "How to Write Your Marriage Contract" by Susan Edmiston, including both Alix Shulman's marital pact and the semi-official Jackie Kennedy/Aristotle Onassis prenuptial deal, the rumored separate bedrooms, $18 million and all. There was Anne Koedt's piece on lesbian love, "Can Women Love Women?", Vivian Gornick's "Why Women Fear Success," Letty Cottin Pogrebin's "Down with Sexist Upbringing," and a rating of the presidential candidates (by the young lawyer Brenda Feigen Fasteau) according to their stand on women's issues and the number of women on their staffs, a mode of assessment that would soon be taken up by women's groups in many other countries. There was Gloria's article "Sisterhood" and the pièce de résistance of the new magazine—Jane O'Reilly's classic feminist awakening, "The Housewife's Moment of Truth." This "click," this light bulb of sudden awareness, dramatized the moment when a woman first realizes that she has spent a lifetime allowing herself to be treated as—even thinking of herself as—auxiliary, lesser, "the little woman."

"In New York last fall, my neighbors—named Jones—had a couple named Smith over for dinner. Mr. Smith kept telling his wife to get up and help Mrs. Jones. Click! Click! Two women radicalized at once . . .

"It will not do for women who are mostly housewives to say that

Women's Liberation is fine for women who work, but has no relevance for them. Equal pay for equal work is only part of the argument —usually described as 'the part I'll go along with.'

"We are all housewives. We would prefer to be persons. That is the part they *don't* go along with . . .

"A woman I know in St. Louis, who had begun to enjoy a little success writing a grain company's newsletter, came home to tell her husband about lunch in the executive dining room. . . . She noticed her husband rocking with laughter. 'Ho, ho, my little wife in an executive dining room.' Click! . . ."

And O'Reilly quoted a male perspective: " 'You can't tell me Women's Lib means I have to wash the dishes?' "

Along with the answer, from a newly liberated woman: " 'Yes.' "

(A far cry, of course, from the women's magazines, with their self-help guides, their soothing balm and encouraging advice for the housewife's role.)

Cynthia Ozick offered a moving personal account that harked back to the skirmish at Town Hall and her doomed attempt, in her struggle against the "woman writer" label with its soap opera image, to root out all signs of personal emotion. The actress-playwright Anselma Dell'Olio (who had objected to cutting her hair at the First Congress) described the sexual revolution and the women's movement as "polar opposites" and took up arms against the male pressure for women to be indiscriminately available.

Most striking of all, however, was a piece that was barely a story at all but a list, compiled by the writer Barbaralee Diamonstein.

The previous year, more than three hundred prominent French-women had publicly declared that they had undergone illegal abortions. Here, in this spring issue of *Ms.*, were the Americans. Along with Gloria and Susan were names that were known throughout the world: Kay Boyle, Hortense Calisher, Nora Ephron, Gael Greene, Lillian Hellman, Dorothy Pitman Hughes, Elizabeth Janeway, Billie Jean King, Maxine Kumin, Viveca Lindfors, Marya Mannes, Anaïs Nin, Grace Paley, Eleanor Perry, Susan Sontag, Barbara W. Tuchman, and many more.

And here, too, was the *Ms.* masthead, its list of editors who had worked so many long hours, days running into nights, time fuzzing. Bina Bernard, Joanne Edgar, Nina Finklestein, Nancy Newhouse, Mary Peacock, Gloria, of course, and her new friend, since the Caucus, Letty Cottin Pogrebin, whose important childrearing article

"Down with Sexist Upbringing" also appeared in that first issue.

Most of the writers and editors rushed out to promote the issue, and one day, as Gloria would remember:

"I was doing one of those local early morning shows in California . . . I was talking about the magazine and the station began getting these telephone calls saying, 'We can't find it.' So I went back to the makeup room and called Clay and said, 'For God's sake, Clay! This is really a disaster. The magazine never got to San Francisco. This is terrible!'

"He called me back and said that it did. . . . It was sold out! Practically the whole issue—250,000 copies—sold out in about eight days!" On top of that, they would all soon discover, they had received 35,000 mailed-in subscriptions, a spectacular response that helped Gloria raise money—$20,000 from Katherine Graham, $1 million from Warner Communications—to start a monthly.

"It was still extremely difficult," she would remember, "because we still had the requirement of being woman-controlled, and no other magazine was. A feminist magazine, you know . . . people thought it was impossible and silly, about burning bras and all that. Harry Reasoner said on television—though he took it back—that we wouldn't last six months."

For the truth was that few foresaw the scope, the unprecedented, oceanic range of this feminist sensibility, the fact that—as would soon be evident—there was nothing about human life on earth (or space, for that matter) that did not concern women. Not love, not birth, not work, not war, art, literature, science, education. In no society had socialism solved "the woman problem"—in spite of the nineteenth-century manifestos of Marx or Engels, in spite of the battles of feminists through the ages. Even in America, the great democratic experiment, sexism skulked, camouflaged, in nearly every corner of life. It lurked at a law firm's annual stag dinner, when the sole female associate, obviously excluded, was sent out on the town with theater tickets, or at a high school track meet where a female runner was jeered from the sidelines with guffaws and sexual innuendo. There was *nothing*, in short, which could not be subjected to that special X-ray vision that would come to be known as "feminist analysis."

Furthermore—and much to the point of this venture—thin were the ranks of the women writers who had never been constrained by editors' views of who, exactly, women were.

329

Fifty-two percent of the population. We are not what you think or make of us. We must speak for ourselves.

It was a hungry, piercing need that would lead, at lighter moments, to the corny, but not altogether far-fetched, mid-seventies joke:

"How many feminists does it take to change a light bulb?"

Answer: "Ten. One to change the bulb and nine to write about it."

And whether or not *Ms.* was edited by consensus, as Gloria and the masthead steadfastly claimed, or whether Gloria herself exercised final editorial control, as Clay and most everyone who worked for it would contend, would not, to most of the country, matter. *Ms.* was destined to be the popular voice of feminism in America.

Among its critics would be a few radicals who considered the magazine soft and middlebrow, even given to exploiting writers. In the Redstockings' book, *Feminist Revolution,* columnist Ellen Willis would describe the *Ms.* "line" as "a mushy, sentimental idea of sisterhood designed to obscure political conflicts between women." The magazine, she would add, being "editor-centered . . . politically and aesthetically bland and predictable," focused on "fantasies of lost matriarchies, female superiority and 'mother right.' "

Many distinguished journalists would find *Ms.* too rigid, its ideology narrow and coarsening to the creative process. One such journalist left *Ms.* unhappy with what she saw as a charade of sisterhood masking a high level of anger. Another complained that in spite of Letty Pogrebin's ongoing series "Stories for Free Children," the magazine's attitudes toward marriage and childbearing were testy. Still another objected to an unrealistic article about the joys of bringing children into the workplace itself, using the magazine's own office as an example.

Susan Brownmiller, for one, quit *Ms.* very quickly:

"The problem was that there were all those women out there who had something to say and couldn't say it in other publications. And Gloria was worried about elitism, terrified of antagonizing blacks and lesbians, burdened by the worry the magazine would say something that would be misinterpreted. Forced sterilization, for example, was not as big an issue as abortion, but it was something blacks had raised, so *Ms.* took it up."

Furthermore, and more problematic for the writer:

"They wanted consensus on every article," Susan would remember. "There was a party line and there were political censors so that stories came back with the notation, 'You must include this or this.' That magazine could have had the best women writers in the city, but stories were being censored by all these journalistic novices, and it inhibited free thinking."

Free thinking—all the new ideas—from Susan's perspective, had already been well developed in the radical groups, and *Ms.* would now publish them secondhand.

Not "blaming the victim," for instance, had emerged intact from the Redstockings' "pro-woman" line—that vision of solidarity that took the woman's side in all instances. It would be used in the future to attack an enormous range of social injustices—the legal defenses that protected rapists and ignored the plight of battered women, discrimination against the underprivileged and underprotected in every walk of life. As a journalistic tool, however—especially in the hands of a painter of portraits—it could be blunt-ended, reductive.

Gloria herself would embark from this premise in profiles of women with whom she was especially empathetic—Jackie Onassis, for instance, the pornography star Linda Lovelace, or the actress Marilyn Monroe. Viewing these women almost exclusively in terms of their victimization, as the passive tools of a sexist society, giving as little weight to their drives and ambitions as she did her own, some critics would note, created thin portraits. Her subjects would sometimes appear, in the words of the lachrymose, turn-of-the-century lyric, "more to be pitied than censured."

And *Ms.* was—and would be—no fan of NOW or its leaders, least of all Betty Friedan, whose presence on these pages would be confined to a cursory mention, at the end of some list, or a dim photo, at the edge of a crowd, of a small, plump figure.

"They rewrote history," in Susan's opinion, "to convey the impression that it all began with *Ms.*"

But *Ms.* would also publish some of the country's finest novelists —Lois Gould, Cynthia Ozick, Mary Gordon among them—and would soon welcome the radical poet Robin Morgan to its staff. It would discover such remarkable unknown talent as the Pulitzer prize–winning Alice Walker. It would pioneer new discussions of women's health care (including a challenge to the indiscriminate use of radical mastectomies), of rape, of battered women and children, of the horrible, exotic practice of genital mutilation, the "clitoridectomy," although not the far more frequent assault on middle-class women—unnecessary hysterectomies.

"We changed the idea of who could be on the cover of a magazine,"

Ms. editor Joanne Edgar would claim. "We ran an old woman on one cover and a black and white together on another." Its "Letters" columns would be packed with heartfelt personal stories from its readers, and its "No Comment" pages with sharp checks on sexist attitudes.

Almost immediately, however, *Ms.*—or Gloria—piqued the interest of the pornographer Al Goldstein, who took to printing the magazine's telephone number next to CALL FOR A PROSTITUTE in big, block letters. Not only did Goldstein run lewd sketches of Gloria in his magazine (*Screw*), but one day, while Gloria was walking past a newsstand near the *Ms.* offices, she was suddenly confronted by a huge photograph of herself—completely naked—plastered across the racks. Or so it appeared. Actually, Goldstein had superimposed a photograph of Gloria's face on another woman's body.

"It was very upsetting," she would recall, as was Leonard Levitt's article, "SHE: The Awesome Power of Gloria Steinem," which was published in *Esquire* in October 1971, even before the first issue of *Ms.* appeared.

This acerbic, detailed profile was strung high and smart with the names of Gloria's highly placed lovers, as well as her connections. Cesar Chavez, Ted Kennedy, George McGovern, Eugene McCarthy.

"Most recently," wrote Levitt, "this woman, who advanced in public favor by appealing to powerful men, has moved to the front ranks of women's liberation, appealing now to women who do not like powerful men."

The article made much of Gloria's sexy presentation of herself, her jewelry, her clothes, her trips to the hairdresser, her makeup. It was a glamorous description that might actually have been labeled—perhaps in another context, another age, perhaps even for some of the founders of NOW—an "appreciation." To so many young radicals, however, these expensive embellishments were nothing so much as the stigmata of the geisha. Woman as *thing.* Gloria herself had often insisted—with some irritation, in fact—that her appearance and style were "irrelevant," that no matter what designer creation she wore, she should not be described by reporters as "chic."

Furthermore, as she had told *Vogue:* "Any woman who spends more than fifteen minutes getting herself ready to face the world is just screwing herself."

And here was Levitt reporting in *Esquire* that Gloria actually spent more than an hour at her makeup! (Even longer, weekend hostesses would report years later. And for television appearances, a personal makeup expert.) He quoted a female observer at one of Gloria's speeches:

"Gloria, these are house cows, secretaries, receptionists. They don't want to know about your male chauvinist pig editors. They want to know how you did it. Tell them how you did it, Gloria, tell them how you did it!"

But that, Gloria would never do. How to get a man, how to enjoy sex, how to "do the best with what you've got" were the province of Helen Gurley Brown and her spectacularly successful *Cosmopolitan,* a magazine that would far outstrip the nearly always financially ailing *Ms.* The philosophic difference between the two editors would eventually be expressed in a daytime television interview Gloria conducted with Helen.

Both the Smith College alumna and the *Cosmo* editor, who had never gone to college at all, would be graciously polite, but Gloria's voice would be hard-edged and stern as she insisted that the sexy *Cosmopolitan* actually posed a danger to women—by telling them to dissemble to men. And, furthermore, why hadn't Helen demanded a seat on the board of the magazine's owner—the Hearst Corporation?

Helen would reply that she did not feel in the least victimized, that she was delighted with her progress and stature at Hearst, that she used her husband's name (movie producer David Brown) because she *wanted* to, and that Gloria was "so steeped in the question of inequality" that she was "always turning everything we talk about" back to her feminist cause. Even more to the point, in Helen's view, was that Gloria should realize that not every girl had men hanging around like she did.

"You've always had men in love with you, Gloria," Helen would say. "It's hard enough, Gloria, to get a man in your life if you're over forty without saying to him, 'Look, I didn't have an orgasm last night, I never have an orgasm with you and the way things are going . . .'"

At Gloria's insistence that "you wouldn't want that man in your life," Helen would suggest that Gloria herself had used many of the subtle, male-flattering techniques that she so abhorred in the pages of *Cosmopolitan,* that like so many intelligent women, she was a good deal more aggressive than she admitted.

But *Cosmo's* cupcake diplomacy (or servile manipulation, depending on, if not your class or pride, certainly your feminist loyalties) was anathema to radical feminists. It seemed to imply, as the women's magazines' "how-tos" always had, that something was wrong with *you,* the woman, something, of course, that *you* could now fix. It was, in short, "blaming the victim," teaching the "victim" to adapt, instead of working to change the system.

And here, it seemed, was Levitt insisting that Gloria had "adapted" herself, thus having her cake and eating it, too! Gloria, he wrote, "gave a man back the image of himself he wanted to see." She could, he continued, quoting one of her friends, "bring out the best in a man because she's so engaging and agreeable and submissive."

And yet, at the same time, there was Gloria's epigram: "A woman needs a man like a fish needs a bicycle."

Like the thousands of tinted aviator glasses that suddenly appeared on thousands of sunburned noses, this message was tacked up bravely on bulletin boards across the country.

"I guess it gave some comfort to the singles," Betty would acknowledge years later. "But really, Gloria was a phony. *She* always *had* a man. And I used to catch her hiding behind a *Vogue* magazine at Kenneth's, having her hair streaked."

But Gloria was "very bothered" by the *Esquire* profile, she told one journalist, because she regarded Levitt's piece "not only as a personal attack but as a particularly offensive instance of machismo journalism . . .

"I don't mind people attacking me on issues, like William Buckley did," she said, "but I mind a sexist attack. It's a character fault, I guess, that I'm upset by this kind of ridicule, but I am."

Buckley, in fact, had addressed the question of fund-raising for Angela Davis, the black, Communist philosophy instructor being tried as an accomplice in the Soledad murders, a woman whom Gloria strongly supported. Only in passing had he noted that Gloria "veers dangerously close to the position that no woman can be held responsible for anything." And, in another column: "the lady's logic has never been her principal contribution to the scene."

"Sexist attacks" such as Levitt's, infrequent as they were, found plenty of space in that wide-open center court known as the "personality profile." There, in that boundlessly expanding locus of celebrity journalism, "the personal is the political" could snarl itself up like a thick ball of wool. If the source of all politics was the personal, then, quite obviously, most especially in feminist terms, the personal life of a visible activist, who graced the covers of magazines—whether leader or spokeswoman or, as Gloria would call herself, "more of a transmitter"—was a vital subject for exploration. (As, more than a decade later, presidential candidate Gary Hart would discover.)

Negative comments on one's personal life could be, of course, upsetting, and Pat Nixon, it was said, had been as disturbed by Gloria's interview of her three years earlier as Gloria had been by Levitt's. Perhaps Mrs. Nixon's connection to politics made her fair game, for indeed, in January, just prior to President Nixon's trip to China, the editor of the brand-new *Ms.* magazine lit into him as well.

"Richard Nixon," Gloria proclaimed, in a speech before the National Press Club in Washington, "is the most sexually insecure political leader since Napoleon."

And though no one labeled this comment "a sexist attack," the columnist James A. Wechsler quipped: "Not even her hardest detractors have accused Miss Steinem of personal research in the realm of Richard Nixon's sexuality."

But since by then Gloria was out on the hustings campaigning for the Democratic front-runner George McGovern, her jab at Nixon seemed to fit into the scheme of things.

For some time now, Gloria had been looking toward something more, "toward a wider role of some sort . . . politics maybe," Clay would recall. She had been moving beyond journalism, and she confessed to him that she wasn't sure that taking on the editorship of *Ms.* was the right step. She had attempted to write movie scripts, and, in 1971, embarked on a collaboration with the actress Marlo Thomas, who was, in her way, already something of a feminist herself.

As a small child, Marlo had mounted her own protest with a little booklet ("Women Are People, Too") addressed to her loving but traditional father, comedian Danny Thomas. She had left the Catholic Church in her twenties because, in her eyes, "it failed to support an independent point of view." For the past five years, the cutesy-poo but independent "That Girl," blaring "Don-*ald*" at her boyfriend while sticking to her guns, had been a nationwide television winner, the first TV heroine to live the single life, alone in an apartment. With the run of "That Girl" at an end, the thirty-three-year-old actress was looking for new projects.

"Gloria and I were going to do a script together," Marlo would recall. "We were just very much aligned with each other. We were absolutely attuned. We were both single and leggy in miniskirts, and had long hair. I had this long black hair; she had this long blond hair.

We both wore sunglasses in our hair and we looked like the flip side of each other.

"There was a kind of kinship and understanding of what you have to go through as a pretty girl. We were really friends. Gloria was beautiful and strong and also charming and funny and soft and kind and sisterly and friendly. All those nice things. I was so happy to meet someone who wasn't married—who like me had made a choice, and there was nothing wrong with her. And we were going to do this movie together."

Instead, however, the two single, leggy, miniskirted dynamos soon found themselves meeting at various functions. Like most of America, Marlo had heard about the new movement, even considered herself "one of them, whatever it was."

"I seemed to fit the profile," Marlo would recall. "I was out there, I was independent, I was working, I wasn't married." And Gloria began to "politicize" her, as Marlo would remember it, to convince her that "feminism wasn't just rising to the top. Feminism was helping other women get to the top."

By then, Marlo was so beloved that it was an article of faith in the women's magazine trade that her picture on the cover almost guaranteed a sellout issue. "That Girl" had been the first glimmer of televised acceptance of a single woman's independence ("Mary Tyler Moore" was the second), and the enormously popular voice of Marlo Thomas was soon heard in behalf of feminism. "A man has to be Joe McCarthy to be called ruthless," Marlo would quip. "All a woman has to do is put you on hold."

The movie fell by the wayside and Gloria's choice—neither scriptwriting nor, as Clay had thought it might be, politics, but the enduring editorship of *Ms.*—was, in his view, the right one.

"I think she just figured it out properly," he would conclude. "Why nail yourself down to political office that would get you involved with a lot of extraneous things? Washington follows where the people tell it to go. The power of opinion is the power of the twentieth century.

"Gloria is out there stirring up opinion. That, in the end, is the ultimate power."

Hartford, Feb. 8, 1972 (UPI)—Gloria Steinem, the glamour girl of the women's liberation movement, is "ripping off the movement for private profit," according to fellow activist Betty Friedan, author of The Feminine

Mystique. Mrs. Friedan, who spoke at the opening of Women's Week at Trinity College yesterday, said Miss Steinem has never been a part of the organized women's liberation movement.

"The media tried to make her a celebrity," Mrs. Friedan said, "but no one should mistake her for a leader."

Miss Steinem, a writer and prominent spokesman for the movement, is editor of Ms., a new women's liberation magazine.

The story was so small that few, perhaps, would have noticed it had the *New York Post* not quickly jumped in with interviews of both women.

"Women's Lib Stars Make Up—Sort Of" was the headlined result.

Betty, it seemed, claimed she was misquoted. She had phoned Gloria about the "misunderstanding." Gloria, it seemed, was not convinced. Betty knew full well that Gloria and the *Ms.* staff were "struggling away, with no salaries," Steinem told the *Post* reporter, and that while she and her friends turned back half their speaking fees to the women's movement, "Betty doesn't think it's fair to expect that she should." Of course, Gloria continued, Betty has children and "we can't get into a position of policing each other's incomes. . . .

"There are obvious ego problems," Gloria added. "If *I* have a lot of problems about my being a leader of the women's movement, I'm sure *she* has even more about me being a leader of the women's movement."

And Betty, with her unfortunate penchant for antagonizing the press, huffed indignantly about the scads of more serious projects she was currently involved in and how she was late for an appointment. *Bang!* the receiver slammed down, after which both women steered off on their speechmaking around the countryside.

21

IF NOT
POWER, WHAT?

To urge the creation of a new morality, a new
"world," does not imply that we will invent new values.

—Marilyn French, *Beyond Power: On Women, Men, and*
Morals, 1985

"This year," Betty proclaimed, "women will make policy, not coffee!"
And, in this "Year of the Woman," 1972, which was also an election
year, she covered ground, talking "mainstream."

On Long Island: "We cannot afford the mental masturbation of
endless consciousness raising."

Upstate, at Grossinger's hotel, with co-panelist Joan Garrity, the
author of *The Sensuous Woman*: "Singles weekends are meat on the
butcher block."

In Peoria: "Men can't be the enemy. They're here to stay."

And in New York, where, at a lawyers' conference on reforming
divorce laws, Betty grew cautious. As if in answer to Gloria's earlier
paean to "no more alimony," she approached the slippery, supercharged subject with the care of a cat on a roof, making a point, in
the process, that was only too prophetic:

"The reality today is that most wives—because of unequal treatment in the past—are not equipped to earn adequate livings for themselves and their children."

She campaigned for the "Chisholm for President" effort as "the opening note of a new politics." She would not, she insisted, trust any of the male candidates until they made definite promises on women's issues.

Gloria, on the other hand, committed herself to McGovern. So wholehearted was her support that she posed for photographers on the arm of McGovern's chair—her miniskirt revealing a dance-hall show of legs—leaving some longtime NOW members to mumble unhappily about the "geisha" look of that shot.

But as even those critics had to admit, the enormous crowds Gloria attracted were surprising even seasoned reporters. Sometimes up to five thousand at a clip, outdrawing Ralph Nader and even McGovern himself. And she revealed—as she would continue to over the years—a remarkable talent, not only for picking up pithy sayings, but for coining them herself. Steinemisms, they would be called, as in "We are becoming the men we wanted to marry," or "Children are just small people; some I like, some I don't."

And now in Georgia: "Most of us are only one man away from welfare."

In New Hampshire: "The most important thing is that George McGovern is not a prisoner of the masculine mystique. He can admit mistakes."

In Queens, just after Communist Angela Davis was freed: "She is a symbol of hope and change for a humanist revolution."

By spring, with spirits as high as the moon, Helen Reddy was warbling her future Grammy winner "I Am Woman." The National Women's Political Caucus, having received letters of support from both Democratic hopefuls, George McGovern and Hubert H. Humphrey, staked its demand for an equal number of female to male delegates at the conventions.

Never had there been so many feminist "highs," as, across the country, one after another, demonstrations continued to swirl . . . protests against a typewriter ad demeaning to secretaries, against a toy fair's Barbie doll for perpetuating the stereotype of girls as mannequins, sex objects, or housekeepers, class-action lawsuits against unfair hiring and promotion practices, especially at universities, a drive to rid textbooks of stereotyped language.

By now, in this "Year of the Woman," a scholarly history of the movement stood proud in the bookstores.

Rebirth of Feminism, written by CBS News staffer Judith Hole and political scientist Ellen Levine, did not, because of the time frame perhaps, mention Gloria, but it did delineate Betty's role in sparking the movement. The book focused mainly on activities in New York— "precisely because," the authors wrote, "the movement in New York is so varied and protean in character it can in some sense serve as a microcosm of the movement as a whole. Moreover, although other cities may not have experienced these problems and transitions, it is most often the case that the changes and growth patterns in New York only precede similar changes elsewhere."

That year, too, ABC newswoman Marlene Sanders, who had finally overcome the embarrassing loss of her film, wrote and narrated the first full-scale documentary feature on women's lib.

Inexorably, inevitably, those "firsts" mounted up. American Heritage published the first dictionary to include "sexism," "liberated women," and "Ms.," and the Feminist Press published a Women's Studies Newsletter. The first international festival of women's films opened in New York, the first women were admitted to the marching band at the University of Minnesota, and Sally Priesand became the first woman rabbi.

On March 22, the ERA, which had already passed the House by an overwhelming vote, sailed through the Senate with a vote of 84 to 8. This time no snickers were heard about men being Playboy Bunnies, or "Can she pitch for the Mets?" The resistant women's organizations and labor unions had seen the light, and Congress had simply followed suit.

EQUALITY OF RIGHTS UNDER THE LAW SHALL NOT BE DENIED OR ABRIDGED BY THE UNITED STATES OR BY ANY STATE ON ACCOUNT OF SEX.

As apparently simple as it was self-evident. Everyone was feeling so strong, by then, that a few brave souls even ventured, publicly, into a bit of self-criticism.

Nora Ephron, the country's funniest feminist, addressed herself, in *Esquire,* to the issue of breasts, the objectification of which having been recently rejected as a male fetish. Ephron had grown up in what she called "the terrible fifties—with rigid stereotypical sex roles, the insistence that men be men and dress like men and women be women and dress like women . . . " and she claimed to be obsessed, still, with feelings of inadequacy over her small breasts. She listened to her girlfriends, "the ones with nice, big breasts . . . go on endlessly about how their lives had been far more miserable than mine. Their bra straps were snapped in class. They couldn't sleep on their stomachs. They were stared at whenever the word 'mountain' cropped up in geography . . ."

She had given thought to their remarks, "tried to put myself in their place, considered their point of view." Then she yanked the personal plum right out of the political pie.

"I think," wrote Ephron, "they are full of shit."

And Lyn Tornabene, who had written a glowing profile of Betty ("a woman who changed my life") a year earlier, hinted at a more serious matter.

"Some Women's Liberation activists make liberation sound as though it's a sorority for working women," Tornabene wrote in *Family Circle*. "They make women ashamed of being housewives. Somewhere in the power structure of the movement there should be someone saying that women should not have to serve industry to feel human any more than a man should."

The point was, Lyn would explain years later, that everybody was denigrating housework. In fact, however, her use of the term "power structure" was, at the time, easily as thorny, for "power" was not a word that came easily to feminist lips. Power, to many theorists, was *supposed* to have been eliminated along with structure and leadership, just as *Ms.* was supposed to be edited by consensus. A decade later, in fact, years after the publication of her influential novel *The Women's Room*, Marilyn French would undertake a massive redefinition of the term, devoting more than six hundred pages to the subject in a book called *Beyond Power*.

But the fact that, in 1972, *some* sort of struggle—and if not power, what?—was simmering within the movement was frankly discussed by Natalie Gittelson in the July issue of *Harpers Bazaar*. In an article called "Betty & Gloria & Shirley & Bella," Gittelson led with the provocative query: "Which Ms. has the movement?" Shirley and Bella, in her view, did not, leaving Betty, who, in Gittelson's words, "makes the hard news and has from the movement's earliest days," and "cool, ever-smiling Gloria, whose bright, glacial surface none can crack . . . as unflappable as Betty is fiery."

Betty "gets things done," wrote Gittelson, even though, "to some women who disdain her moral leadership," she seems "simply 'an accident of history' who, having served her purpose, is now therefore expendable."

Gloria was the "media's darling," this writer observed, quoting one "irate" member of the National Women's Political Caucus who insisted that while Gloria "was piously proclaiming *on* the platform that the movement should have no 'stars,' she spent a lot of time *off* the platform with reporters and photographers from *Time* and *Newsweek*," one of whom was "doing a star story on her."

Gloria was indeed a star, as magnetic a presence as such box office draws as Warren Beatty and Shirley MacLaine, who joined her in the McGovern camp. Hollywood, which had often dabbled in politics—in both films and reality—was much involved in the issue of the Vietnam War, and as it dragged on, and as Nixon mined Haiphong harbor and bombed rail lines to China, much of Hollywood's film community—along with many other liberal American groups—was outraged.

"This new escalation is reckless . . . a flirtation with World War III," candidate McGovern protested, thereby heaving some of the movie world's brightest lights aboard his antiwar campaign. And some of these war protestors were, by this time, budding feminists as well.

The actress Jane Fonda, whose mid-seventies antiwar film *Coming Home* would reveal a moving feminist sensibility, had already been grounded in the women's movement by Flo Kennedy. Jane and Flo had met while Fonda was researching *Klute,* her film portrayal of a prostitute, which debuted in 1971. Flo—champion battler for the underdog—would go on to form Coyote (Cut Out Your Old Tired Ethics), which would defend the rights of prostitutes, but prior to the making of *Klute,* she had helped Jane explore the tenuous, seamy lives of the "red-light" districts.

Now, with *Klute* (along with *Barbarella* and Roger Vadim) behind her, Fonda was married to antiwar New Left activist Tom Hayden, and in July 1972 she traveled to North Vietnam and broadcast an appeal to U.S. pilots over the Voice of Vietnam Radio.

"I implore you, I beg you, to consider what you are doing," she said. "In the area where I went, it was easy to see that there are no military targets, there is no important highway, there is no communications network. . . . These are peasants. They grow rice and they rear pigs. They are similar to the farmers in the Midwest many years ago. . . . Are these people your enemy? What will you say to your children years from now when they ask you why you fought the war?"

Many who sympathized with Fonda's motives questioned her

methods. Others, far angrier, called her "Hanoi Jane," even accused her of treason.

Actress Shirley MacLaine, far less controversially, campaigned on television for George McGovern, forming, in the process, a friendship with Bella Abzug. As did Marlo Thomas, who would soon prove one of the most attractive voices of feminism in the country.

"Nineteen seventy-two is the year for women," Bella announced. "Whatever happens in '72, things will never be the same."

Whatever happens, Bella meant, in this election. Or first of all—and more to the point, since, as most everyone agreed, it would be the Democrats, the progressives, who would surely bow first to women's pressure—at the Democratic National Convention in Miami.

The signs were all there. Anyone watching that heat-toughened playground that summer could see it about to happen. The disorder, the self-indulgence, the rebellious hope of the sixties were over. Abbie Hoffman, Jerry Rubin, the poet Allen Ginsberg, the yippies and the hippies were hanging out—amid Quaaludes, poinsettias, and tired, lackluster complacency—in Flamingo Park. Their era, clearly, was ending. Women, with their enthusiasm high as that shimmering, bleaching sun and hopes so contagious that they all seemed to buzz aloud with it, were, in a whole new way, just beginning.

And so what if the accommodations were not exactly presidential, if, at the $8-a-night headquarters of the National Women's Political Caucus, fuses blew, elevators got stuck, phones overloaded, and the dank, dismal place was full of cockroaches. The "boiler room" was steaming away, and a brand-new gang was in the game. When Flo Kennedy and her Feminist Party found their hotel reservations had gone to somebody else, Flo simply plunked down bag and baggage in the lobby. There, to the delight of reporters, she promptly burst forth into the song she had been singing and leading on college campuses around the country.

"Move on over or we'll move on over you. . . . I'm tired of these bastards fuckin' over me."

With a turban on her head, medallions clanging around her neck, and a money pouch buckled around her hips like a gun holster, Flo, with her penchant for street theater, jazzed the joint daily. Throughout the run of the convention, the press would find her, under that flat, cloudless Florida sky, commandeering a six-lane thoroughfare for a parade or posing for a movie crew in the churning surf of the blue Atlantic. The surf bit—and for this Flo was wrapped in a white bed sheet and propped in a beach chair—was for Sandra Hochman's witty movie, called *The Year of the Woman,* of course, in which Flo would appear looking for all the world like a fallen angel.

And, as usual, Flo dished out the copy for the press:

"Little boys are taught to hit and little girls are taught to cry."

"Housework is the nearest thing to slavery except the real thing. Nothing is quite so debilitating and imprisoning as a child, but if you're going to be kept in a position where you think slavery is a good deal, you'd better hope you'll get a good master."

"Child-care facilities are just like rest rooms. If you need them, you should have them."

"First you're on the pedestal and then you're in the boiling water. First you're sprayed with Chanel No. 5 and then you're getting it in the eye."

By now, the entire presidential nominating ritual was media fix-ated, and though few foresaw that the country would one day actually elect a movie actor to the nation's highest office, this year the presidential campaign was the most camera-conscious, star-struck in the nation's history.

Betty had arrived at the convention in an awkward position. Through some "maneuver," as she would describe it, Gloria seemed to be the spokesperson (a newly accepted term that year) for the National Women's Political Caucus. Just as she had at that first meeting of the Caucus a year earlier, Gloria had pressed to have *other women*—not just the women's lib "stars"—come forward. But that "command," Betty would complain, only allowed Gloria herself the full access. "In the end it was somehow Gloria who would speak to the press."

And the press, of course, was everywhere. This convention was so electric—and the new role of women so revolutionary—that major magazines were actually sending *feminists* to cover it.

Nora Ephron, on assignment for *Esquire,* would depict Betty's entrance on the scene this way:

"The cameras are clicking at Gloria and Bella has swept in trailed by a vortex of television crews, and there is Betty, off to the side, just slightly out of frame. The cameras will occasionally catch a shoulder of her flowered granny dress or a stray wisp of her chaotic graying hair or one of her hands churning up the air; but it will be accidental, background in a photograph of Gloria, or a photograph of Bella, or a photograph of Gloria and Bella. Betty's eyes are darting back and forth trying to catch someone's attention, anyone's attention. No use."

And then Betty griped, according to Ephron: "I'm so disgusted with Gloria." (Exactly *how* disgusted, nobody yet knew.)

Meanwhile, like *Esquire*, *Harper's* had assigned a feminist writer as well. Here on the scene, along with Betty and Gloria and Shirley and Bella and Flo, was Germaine, wearing, for this momentous occasion, denim overalls.

And while Germaine was covering the convention for *Harper's*, the press was covering her. One story reported that the six-foot-tall literary guerrilla with the high cheekbones and the luxuriant cascade of hair had asked—out of feminist curiosity, apparently—to meet a prostitute at the Poodle Bar. There Germaine had found herself confronted with nothing more—or less—than irritating, maternal queries about her attire.

"But why do you dress like that?" the hooker asked.

"I make more money than you do," Germaine replied.

"You look terrible," the woman persisted.

"Look," said Germaine, her jaw firming up, "I'm tired of this shit. I wear this, it feels good, it's got pockets and I carry lots of things and I've always had this haggard look and lots of people like it." (One notable exception being Harriet Van Horne, who, still complaining that the women's libbers were "sweaty and unwomanly," took Germaine to task for "discussing her menses" on the "Dick Cavett Show.")

Germaine was not entirely captivated by the democratic hoopla, either—or, to be precise, by the women's role in it. And as the convention progressed, with its wheeling and dealing, button-holing, pleading, lobbying, she grew suspicious.

"Gloria's relentless prominence in all affairs began to disturb me," Germaine would report in *Harper's*, "and most of all her [Gloria's] occasional wistful mentions of 'the smoke-filled rooms where the decisions are made . . .' And all the while, McGovern seemed to be ignoring the central women's issue—abortion—and instead, even addressing the Caucus, gave his stock speech on Vietnam."

Nor could this outspoken young woman make sense of why, at that same meeting, Jacqui Ceballos, the NOW official who had braved the first speaker's role at Town Hall, was left out on a limb.

"Suddenly, there was an interruption," Germaine would write. "Jacqui Ceballos, deadly pale, was on her feet just below the stage.

" 'What about the right to control our own bodies?' she cried. 'We'll never be free till we have that!'

"Bella and Gloria stared glassily out into the room, as if they were deaf or entranced," leaving Germaine to wonder "if they had already made some sort of deal. . . . What could be worth it? . . .

"The women were in Miami as cards in McGovern's hand," she concluded sadly, "to be discarded as he wished, not as players at the table."

Years later, in fact, Germaine would *still* look back on the whole thing as a disaster.

"The women really broke my heart," she would remember, "because they had fallen for the idea that they'd be accepted into the power structure. They hadn't and they never would be. But there was Gloria. She was being invited into the smoke-filled rooms, but what the hell did she have to deal with? She couldn't deliver a vote. She couldn't deliver shit!

"I think all Americans are politically illiterate. They have no idea of history or historical process, of the class struggle, or even any version of what it might be. They have this mad optimism which says 'Anybody can make it, they can pull themselves up by the bootstraps.' And that is a lie. McGovern knew that he had them because where the fuck else did they have to go? They were just sitting ducks and they couldn't see it. They kept on talking big. If they had big cigars with bands on them, they would have puffed them. I thought I was going to disgrace myself by having—well, not hysterics—by just crying uncontrollably in front of the TV cameras."

Gloria, in fact, did cry. On the convention floor and then later, walking down Collins Avenue. Gloria was very upset at not being taken seriously, Nora Ephron would report.

"I'm just tired of being screwed," she said, "and screwed by my friends. We're just walking wombs."

Ephron, according to that same *Esquire* piece, was somewhat baffled by Gloria's tears, never herself, she noted, having cried "over anything remotely political" in her life. But, as she also reflected, "Gloria Steinem has in the past year undergone a total metamorphosis, one that makes her critics extremely uncomfortable. Like Jane Fonda, she has become dedicated in a way that is a little frightening and awe-inspiring . . ."

As for the conflict between Gloria and Betty:

"It is probably too easy to go on about the two of them this way," Ephron wrote. "Betty as Wicked Witch of the West, Gloria as Ozma, Glinda, Dorothy—take your pick. To talk this way ignores the subtleties, right? Gloria is not, after all, uninterested in power. And yes, she manages to remain above the feud, but that is partly because, unlike Betty, she has friends who will fight dirty for her. Still, it is hard to come out anywhere but squarely on her side. Betty Friedan, in her thoroughly irrational hatred of Steinem, has ceased caring whether or not the effects of that hatred are good or bad for the women's movement."

Betty cringed at the media coverage—not just Nora's "especially bitchy account," she would write, "but all those reporters who suggested that I was jealous of Gloria because she was blonde and pretty and I was not (illustrated by one of those monstrous, ugly pictures of me, mouth open, fist clenched) . . . Gloria is assuredly blonder, younger and prettier than I am—although I never thought of myself as quite so ugly as those pictures made me . . ."

And Betty would also report having it out with Gloria behind the stadium, on the same night that George McGovern was nominated.

"Open conflict," Betty would write, "or rather I shouted and she said sweetly, in effect, that I had to get out or else. I shouted because the meeting of the women delegates which should have been called by the Caucus so that all of us could swing our power behind Shirley Chisholm had been called off, evidently at Gloria's instruction . . .

"I was no match for her, not only because of that matter of looks—which somehow paralyzed me—but because I don't know how to manipulate . . . "

But as it would turn out, Betty was not *completely* paralyzed. By the convention's close, she had called for and won—against great opposition—a roll-call vote on abortion. ("We have to find out," she insisted, "who our enemies are.") The abortion plank was defeated, but for the first time in history, the prickly, divisive subject was openly debated on a convention floor, in the presence of network television cameras.

And though Shirley Chisholm's candidacy got lost in the fray, skillful last-minute politicking brought substantial votes for the vice-presidential nomination of Sissy Farenthold. Furthermore, instead of appearing—as they had in the past—as greeters, ornaments, invisible auxiliaries, women had challenged seating rules and won a 40 percent share of the delegates.

(Not *everyone* saw that as a win. In Sandy Hochman's film, columnist Art Buchwald was inconsolable. Observing that "it was the first time girls were not just being used to keep men happy at conventions," he confessed that he missed the "hurdy-gurdy pretty girls in their shirts and saddle shoes.")

Nothing, as Bella had said, would ever be the same, even if, in November, the American people, resolutely ignoring—for the moment—the *Washington Post* stories about an odd little burglary in the Watergate, would proceed to elect Richard Nixon by the biggest landslide in history. That year, more women than ever before ran for political office, 28 percent more women were elected to state legislatures, and five new women—Pat Schroeder, Elizabeth Holtzman, Barbara Jordan, Yvonne Brathwaite Burke, and Marjorie Holt, formidable legislators who would help to change the face of Washington politics —would be elected to Congress.

"I have a brain *and* a uterus," Schroeder would soon announce. "I intend to use both."

22

COME THE
REVOLUTION

Lily Tomlin:
And maybe one day we'll do something so magnificent,
everyone in the universe will get goose bumps.

—Jane Wagner, *The Search for Signs of Intelligent Life in*
the Universe, 1986

Before that happened, however, quick on the heels of the convention (but written, obviously, many weeks earlier), Betty let Gloria have it.

McCall's called a full-scale press conference to announce Betty's bombshell, and at that gathering, on July 18, at the Biltmore Hotel in New York, Betty Friedan, author of *The Feminine Mystique,* founder of NOW, wearing for the occasion a plaid summer dress with a ruffle around the neck and dangle earrings, took the stand.

All of the journalists present had read an advance copy of Betty's upcoming article, and within seconds, the conference erupted.

Hisses. Hands waving angrily in the air. A barrage of furious questions burst forth from women reporters, most notably a contingent from *Ms.* They produced a scene, as *Newsday* reported, that was "almost without precedent at American press conferences."

"I deliberated for months before writing this," Betty announced over the din, "because it had been our practice up to now to keep to ourselves differences within the movement. But the movement has become too big to hide or dismiss these differences."

Immediately, there were rude noises.

Why hadn't she taken these "differences" up directly? someone demanded.

"I have asked Gloria several times to debate these ideological issues publicly with me," Betty responded, "but she doesn't seem to want to do this."

For indeed, as Clay had remarked, Gloria was "not confrontational." Even in the age of confrontation politics, debate was never her style. And yet, she had recently proclaimed, "I think we should express our differences. We still agree too much. We're afraid not to —it's our stereotype. We're afraid to eat watermelon."

Stolidly, Betty now chomped on that watermelon, making her points, those same complaints she had raised in her article.

Barring male reporters from meetings, elevating women as a class was *female chauvinism*.

"The assumption that women have any moral or spiritual superiority as a class or that men share some brute insensitivity as a class," she had written, "is female sexism. If I were a man, I would object strenuously . . ."

"Does this mean," she now argued, the hoarse voice rising, "that any woman who admits tenderness or passion for her husband, or any man, has sold out to the enemy? . . .

"If we make men the enemy they will surely lash back at us. If we demand equal treatment from them and still insist on special privilege, we deserve the backlash. . . .

"Men *can* and *must* be with us if we are to change society."

And she did not—no, she would not—back down from the direct personal attacks she had made in her article:

That Bella had chosen to run for Congress against a man (William Ryan) whose record on women's issues was as strong as any woman's. That was *female chauvinism!*

That there was a tone in Gloria's articles in *Ms.* that implied that "women are special and pure, forever wronged by men." That Gloria was promoting "a female chauvinism that makes a woman apologize for loving her husband and children." That she had dismissed marriage as prostitution and assumed that "no woman would ever want to go to bed with a man if she didn't need to sell her body for bread or a mink coat!"

But by then Betty was hitting wild, scattershot. A tangle of intensities, a war of words in which words were obviously beside the point. Whatever her emotional needs, whatever the issues, Betty was marching into battle—with inevitable futility—against a woman who not only commanded a loyal following, a power base, in short, but who also, by now, as Clay had put it, "personified the movement."

Yet in the heat of this moment, for better or for worse, notably absent from the images projected by the latest thrust of the women's movement was not merely *wife* but *mother*. Neither role was one by which most young feminists chose to define themselves. The foolish, tormented, passive, *exclusive* overload of the "Mom" role of the fifties had done its work, and even Betty herself had bristled at the label "mother of the movement." All too often had women been relegated to secondary roles or menial jobs on the ground that they—unlike men—were needed in the home to care for children. All too often had these restrictions led to self-perceptions of the somehow "lesser."

Furthermore, "wife and mother," in this decade of the launch of *People* magazine and the *National Star,* had the sound and smell of an artifact, a has-been. "Mother of the movement," especially one who happened to be a forty-seven-year-old mother of three, would never prompt a flurry of requests to appear on the "Dick Cavett Show"; she would not float magazines, by the millions, off the newsstands. Whatever was *said* by feminists about the need for child care, for maternity leave, for accommodations in the workplace (and, contrary to later criticism, a great deal *was* said), the pervasive *image* of the liberated woman emerged exactly as Marlo Thomas had seen it: independent, unmarried, and, obviously, childless.

"Betty Friedan is glad she likes men and thinks everybody should," wrote the *Daily News.* And in response to Betty's well-covered tirade, Gloria, pleading a case of laryngitis, issued a press release:

"Having been falsely accused by the male Establishment journalists of liking men too much, I am now being falsely accused by a woman Establishment journalist of not liking them enough."

"Gloria wanted me to disappear," Betty would conclude in retrospect. "She just wanted to *disappear* me."

"Some older women," Gloria would remark, "think they own the movement."

"Establishment journalist" served as a well-placed blow at the author of *The Feminine Mystique,* and soon many women, distressed at this public display of division, openly denounced Betty's remarks as

"unfortunate" and "distasteful." Some even predicted that this skirmish, this scratchy little war whoop, tolled the demise of the movement. And, as usual by now, some—both men *and* women—would
not be sorry to see it go.

Given this great splash of interest in the subject, there was, of
course, criticism, even one long article in the *New York Times Magazine* that lumped "women's lib" with such ephemeral ideological fads
as Timothy Leary's drug cult and Charles Reich's "Consciousness III."
Mostly, the male objectors bemoaned the certain death of the family.
Less hysterically, they pointed to the movement's middle-class, intellectual origins, to its lack of appeal outside this "narrow class structure."

William F. Buckley, Jr., waxed wittily splenetic over a textbook
publisher's pamphlet urging the elimination of sexist language from
textbooks. Since 1970, publishing companies—American Heritage
and its dictionary among them—had been examining the use of sexually prejudicial words in the language: "jockette" for female jockey,
or "poetess," or the male pronoun "he" to mean either sex, or the use
of "man" whenever action was implied.

"Early man" now had to be changed to "early human"? Buckley
wailed. "When man invented the wheel" must be switched to "When
people invented the wheel"? So " 'businessmen' is out; and 'business-
people' is in. Presumably the singular is a 'businessperson.' What do
you want to be when you grow up, Johnny? A businessperson. What
do you do with 'repairmen'? Repairperson? . . . The use of the pronoun 'he' to do androgynous duty is out. For instance, you can't say,
'The motorist should slow down if he is hailed by the police.' You
have to say: 'The motorist should slow down if he or she is hailed by
the police.'

" 'Galileo was the astronomer who discovered the moons of Jupiter.
Marie Curie was the beautiful chemist who discovered radium.'
WRONG. Try: 'Galileo was the handsome astronomer who discovered
the moons of Jupiter. Marie Curie was the beautiful chemist who
discovered radium.'

"But what if Galileo was ugly? Or, heaven forfend, what if Galileo
was really handsome and Marie Curie was really ugly (which I happen
to know was the case)?"

As usual, Buckley's objections weren't aimed at the movement itself. Instead, he suggested that *it* should be saved from the mutilation of language.

By?

None other than Germaine Greer, the Shakespearean scholar and "everybody's favorite feminist." Like Mailer before him, Buckley was impressed.

"Miss Greer," he wrote, "is a very brilliant woman who . . . in the course of making her case against 'sexism' exploits the hell out of sex. The kind of attention devoted to her in *Playboy, Evergreen Review,* et al., is inconceivable except that she obligingly spices her remarks with lascivious sexual detail as reliably as the boilerplate pornographers."

Germaine should rush to the rescue of the English language, Buckley prescribed, because "I think—I am not absolutely certain—but I suspect that she is capable of humor" (implying, of course, that there were others who weren't).

And perhaps it was true in those days that, in certain circles, with the purity of one's feminism constantly under a microscope, and with the exception of a few weak jokes about men, humor was in short supply. Everything, as Marlo Thomas would soon discover, was so deadly *solemn,* and many of the American feminists—as Germaine would recall many years later—took up the hunt for veiled sexism with something less than debonair charm.

"They were so fucking self-centered," Germaine eventually would complain, "and we still do not have a basic strategy. We're a movement that hasn't had its Marx, let alone its Lenin.

"Instead of being political, it [the movement] became a religion. There were things you couldn't say. There were observances you had to carry out. You had to dress your little girl in trousers and you took away dolls and you tried to get special language books for them, like the Ayatollah in the schools in Iran . . .

"I mean all that stuff about . . . let's have castration for rape; let's get the pornographers off the streets, string 'em up by the thumbs; let's start burning books; let's say 'Yecch!' women are badly treated in this movie, so we won't see it. There's crypto-fascism in that position."

By then, Germaine would confess as well that she, like Buckley, had winced at the "brutalizing" of her beloved language. ("Spokesperson" was, after all, a mouthful, and "manhole" was threatening to mutate to "personhole" or "accesshole." "Ms.," Germaine would eventually insist, "is not a *word.*")

At the moment, though, with the movement so young, Germaine

remained silent on these issues; even challenged Buckley himself—that formidable debater—before the Cambridge Union in England (taped and broadcast by America's Public Broadcasting Service). The subject was "The Women's Liberation Movement," and Germaine managed to sweep the debate (with an audience vote of 546 to 156) by turning her sympathies for Buckley to her own—and the movement's—advantage.

"Now I am sorry to disappoint you," she told the audience, "but I am not interested in delighting you with a song-and-dance routine with William Buckley, for whom I have rather more respect than you would be prepared to allow. I regard him as a man of intellectual probity, and part of my problem now is that I cannot understand altogether why Mr. Buckley is on the other side of the hall."

Buckley's attacks, after all, were mere pinpricks compared to the full-scale barrage just launched by a woman.

Conservative editor/writer Midge Decter had been heard from on the subject before, but in 1972 she devoted an entire book to the attack.

The New Chastity and Other Arguments Against Women's Liberation, densely written and doggedly psychoanalytic, was not much interested in such issues as equal pay for equal work or any manner of social inequities. (Women, Decter claimed, could always *go home.*) Like Mailer, whom she had urged to write *The Prisoner of Sex,* Decter went for the psyche, an easy target in those heady days of zeal for personhood, when, in certain feminist circles, husbands and babies were viewed not only as entrapments, but as cop-outs, a retreat to a dependent-enslaved way of life. Decter, though often setting up straw women, also landed some zingers.

The liberated woman covertly longs for maidenhood, this wife and mother argued. Feminists were resisting motherhood, and that resistance was nothing less than "an expression of self-hatred . . . a dirty little secret." The maternal urge, she insisted, was to be denied at women's peril.

Furthermore, the sexual revolution had assigned to women "the obligations of an impersonal lust they did not feel but only believed in," and instead of dealing with the choices it presented, they retreated into the comforting role of the victim. Women could be happy *without* orgasms, Decter claimed, and taking as a universal one placard she had seen—"Don't Fuck, Masturbate"—she saw the "founding passion" of women's liberation as an enmity for men.

The new feminism, in Decter's view, was "perversely" drifting toward a world without sex, a withdrawal from the trials and responsibilities of heterosexuality. Betty was a "would-be intellectual," and Kate's *Sexual Politics* was "vulgarity almost not to be credited."

A cold assault, surely, but in this year of empowerment, it seemed no more telling than that March 22 headline in the *New York Times*:

"In Small Town, U.S.A., Women's Liberation Is Either a Joke or a Bore."

Reporting from Hope, Indiana, Judy Klemesrud wrote that hardly anyone in that farming town of 1,500 would recognize either Betty Friedan *or* Gloria Steinem. "The term 'consciousness raising' is likely to elicit a furrowed brow and a 'Huh?' while a male chauvinist pig would probably be identified as just another breed to haul to next summer's Bartholomew County Fair."

People in Hope had certainly *heard* about women's lib, from "their beloved Johnny Carson" or their favorite magazines, *Life, Redbook,* and *Good Housekeeping,* but, as Klemesrud noted: "It's just that they don't care enough about it or don't understand it, to want to know more of the specifics. . . .

" 'What,' asked one of them, 'does burning bras have to do with making us equal?' "

And a certain lawyer in St. Louis (few feminists even noticed her name), who in October was apparently asking a similar question about equal rights in general.

That powerful amendment was already breezing through state legislatures across the country. By the end of the year, after twenty-two states had ratified, projections were clear for passage by—at the latest —the following summer.

"Things will never be the same again," columnist Max Lerner wrote, "in women's minds, and between women and men."

Everything was changing completely.

In the bookstores, Phyllis Chesler's *Women and Madness* argued that what was diagnosed as mental illness in women was often simply a healthy response to a sexist environment. Jessie Bernard's *The Future of Marriage* revealed that marriage was more beneficial for men than women. Barbara Seaman's *Free and Female* offered witty advice for a healthy, unrestrained sex life for women. Sidney Abbot and Barbara Love wrote an intelligent account of lesbian sensibilities in *Sappho Was a Right-On Woman.* Elizabeth Janeway analyzed the myth of woman's frailty in *Man's World, Woman's Place.* Even editor/writer

Michael Korda rode the wave in his book called *Male Chauvinism,* which cleverly pointed out the corporate advantages of women's equality.

In New York, the state penal law was amended to allow conviction of a rapist on the testimony of the victim if her testimony was supported by evidence that she did not consent to sex but was forcibly compelled to submit. On the federal level, the EEOC was empowered to take sex discrimination cases to court, thus providing the means by which employers could be sued by a federal agency. And another, and perhaps the most powerful of legal actions—Title IX of the Educational Amendments—prohibited sex discrimination in most federally funded educational programs, thus providing, among other things, the funding for collegiate women's sports that would eventually produce dazzling winners at the 1984 Olympics.

Those laws were essential, but so was the personal strength needed to use them, as both Ti-Grace Atkinson and Marlo Thomas insisted that year.

Ti-Grace returned from her hospital vigil over Joe Colombo to tell a jam-packed audience "the brutal truth: older women are the garbage of society, a stockpile of losses. Hope is what has done women in. Women in their fifties and sixties know the truth. Housewives have no place to go but revenge. Come the revolution, I want one housewife for every ten revolutionaries."

Marlo took a different approach.

For some time she had searched for a book for her three-year-old niece, something to replace *Sleeping Beauty* or *Cinderella,* with their passive messages of savior princes and glass slippers, or other stories that announced: "I'm a boy, I'm a doctor. I'm a girl, I'm a nurse." Failing to find such a book, Marlo set out to make a record for her niece that included more positive stories.

"I was on an airplane going somewhere for McGovern," the actress would recall years later. "I was reading *Ms.* and Letty had done an article, something to do with what she called 'Stories for Free Children.' When I got off the plane, I called Gloria and asked to meet Letty."

And Letty had helped—or tried to—by gathering stories from writers and editors she knew.

"But when we got all those stories back," Marlo would remember, "they were awful! Just terrible. They were message-y and not fun or entertaining or anything. I knew my niece wouldn't laugh at all, and I was brokenhearted."

Marlo turned to her current boyfriend, Herb Gardner, and to such show business pros as Mel Brooks, Carl Reiner, Peter Stone, and Sheldon Harnick, to performers Harry Belafonte, Dick Cavett, Carol Channing, and Diana Ross. With their help, she produced eighteen charming consciousness-raising songs, a children's celebration of self and of equality, of girls who were athletic and mechanical and boys who played with dolls and cried. And the football star Rosey Grier sang, on this record entitled *Free to Be . . . You and Me*: "It's all right to cry. Crying gets the sad out of you."

By the end of the year, Marlo's record was selling by the thousands to parents and children across the country, its proceeds funding the Free to Be Foundation, the heart and pocketbook of the Ms. Foundation for Women, which would eventually allocate hundreds of thousands of dollars to projects for women and children.

Even now independent centers were sprouting in cities and towns across the land, some bearing names that had never been heard before. Rape crisis, battered women, women's health centers, counseling centers, networking organizations. Already, these projects were changing the environment of women.

"As lovely as Aphrodite—as wise as Athena—with the speed of Mercury and the strength of Hercules—she is known only as WONDER WOMAN!"

Gloria brought the comic strip heroine aboard and everything, it seemed, was moving into place. Everywhere that feminists gathered you could feel it happening, a rushing, gathering-in momentum, camaraderie. Arm-in-arm solidarity. Since the country now understood the *justice* of the women's protest, everything else was sure to follow.

Almost as if to prove the point, on January 22, 1973, the word came down from Washington:

"The Supreme Court overruled today all state laws that prohibit or restrict a woman's right to obtain an abortion during the first three months of pregnancy. The vote was 7 to 2."

Roe v. *Wade*. The legalization of abortion. It seemed—in those giddy, triumphant days—nothing less than the natural course of events.

"NEVER AGAIN," crowed *Ms.* magazine, in two-and-a-half-inch block letters superimposed over a horrifying photograph of a woman who had bled to death in a back-alley abortion.

Ten years had passed since the publication of *The Feminine Mystique,* seven since the founding of NOW, five since the rear-flank attack on the Miss America contest, nearly a decade of battle, of cries in the streets, of rousing messages heard round the world.

Yes, sister, yes!

There was no stopping it now. The signs of affirmation were everywhere. John Mack Carter, the besieged editor of *Ladies' Home Journal,* providing mailing facilities for the National Women's Political Caucus; a bank promoting itself: "If you don't get a mortgage at Lincoln, it's not because you're a woman." Everybody thinking about it. *Everybody* coming around!

Or so it appeared.

Barely heard was that scratching calliope sounding from the Midwest, that lawyer from St. Louis whose organization was known by the command:

STOP ERA.

23

EPILOGUE

The ERA did not pass that summer.

Nor the next.

Eventually, after nearly a decade of hope and tireless campaigning, it would fail. A stunning defeat, both symbolic and real, leaving America one of the few industrialized countries in the world without permanent national protection for women.

Already, in that glorious year of *Roe* v. *Wade,* a certain murkiness had begun to descend on the American movement. The show—the remarkable spectacle of the Golden Age of Feminism that so captivated the world—had begun to shift into the shadows. The flash and the dazzle were fading, the theater lights turning down.

Phyllis Schlafly—that St. Louis lawyer—was, as the unwary feminists quickly discovered, the founder of STOP ERA. She was conservative, upper middle class, Catholic, holder of a master's degree from Harvard, a wife and mother of four sons and two daughters. She claimed that the amendment would destroy the "right to be a woman," that it would "deprive the American woman of many of the fundamental special privileges we now enjoy," and especially the greatest rights of all: *not* to take a job, to keep her baby, and to be supported by her husband.

Those "selfish and misguided" women on television talk shows and picket lines, Schlafly insisted, were intent on "taking our husbands' jobs away," and she was soon delivering apple pies, jars of homemade jam tied round with ribbons, and steaming loaves of home-baked bread to state legislators. Bearing the slogan "From the breadmakers to the breadwinners," a disciplined cadre of women in granny gowns trilled the message that *they*—not those ugly, unhappy feminists who were "out to destroy the family"—spoke for the American female.

Schlafly was crisp, straight-backed, a clever communicator, and, unlike so many of the hot-eyed feminists, as familiarly "American," as "normal" as a soap opera matron. And though she did not, in and of herself, cause the loss of momentum in the women's movement or, for that matter, even with her threats of coed bathrooms, doom the ERA, what she did instead, most successfully, was to touch—and to play on—hidden fears: the fears of women who were growing older, women who believed they *needed* the protection of their husbands, women who stayed at home to raise their children, or who hated their lives in the workforce and, more than anything else, still dreamed of the split-level ranch and the man who would take them there.

The divorced homemaker in Los Angeles, for instance, unskilled, untrained for the workforce, who was desperately seeking a new man; the mother of two teenagers in Boston, resisting the movement's implication that she had wasted her life; the saleswoman in San Diego, who had no intention of offending her boss with talk of a "patriarchy"; and the PTA president in El Paso, who not only adored caring for her home and kids but enjoyed her status as a community leader.

To many of these women, those assertive, verbal feminists touting the ERA—the entire feminist movement, in fact—seemed not only exclusionary but decidedly threatening, especially as word seeped out that meetings of NOW were brawls of claims and counterclaims, most of them centering on lesbianism.

"Dykes."

Far from being put to rest, that subject flared again.

"The lesbian is the rage of all women condensed to the point of explosion," read an early radical tract, and in the decade that followed *Roe* v. *Wade*, the mid-seventies through the mid-eighties, this seemed to be true. On many college campuses, where most young men were by then at least paying lip service to feminist aims, what activating anger remained from the early days was supplied by the lesbians. The implication in certain quarters was that feminist actually *meant* lesbian, and that the only way to become a true feminist was to be lesbian. Or to hate men. To many college students, in the throes of the mating game, the campus activists seemed threatening—too serious, too hard, politicized, masculine, even abnormal and scary.

"No, I'm not one of them. Heavens, no!"

These words, accompanied by raised eyebrows and shrugs of disgust, could be heard clearly through those years out in the heartland. (But far from the powerful centers of publishing and government.) Suburban NOW recruiters were hard put to get women to join, and the unaligned phrased their resistance in the terms that Betty herself had used to describe—and to warn—the radicals: "extremist," "anti-male," "anti-family."

Once again, as in ages past, certain vague but to many women menacing connotations had attached themselves like a thicket of barnacles to the very word "feminist."

"Can't you think of another *word*?" one young woman quéried. "Feminist sounds so polarizing, so *one-sexist*, so anti-love."

But most women certainly weren't anti-love. Surely not anti their hard-working husbands, their beloved sons. Nor were they, for the most part, anti-domestic, another tenacious impression linked to the feminists, a sense that baking brownies for your family was somehow pathetically retrograde.

Most women, in short, were not ideologues, and they were put off by the rigidities that developed in those quieter years.

You must *never* say "girl"; you must *never* let your daughter play with a Barbie doll; you must *never* say "chair*man*," "mail*man*," "fire*man*."

Many began to question what all this "independence" would lead to anyway. Was the rebellion of a Patty Hearst the end result? Or the rape and murder that awaited the hapless adventurer in *Looking for Mr. Goodbar*? Or was the reality, after all, that in order to achieve the prescribed heights of strength an ordinary female required spare parts like the Bionic Woman?

What was it all about, anyhow?

Confusion reigned as the discussion moved from cocktail party chatter into the intimacy of kitchens and coffee shops.

Should men open doors for you or shouldn't they? Should they diaper the baby or not? Are women turned on by male pinups? Should you have an extramarital affair? And what about your husband?

Most damaging of all, didn't this level of questioning seem, given the temper of the times, somehow . . . trivial?

Here, after all, the very same year as the abortion ruling, the real significance of that break-in at the Watergate began to grip the country. Then the television hearings themselves, with their grim and powerful dramatis personae: Haldeman, Ehrlichman, Kleindienst, John Mitchell, John Dean. Americans were drawn to their screens as that tale of deception at the highest level of government played itself out like a perfectly crafted mystery story. Nor did the denouement— a president of the United States as good as impeached—relax the nation's tense fascination with day-to-day events. By the mid-seventies, the first signs of our bizarre vulnerability to small groups of fanatics from small, perhaps equally fanatic countries in the Middle East began to appear along with new, disquieting names: Palestine Liberation Organization, Khadafy, Khomeini—terrorism.

As the decade wore on and, with it, the ominous, burgeoning threat of the oil crisis, a series of inflationary spirals wore away at the nation's confidence. Americans began to worry about their jobs and their livelihoods, which still meant, to most families, *men's* jobs and *men's* livelihoods. *An Unmarried Woman* struck a nerve as rumors circulated that this inspiring, feminist-oriented film had led many women to leave their husbands. And then—since these ex-wives were not, after all, quite so magnetic as Jill Clayburgh, the movie's heroine (or so their friends speculated)—they had found themselves in trouble.

Even more alarming—to mothers and fathers—was the growing cloud of religious cultism. After nearly one thousand died in the Jonestown massacre, and as uncounted numbers of adolescents were "brainwashed" by groups like the Moonies, parents worried about what sort of family structures would protect their children. It did seem, in those years when the dulcet southern voice of Jimmy Carter dispensed apparent sweet reason, that such traditional values deserved far greater concern than the question of whether or not Mother was "fulfilling" herself. As did, surely—after Love Canal and the accident at Three Mile Island—the possibility that toxic waste and nuclear power were threatening all life on the planet.

Meanwhile, however, in what seemed to so many a peripheral, faraway place, the political struggle of feminism continued. Betty, Gloria, Germaine, and the rest pressed on through a series of major women's conferences. The First National Women's Conference, for example, held in Houston in 1977, not only drew nearly 15,000 women but First Ladies Betty Ford, Rosalynn Carter, and Lady Bird Johnson.

To those who attended, the Houston conference was the height, the heady, climactic celebration of the women's movement. Few Americans sensed its import, however. Houston was blitzed from the front pages by a sudden, heartening vision of peace in the Middle East: the Egyptian president Anwar Sadat, reflecting the mood of Carter's Camp David accords, appeared on Israeli soil, clasping hands with his former archenemy.

And so the political center of the feminist rebellion moved even farther from the daily lives of most women. Especially since it seemed —if one happened to catch a newspaper item or a piece of some chatter on a television show—such a dense thicket, such a wilderness of theory.

Feminism always was, perhaps always will be, maddeningly complex, and the movement itself as disputatious as any in history. For every flag flown high, there was opposition from within.

Not every woman who considered herself an ardent feminist, as it turned out, was in favor of legal abortion. Major splits developed as those years wore on, over supporting all women, whatever their politics or character; over mimicking men instead of adhering to women's values; over the dangers of pornography versus the threat of censorship.

Definitions, in a complex industrial society, became very important. Women's experience was different, but did "unique" also imply "separate"? Premenstrual syndrome: What did this female "disability" augur for women's ability to hold power? Comparable worth: Why were the jobs women held inevitably the ones with lower salaries? Should pregnancy be defined, for employment purposes, as ordinary illness? There was wariness, in certain feminist circles, of singling out women for special treatment.

New technologies rose to remedy infertility, most of them having to do, of course, not with men's bodies, but with women's. Just as the pill had raised doubts in the sixties, the question of whether these new techniques were boon or exploitation elevated temperatures.

Throughout those years, the internecine warfare of the movement did not—perhaps *could not*—cease. Not only was its ideology rich with paradox, not only did it contain elements completely unknown to any previous social movements (the exact mechanics of a woman's

363

orgasm, for instance, or, as *Ms.* editor Andrea Dworkin would insist, the entire role of sexual intercourse), but it sought for its constituency over half the world's population!

"The woman problem" was, obviously, worldwide and as feminists began to explore international waters (though never extensively enough, in Germaine's view), ugly statistics emerged. Women performed two-thirds of the world's work, yet everywhere they were always, in the aggregate, the poorest people, receiving only 10 percent of the income, owning only 1 percent of the property. Sometimes, in certain parts of the world, things only got worse. The resurgence of Islamic fundamentalism set back women's rights in the Middle East; the battles over apartheid in South Africa kept women from their children.

Most discouraging of all was the fact that most of the international conferences designed to address these issues were controlled by cynical, dominating national interests, hiding behind—more often than not—brutal, inflammatory anti-Semitism. The first such conference, opening the United Nations International Women's Year and its Decade of Women, held in Mexico, was headed by that country's president—a man. The delegates were addressed by women who had, at best, questionable credentials: Princess Ashraf of Iran, for instance, the twin sister of a potentate who had divorced his wife when she could not bear him a son; Imelda Marcos, a woman who was not only in power solely by virtue of her marriage to the president of the Philippines, but who, along with her husband, would soon be revealed as staggeringly corrupt.

Furthermore, though "anatomy is not destiny" was, like so many other slogans, a catchy phrase, the fact was that anatomy—or, at least, biology—did indeed play a role in a woman's condition. As the definition of "woman" was explored further, sparks flew within the movement itself.

Was the role of the nurturing mother one that brought pleasure and self-fulfillment, or was it foisted on women by men unwilling to relinquish power in the workplace? Not only did American feminists sometimes fail to understand the needs of women in third world countries, where climbing the corporate ladder was not a goal, but problems were developing in this country as well. Women were beginning to confront serious stresses, not the *result* of the women's movement necessarily but closely connected to it: an economy in which two incomes were often a necessity, not a choice; the suffering

364

—known by that grim phrase, the "feminization of poverty"—in so many female-headed households (an explosion, from 1970 to 1984, of over 80 percent). The new "equal" divorce laws of the late seventies and early eighties, building on an illusion of equality, eliminating alimony, wreaking havoc on already inadequate child support, threw thousands of middle-class women, for varying periods, into impoverished states.

"These are the women," a lobbyist for the growing ranks of "displaced homemakers" would eventually note with anger, "who drove the car pools, ran the bake sales, and organized the Scout troops." These women, who ranged from divorced welfare mothers to widowed country club matrons, she would add, "have gotten a very raw deal."

That the bearing and raising of children should not be solely the concern of women was axiomatic, but there, in reality, it would be. Older women untrained for the workforce. What about them? Younger women at work. What about the kids? What had happened to those demands for child care that NOW had raised in the late sixties?

"This country is drifting toward a fascist state," Kate Millett warned, and once again, she blamed the media. "The media make everything two inches long so it will be really stupid and unimportant. Obfuscation is the name of the game, so the ERA becomes something about toilets, something like civil rights becomes a matter of personal preference, and male chauvinism is just a cute, permissible attitude."

An insightful statement, a lively voice. And yet it was just that—a voice. Not political leadership.

Like the voices of all the other feminist oracles, Kate's had been, one way or another, carried by the media, that magic carpet that she, along with so many other feminists, now blamed for the movement's failures.

The criticism was usually fair and to the point, applied as it was to the media's short and fickle attention span, and yet what few seemed to notice at the time—or even admit, for that matter—was the incomparable role of that incomparable force.

No other social movement in history had swept through the world in quite this way. Never had so many activists plied their trade—not as dockworkers or ministers or politicians, but as writers and journalists. Never had there been a *mass* magazine completely dedicated to a cause; never had there been so many books and articles; never had such a booming, omnivorous power so quickly translated the written word into an immediate presence in so many homes.

The media, with their hunger for conflict and sex appeal, had indeed created stars.

But the media moved on.

And so did these articulate feminists, their names blending by now with dozens of others: Ellie Smeal, Donna Shalala, Carol Bellamy, Judy Goldsmith, Molly Yard. For one reason or another, no one of them rose in those years to unite all women behind her banner.

There was, for instance, Kate herself, a woman who, almost from the very beginning, had chafed at her leadership role.

After Kate's release from the mental hospital, she did not return to the public arena. Instead she retired to her loft in the Bowery and to her farm outside Poughkeepsie, to sculpt and to write books, the first two of them autobiographical works of deep despair, of dependent love for her women lovers, of unfinished manuscripts and suicide attempts.

The books won scant praise from critics, and after the publication of one of them, Kate complained to a reporter: "We're supposed to be strong all the time—*Be strong or I'll punch you.*"

Unable, or unwilling, to cope with the idea that she could not control the image of herself that was projected by the press, Kate withdrew from the scene. And when, in the early eighties, she did embark on a trip to Iran on behalf of women's liberation, in the midst of the Khomeini revolution, she was expelled. Her published account of her trip, though lively and interesting, did little to solve the problems of women there.

Susan Brownmiller triumphed with her best-selling book *Against Our Will: Men, Women and Rape,* but Susan (who had very much enjoyed the political fray) also retired to the literary life, only venturing forth, in the late seventies, to form the activist group Women Against Pornography. ("A last gasp," as she would describe it.) But to Susan, the women's movement—with its core of urban intellectualism and energizing ideas—had ended by then, and she mourned the loss of her participation in it.

"I had done what I could," she would recall. "My particular talents were useful at a particular time and the realization that I had outlived my usefulness was painful."

Susan herself had one encounter with a former radical leader who had become a Rosicrucian, adhering to that seventeenth-century spiritual movement.

"She had been so strong and sturdy, but now she was like a wraith, haunting Forty-second Street and the Lower East Side, this pathetic little creature in tattered clothes, looking up Rosicrucian symbols in the library. She had written this prescient book and she thought she would be the Simone de Beauvoir of the American movement. 'Look at me now,' she said to me. 'You did this to me.' "

Ti-Grace Atkinson's decline, though far less personally hurtful, was also precipitous. In the mid-seventies, just after *Newsweek* hailed *Amazon Odyssey*, her collection of speeches and essays, as "intense and often brilliant," its author "one of the most radical and original thinkers in the women's movement," she found herself collecting welfare payments. As the theater lights began to dim—or as, more to the point, the shock value wore off—so did requests for Ti-Grace's appearance on the lecture circuit.

And for Flo Kennedy's as well. Even, in fact, for the "literary guerrilla" Germaine Greer's.

Not being an American citizen (though she did spend three fall semesters as director of the Center for Women's Studies in Tulsa, Oklahoma), Germaine could hardly have united the forces here . . . had she cared to, which, quite obviously, she did not.

Being far too restless an intelligence, far too intolerant of mediocrity for any political role, Germaine preferred to remain a gadfly, a critic. As gloriously verbal as ever, she could not, in the long run, resist sniping at the American movement not only for its "religious" tendencies but for its "dress-for-success" image:

"Feminism became a marketing strategy in the States, to the independent woman who had high spending power. If I have one more executive wardrobe described to me, I will go stark, staring insane. I'm not interested in executives of either sex. As far as I'm concerned, they're all male. I don't think it's any hardship not to be able to get a seat on the board of General Motors or Bendix. If you're enough like a man, you'll get one."

The women's movement, in Germaine's view, had failed in its efforts to define a proper role for a woman. ("We never really escaped from our own narrow, self-gratifying, spinsterish sort of mind.") In her search for a society in which her vision of community and solidarity among women could flourish, she traveled extensively—to India, and, eventually, to Brazil and to Cuba—always writing about the lives of the poorest women, their ties to men and children.

Peripatetic, endlessly curious, Germaine remained the brilliant observer, the outsider.

Which left, of course, Gloria Steinem and Betty Friedan.

From 1973 on, the paths of Gloria Steinem and Betty Friedan seldom crossed. Only for such rare events as that great celebration in Houston did they share a podium. *Ms.* continued either to ignore Betty entirely or to note her efforts only in passing, one such reference, in a book review column, lumping the author of *The Feminine Mystique* with archenemy Phyllis Schlafly as an equally "wrongheaded" revisionist.

No longer courted by the media, no longer the president of NOW, Betty's visibility faded. Her fiery demeanor, however, did not. Some believed that Betty's impatience, which seemed, at times, increasingly vocal, had caused her eclipse, others that it was simply the result of what must surely have been, to her, an irritating shift into the shadows. Still others saw Betty's explosive manner as stemming from passionate conviction, from her insistence, in one writer's view, on "seizing an idea by the scruff of the neck and shaking loose its fleas."

One way or another, however, this volatile battler had made enemies, many of whom would be far from reluctant to speak their minds.

"Betty represents the failure of nerve of the women's movement" was Ti-Grace Atkinson's caustic assessment in the early eighties. "Her driving force was pathological, a sort of manic energy that seemed to rise off her and that we *interpreted* as inspirational."

Susan Brownmiller, too, was troubled by Betty, by what Susan saw as her "flow of venom . . . such a failing of character that she cannot give anyone anything because she doesn't feel she's gotten enough herself." But Muriel Fox, so often called upon to smooth the waters behind that churning motor, would wonder if Betty's "terrible" behavior didn't just happen to be exactly the impetus needed to start a revolution. (If not, perhaps, to sustain it, or, most tellingly, to maintain her leadership role.)

Outspoken as always, Betty continued to say—and write—her piece. Not only did she object to "sexual politics," as she called it, but she would always maintain that she should have spoken up louder and more effectively against it, against, in particular, using the lesbian issue to disrupt the mainstream thrust of the movement.

Betty's raised voice was undoubtedly heard, but it was also, in those days, unheeded.

By the mid-seventies, as women's issues became an accepted part of public awareness—the idea of the movement becoming, in typically American fashion, absorbed into the culture, in effect institutionalized—Betty's reputation for point-blank expression and a flaring temper cost her severely. By then, Bella Abzug had clearly come to the fore. No shrinking violet herself, but a less rambling speaker than Betty, more politic and far more popular with the Ms. contingent, Bella's feisty and relentless campaigning for women's rights, along with her high visibility in Congress, her unforgettable hat, and her tough New York straight talk, made her a popular symbol of feminism. She was appointed by President Ford to head the National Commission on the Observance of International Women's Year, and by President Carter to co-chair the National Advisory Committee for Women. After a few short years in the sun, however, Bella was abruptly fired by Carter amid rumors that she had been critical of certain administration policies. Many important committee members resigned, and Bella herself—subsequently defeated in several elections—never quite managed to regain her national popularity.

Meanwhile, however, Betty was named to neither of those major governmental bodies headed by Bella, and when the author of *The Feminine Mystique* arrived at the great celebration in Houston with no official position, she could only offer a humble speech. In a conciliatory gesture, she welcomed the large lesbian contingent, "just to end the division," she would one day explain, but her name was conspicuously absent from the heavy publicity that followed that event. .

Furthermore, Betty's 1981 book, *The Second Stage*, with its emphasis on male and family cooperation, irritated many feminists, adding definition to what was a growing tendency to distinguish between "liberal" and "radical" feminism. Many activists, feeling strongly that "the first stage" had not yet been won, regarded the book as a step backward. Simone de Beauvoir was among the detractors, and just a few years before she died, this influential writer told the *New York Times Book Review* that, though she respected *The Feminine Mystique,* she was so angered by *The Second Stage* that she tossed the book across the room. Since, like her many followers, de Beauvoir regarded marriage, the family, and especially housework all as entities of enslavement, it seemed to her that *The Second Stage* promoted a return to traditional relationships and behavior.

And yet, as time would tell, most women did not intend to give up those values. Betty—with her feet planted firmly in Peoria, with her maternal pride in her three accomplished children—understood that. She understood as well, and subscribed to, an ethic of achievement and, unlike some feminists, never failed to delight in the company of the growing contingent of successful, high-achieving women who, in her words, "played hardball." Her instincts, in short, were middle-class American; her philosophy (if not always her behavior) was political.

But Betty spent most of that decade out of the public eye, lecturing and teaching at many universities, Harvard and Yale among them. It would be the mid-eighties before she became once again the feminist authority, sought out by reporters for her opinion on major issues.

Throughout that quieter era, Gloria alone maintained her visibility. She was far and away the country's most popular feminist, her impact reaching so far that when Sally Ride, the first female astronaut, blasted off into space, the young woman's mother exclaimed, "Thank God for Gloria Steinem." She was the "princess of the women's movement," as the *Ladies' Home Journal* put it, "an unquestioned beauty, with . . . the follow-me-onto-the-barricades charisma that makes the myth."

The myth could not have survived, of course, without Gloria's absolute dedication to her feminist vision (or dogma, as some critics would see it), along with her ready wit, that gender switch that flashed her message:

"How would you feel if you got a spinster of arts degree when you graduated?" she once asked a college audience. "Or then got a mistress of science and had to work very hard to get a sistership?" And, in her article "If Men Could Menstruate," how males would then brag about being "a three-pad man," or "Yeah, man, I'm on the rag."

She was clever as well about when to use her talent for quick, sharp communication and when to withhold it.

When the CIA funding of the agency Gloria had co-founded back in the late fifties was exposed in the press, she admitted that the organization received funds from the CIA, denied being an agent of the CIA, and dismissed those Helsinki youth conferences as "the CIA's finest hour." And though this answer did not satisfy everyone (a group of Redstocking members mounted an attack on this question, drawing out, in the process, the impassioned interest of Betty Friedan), the flurry soon passed.

Both these attacks had occurred because, in Gloria's view: "We are all damaged as women. If we are old-style women, we come into the movement and say: 'This is mine. I invented it.' The new-style, New Left women say: 'I never had anything in my life. Nobody else is going to have it either.' "

But "it"—whether the movement or Gloria's own friendly, polished, star-quality glow—could never be taken away from her. On her fortieth birthday, looking as beautiful as ever—and almost as youthful—she delighted reporters (and many women) with the succinct reply to surprised comments about her age: "This is what forty looks like."

But, of course, for most women it was not.

And therein, in a strange way, lay both the inspiration and the problem.

No one could ever doubt Gloria's commitment to her feminist principles. Much of the money she earned (from lectures alone—about two every week, according to her count, at least one of them drawing her standard price of $6,000 to $7,000) went to her favorite causes. In 1984, the Ms. Foundation was once again a recipient—this time of the proceeds from an elaborate gala party, with tickets at $250 a head, celebrating Gloria's fiftieth birthday at the Waldorf-Astoria. The party, duly covered by *Time,* was hosted by Marlo Thomas and Phil Donahue, and the list of guests and committee members included Betty Ford, Rosalynn Carter, and Jacqueline Kennedy Onassis.

But though Gloria's celebrity status was glamorous enough to attract such stars, and her appeal sexy enough to have her *Show* magazine article "A Bunny's Tale" made into a TV movie, her politics remained as staunchly leftist as they had been in the sixties. As did, for the most part, *Ms.*

"We must not support those who look like *us* and sound like them," she told the women gathered at the 1982 Democratic Convention, a reference to Britain's prime minister Margaret Thatcher and India's Indira Gandhi. (None of these Democratic women, however, in their practical suits and modest haircuts, looked very much like Gloria, who was dressed, as usual, in a short skirt, her long hair flowing below her shoulders.) "Sounding like 'them'" was Gloria's euphemism for conservatism, and she continued to avoid endorsing anyone —even a woman—who could in any way be tarred with that brush. One of the great failures of the women's movement, to Gloria's mind, was its middle-class image, and she was always critical of what she called the "suburban" impression created by Betty and *The Feminine Mystique.*

A true conservative might indeed be beyond the pale. A demand that a leader of an American movement capture the loyalty of the wide spectrum of this country's middle classes might also overstate the case. But middle-class energies are not an uncommon genesis for social change, and they can't be ignored, either by a social crusade or, surely, by an American mass magazine. This was one of the salient lessons of the sixties, but Gloria—and *Ms.*—relentlessly disregarded it, which was one reason the magazine was left continually short of funds, and was forced to be sold, in 1987, to the Australian publisher John Fairfax Ltd.

Meanwhile, Gloria worked tirelessly to improve the lot of women, helping, in the process, to make the movement respectable to the country's "establishment," broadening its base of support. Many believed, however, that the contrast between her glamorous life and her public pronouncements that she—like all other women—was still an oppressed victim of a patriarchal system, while endlessly appealing to the heart, was also disorienting.

Much as both men and women conceived great loyalty to Gloria, much as they flocked to her lectures, bought her books (her collection of essays, *Outrageous Acts and Everyday Rebellions,* was a national best-seller in 1983), few women could identify with this beautiful creature, who posed in a bubble bath for *People* and in a very short miniskirt for *Vanity Fair,* the latter photo signaling—to Susan Brownmiller at least—"the end of the movement." Not only had Gloria managed to remain remarkably uncommitted in personal matters, but she also seemed to deny both her own ambitions and her own remarkable achievements, thus becoming, to many, a devoted, compassionate, and inspiring heroine, and also a fantasy figure who lived in a world that was far beyond them.

"I'm not Gloria Steinem," most women shrewdly reminded themselves. "What's good for her is not necessarily good for me."

Even if—or perhaps especially if—what she espoused was a constitutional amendment.

The ERA failed, as Gloria would insist, because feminists were politically naive, unaware of the threat of such organized forces as insurance companies, real estate lobbies, and the special interests that influence state legislatures.

It failed, too, because the movement itself had lost its momentum. It failed because constitutional amendments are far more difficult to create than most people imagine. It failed because of the mood of the country in the early eighties, when time was quickly running out for ratification and most Americans were focused on the fact that Jimmy Carter could not manage to extricate our own American citizens from one of those small, supposedly powerless Middle Eastern nations. People had begun talking about the country's loss of "guts," "courage," and, yes, "machismo."

It failed for all of those reasons but it also failed because of a certain degree of public suspicion, a lack of trust and a resistance to following the dictates of what were, in fact, media figures.

"Women's liberation is very much a minority movement," the social anthropologist Lionel Tiger had claimed from the earliest days. "It's evangelical. It's a movement that makes people feel good . . . they like reading about revolution."

And listening to it on the radio, and watching it on television. . . .

It had been, in those early days, a media circus—a crazy time of outrage, discovery, and risk, when fame and fortunes rose and when hopes were stratospheric—when theories were brutally attacked, leadership skirmishes exploited, names called, egos demolished, and retaliation swift and public. When battles were fought with emotional blood and real tears. When images—so expensively groomed and polished for male political candidates—were left in the hands of novice proponents of a social movement, to be flashed across millions of television screens willy-nilly.

For all that—and for all the talk and flirtation with revolution and violence—no one was ever shot at. No one was murdered in the fray or beaten in jail cells or left to rot as a political prisoner. Instead, these feminist oracles were given a platform, and perhaps, as Germaine would claim, they got as much out of the feminist movement as they gave. Surely, in many ways, they had fallen short.

They had been indeed—as geographically isolated Americans—ethnocentric, often unaware of the needs of women in those countries where the extended family was woven more tightly into the social fabric. Too many had even ignored the demands and emotions of their own middle- and working-class women, especially those with children, and when, in the mid-eighties, they found themselves openly criticized by feminists here, the attacks had some merit. As late as 1988, America would still lack any form of guaranteed leave for parents. In those countries which did have such protection—Sweden, Norway, Finland, Austria—women's salaries would be far higher than the still-languishing seventy cents to every man's dollar in America.

Sex discrimination would not disappear—from the workplace, the courts, or the public eye. Except for the exciting but brief, ill-fated bid of vice-presidential candidate Geraldine Ferraro, no woman would run for the country's highest offices or, for that matter, hold appointments to such high-level posts as Secretary of Defense or State. Talented television reporters such as Jane Pauley, Diane Sawyer, and Connie Chung would rise to the top of their professions, but there would still be no woman who served as full-time solo anchor on a network news show. Few besides super-lawyer Carla Hill or advertising chief Mary Wells Lawrence would break through what had come to be known as "the glass ceiling," the barrier to the very top of the nation's most powerful corporations. Most women were still—though perhaps to a lesser degree—responsible for home and children, leading many exhausted mothers to blame the women's movement for their added responsibilities in the workplace. And by 1988, given the absence of constitutional protection, many advances would be threatened by the appointment of the conservative Anthony M. Kennedy to the United States Supreme Court.

The Golden Age of Feminism had indeed been a media event, and this, of course, was the movement's greatest failure.

But perhaps it was also its greatest strength.

In the lull of the seventies, the movement—if such could still be said to exist—had set out on a different journey, one that was, if not the "second stage," an unwavering, peripatetic quest. It had begun its travels then into our separate, singular minds and psyches, where, according to the rules of each realm, ideas do—or do not—find their space.

Across the nation and around the world, ordinary women and men began to permit those voices, those shattering arguments of "sexual politics," "the feminine mystique," "the female eunuch," to sift quietly into their lives. They began to test them, to think about how and what part and in what way these notions applied to each one of them.

Yes, I can do this work as well as a man. Maybe those too-serious, "masculine" women at college were partly right. No, I don't want to do without lipstick. No, I don't mind if a man whistles at me. Yes, I'm as smart as my boyfriend. No, I don't want my son to play with dolls.

In living rooms, bedrooms, offices, and courtrooms, studios and classrooms, clinics and playing fields across the country, the *sense* of feminism, though seldom that word itself (the "F-word" as it was called, wryly, in *Ms.*), began to permeate all of our lives.

In their own way, at their own pace, using their own judgment, individual women began to move, and as they did, their hopes, dreams, and accomplishments bubbled up like underground springs. Tentatively at first ("Can I really handle medical school?"), but steadily ("Do I dare to hire a male secretary?"), their numbers growing into a rushing river, they flowed into every field, every profession, and nearly every formerly all-male enclave. One by one and inch by inch, women broke through into plains so vast that the social landscape was completely transformed.

Like it, understand it, admit it or not, barely a human being on earth would be untouched by feminism.

Here, in the late eighties, was a world in which a woman—Sandra Day O'Connor—sat on the U.S. Supreme Court. It was also a world where women installed telephone wires and TV cables; where women drove cabs, where hundreds of women were physicians, hundreds more were lawyers, accountants, architects, executives, bankers, judges, television commentators.

In place of "Father Knows Best" and the wife-in-the-kitchen, "Cagney and Lacey"—female cops chasing the bad guys; in place of a gray male lineup in the state and local, even national governing bodies, a bright and various medley—skirts, stockings, high heels, and women's voices, setting their own agendas. At your mailbox, a woman carrier; at your bank, a woman president; at your church, a woman minister; at your newspaper, a woman publisher; at the sports arena, a women's basketball team; at the Olympics, a string of gold medals

won by fearless, determined women, rapidly decreasing the performance gap between the sexes. Should anyone doubt this historic
change, they had only to note the diminished fortunes of the Avon
company, that formerly ubiquitous cosmetics firm that once had re-
lied, to its chagrin, solely on door-to-door sales to the woman at
home. Or the proliferation of serious, successful, mass magazines that
—far from denying women's expansive interests—were completely
devoted to them. *Working Woman. Working Mother. Savvy.*

By now, barely a day could pass in which the story of women's
progress—a string of dazzling statistics—did not appear in some
publication in some part of the world:

• For the first time in history, the pay gap between men and women has
narrowed to 30 percent.
• Women now hold 38 percent of management positions, almost twice what
they held in 1972.
• The average salaries of 60 percent of women officers in Fortune 500 (and
Service 500) companies is $117,000.
• Almost half of all graduating accountants and one-third of all MBAs are
women, an increase of more than 300 percent in the last ten years. More
than one-fourth of all graduating lawyers and almost one-fourth of all graduating physicians are women.
• Every major investment bank has at least one woman partner, and in the
fifty largest commercial banks in the country 50 percent of the officers,
managers, and professionals are women.
• The number of women graduating with engineering degrees increased
thirteenfold since 1975.
• Approximately 18,000 women hold elected office.

By now, the feminist Marlo Thomas would be married to a man
whose voice—through the seventies—may well have carried the message of women's concerns farther and wider than any other. Phil
Donahue, the enormously popular television host, not only sympathized and understood, but lent his stage and microphone to an ongoing stream of feminist writers, that fountain which did not falter.

The poet Adrienne Rich's enduring treatise, *Of Woman Born*, appeared in the mid-seventies and Carol Gilligan's *In a Different Voice*
in the early eighties. Strong-minded historians like Elaine Showalter,
unfailingly reasonable journalists such as Ellen Goodman, feminist

sociologists, anthropologists, physical scientists, and literary critics made themselves felt.

Nor did the stream of feminist novels cease. What had begun in the sixties and seventies with books such as Doris Lessing's *The Golden Notebook,* Lois Gould's *Such Good Friends,* and Erica Jong's *Fear of Flying* continued in the eighties with Alice Walker's *The Color Purple,* Sue Miller's *The Good Mother,* and Marilyn French's *Her Mother's Daughter.* Significant works poured from the pens of Cynthia Ozick, Margaret Atwood, Marguerite Duras, Isabel Allende, Toni Morrison, Mary Gordon, Ntozake Shange. Few serious novels written by women were anything *but* feminist.

And this time, unlike the buried creations of earlier feminist efforts, and thanks to expansion in women's libraries and women's studies departments, the ink was indelible. So thoroughly grounded was the new scholarship that many academics considered philosophic feminism an analytic tool as viable as Marxism or existentialism.

Short of a worldwide holocaust, or a burning of books, the rebellion that began when Betty Friedan ambled shamefaced into her Smith College reunion, when the women from SNCC wrote their cautiously anonymous "position paper" on women, would not be allowed to die.

It had been, as Betty would put it, "a miracle."

The miracle, in her view, was that "women with no money and no experience . . . were able to find each other."

And the glory was that the world was transformed. Without guns, without strikes, and without bloodshed.

In the mid-eighties, an age that the *New York Times* labeled "post-feminist," the Supreme Court applied its stamp to a state's compensatory promotions for women, to a guarantee of their jobs after they return from maternity leave, to their acceptance into certain all-male clubs, even to a ruling against sexual harassment. Uninsured by the ERA these rulings might be, but they were hammered in place by practice and by custom—by women lawyers, by women legislators, by a historic range of women's pressure groups, and, most important of all, by what women now expected and demanded for themselves.

So perhaps that constitutional amendment did not, after all, matter *quite* so much. By 1988, the Pentagon itself, the symbolic core of male supremacy, was demanding more jobs for women and an end to sexual harassment in the military. By then, in fact, middle-class women would have choices their mothers could barely imagine. Some of them would decide to step off the fast track to raise their children.

Some would manage both, and some would choose career over family. Working-class women would face their bosses with an assurance so strong as to lead Barbara Ehrenreich to predict a new wave of feminism springing from their ranks.

Choices, options—where they had never before existed.

Self-assurance. Self-esteem.

Women were not, as they once had believed, "over the hill" at thirty years of age—or forty, or fifty, or sixty. They were not, in short, solely marketable items. They could support themselves financially, and that, perhaps, was the most strengthening change of all.

Confidently now they marched into hotels or bars "without an escort," never imagining for a moment that their healthy desire for a social life could be expressed only as some man's guest. They filled the tables of restaurants. They listened and talked to each other, recognizing—without a moment's reservation—each other's value, each other's worth, each other's right to fulfill her potential.

Most important, a new generation of women had emerged, and it was this group that, in the early eighties, in a great surge, wrenched those job statistics and pay scales to such remarkable heights. They had used the access to education and job opportunities fought for and won by the early feminists, and they had handled it all with a new self-image. Among them—molded by hundreds of "consciousness-raised" teachers—were bright comers who could accomplish what management theorists often claim is the keystone to success: They could picture themselves in the top honcho's job.

The new woman—as dozens of psychological surveys proved— was *different*.

As was (whether he did the dishes, stayed home with sick kids or not) the new man.

He did not suppose "You're so cute when you're mad" would win him points in charm and seduction, or that sprinkled references to "dumb broads" would convince polite company of his masculine prowess. He knew he could work for a female boss and he did not immediately assume that a woman he hired should be chained to her entering job slot because she was sure to leave to get married or have babies.

By now, in fact, if you asked a *father* what he hoped for his daughter, his answers—though undoubtedly not defined as such—would be *feminist*:

"Yes, I want my daughter to have equal pay and maternity leave."

"No, I do not want her sexually harassed on the job."

This father might well remember those days when such terms were unknown, when his daughter would have been barred from a course in woodworking or auto mechanics, from delivering a newspaper or winning a sports scholarship; when his unmarried sister could not hold a credit card, buy a house or insurance; when his wife had no recourse if an employer announced that women weren't suited for the job; or when someone he knew very well hid the secret of violence at home, or rape.

Somewhere in the mirror of this man's mind was a scene he might prefer to forget. In this fading panorama, the places of decision and the faces of respect—on juries, on television, in colleges and offices and pulpits—are solidly and resolutely male. They hide the tears and outrage of millions of women, tears he knows that his daughter will not shed.

Yes, the ERA failed, but by then not hundreds, as Mao had directed, not thousands, but millions of flowers had bloomed.

And if you asked some of these strong young blossoms to quit their analyses of international interest rates for a minute, or their preparations for court, or their Jane Fonda exercises, or their "quality time" with the baby, just to tell you if they recognized these names—Betty Friedan; Germaine Greer; Kate Millett; Gloria Steinem; Susan Brownmiller; Kay Clarenbach; Catherine East; Shirley Chisholm; Bella Abzug; Flo Kennedy; Letty Cottin Pogrebin; Barbara Seaman; Ti-Grace Atkinson—many of them would set their work aside for that moment and then they would answer vaguely, as if from a distant cloud, as they tried to capture the faces, the names, the *connection* . . .

"Well, I think so. Gloria Steinem, yes. I've seen her on the 'Today' show. But the rest . . . I *think,* but to tell you the truth, I'm not altogether sure.

"Weren't they the ones who burned their bras?"

Afterword

BETTY FRIEDAN

In 1975, Betty was awarded an honorary doctorate of letters (an L.H.D.) from her beloved Smith College. A year later, she published *It Changed My Life: Writings on the Women's Movement*, an autobiographical account of her trials and insights, and in 1981, *The Second Stage*. She has attended most international women's conferences, including the relatively successful 1985 conference in Nairobi, and in the mid-eighties she formed a "think tank" at the University of Southern California to examine women's issues.

In 1987, a committee of Betty's most devoted friends—Marlene Sanders, Ellie Guggenheimer, songwriters Betty Comden and Adolph Green among them—threw a *gemütlich* sixty-fifth birthday party for her at the Palladium, a cavernous Manhattan disco. Jokes and satirical songs abounded—about Betty's love for men ("who have something I enjoy"), about her temperament ("shy, demure, and sentimental"), her organization ("Even Betty needs a wife"), about her busy social life in the Long Island waterfront town of Sag Harbor. There, where her children often visit and plant vegetable gardens, Betty sometimes cooks up large pots of soup for crowds of animated conversationalists, usually featuring among them, as one of the birthday songs reported, "a house guest who's distinguished, also famous . . ."

At this birthday celebration, however, there were also paeans of gratitude:

"She has changed our world and nation . . ."

AFTERWORD

"Since Betty set us free . . ."

Betty's Manhattan apartment—across from Lincoln Center, with a high, airy view—is filled with books and relics of her travels around the world, brightly upholstered Victorian furniture, and modern paintings (one by her sister, Amy) slashed with brilliant color. She frequently entertains here for authors of new books or on behalf of those feminist issues with which she is sympathetic.

Betty's daughter, Emily, a graduate of Harvard Medical School, is a practicing pediatrician, married to a physician on the faculty of the University of Buffalo Medical School. Her son Jonathan, an engineer, and his wife, a free-lance editor and writer, have two small sons. Daniel, a theoretical physicist on the faculty of the University of Chicago, has won a MacArthur Award.

Betty has not remarried, but she still dates frequently and has been known to appear at parties with more than one date in tow, blithely announcing, after suitable introductions, that she has met the second one "on the plane." She has also recently grown interested in the study of Torah and is active in Jewish affairs.

Her perspective on the women's movement, while passionate, remains moderate, the lesbian issue, as she sees it, having created a stumbling block, but the future hopeful. She was a strong supporter of the aborted presidential candidacy of Representative Patricia Schroeder, and she is writing a book about aging called *The Fountain of Age*.

GLORIA STEINEM

Gloria remained as editor of *Ms.* until the fall of 1987, when the magazine was purchased by John Fairfax Ltd., an Australian publisher. *Ms.*'s financial difficulties, in her view, stemmed in major part from its independence. Unlike other women's magazines, she contends, *Ms.* refused to allow advertisers to dictate editorial policy.

Throughout her years as editor, Gloria wrote many articles for the magazine and spent a year at the Woodrow Wilson International Center for Scholars in Washington, D.C., attempting to formulate an overall philosophy for the women's movement. The essays she wrote that year are included in a collection of her articles that was gathered together by Letty Cottin Pogrebin and published as a book, *Outrageous Acts and Everyday Rebellions,* in 1983. When, as publicity for the book, Gloria posed for *People* magazine in a bubble bath, both men and women wrote irate letters. "Feminism finds absolutely no shame in women's bodies," Gloria responded, "only in the powerlessness that often allows them to be used against our will."

In 1987, she wrote the accompanying text for *Marilyn,* a coffee-table picture book of Marilyn Monroe. That same year, Letty Cottin Pogrebin, acting as Gloria's agent in a remarkable three-day auction, drew a high bid of $700,000 from Little, Brown for a proposed book by Gloria called *The Bedside Book of Self-Esteem.* A second work, untitled, on the subject of women in America's richest, most powerful families, brought $500,000 from Simon & Schuster. Instead of charging her friend an agent's fee, customarily 10 to 15 percent, Letty donated her fee to two *Ms.* foundations.

In the 1970s, Gloria maintained one unusually long relationship with the lawyer Stanley Pottinger. Her subsequent romance—with the publishing and real estate tycoon Mort Zuckerman—lasted about three years.

Gloria still lives on East 73rd Street in the same apartment in which the idea for *Ms.* was hatched. She seldom entertains but is often seen at Manhattan's most glamorous parties or lunching with friends such as Jacqueline Kennedy Onassis. She appears as a television interviewer on NBC's "Today" show, but she is no longer active at *Ms.* In 1988, she raised funds for presidential candidate Jesse Jackson.

Women's self-respect, in Gloria's view, is the most important change created by the women's movement, but she remains critical of male attitudes. Since, in her assessment, women are only twenty years into one hundred years of change, they have eighty years to go.

KATE MILLETT

After *Flying,* Kate published the autobiographical *Sita* and, in 1979, the most grisly of all her books, *The Basement*—about the murder of Sylvia Likens, a sixteen-year-old who was beaten, starved, burned by cigarettes, and left to die with the words "I am a prostitute and proud of it" carved on her stomach.

Less gruesome by far, more of an adventure story, in fact, was *Going to Iran,* published in 1982.

Kate also continues to produce sculpture, paintings, and photographs, working from both her studio in the Bowery and her farm near Poughkeepsie. On the farm, in one of the buildings, is a long, narrow, white-walled room spanned by old beams, old wooden floors covered with bright rugs, and graceful, comfortable furniture. At one end of the room is a kitchen, where Kate, an elegant cook, often prepares country dinners. Near this building are two pine trees planted in honor of Simone de Beauvoir, whose funeral Kate attended in Paris in 1986.

Kate, who is currently at work on a book about political torture, recognizes that her "private solution," as she calls it, is not the answer, but believes that the women's movement is not only very strong, but "inventively spreading and growing." Many feminist academics consider her writing—especially *Sexual Politics*—the central canon of this wave of feminism.

GERMAINE GREER

In the early seventies, with royalties from *The Female Eunuch,* Germaine bought an old farmhouse in the Tuscany region of Italy. There, at Villa la Germaine, as the locals call it, amidst a profusion of flowers, which she plants, and sloe berries, which she harvests and sends off to a laboratory for medicinal use, Germaine spends most of her summers. Until the mid-eighties, when she moved to the countryside south of Cambridge, she spent most winters in London.

In 1979, in *The Obstacle Race,* Germaine addressed the prickly question of the absence, in the world of art, of the female genius. *Sex and Destiny,* published in 1984, attacked "the population control apparatchiks" who seek to impose birth control on underdeveloped countries, thereby, in Germaine's view, riding roughshod over the family social structure. Her book of essays, *The Madwoman's Underclothes,* published in 1987 and frequently described as "Shavian," includes deeply detailed observations of the life of women in Brazil and Cuba as well as an examination of the famine in Ethiopia.

Germaine is currently at work on two projects: a book of seventeenth-century women's verse called *Kissing the Rod* and a study of the 1986 English election campaign of Prime Minister Margaret Thatcher, entitled *Fortune's Maggot.* She has not remarried but has twelve godchildren and has recently remarked that a woman's greatest love affair is with her children.

Though Great Britain's renewed interest in feminism has made her a popular public figure, she is not pleased with the results of the women's movement in England. The rhetoric has changed, she insists, but the economic recession may have created worse hardships for women, especially for female blue-collar workers and single-parent families.

SUSAN BROWNMILLER

Susan lives in a small penthouse apartment in Greenwich Village with a terrace on which, in summers, a peach tree and a blueberry bush blossom, tomatoes grow hardy, and roses glow against the city brick. She shares this urban oasis with Paul Johnson, a carpenter and novelist who had been active in the peace movement in the sixties.

In 1984, nine years after her successful *Against Our Will: Men, Women and Rape,* Susan published *Femininity,* a critical analysis of that syndrome of qualities that suggested, essentially, that women would be well advised to give it up.

Analyses such as this, Susan believes, are no longer welcome, the women's movement itself no longer relevant.

TI-GRACE ATKINSON

In the late seventies, Ti-Grace began teaching introductory philosophy at Parsons, and eventually, at Columbia, courses both in contemporary civilization and feminism, and in political philosophy. She continues to work on her Ph.D. thesis, using women's oppression as a paradigm for the oppression of all other groups.

A revival in the form of a rare but enthusiastic meeting of radical women in 1987 has given Ti-Grace new hope for the women's movement, especially since it included some of the older activists. These women, she believes, can offer a rich legacy, if only to alert younger women to mistakes of earlier days.

FLORYNCE KENNEDY

Like Ti-Grace, Flo suffered financially from the drop-off in public interest in feminism. Through the mid-seventies she traveled the country drawing such headlines as "Here Comes Trouble" and "Flo Kennedy's Not Going Gently." In 1976, she published her autobiography, *Color Me Flo: My Hard Life and Good Times,* and in 1986 she appeared in "The Flo Kennedy Show," an interview series on cable television. Flo's small, cluttered apartment on East 48th Street is often home to advocates of various causes, early support for presidential candidate Jesse Jackson among them.

Bella Abzug lost another bid for a congressional seat in 1986, but maintains her law practice and continues to lecture and to co-chair the Women's Foreign Policy Council, an organization she founded in 1985 to make women more visible in public debate. Her 1984 book *The Gender Gap* is both an autobiographical account of her career and a guide to political power for women.

Shirley Chisholm was named to the House Rules Committee in 1977. She remained in Congress until 1982, taught at Mount Holyoke College for five years, and retired to her home in Williamsville, New York.

Marlo Thomas's television special "Free to Be . . . You and Me" won an Emmy Award in 1974, and in 1980 "The Body Human: Facts for Girls" won another. *Free to Be . . . A Family,* a book which she edited, along with Christopher Cerf and Letty Cottin Pogrebin, became a best-seller, and Letty herself was established as an authority on nonsexist childrearing with her book *Growing Up Free*. Notable among Letty's recent work is the book *Family Politics* as well as articles examining her own position as a Jewish feminist who found that "anti-feminism exists among Jews" and "anti-Semitism exists among feminists." She is married, with three grown children, and lives in New York. As does Barbara Seaman, who is also a mother of three and who, in 1987, published *Lovely Me*, a biography of the novelist Jacqueline Susann.

Kay Clarenbach is a professor of political science at the University of Wisconsin in Madison. Dolores Alexander is a copy editor at *People*; Muriel Fox, who in 1976 was named by *BusinessWeek* as the top-ranking woman in public relations, serves on the boards of two major corporations and chairs the NOW Legal Defense and Education Fund. Mary Eastwood heads a Maryland company that investigates discrimination complaints by federal employees against federal agencies. Catherine East lobbies in Washington for civil rights. Jean Faust volunteers at the New York City Ballet Company. Ivy Bottini is a gay rights activist giving much of her time to the creation of a hospice for AIDS patients in Los Angeles.

Most of the authors continue to write, although the demand for feminist nonfiction has given way, in recent years, to works that deal with the problems between women and their lovers.

Chronology

1777

Abigail Adams's letter to her husband, John, insists that if, in the new American Constitution, "care and attention are not paid to the ladies," they will foment a rebellion.

1848

Women draft a Declaration of Sentiments and Resolutions at Seneca Falls Convention in New York, officially opening the drive for women's suffrage in the United States.

1916

Jeanette Rankin is the first woman elected to the United States Congress.

1920

Susan B. Anthony, Elizabeth Cady Stanton, Lucy Stone, Sojourner Truth, and others win national suffrage for women.

1923

Equal Rights Amendment introduced in Congress by Alice Paul's National Women's Party.

1937

Eleanor Roosevelt claims that housewives, like many other workers, should receive salaries.

CHRONOLOGY

1945

Representative Helen Gahagan Douglas introduces Equal Pay Act in Congress. Act stipulates equal pay for employees performing the same work.

1949

The Second Sex by Simone de Beauvoir published in France. (In United States: 1953.)

1953

Sexual Behavior of the Human Female by Alfred C. Kinsey published.

1960

Birth control pill approved for marketing.

1961

President John F. Kennedy appoints President's Commission on the Status of Women, chaired by Eleanor Roosevelt.

1963

The Feminine Mystique by Betty Friedan published.
"I Was a Playboy Bunny" by Gloria Steinem published in *Show* magazine.
Equal Pay Act, first major legislation against sex discrimination, passed. President's Commission on the Status of Women recommends twenty-four ways to combat sex discrimination, among them the installation of permanent bodies. Interdepartmental Committee on the Status of Women (made up of cabinet-level officials) and Citizen's Advisory Council on the Status of Women (made up of private citizens) subsequently appointed.

1964

Congress passes Civil Rights Act. Title VII prevents sex discrimination in employment in businesses of twenty-five or more employees.

1965

Sex provision in Civil Rights Act dubbed "Bunny law" at White House conference on equal opportunity.
Members of Student Nonviolent Coordinating Committee write a position paper objecting to women's subordinate role in civil rights movement. ("Sex and Caste" by Mary King and Casey Hayden published in newsletter *Liberation* in 1966.)

CHRONOLOGY

1966

Funding for family planning and birth control information provided through President Lyndon B. Johnson's Department of Health, Education and Welfare.

William H. Masters and Virginia E. Johnson's *Human Sexual Response* published.

June 29: National Organization for Women (NOW) formed at Washington Hilton Hotel during third National Conference of State Commissions on the Status of Women (Formal Founding: October 29, 1966).

Women demanding equal rights are booed out of conference of Students for a Democratic Society.

NOW, in its first official act, petitions Equal Opportunity Commission to ban separate male/female want ads. Demonstrations against the firing of stewardesses if they marry or reach age thirty-two also begin.

1967

Consciousness raising probably begins this year.

Colorado is first state to reform its abortion law.

EEOC begins to hold hearings on sex discrimination.

NOW pickets *New York Times* classified office to demand elimination of male/female want ads.

President Lyndon B. Johnson signs order banning sex discrimination in federal employment, also one which removes restrictions that prohibit women in armed services from attaining rank higher than colonel.

New York Radical Women formed; eventually splits into Redstockings and WITCH.

NOW presents Bill of Rights at second annual convention. Some women resign over inclusion of legalization of abortion.

Lack of response from EEOC leads NOW to picket the commission's regional offices across the country.

1968

Jeanette Rankin Brigade and New York Radical Women demonstrate at antiwar protest in Washington, D.C. First use of slogan "Sisterhood is powerful."

NOW files suit against EEOC "to force it to comply with its own governmental rules."

Voices of Women's Liberation Movement newsletter published in Chicago.

TWA stewardesses file complaint against sex discrimination with EEOC.

Caroline Bird's *Born Female: The High Cost of Keeping Women Down* published.

Notes from the First Year, radical theoretical journal edited by Shulamith Firestone, published.

Valeria Solanis, author of "The SCUM Manifesto," shoots and wounds artist Andy Warhol.

EEOC issues guidelines and forbids male/female want ads.

September 7: Women demonstrate against Miss America contest in Atlantic City.

Ti-Grace Atkinson's attempt to restructure New York NOW is defeated. She resigns and, along with Florynce Kennedy, forms the October 17th Movement, later called the Feminists.

WITCH hexes the New York Stock Exchange.

Shirley Chisholm becomes first black woman elected to House of Representatives.

In landmark case, Title VII supersedes state law restricting women from working overtime and lifting weights over prescribed limits (*Rosenfeld* v. *Southern Pacific*).

About two hundred women attend first national women's liberation conference in Chicago.

Women's Equity Action League (WEAL) formed to fight sex discrimination in education.

Radical feminists begin using the term "sexism."

1969

At dramatized "counter-inaugural" of Richard Nixon, women attack "male chauvinism" and are booed off the stage.

Sheila Tobias leads Women's Conference at Cornell University and initiates ideas for women's studies courses.

Redstockings formed and, along with NOW, protest at New York legislative hearings on abortion.

February 12: NOW invades Oak Room of the Plaza Hotel in New York City.

Redstockings begin to hold public meetings on abortion and, this summer, issue their "pro-woman" manifesto.

EEOC issues guidelines against state protective labor laws which apply only to women.

The Feminists picket New York City Marriage Bureau claiming that marriage demeans women.

President Richard Nixon establishes Task Force on Women's Rights and Responsibilities to make recommendations on legislation.

First Congress to Unite Women meets in New York City.
Junior high school student in New York sues Board of Education because she was barred from metal shopwork class.
New York Radical Feminists formed.

1970
The Doctors' Case Against the Pill by Barbara Seaman published.
Women protest at Senate subcommittee hearings on birth control pill.
WEAL files class-action suit to end discrimination in higher education, including sports.
NOW demands congressional hearings on ERA.
Hawaii is first state to repeal abortion law.
Women charge *Newsweek* magazine with sex discrimination.
NOW elects Aileen Hernandez as its new president.
March 18: Susan Brownmiller leads sit-in at the *Ladies' Home Journal.*
Women jailed overnight for invading Grove Press, publishers of erotica.
Meeting and information centers for women activists open across the country, especially in big cities.
United Auto Workers is first union to endorse ERA.
May 1–3: Second Congress to Unite Women takes place.
Women sue Time, Inc. for sex discrimination.
Representative Martha Griffiths forces ERA out of House Judiciary Committee (where it had languished since 1948) to floor of House of Representatives.
Cornell University offers first major course in women's studies.
Kate Millett's *Sexual Politics* published.
The U.S. Department of Labor, in a complete reversal, announces support of the ERA, followed by issuance of guidelines against sex discrimination.
NOW files blanket complaint against more than thirteen hundred corporations and three hundred colleges and universities receiving federal funds.
House Special Subcommittee on Education holds unprecedented hearings on sex discrimination in education.
The Department of Health, Education and Welfare tells field personnel to include sex discrimination in all contract investigations.
The Department of Justice files first sex discrimination suit under Title VII of the Civil Rights Act.
New York State liberalizes abortion law.
Ladies' Home Journal publishes feminist supplement written by March 18th demonstrators.
Time runs women's liberation issue with Kate Millett on cover.

August 26: Women's Strike for Equality takes place nationwide, commemorating the fiftieth anniversary of women's suffrage. Betty Friedan, organizer of the "strike," leads Fifth Avenue march.

Twelve TWA stewardesses, dissatisfied with EEOC action, file multimillion-dollar suit against the airline.

Sisterhood Is Powerful, edited by Robin Morgan, published.

WEAL files class-action suit against all U.S. medical schools on grounds of sex discrimination.

Bella Abzug elected to Congress.

First women's professional tennis tour begins.

Lavender armbands worn in support of lesbians.

Public Health Service Act passed. Title X of the act provides funds for family planning and contraception information for low-income women.

1971

"Speak-out on rape" held by New York Radical Feminists.

In landmark case, U.S. Supreme Court rules that businesses cannot refuse to hire women with small children unless this policy applies to men as well.

Professional Women's Caucus files class-action suit against all American law schools.

Ti-Grace Atkinson attacked at Catholic University in Washington, D.C.

University of Michigan becomes first school to incorporate an affirmative action plan for women.

The Female Eunuch by Germaine Greer published in United States. (In England: 1970.)

Gynecological self-examination begins at a bookstore in Los Angeles, continues at a NOW convention in that city a few months later.

April 30: "A Dialogue on Women's Liberation" ("Town Bloody Hall") held at New York City's Town Hall.

Senate Rules Committee votes to allow girls to become pages as long as their sponsoring senators assume responsibility for their safety. First girls subsequently appointed.

July 10–12: First official meeting of National Women's Political Caucus held at Statler Hilton Hotel in Washington, D.C.

Panel on Violence in the Women's Movement meets.

October 12: ERA passes House of Representatives by a vote of 354 to 23.

Supreme Court invalidates discriminatory state law involving estates.

December 9: President Nixon vetoes Comprehensive Child Development Act which would have provided federally funded day-care centers.

December 20: Ms. magazine appears as a forty-page insert in *New York* magazine.

Our Bodies, Ourselves: A Course by and for Women by the Boston Women's Health Collective published.

1972

Formation of Women's Action Alliance announced to press.

First full issue of *Ms.* (Spring) published.

March 22: ERA passes Senate, 84 to 8.

Equal Employment Opportunity Act passed, with provision against sex discrimination.

National Commission on Consumer Finance challenges discriminatory refusal of credit to women.

July 10–14: Issue of abortion rights raised publicly at the Democratic National Convention in Miami. Also, women make up 40 percent of delegates versus 13 percent in 1968.

Title IX of the Education Amendments Act outlaws sex discrimination in most educational institutions. This legislation facilitates funding for women's athletics.

Pat Schroeder, Elizabeth Holtzman, Barbara Jordan, Yvonne Brathwaite Burke, and Marjorie Holt elected to Congress. Total of sixteen women win seats in House of Representatives.

Marlo Thomas releases record *Free to Be . . . You and Me.*

1973

January 22: Roe v. *Wade.* The Supreme Court legalizes abortion through first trimester of pregnancy.

Singer Helen Reddy wins Grammy Award for the song "I Am Woman."

Universities begin to establish academic-athletic scholarships for women.

Congress appoints first female page in U.S. House of Representatives.

Senate committee approves truth-in-lending amendments which prohibit sex discrimination in retail and mortgage credit.

NOW Legal Defense and Education Fund launches national Public Service Advertising Campaign on equality for women.

Hofstra University in New York hosts the first Sports Symposium for Women.

Representative Martha Griffiths, chairperson of the House Joint Economic Committee, holds the first hearings on the economic problems of U.S. women.

Aging male tennis star Bobby Riggs, claiming that any man can beat any woman in a match and that, therefore, women should not be paid as much prize money as men, challenges world champion Billie Jean King. Billie Jean wins, 6–4/6–3/6–3, in widely heralded "battle of the sexes."

AFL-CIO endorses ERA.

New Jersey Division of Civil Rights rules that exclusion of girls by Little Leagues is illegal.

1974

New York State legislation ends requirement for corroboration in rape cases.

Françoise Giroud appointed as France's Secretary of State for the Status of Women, a cabinet-rank position.

Equal Credit Opportunity Act prohibits credit discrimination based on sex or marital status.

Ella Grasso wins governorship of Connecticut; first woman governor elected in her own right, not as widow or wife of previous governor.

Mary Ann Krupsak is elected lieutenant governor of New York.

At age sixty-four, New Jersey's Millicent Fenwick wins seat in House of Representatives.

Record number of women (eighteen) are elected to the House of Representatives. Number includes all twelve who sought reelection. Also: State legislatures gain 130 women to bring total to 600, almost double that of five years earlier.

1975

President Gerald Ford creates National Commission on Observance of International Women's Year, as proclaimed by United Nations General Assembly.

Supreme Court rules that women may not be excluded from jury duty because of sex.

United Nations sponsors first world conference on women in Mexico City.

Time magazine's Man of the Year is twelve women.

Against Our Will: Men, Women and Rape by Susan Brownmiller published.

ERA is defeated in New York and New Jersey.

1976

United Nations Decade for Women begins.

Sarah Caldwell becomes first woman to conduct at Metropolitan Opera.

Dr. Benjamin Spock revises his *Baby and Child Care* to eliminate sexist bias.

Barbara Walters becomes the first woman network news anchor at an annual salary of $1 million.

Supreme Court extends abortion rights so that a woman need not have her husband's or parent's consent to undergo an abortion.

1977
November 18–21: First National Women's Conference in Houston chaired by Bella Abzug and attended by three First Ladies.

1978
Pregnancy Disability Act (amending Title VII of the Civil Rights Act) prohibits firing a woman on the basis of pregnancy or childbirth and requires health benefits coverage of pregnancy.
Congress extends ERA ratification date to June 30, 1982.
NASA names its first women astronauts.

1979
Thirty-six U.S. women's magazines run pro-ERA articles.
President Jimmy Carter creates the National Women's Business Enterprise Policy to support women's businesses through technical and management assistance, training, and counseling.

1980
President Carter proposes that women register for the draft, thus creating provocative issue for feminist foe Phyllis Schlafly.
United Nations sponsors the second world conference on women in Copenhagen, Denmark.
Twenty-two women elected to House of Representatives. Record number (fifty-seven) run for Congress.

1981
Arizona judge Sandra Day O'Connor confirmed as first woman to serve on the Supreme Court.
The Second Stage by Betty Friedan published.

1982
Deadline for seven-year extension of ERA ratification runs out, three states short of thirty-eight needed for ratification.

1983
Sally Ride is first American woman astronaut to go into space.
Total of 992 women in state legislatures, triple that of ten years earlier.

NOW endorses Walter Mondale as Democratic presidential candidate.
Outrageous Acts and Everyday Rebellions by Gloria Steinem published.

1984

Supreme Court weakens Title IX's effectiveness by limiting its applications to affect only those programs receiving direct federal funds—that is, student aid programs.

Geraldine Ferraro wins nomination for U.S. vice-president at the Democratic National Convention in San Francisco, the first woman in history to be named to a major national ticket.

1985

United Nations sponsors third women's conference in Nairobi, Kenya.

Montana is first state to require gender-neutral rates for all types of personal insurance.

1986

One hundred fifty thousand people march in pro-choice "Marches for Women's Lives" in Washington, D.C., and Los Angeles.

Supreme Court rules that sexual harassment that creates a hostile environment is a form of sex discrimination actionable under Title VII.

1987

Supreme Court ruling upholds California statute which requires employers to provide maternity leave and job reinstatement.

Supreme Court upholds promotion of a woman over a marginally more qualified man in employer's affirmative action program.

Supreme Court rules that states may require all-male private clubs to allow female members.

Notes

CHAPTER 1

13   "Wake Up Plaza!": *NOW Acts,* Winter/Spring 1969, p. 7.

14   from twelve till three: *New York Times,* Feb. 13, 1969; Bill Harris, *The Plaza* (1981), p. 56. In 1969, both New York stock exchanges closed well before 4 P.M. Although Muriel Siebert had owned a seat since 1967, neither she nor any other woman would work on either floor until 1976.

15   "No, madam . . .": Betty Friedan, *It Changed My Life: Writings on the Women's Movement* (1977), p. 52.

16   unable even to believe: Later, after Friedan's agent convinced her that Felker was serious, she did edit a section of the *Ladies' Home Journal.*

20   "We have reservations": New York *Daily News,* Feb. 13, 1969.

20   the refusal of service: *New York Times,* Feb. 13, 1969.

21   Betty held forth: Ibid.

21   "For a woman . . .": Harriet Van Horne, "The Feminine Mistake," *New York Post,* Feb. 14, 1969.

CHAPTER 2

25   At the Polo Lounge: *NOW Acts,* Winter/Spring 1969, p. 8.

CHAPTER 3

28   "Her essential quality . . .": Germaine Greer, *The Female Eunuch,* (1971), p. 57.

CHAPTER 4

41   "My father had two points . . .": *Time,* Jan. 3, 1969, p. 38; *USA Today,* July 29, 1986.

41 Pauline had been: *Toledo Blade*, Oct. 26, 1970.

42 their own thing: Ibid.

43 "from candy wrappers . . .": *Toledo Blade*, Nov. 14, 1965.

45 she would talk about the rats: *Newsweek*, Aug. 16, 1971, p. 53.

46 The rats, she told a reporter: *Toledo Blade*, May 10, 1972.

46 "an invalid who lay in bed . . .": Gloria Steinem, *Outrageous Acts and Everyday Rebellions* (1983), p. 130.

50 "I sometimes imagined . . .": Ibid., p. 135.

50 "anxiety neurosis": Ibid., p. 140.

50 "My mother was not mentally ill": *USA Today*, May 20, 1985.

51 "In fact . . .": Ibid.

CHAPTER 5

54 "If I am right . . .": Betty Friedan, *The Feminine Mystique* (1963), p. 32.

57 an old, overgrown cemetery: Paul Wilkes, "Mother Superior to Women's Lib," *New York Times Magazine*, Nov. 29, 1970, p. 27.

59 "belittled, cut down my father . . .": Ibid., p. 29.

60 Miriam took them to a psychologist: *New York Times*, Nov. 19, 1971.

63 journalists would colorfully recount: *Chicago Tribune Magazine*, Oct. 25, 1981, p. 14. The story first appeared, however, in *The Feminine Mystique*.

63 how the love-torn: Wilkes, "Mother Superior," p. 27.

65 "The American Woman? Not for This GI": Victor Dallaire, "The American Woman? Not for This GI," *New York Times Magazine*, March 10, 1946, p. 15.

65 for an early investigation: Margaret Mead, "What Women Want," *Fortune*, December 1946, p. 173.

67 Betty devoted herself to making a home: Betty Friedan, *It Changed My Life: Writings on the Women's Movement* (1977), p. 35.

67 "The independent woman . . .": Ferdinand Lundberg and Marynia F. Farnham, M.D., *Modern Woman: The Lost Sex* (1947), p. 319.

67 denial of femininity: Ibid., pp. 266–267.

67 a footnote citing Dr. Helene Deutsch: Ibid., p. 264.

68 "psychiatric case histories": Ibid., p. 149.

68 It was a tale: Friedan, *It Changed My Life*, p. 29.

68 "And I understood . . .": Ibid.

69 "Women should begin . . .": Lundberg and Farnham, *Modern Woman*, p. 370.

CHAPTER 6

72 "Freud assumed . . .": Kate Millett, *Sexual Politics* (1970), p. 180.

77 "the time of recriminations": Kate Millett, *Flying* (1974), p. 230.

77 "And still now . . .": Ibid.

78 "Wouldn't it be wonderful . . . ": Ibid., p. 231.

78 "Now I realized . . .": Ibid., p. 225.

78 "I was smart and ugly . . .": *New York Post*, Aug. 1, 1970, p. 17.

NOTES

CHAPTER 7

83 "It was a strange stirring . . .": Betty Friedan, *The Feminine Mystique* (1963), p. 15.

84 "masculinized . . . her warm, intuitive . . .": Ferdinand Lundberg and Marynia F. Farnham, M.D., *Modern Woman: The Lost Sex* (1947), p. 175.

85 "fields belonging to the . . .": Ibid., p. 370.

89 "What difficulties have . . .": Friedan, *Feminine Mystique*, p. 357.

89 "How have you changed inside?": Ibid., pp. 357–358.

90 words that bore no resemblance: Betty Friedan, "Millionaire's Wife," *Cosmopolitan*, Sept. 1956, pp. 78–87; Friedan, "Two Are an Island," *Mademoiselle*, July 1955, pp. 88, 100–103.

92 "this calm, strange sureness . . .": Betty Friedan, *It Changed My Life: Writings on the Women's Movement* (1977), p. 39.

92 "The Coming Ice Age": Betty Friedan, "The Coming Ice Age," *Harper's*, Sept. 1958, p. 39.

94 "Neither my husband . . .": Friedan, *It Changed My Life*, p. 38.

94 "It is a Freudian idea . . .": Friedan, *Feminine Mystique*, p. 103.

94 "The role of Margaret Mead . . .": Ibid., p. 145.

94 "to spend their days . . .": Ibid., p. 256.

94 "I helped create . . .": Ibid., p. 66.

95 "The big lie . . .": Ibid., p. 48.

95 "as if waking from a coma . . .": Ibid., p. 79.

95 "comfortable concentration camp": Ibid., p. 307.

95 "the high-dominance . . .": Ibid., p. 320.

95 "ugly duckling adolescence": Ibid., p. 356.

95 "the problem lay buried . . .": Ibid., p. 15.

96 "I remember him pleading with me . . .": Paul Wilkes, "Mother Superior of Women's Lib," *New York Times Magazine*, Nov. 29, 1970.

96 "angry battler for her sex": Jane Howard, "Angry Battler for Her Sex," *Life*, Nov. 1, 1963.

97 "Nice single girls . . .": Helen Gurley Brown, *Sex and the Single Girl* (1962), p. 204.

98 "If you don't let me . . .": Wilkes, "Mother Superior."

98 "Girls, how many of us . . .": Friedan, *It Changed My Life*, p. 40.

99 "small acts of domesticity": Joyce Kissock Lubold, "The Feminine Mistake," *Reader's Digest*, June 1965, p. 55.

99 "superficial . . .": *New York Times*, April 7, 1963.

99 "*Where* are all these women . . .": *Commonweal*, Jan. 10, 1964, p. 428.

99 hundreds of letters: Friedan, *It Changed My Life*, p. 39.

99 "In the last analysis . . .": Friedan, *Feminine Mystique*, p. 181.

CHAPTER 8

100 "Literally millions of women . . .": Gloria Steinem, *Outrageous Acts and Everyday Rebellions* (1983), p. 244.

100 "A landing party from Aristotle Onassis' . . .": Gloria Steinem, *The Beach Book* (1963), p. 97.

NOTES

101 "red balloons . . .": Joan Didion, "New York: The Great Reprieve," *Mademoiselle*, Feb. 1961, pp. 102–103, 147–150.

104 she left it: Leonard Levitt, "SHE: The Awesome Power of Gloria Steinem," *Esquire*, Oct. 1971, p. 210.

108 "not ours, was the norm . . .": Steinem, *Outrageous Acts*, p. 15.

109 with Paul Sigmund: New York *Daily News*, June 19, 1975.

110 in 1962 in Helsinki: Ibid.

110 would anger many feminists: Ibid. (The Redstockings issued a 16-page press release accusing Gloria Steinem of covering up her involvement with the CIA.)

111 "a midsummer night's dream!": "The New Woman," *Newsweek*, Aug. 16, 1971, p. 51.

111 "a series of little marriages": Ibid., p. 54.

113 "The Moral Disarmament of Betty Co-Ed": Gloria Steinem, "The Moral Disarmament of Betty Co-Ed," *Esquire*, Sept. 1962, p. 97.

114 "A blue satin band . . .": Steinem, *Outrageous Acts*, p. 35.

116 "Except that I like . . .": Steinem, *Beach Book*, Introduction, p. ix.

116 "Sun Bather": Nora Ephron, "Sun Bather," *New York Post*, Jan. 10, 1964.

CHAPTER 9

117 "Perhaps I am not . . .": Germaine Greer, *The Female Eunuch* (1971), p. 160.

119 "She's a remarkable woman": Mel Gussow, "David Hare: Playwright as Provocateur," *New York Times Magazine*, Sept. 29, 1985, p. 46.

121 "Nice Time," a television show: *Daily Mail* (London), Oct. 8, 1970.

123 "women made peanut butter . . .": Sara Evans, *Personal Politics*, (1979), p. 160.

123 "a common-law caste system": Ibid., p. 98.

125 "a Greek god sprung . . .": *New York Times*, April 4, 1972.

125 "the lower-class life . . .": New York *Daily News*, April 14, 1972.

126 "I suspected she wanted to . . .": Ibid.

126 "That legal paper . . .": Ibid.

128 The book would be called *The Female Eunuch*: Germaine Greer's book proposal begins: "It is odd that the white liberal of 1969 has accepted the idea that negroes, whom he does not know, must free themselves by establishing their own dignity on their own terms, when he would be surprised to hear that the women who live in his house are unfree and unrealized."

CHAPTER 10

129 "It is a mystery . . .": Betty Friedan, *It Changed My Life: Writings on the Women's Movement* (1977), p. 23.

129 "I'm nasty, I'm bitchy . . .": Jane Howard, "Angry Battler for Her Sex," *Life*, Nov. 1, 1963.

130 "an orgasm from shining . . .": *New York Newsday*, April 23, 1975.

130 "If you ever . . .": Friedan, *It Changed My Life*, p. 92.

130 She was going to write: Ibid., p. 60.

131 Catherine East: Ibid., p. 111.

131 One woman, she would later write: Ibid., p. 113.

132 "march on Washington . . .": Ibid., p. 112.

132 Dick Graham had cautiously: Ibid., p. 115.

132 "existential dread": Ibid., p. 118.

133 About twenty-five women filed: Toni Carabillo, "A Passion for the Possible," *Do It Now*, Oct.1976.

134 "I was very naive": Friedan, *It Changed My Life*, p. 117.

135 "Who invited *you*?": Carabillo, "A Passion for the Possible," p. 6.

137 on her paper cocktail napkin: *Wall Street Journal*, April 1, 1977.

138 the twenty-eight-member board: Ibid.

138 NOW was not a club for women: *World Journal Tribune*, Nov. 22, 1966.

138 listing Kay Clarenbach as temporary "chairman": *Sentinel*, Aug. 1, 1966.

139 Muriel's official release: Friedan, *It Changed My Life*, p. 121.

139 NOW formed task forces: Carabillo, "A Passion for the Possible," p. 8.

139 That fall, they began to meet: Ibid.

140 a lawsuit from the American Newspaper Publishers Association: New York NOW—New York Reports, Nov. 4, 1968, p. 1.

140 "absolutely unbending": Memo to Pat Trainor and Dolores Alexander from Jean Faust, Sept. 16, 1968.

140 "I got my job . . .": New York NOW Newsletter, 1968, p. 2.

140 "A Death Watch at ANPA": Jean Faust, New York NOW memo.

141 Bill of Rights: Friedan, *It Changed My Life*, pp. 143–145.

142 a mass march on Washington: *National Observer*, Dec. 26, 1966.

143 "The best minds . . .": Kate Millett, *Flying* (1974), p. 502.

143 "increasingly apparent tendency to flout convention": *Current Biography Yearbook 1971*, p. 271.

CHAPTER 11

150 from male put-downs: Robin Morgan, *Going Too Far* (1977), p. 66.

150 the only program: Frank Deford, *There She Is: The Life and Times of Miss America* (1971), p. 5.

150 "No More Miss America": "No More Miss America" flier, New York, Aug. 22, 1968, p. 1.

150 "Atlantic City is a town with class . . .": New York *Free Press*, Sept. 12, 1968.

151 "Miss America Sells It": Frank Deford, *There She Is: The Life and Times of Miss America* (1971), p. 257.

151 "If you got married . . .": New York *Free Press*, Sept. 12, 1968.

151 "Ain't she sweet?": Peter Babcox, "Meet the Women of the Revolution, 1969," *New York Times Magazine*, Feb. 9, 1969.

151 "We all felt, well, *grown-up* . . .": Morgan, *Going Too Far*, p. 62.

152 "the best fun I can . . .": Flo Kennedy, *Color Me Flo: My Hard Life and Good Times* (1976), p. 62.

153 "The only real concern . . .": Deford, *There She Is*, p. 256.

153 a coalition of women's peace groups: *New York Times*, Jan. 16, 1968. (Jeanette Rankin, eighty-seven years old and the first woman elected to Congress (1916), led one small delegation, which was part of a large but orderly demonstration, into the office of the Senate Democratic leader Mike Mansfield. Among those

demonstrating were Coretta King, widow of Martin Luther King, Jr., singer Judy Collins, and actress Viveca Lindfors.)

153 a Gallup poll: *New York Times,* March 10, 1968.

154 "Voice of the Women's Liberation Movement": Edited by Joreen and Shulamith Firestone.

154 "The Second Feminist Wave": Martha Weinman Lear, "The Second Feminist Wave," *New York Times Magazine,* March 10, 1968.

156 " 'commit suicide' . . .": Ti-Grace Atkinson, *Amazon Odyssey* (1974), p. 47. From a paper written in April 1969: "The feminist dilemma is that it is as women— or 'females'—that women are persecuted, just as it was as slaves—or 'blacks'—that slaves were persecuted in America. In order to improve their condition, those individuals who are today defined as women must eradicate their own definition."

158 Valeria Solanis: New York *Daily News,* June 4, 1968.

158 "mad, mad world . . .": Ibid.

158 "The SCUM [Society for Cutting Up Men] Manifesto": Valeria Solanis, SCUM manifesto, reprinted in Robin Morgan, ed., *Sisterhood Is Powerful: An Anthology of Writings from the Women's Liberation Movement* (1970), p. 514.

158 Solanis was not a lesbian: *New York Post,* June 4, 1968.

158 Maurice Girodias, who had paid Valeria $500: Ibid.

159 Friends of Warhol: Ibid.

159 to have photographs: Jean Stein, *Edie: An American Biography* (1982), p. 238.

159 ". . . a Heroine to Feminists": *New York Times,* June 14, 1968.

159 "TG has badly damaged NOW . . .": New York NOW memo from emergency meeting of Executive Committee, June 17, 1968.

159 "The oppression of women by men . . .": Ti-Grace Atkinson, *Amazon Odyssey* (1974), p. 5. Vaginal orgasm as a Mass Hysterical Response. From a speech delivered to the National Conference Medical Committee for Human Rights in Philadelphia, April 5, 1968.

160 "By God, you'd better learn it . . .": Atkinson, *Amazon Odyssey,* p.7.

160 Born black and poor in Kansas City: Kennedy, *Color Me Flo,* p. 24.

161 Zella cut out patterns: Ibid., p. 25.

161 As Flo would tell the story: Ibid., p. 31.

162 "The Case Against Marriage": Ibid., p. 2.

162 "A Comparative Study . . .": Ibid., p. 120.

162 "Most people are not taught . . .": Ibid., p. 97.

163 A toilet bowl: *Newsday,* Sept. 10, 1968.

164 "When I said something about the war": Kennedy, *Color Me Flo,* p. 62.

164 "Desist immediately . . .": New York NOW memo from Muriel Fox to Jean Faust, Dolores Alexander, and Joan Hull, June 1968.

165 "irreconcilable ideological conflicts . . .": Atkinson, *Amazon Odyssey,* p. 9.

165 the "finest mind" of all: Kate Millett, *Flying* (1974), p. 509.

165 "We must not seem intellectually arrogant . . .": New York NOW memo from Jean Faust to Kate Millett, March 5, 1969.

166 "Women who grasp . . .": Atkinson, *Amazon Odyssey,* p. 25.

166 She had cut herself off: *New York Post,* April 1, 1970.

167 "My impression is that the prostitute . . .": *New York Times,* May 29, 1970.

168   *The Second Sex:* Simone de Beauvoir, *The Second Sex* (1953).

168   "Men have always kept . . .": Ibid., p. 157.

169   "We are exploited . . .": Morgan, *Sisterhood Is Powerful,* p. 533.

169   "Frigidity has generally . . .": Ann Koedt, "The Myth of the Vaginal Orgasm," in Shulamith Firestone, ed., *Notes From the First Year,* New York Radical Women, (1968), p. 1.

170   "metaphysical cannibalism": Atkinson, *Amazon Odyssey,* p. 57.

170   "The Grand Coolie Damn": Marge Piercy, in Morgan, *Sisterhood Is Powerful,* p. 421.

170   " 'Kinder, Küche, Kirche' . . .": Dr. Naomi Weisstein. Ibid., p. 20.

170   WITCH street theater group "hexing" Wall Street: Sara Davidson, "An 'Oppressed Minority' Demands Its Rights," *Life,* Dec. 12, 1969.

170   picketing the New York City marriage: Ibid.

170   "Witness the Liberated Woman . . .": Julie Baumgold, "You've Come a Long Way, Baby," *New York,* June 9, 1969.

171   "Oh, my God": Davidson, "An 'Oppressed Minority.' "

171   "The more I understand . . .": Ibid.

171   Fact: Only 1 percent of the nation's engineers . . .": *Time,* Nov. 21, 1969, p. 54. All of these points, with the sole exception of the last one, appear in the *Time* article.

172   paralleled the black movement: Vivian Gornick, "The Next Great Moment in History Is Theirs," *Village Voice,* Nov. 27, 1969.

CHAPTER 12

174   "women preoccupied with desperate . . .": Betty Friedan, *The Feminine Mystique* (1963), p. 26.

179   And then she sued: *New York Times,* Oct. 8, 1969.

179   Flo and Diane wrote about the hearings: Diane Schulder and Florynce Kennedy, *Abortion Rap* (1971).

180   Barbara Seaman addressed that subject: Barbara Seaman, *The Doctors' Case Against the Pill* (1969).

181   "The Terrible Trouble with the Birth Control Pills": Lois Chevalier and Leonard Cohen, *Ladies' Home Journal,* July 1967.

181   *McCall's* followed with: Alice Lake, "The Pill," *McCall's,* Nov. 1967.

182   Barbara testified: Seaman, *The Doctors' Case,* back leaf.

182   wrote letters to Congress: Letter to Senator Gaylord Nelson from Jean Faust, Jan. 23, 1970.

182   "disorganized, scatterbrained": *New York Times,* Jan. 2, 1970.

183   only 7.5 percent of whom: Sheryl Burt Ruzek, *The Women's Health Movement* (1979), p. 99.

183   twelve women who: *New York Times,* April 11, 1985.

183   "Cunt is beautiful": Germaine Greer, "Lady, Love Your Cunt," *Suck,* 1971; reprinted in *The Madwoman's Underclothes* (1987), p. 77.

183   "That tiny slit . . .": Colette Price, "The First Self-Help Clinic," in Redstockings' *Feminist Revolution* (1975), pp. 136–137.

187   the Weathermen accidentally detonated: *New York Times,* March 18, 1970.

187 Jane Alpert was arrested: Jane Alpert, *Growing Up Underground* (1981), p. 227.

187 her camouflage: Ibid., p. 253.

187 "Goodbye to All That": Robin Morgan, "Goodbye to All That," *Rat*, January 1970, reprinted in *Going Too Far* (1977), p. 121.

187 "Free Our Sisters!": Ibid., p. 131.

188 a sensitive recounting: Susan Brownmiller, "Sisterhood Is Powerful," *New York Times Magazine*, March 15, 1970.

188 "hopelessly bourgeois": Ibid.

189 Down the corridor where the secretaries: Marcia Cohen, "Ladies' Men," New York *Daily News*, Oct. 26, 1980.

191 "Why hasn't the magazine . . .": Claudia Dreifus, *East Village Other*, April 1970.

192 "We've had enough of this . . .": *Daily News*, March 19, 1970.

193 "They have a point . . .": *Time*, March 30, 1970.

193 "one of the most interesting . . .": *Daily News*, March 19, 1970.

194 For the *Journal*: A month later, in Holland, the "Dolle Minas" were swarming into the offices of sedate women's magazines dressed as cleaning women. Also, in an attempt to be amusing, they sat on bicycles and beside bridges whistling and hooting at startled men.

194 *Newsweek*: "Women's Lib: The War on 'Sexism,' " March 23, 1970, p. 71.

194 *Atlantic Monthly*: "A Woman's Place," Special Issue of the *Atlantic Monthly*, March 3, 1970.

194 *Mademoiselle*: "Women Re Women," Special Issue of *Mademoiselle*, February 1970.

196 One small step: *New York Times*, March 19, 1970.

CHAPTER 13

198 "They've got the fucking fantasy . . .": Barbara Kevles, "Raising My Fist for Feminism: I Discovered the Movement in Jail," *Works in Progress*, No. 5, 1972, p. 153.

198 "My long hair catches in the zipper": Ibid, p. 167.

198 " 'Take off your underpants' ": Ibid., p. 169.

199 "sobbing and gasping . . .": Ibid., p. 168.

200 As so many of the young radicals: The reverse was also true. In some minds, the student antiwar movement was indistinguishable from the feminists, both provoking violence. On May 9, 1970, the *New York Post* reported that a young woman, an administrative assistant to Mayor John Lindsay, was roughed up by construction workers when she attempted to ease a conflict with students. "If you want to be treated like an equal, we'll treat you like one," the workers shouted.

200 Kevles, too, would make: "Raising My Fist for Feminism: I Discovered the Movement in Jail," *Works in Progress*, No. 5, 1972, p. 169.

200 "As the air climbs my squatting cheeks . . .": Ibid., p. 169.

201 "Sister Joe Colombo": Ti-Grace Atkinson, *Amazon Odyssey* (1974), p. 199.

201 "I, Ti-Grace Atkinson, in the name of all women . . .": Ibid., p. 169.

202 "the greatest organized crime ring . . .": Ibid., p. 191.

202 "the virginity of the Blessed Mother": *New York Post Weekend Magazine,* March 20, 1971, p. 25.

202 "I can't let her say that!": New York *Daily News,* March 12, 1971.

203 "I'm only sorry I missed": *New York Post,* March 12, 1971.

203 "forty-eight-year-old reputed chief . . .": *New York Times,* June 29, 1971.

204 Ti-Grace appeared wearing black pajamas: Kate Millett, *Flying* (1974), p. 509.

204 "I am dedicating my remarks tonight . . .": Atkinson, *Amazon Odyssey,* p. 199.

204 she found the Mafia "morally refreshing": *New York Post,* Sept. 3, 1971.

204 "Maybe she's right . . .": Ibid.

205 " 'We have just begun to discuss strategy' . . .": New York *Daily News,* Nov. 22, 1966. Joe Cassidy's Offbeat column is headlined "Plan to Revolt Is Bared in Gals' Den of Inequity."

205 "Women Are Revolting": Jean Faust, in a letter to WNEW-TV, objects to their programming of "Women are revolting" as mocking the women's movement (Nov. 13, 1970).

206 an innocent beauty in hotpants: *Saturday Review,* Dec. 4, 1971, p. 72.

206 "I don't want to be used as an object . . .": Sara Davidson, "An 'Oppressed Minority' Demands Its Rights," *Life,* Dec. 12, 1969.

214 Lucy in the *Saturday Review:* Lucy Komisar, "New Feminism," *Saturday Review,* Feb. 21, 1970, pp. 27–30.

215 "Members of women's groups . . .": Sara Davidson, "Foremothers," *Esquire,* July 1973, p. 70.

215 "There is something every woman wears . . .": Robin Morgan, *Going Too Far* (1977), p. 129.

CHAPTER 14

217 "That's it, that's her . . .": *Toledo Blade,* Nov. 14, 1965.

218 "Just sitting in a restaurant . . .": Ibid.

219 "girl writer assignments": Gloria Steinem, *Outrageous Acts and Everyday Rebellions* (1983), p. 14.

220 " 'I never had time . . .' ": Ibid., p. 241.

220 "Well, what I would do . . .": *Detroit Free Press,* Aug. 15, 1971.

221 "Marriage is like a door . . .": Eugene Boe, "I Want to Come Back as a New Woman," *New Woman Magazine,* Feb. 1972, p. 71.

222 "radical chic": Tom Wolfe, "Radical Chic: That Party at Lenny's," *New York,* p. 27.

222 "One of the best dates . . .": *Time,* Jan. 3, 1969, p. 38.

223 "I try to charm everybody . . .": *Toledo Blade,* Nov. 14, 1965.

223 "With legs like those . . .": Boe, "I Want to Come Back," p. 69.

223 "I had canceled out . . .": Steinem, *Outrageous Acts,* p. 9.

223 "Though I wasn't shy . . .": Ibid.

225 "After Black Power . . .": Gloria Steinem, "City Politic," *New York,* April 7, 1969, p. 8.

226 Information on NOW's efforts in the battle for abortion rights, the Colgate-

Palmolive demonstrations, and the battle to end gender-based help-wanted ads was sent to Gloria under a cover letter from Jean Faust to Gloria Steinem, dated January 8, 1969.

227   according to Mailer, it was Gloria herself: Norman Mailer, *The Prisoner of Sex* (1971), p. 19.

227   those who wondered: Boe, "I Want to Come Back," p. 71.

227   "a voice that doesn't want . . .": Joe Flaherty, *Managing Mailer* (1970).

229   "In my experience, commencement speakers . . .": Caroline Bird, "Gloria Steinem: New Woman's New Woman," *New Woman*, Dec. 1970, p. 48.

229–30   "great moment in history . . .": Charles A. Reich, *The Greening of America* (1971), p. 179.

230   ". . . Gloria Steinem, a contributing editor . . .": Gloria Steinem, "What It Would Be Like If Women Win," *Time*, Aug. 31, 1970, p. 22.

CHAPTER 15

232   *Sexual Politics:* Kate Millett, *Sexual Politics* (1970).

233   working up to eighteen hours a day: "Who's Come a Long Way, Baby?" *Time*, Aug. 31, 1970, p. 19.

233   "I was really afraid . . .": Ibid.

234   "Fumio, I love you": *New York Post*, Aug. 1, 1970.

234   "I wrote it bang, bang, bang": *Life*, Sept. 4, 1970, p. 22.

234   "My mother had a college degree . . .": *New York Post*, Aug. 1, 1970.

234   "You go around feeling neurotic . . .": *Life*, Sept. 4, 1970, p. 22.

234   Kate's membership in the Radical Lesbians: Ibid.; *New York Times*, July 20, 1970.

235   written *two* reviews: *New York Times*, Aug. 5 & 6, 1970.

237   "We were constantly reminded . . .": *Life*, Sept. 4, 1970, p. 22.

237   "I was smart and ugly . . .": *New York Post*, Aug. 1, 1970.

237   "All my life, guys said I . . .": *Time*, Aug. 31, 1970, p. 19.

239   "Kate's missing the boat . . .": Ibid.

239   "I'll only keep enough to live . . .": *New York Newsday*, July 24, 1970.

239   "If I am bored . . .": Kate Millett, *Flying* (1974), p. 12.

240   she thought of Betty Friedan: Ibid., p. 22.

240   "I'm not into that": *Life*, Sept. 4, 1970, p. 22.

242   Teresa Juarez, a member of the Radical Lesbians: Millett, *Flying*, p. 14.

242   Kate had actually been waiting: Ibid.

242   "Are you a lesbian? Say it!": Ibid.

243   "I hear them not breathe": Ibid., p. 15.

245   "like sitting with your testicles . . .": *Time*, Aug. 31, 1970, p. 16.

245   "Mao Tse-tung of Women's Liberation": Ibid.

245   " 'There it goes down the tube . . .": Millett, *Flying*, p. 17.

245   "A Second Look" at women's lib: *Time*, Dec. 14, 1970, p. 50.

247   "The disclosure . . .": Ibid.

249   the Women's Strike Coalition: *New York Times*, Dec. 13, 1970.

249   "we're ALL wearing lavender . . .": Betty Friedan: *It Changed My Life: Writings on the Women's Movement* (1977), p. 211.

249 "Sexual politics is highly dangerous . . .": Ibid., p. 217.

250 she phoned the offices: Ibid., p. 213.

250 "Kate Is Great" press conference: *New York Times,* Dec. 18, 1970.

250 In the group were: Ibid.

250 "Women's liberation and homosexual liberation . . .": Ibid.

251 "Shamefully, pointlessly rich": Millett, *Flying,* p. 4.

251 "Asking women to disguise . . .": *New York Times,* Dec. 12, 1971; Sidney Abbott and Barbara Love, *Sappho Was a Right-on Woman* (1972), p. 134.

253 "Author Commitment Papers Withdrawn": *St. Paul Dispatch,* Aug. 8, 1973.

254 six attempts at suicide: Kate Millett, *Sita* (1978), p. 130.

CHAPTER 16

255 "everybody's favorite feminist": Mary Cantwell, "An Opinion," *Mademoiselle,* July 1971, p. 36.

255 "The struggle which is . . .": Germaine Greer, *The Female Eunuch* (1971), pp. 10, 58.

257 "But I'm sure . . .": *Daily Mirror* (London), Feb. 1, 1971.

257 "To refuse hobbles . . .": Greer, *Female Eunuch,* p. 351.

257 "Women who fancy . . .": Ibid., p. 349.

258 the male prerogatives: Ibid., p. 64.

258 "Many men are almost . . .": Ibid., p. 342.

258 "Men are tired of having . . .": Ibid., p. 338.

258 "but for ecstasy": Ibid., p. 37.

259 "I only wish . . .": Christopher Lehmann-Haupt, "The Best Feminist Book So Far," *New York Times,* April 20, 1971.

259 Warwick's "most popular lecturer": Jordan Bonfante, "Germaine Greer," *Life,* May 7, 1971, p. 32.

259 "Pregnancy is barbaric.": Shulamith Firestone, *Dialectic of Sex: The Case for Feminist Revolution* (1972), p. 198.

260 "Women's Liberation has been . . .": Pete Hamill, *New York Post,* Dec. 22, 1970.

260 "You might have to . . .": Helen Lawrenson, "The Feminine Mistake," *Esquire,* January 1971, p. 83.

260 "not a liberation movement . . .": Arlene Croce, "Sexism in the Head," *Commentary,* March 1971, p. 63.

261 "sick of pretending . . .": Greer, *Female Eunuch,* p. 58.

261 "a prisoner of the virility cult": Kate Millett, *Sexual Politics* (1970), p. 314.

261 "It's absolutely philistine . . .": *New York Times,* March 22, 1971.

262 "I was in training": Germaine Greer, "My Mailer Problem," *Esquire,* September 1971, p. 92.

262 "a voice which could have boiled . . .": Norman Mailer, *The Prisoner of Sex* (1971), p. 20.

262 "a future leader . . .": Ibid., p. 71.

262 The land of Millett: Ibid., p. 72.

263 "an honor student . . .": Ibid.

263 Robin Morgan, according to Germaine's, "My Mailer Problem," p. 92.

264   "the themes of his life . . .": Mailer, *Prisoner of Sex*, p. 25.

264   "A wind in this prose . . .": Ibid., p. 34.

264   "She wished to meet Norman . . .": Diana Trilling, *We Must March, My Darlings* (1977), p. 200.

264   To fuck him ("She had already told me she wouldn't mind fucking him"): Jill Johnston, *Lesbian Nation: The Feminist Solution* (1973), p. 24.

264   "Norman Mailer is his own worst enemy": *New York Times*, March 22, 1971.

CHAPTER 17

267   she feared that the bruises: Paul Wilkes, "Mother Superior to Women's Lib," *New York Times Magazine*, Nov. 29, 1970.

268   "Betty has a great need . . .": Myra MacPherson, "The Other Friedan," *Washington Post*, Feb. 27, 1971.

269   In 1972, he would petition Family Court: *New York Post*, March 15, 1975.

269–70   "Space? NOW Women Ask to Go There Too": *New York Post*, Dec. 8, 1969.

270   argued vehemently against: *New York Post*, Jan. 26, 1970.

270   "Over 25 percent of mothers . . .": Ibid.

272   a lesbian had been assigned to seduce *her*: Betty Friedan, "Up from the Kitchen Floor," *New York Times Magazine*, March 4, 1973, p. 34.

272   "Our sisterhood . . .": *New York Times*, March 21, 1970.

276   dazzling array of influential co-hostesses: *New York Times*, Aug. 10, 1970.

276   "she of the feminine mystique . . .": Harriet Van Horne, "The Feminine Mistake," *New York Post*, Feb. 14, 1969.

276   She wasn't a women's liberationist: *New York Times*, Aug. 10, 1970.

278   "One of the biggest enemies . . .": Ibid.

278   "star complex": Wilkes, "Mother Superior."

278   Up to Boston: Betty Friedan, *It Changed My Life: Writings on the Women's Movement* (1977), p. 199.

279   "Betty's baby": Judy Klemesrud, "A Herstory-Making Event," *New York Times Magazine*, Aug. 23, 1970, p. 15.

279   Most women, she and her colleagues: *New York Post*, Aug. 26, 1970.

279   "fought in the bedroom": *New York Post*, Aug. 24, 1970.

279   *Lysistrata*: New York *Daily News*, Aug. 5, 1970.

280   impressive array of sponsors: Klemesrud, "A Herstory-Making Event," p. 15.

280   "How could we have . . .": Friedan, *It Changed My Life*, p. 199.

281   at the Statue of Liberty: *Daily News*, Aug. 11, 1970.

281   "This is our hour . . .": *New York Post*, Aug. 25, 1970.

281   "a gray-haired combination . . .": Klemesrud, "A Herstory-Making Event," p. 16.

281   "ridiculous exhibitionists": *New York Times*, Aug. 26, 1970.

282   women's libbers were uncombed: *New York Post*, Aug. 26, 1970.

282   "I don't want people to think . . .": *New York Times*, Aug. 27, 1970.

282   the microphone: *New York Post*, Aug. 27, 1970.

282   "The men in this country fight the wars . . .": Ibid.

282   she seemed like a Civil War general: Ibid.

NOTES

283 one of the men presents her: *New York Post,* Aug. 26, 1970.

283 "Hey, I'd like to liberate *that*": Pete Hamill, "The Women March," *New York Post,* Aug. 27, 1970.

283 Betty promenades into: *New York Post,* Aug. 27, 1970.

284 "Marvelous . . .": Ibid.

285 "MOM—Men Our Masters": *New York Post,* Aug. 26, 1970.

286 "In the religion of my ancestors . . .": Friedan, *It Changed My Life,* p. 206.

287 New York governor Nelson Rockefeller: *New York Post,* Aug. 26, 1970.

287 "Don't joke about women's liberation": Clayton Fritchey, "New Deal for Women," *New York Post,* Aug. 31, 1970.

287 "Despite the humorous outlook . . .": Ibid.

287 "the remnants of what . . .": Hamill, "The Women March."

287 "From now on . . .": *New York Post,* Aug. 27, 1970.

CHAPTER 18

290 "An extremely hostile . . .": Peter Manso, *Mailer: His Life and Times* (1985), p. 524.

290 "like an Irish bartender": Mary Cantwell, "An Opinion," *Mademoiselle,* July 1971, p. 36.

291 ". . . a floozy kind of fox fur": Manso, *Mailer,* p. 520.

293 "I was so tense . . .": Germaine Greer, "My Mailer Problem," *Esquire,* Sept. 1971, p. 214.

297 "I just hissed at him . . .": Manso, *Mailer,* p. 522.

298 to oppose contraception: Norman Mailer had often expressed his conviction that women had a biological imperative to bear children.

299 ". . . the token straight": Ibid., p. 520.

302 "as if they're going to get shot . . .": Manso, *Mailer,* p. 524.

303 Norman had treated her badly: Ibid., p. 523.

304 "terribly taken with her . . .": Ibid.

304 "strutting and smirking . . .": Greer, "My Mailer Problem," p. 214.

305 luncheon at the staid National Press Club: *Washington Post,* May 19, 1971.

305 "Dealing with the, uh, Problem": Nora Ephron, *Crazy Salad* (1975), p. 76.

CHAPTER 19

309 "like some great Shakespearean performer": Paul Wilkes, "Mother Superior to Women's Lib," *New York Times Magazine,* Nov. 29, 1970, p. 28.

311 "those navel-gazing rap sessions": "Women's Lib Shifts Aim to Congress," *New York Post,* Aug. 27, 1970.

312 "In 1972, we will go to the national conventions of both major parties . . .": Friedan's blank check in Muriel Fox's personal files.

313 "came from Betty Friedan . . .": *Draft of Proposed Explanatory Literature:* ". . . The original conception of the Caucus came from Betty Friedan, well known author of *The Feminine Mystique* and a leading feminist thinker and lecturer, who suggested it to several women's groups in New York City. . . . On March 21, 1971, about 100 women from many different civic, political, labor and service groups, as well as unaffiliated housewives met and voted to set up a committee to organize a

National Women's Political Caucus." (As stated in this release, one aim of the group was to have women fill 50 percent of all delegations and slates.)

313 "screamed at me over the phone . . .": Betty Friedan, *It Changed My Life: Writings on the Women's Movement* (1977), p. 222.

313 "She stirs up the people . . .": Carey Winfrey, "Abzug," *New York Times Magazine*, Aug. 21, 1977, p. 59.

313 "I and the people . . .": Penelope McMillan, "Bella Isn't Funny Anymore," *New York Daily News*, May 28, 1972, p. 15.

314 "Bella's politics appeal . . .": Tom Burke, "The Bella Abzug Show," *New Times*, Sept. 16, 1977, p. 43.

314 "My election goes beyond . . .": *New Woman*, June 1971, p. 47.

315 the Rockefeller Commission: *Report to the President by the Commission on CIA Activities Within the United States*, June 1975, pp. 130–150.

315 "The faces of those white women . . .": Toni Morrison, "What the Black Woman Thinks About Women's Lib," *New York Times Magazine*, Aug. 22, 1971, p. 15.

316 Fannie Lou Hamer: *New York Times*, July 11, 1971.

316 "certainly not my purpose to replace . . .": Ibid.

316 "Our aim should be to humanize . . .": *New York Times*, July 11, 1971.

317 "a scheme . . .": Friedan, *It Changed My Life*, p. 222.

318 "augment what NOW is doing": *New York Post*, Oct. 19, 1971.

318 "Maybe political feminism . . .": Friedan, *It Changed My Life*, p. 234.

318 "One more woman . . .": *New York Post*, Aug. 25, 1971.

318 "What did it look like?": *New York Times*, July 14, 1971; *New York Post*, July 15, 1971.

CHAPTER 20

321 "the idea of ownership . . .": William F. Buckley, Jr., "Gloria Steinem," *New York Post*, Oct. 19, 1971.

322 "Friends, sisters . . .": "Gloria Steinem Bares Sex Myths," *Toledo Times*, October 7, 1970.

322 "So many men . . .": Ibid.

322 "It's a myth . . .": Ibid.

322 "What gets nearly everyone . . .": *Newsweek*, Aug. 16, 1971, p. 51.

323 "Why Gloria Steinem?": Marilyn Mercer, "Woman of the Year," *McCall's*, January 1972, p. 67.

326 "I get the feeling . . .": Gloria Steinem, "Sisterhood," first issue of *Ms.* in *New York*, Dec. 20, 1971, p. 48.

327 "In New York last fall . . .": Jane O'Reilly, "The Housewife's Moment of Truth," first issue of *Ms.* in *New York*, Dec. 20, 1971, p. 55.

329 "a mushy, sentimental idea . . .": Ellen Willis, "The Conservatism of *Ms.*," in *Redstockings: Feminist Revolution* (1978), p. 170.

332 "Most recently . . .": Leonard Levitt, "SHE: The Awesome Power of Gloria Steinem," *Esquire*, October 1971, p. 87.

332 "I don't mind people . . .": Mercer, "Woman of the Year," p. 125.

334   "veers dangerously close . . .": William F. Buckley, Jr., "Mss. Davis and Steinem," *New York Post*, Dec. 9, 1971.

334   "the lady's logic . . .": Buckley, "Gloria Steinem."

335   "Richard Nixon . . .": New York *Daily News*, Jan. 25, 1972.

335   "Not even her hardest detractors . . .": James A. Wechsler, "Sex and Campaign 72," *New York Post*, Feb. 15, 1972.

337   "struggling away . . .": *New York Post*, Feb. 10, 1972.

CHAPTER 21

338   "This year . . .": *Daily News*, July 10, 1972.

338   "We cannot afford . . .": *New York Newsday*, March 20, 1972.

338   "Singles weekends are . . .": *New York Post*, Jan. 31, 1972.

338   "Men can't be the enemy": *Peoria Journal Star*, Sept. 29, 1972.

338   "The reality today . . .": *New York Times*, Jan. 14, 1972.

339   "the opening note . . .": *New York Post*, May 15, 1972.

339   "Most of us . . .": *Daily News*, May 3, 1972.

339   "The most important . . .": *New York Times*, Feb. 12, 1972.

339   "She is a symbol of hope . . .": *New York Post*, June 5, 1972.

340   "precisely because . . .": Judith Hole and Ellen Levine, *Rebirth of Feminism* (1971), p. 135.

341   "the terrible fifties . . .": Nora Ephron, "A Few Words About Breasts," in *Crazy Salad* (1975), pp. 3–12. Originally appeared in *Esquire*, May 1972.

341   "Some Women's Liberation activists . . .": Lyn Tornabene, "Does Women's Liberation Make You Feel Inferior?" *Family Circle*, July 1972, p. 82.

341   "Which Ms. Has the Movement?": Natalie Gittelson, "Betty & Gloria & Shirley & Bella," *Harper's Bazaar*, July 1972, p. 80.

342   "I implore you, I beg you . . .": *New York Times*, July 15, 1972.

343   "Nineteen seventy-two . . .": *New York Post*, Feb. 14, 1972.

343   "Move on over . . .": *Miami Herald*, July 16, 1972.

344   "Little boys are taught . . .": Ibid.

344   "Housework is the nearest . . .": Ibid.

344   "Child care facilities . . .": Ibid.

344   "First you're on the pedestal . . .": Ibid.

344   "In the end . . .": Betty Friedan, *It Changed My Life: Writings on the Women's Movement* (1977), p. 235.

344   "The cameras are clicking . . .": Ephron, *Crazy Salad*, p. 37.

345   "But why do you dress like that?": *New York Post*, July 10, 1972.

345   "Gloria's relentless prominence . . .": Germaine Greer, "McGovern, the Big Tease," *Harper's*, October 1972, p. 62.

346   "I'm just tired of being screwed . . .": Ephron, *Crazy Salad*, p. 45.

347   "especially bitchy account . . .": Friedan, *It Changed My Life*, p. 234.

347   roll-call vote: New York *Daily News*, Aug. 24, 1972. Betty Friedan's demands at the Republican Women's Caucus were also well covered in the *Washington Post*, Aug. 25, 1972.

347   "We have to find out . . .": Ephron, *Crazy Salad*, p. 44.

348   "I have a brain *and* a uterus": *New York Times*, Aug. 23, 1987, p. 24.

CHAPTER 22

349 "almost without precedent . . .": *Newsday,* July 19, 1972.

350 "The assumption that women . . .": Betty Friedan, *McCall's,* August 1972, p. 83.

350 "Does this mean . . .": Ibid.

351 "Having been falsely accused . . .": *New York Times,* July 19, 1972.

352 one long article: Joseph Adelson, "Is Women's Lib a Passing Fad?" *New York Times Magazine,* March 19, 1972.

352 "Early man": William F. Buckley, Jr., "Textbook Sexism," *New York Post,* Nov. 25, 1972.

354 "Now I am sorry . . .": *New York Times,* Feb. 24, 1973.

354 she devoted an entire book: Midge Decter, *The New Chastity and Other Arguments Against Women's Liberation* (1972).

355 "Things will never be the same again": Max Lerner, "Woman Unbound," *New York Post,* June 1, 1971.

356 "the brutal truth": New York *Daily News,* June 9, 1972.

357 "As lovely as Aphrodite . . .": *New York Times,* Oct. 19, 1972.

357 "The Supreme Court . . .": *New York Times,* Jan. 23, 1973.

CHAPTER 23

359 "right to be a woman": *Christian Science Monitor,* June 25, 1982, p. 22.

359 "selfish and misguided": *Daily News,* Feb. 19, 1981. (Excerpted from the book *The Sweetheart of the Silent Majority: The Biography of Phyllis Schlafly* by Carol Felsenthal.)

360 "From the breadmakers to the breadwinners": *New York Times,* Dec. 15, 1975.

365 "These are the women . . .": *USA Today,* July 30, 1987.

367 "intense and often brilliant": Margo Jefferson, "Sexual Mine Field" (book review), *Newsweek,* Sept. 30, 1974, p. 99.

368 "seizing an idea . . .": James Wolcott, "Power and Gloria," *Vanity Fair,* Nov. 1986, p. 20.

370 she tossed the book: Deirdre Bair, "Simone de Beauvoir in Paris and America," *New York Times Book Review,* May 6, 1984.

370 "Thank God for Gloria Steinem": New York *Daily News,* Nov. 30, 1986.

370 the "princess of the women's movement": *Ladies' Home Journal,* March 1981, p. 141.

371 "the CIA's finest hour": *New York Times,* Feb. 21, 1967.

371 the flurry soon passed: *New York Times* News Service, Sept. 28, 1975; *Color Me Flo, My Life and Good Times,* p. 78. (The Redstockings charges were made in May 1975, a year of great dissension in the movement. That summer, several feminists, Ti-Grace Atkinson among them, walked out of Sagaris, a feminist study group in Vermont, because they were suspicious of Gloria Steinem's failure to respond to the charges. Barbara Seaman, who also attended Sagaris, was convinced that most of the internal strife was caused by CIA operatives acting as *agents provocateurs,* and Betty

Friedan reported that she felt physically threatened at the International Women's Conference in Mexico City. By fall, Steinem acceded to feminist pressure and wrote a reply to the Redstocking charges describing her association with the International Research Service as a mistake which she had not realized at the time. At the same time, *Ms.* was also under fire from Elizabeth Forsling Harris, one of the magazine's founders, for what she contended was a misrepresentation of stock values. Meanwhile, too, underground radical Jane Alpert, having surrendered to authorities, wrote a description of her conversion to radical feminism in *Ms.*, thereby, according to some, betraying the underground. Flo Kennedy and Atkinson took this position; Steinem, Kate Millett, Grace Paley, and Phyllis Chesler, among others, defended Alpert.)

371 "This is what forty looks like": *New York Times,* May 24, 1984.

373 "Women's liberation is very much . . .": "An Unchauvinist Male Replies," *Time,* Aug. 31, 1970, p. 21.

376 For the first time in history: *New York Times,* Feb. 2, 1988.

376 Women now hold approximately 35 percent: Bureau of Labor Statistics, from *Fortune,* August 3, 1987.

376 The average salaries: Ibid.

376 Almost half of all: Ibid.

376 Every major investment bank: Ibid.

377 By 1988, the Pentagon itself: *New York Times,* Feb. 3, 1988.

378 a new wave of feminism: Barbara Ehrenreich, "The Next Wave," *Ms.*, July/August 1987, p. 166.

Selected Bibliography

Abbott, Sidney, and Love, Barbara. *Sappho Was a Right-On Woman: A Liberated View of Lesbianism.* New York: Stein and Day, 1972.

Abzug, Bella, and Kelber, Mimi. *Gender Gap: Bella Abzug's Guide to Political Power for American Women.* Boston: Houghton Mifflin, 1984.

Adams, Jane. *Women On Top.* New York: Berkley Books, 1981.

Adamson, Madeleine, and Borgos, Seth. *This Mighty Dream.* Boston: Routledge and Kegan Paul, 1984.

Alpert, Jane. *Growing Up Underground.* New York: Morrow, 1981.

Banner, Lois W. *Women in Modern America: A Brief History.* New York: Harcourt Brace Jovanovich, 1974.

Barlow, Judith E., ed. *Plays by American Women.* New York: Avon, 1981.

Bell, Anne Olivier, ed. *The Diary of Virginia Woolf: Volume Three: 1925–1930.* New York: Harcourt Brace Jovanovich, 1980.

Bellow, Saul. *Mosby's Memoirs and Other Stories.* New York: Viking, 1968.

Bernard, Jessie. *The Future of Marriage.* New Haven, Conn.: Yale University Press, 1982.

Bernstein, Paula. *Family Ties, Corporate Bonds.* Garden City, N.Y.: Doubleday, 1985.

Bird, Caroline. *Born Female: The High Cost of Keeping Women Down.* New York: Pocket Books, 1968.

Bolen, Jean Shinoda, M.D., *Goddesses in Everywoman: A New Psychology of Women.* New York: Harper & Row, 1984.

Boston Women's Health Book Collective. *Our Bodies, Ourselves: A Book by and for Women.* Boston Women's Health Book Collective: 1971.

Boston Women's Health Book Collective. *The New Our Bodies, Ourselves: A Book by and for Women.* New York: Simon & Schuster, 1984.

Brown, Helen Gurley. *Having It All: The Ultimate Women's Guide to Love,*

Sex, Money—Even If You're Starting With Nothing. New York: Pocket Books, 1983.

Brown, Helen Gurley. *Sex and the Single Girl.* New York: Bernard Geis, 1962.

Brown, Rita Mae. *Rubyfruit Jungle.* New York: Daughters, 1973.

Brownmiller, Susan. *Against Our Will: Men, Women and Rape.* New York: Bantam, 1976.

Brownmiller, Susan. *Femininity.* New York: Linden Press/Simon & Schuster, 1984.

Burg, Kathleen Keefe. *The Womanly Art of Self-Defense: A Common Sense Approach.* New York: A & W Visual Library, 1979.

Cable, Mary. *American Manners and Morals.* New York: American Heritage, 1969.

Campbell, D'Ann. *Women at War with America: Private Lives in a Patriotic Era.* Cambridge, Mass.: Harvard University Press, 1984.

Carmichael, Carrie. *Non-Sexist Childraising: How You Can Help Your Children Grow Up Free to Be Themselves.* Boston: Beacon Press, 1977.

Carroll, Peter N. *It Seemed Like Nothing Happened: The Tragedy and Promise of America in the 1970's.* New York: Holt, Rinehart and Winston, 1982.

Chafe, William H. *The American Woman: Her Changing Social, Economic, and Political Roles, 1920–1972.* London: Oxford University Press, 1972.

Charvet, John. *Feminism.* London: J. M. Dent and Sons, 1982.

Cherow-O'Leary, Dr. Renee, and NOW LDEF. *The State-by-State Guide to Women's Legal Rights.* New York: McGraw-Hill, 1987.

Chesler, Phyllis. *Women and Madness.* New York: Avon, 1973.

Chicago, Judy. *Through the Flower: My Struggle as a Woman Artist.* Garden City, N.Y.: Doubleday, 1975.

Cleaver, Eldridge. *Soul on Ice.* New York: Dell, 1968.

Cole, K. C. *Between the Lines.* Garden City, N.Y.: Anchor/Doubleday, 1982.

Comfort, Alex, Ph.D., ed. *The Joy of Sex. A Gourmet Guide to Lovemaking.* New York: Crown, 1972.

Cooper, Jane, et al., eds. *Extended Outlooks.* New York: Collier, 1982.

Corea, Gena. *The Mother Machine: Reproductive Technologies from Artificial Insemination to Artificial Wombs.* New York: Harper & Row, 1985.

Cornford, Francis MacDonald, ed. *The Republic of Plato.* London: Oxford University Press, 1945.

Cowan, Paul. *An Orphan in History: Retrieving a Jewish Legacy.* Garden City, N.Y.: Doubleday, 1982.

Daly, Mary. *Beyond God the Father: Toward a Philosophy of Women's Liberation.* Boston: Beacon Press, 1973.

Daly, Mary. *Pure Lust: Elemental Feminist Philosophy.* Boston: Beacon Press, 1984.

Davis, Angela Y. *Women, Race and Class.* New York: Vintage, 1983. (Random House, 1981.)

de Beauvoir, Simone. *Adieux: A Farewell to Sartre.* New York: Pantheon, 1984 edition.

de Beauvoir, Simone. *The Second Sex: The Classic Manifesto of the Liberated Woman.* New York: Vintage, 1974.

de Tocqueville, Alexis. *Democracy in America.* New York: Vintage, 1945.

Deckard, Barbara Sinclair. *The Women's Movement: Political, Socioeconomic and Psychological Issues.* New York: Harper & Row, 1983.

Decter, Midge. *The Liberated Woman and Other Americans.* New York: Coward, McCann and Geoghegan, 1971.

Decter, Midge. *The New Chastity.* New York: Berkley Medallion Books, 1972.

Deford, Frank. *There She Is: The Life and Tiimes of Miss America.* New York: Viking, 1971.

Deutsch, Helene, M.D. *The Psychology of Women: A Psychoanalytic Interpretation.* London: Research Books, 1947.

Dinnerstein, Dorothy. *The Mermaid and The Minotaur: Sexual Arrangements and Human Malaise.* New York: Harper Colophon, 1977.

Djerassi, Carl. *The Politics of Contraception: Birth Control in the Year 2001.* San Francisco: Freeman, 1981.

Dowling, Colette. *The Cinderella Complex: Women's Hidden Fear of Independence.* New York: Summit, 1981.

Dworkin, Andrea. *Pornography: Men Possessing Women.* London: Women's Press, 1981.

Ehrenreich, Barbara. *The Hearts of Men: American Dreams and the Flight from Commitment.* Garden City, N.Y.: Anchor/Doubleday, 1983.

Ehrenreich, Barbara, and English, Deirdre. *For Her Own Good: 150 Years of the Experts' Advice to Women.* Garden City, N.Y.: Anchor/Doubleday, 1978.

Ehrenreich, Barbara, et al. *Re-Making Love: The Feminization of Sex.* Garden City, N.Y.: Anchor/Doubleday, 1986.

Eisenstein, Hester. *Contemporary Feminist Thought.* Boston: G. K. Hall, 1983.

Eliot, George. *Letters.* Gordon S. Haight, ed. Oxford: Oxford University Press, 12 vol., 1955–66.

Engels, Friedrich. *The Origins of the Family.* New York: Harcourt Brace Jovanovich, 1968.

Ephron, Nora. *Crazy Salad.* New York: Knopf, 1975.

Ephron, Nora. *Scribble, Scribble: Notes on the Media.* New York: Knopf, 1978.

Epstein, Joseph. *Ambition: The Secret Passion.* New York: Dutton, 1980.

Evans, Sara. *Personal Politics: The Roots of Women's Liberation in the Civil Rights Movement and the New Left.* New York: Vintage, 1980.

Farber, Seymour M., and Wilson, Roger H. L. *The Potential of Woman.* New York: McGraw-Hill, 1963.

Ferree, Myra Marx, and Hess, Beth B. *Controversy and Coalition. The New Feminist Movement.* Boston: Twayne, 1985.

Fields, Suzanne. *Like Father, Like Daughter: How Father Shapes the Woman His Daughter Becomes.* Boston: Little, Brown, 1983.

Felsenthal, Carol. *The Sweetheart of the Silent Majority: The Biography of Phyllis Schlafly.* New York: Doubleday, 1981.

Firestone, Shulamith. *The Dialectic of Sex: The Call for Feminist Revolution.* New York: Bantam, 1981 edition.

Flexner, Eleanor. *A Century of Struggle.* New York: Atheneum, 1971.

Forster, Margaret. *Significant Sisters: The Grassroots of Active Feminism 1839–1939.* New York: Knopf, 1985.

Frankfort, Ellen. *Kathy Boudin and the Dance of Death*. New York: Stein and Day, 1983.

Frankfort, Ellen. *Vaginal Politics*. New York: Bantam, 1973.

French, Brandon. *On the Verge of Revolt: Women in American Films of the Fifties*. New York: Frederick Ungar, 1978.

French, Marilyn. *The Women's Room*. New York: Summit, 1977.

French, Marilyn. *Beyond Power: On Women, Men and Morals*. New York: Summit, 1985.

Friedan, Betty. *It Changed My Life: Writings on the Women's Movement*. New York: Dell, 1977.

Friedan, Betty. *The Feminine Mystique*. New York: Norton, 1963.

Friedan, Betty. *The Second Stage*. New York: Summit, 1981.

Fromm, Erich. *The Sane Society*. New York: Holt, Rinehart & Winston, 1955.

Galbraith, John Kenneth. *The Anatomy of Power*. Boston: Houghton Mifflin, 1983.

Gallop, Jane. *The Daughter's Seduction: Feminism and Psychoanalysis*. Ithaca, N.Y.: Cornell University Press, 1983.

Gilbert, Lynn, and Moore, Gaylen. *Particular Passions: Talks with Women Who Have Shaped Our Times*. New York: Clarkson N. Potter, 1981.

Gilliatt, Penelope. *Unholy Fools: Wits, Comics, Disturbers of the Peace*. New York: Viking, 1973.

Gilligan, Carol. *In a Different Voice*. Cambridge, Mass.: Harvard University Press, 1982.

Gittelson, Natalie. *Dominus: A Woman Looks at Men's Lives*. New York: Farrar, Straus & Giroux, 1978.

Goodman, Ellen. *Turning Points: How People Change Through Crisis and Commitment*. Garden City, N.Y.: Doubleday, 1979.

Gornick, Vivian. *Women in Science: Portraits from a World in Transition*. New York: Simon & Schuster, 1983.

Gornick, Vivian, and Moran, Barbara K. *Woman in Sexist Society: Studies in Power and Powerlessness*. New York: New American Library, 1972.

Gould, Lois. *Not Responsible for Personal Articles*. New York: Warner, 1979.

Gould, Lois. *A Sea-Change*. New York: Simon & Schuster, 1976.

Gould, Lois. *Such Good Friends*. New York: Random House, 1970.

Greenfield, Jeffrey. *No Peace, No Place: Excavations Along the Generational Fault*. Garden City, N.Y.: Doubleday, 1973.

Greer, Germaine. *The Female Eunuch*. New York: Bantam, 1972.

Greer, Germaine. *The Madwoman's Underclothes: Essays & Occasional Writings*. New York: Atlantic Monthly Press, 1987.

Greer, Germaine. *The Obstacle Race*. New York: Farrar, Straus & Giroux, 1979.

Greer, Germaine. *Sex and Destiny: The Politics of Human Fertility*. New York: Harper & Row, 1984.

Griffith, Elisabeth. *In Her Own Right: The Life of Elizabeth Cady Stanton*. New York: Oxford University Press, 1984.

Griffith, Richard, et al. *The Movies*. New York: Simon & Schuster, 1983.

Halberstam, David. *The Powers That Be*. New York: Dell, 1979.

SELECTED BIBLIOGRAPHY

Handlin, Oscar. *The Americans: A New History of the People of the United States.* Boston: Atlantic Monthly Press, 1963.

Haskell, Molly. *From Reverence to Rape: The Treatment of Women in the Movies.* New York: Holt, Rinehart and Winston, 1974.

Hawkes, Ellen. *Feminism on Trial.* New York: Morrow, 1986.

Hennig, Margaret, and Jardim, Anne. *The Managerial Woman.* Garden City, N.Y.: Anchor/Doubleday, 1977.

Hewlett, Sylvia Ann. *A Lesser Life: The Myth of Women's Liberation in America.* New York: Morrow, 1986.

Higginson, Margaret V., and Quick, Thomas L. *The Ambitious Woman's Guide to a Successful Career.* New York: AMACOM, 1975.

Hite, Shere, ed. *Sexual Honesty: By Women for Women.* New York: Warner, 1974.

Hole, Judith, and Levine, Ellen. *Rebirth of Feminism.* New York: Quadrangle, 1971.

Holme, Bryan, ed. *The Journal of the Century.* New York: Viking, 1976.

Hughes, Ted, and McCullough, Frances, eds. *The Journals of Sylvia Plath.* New York: Ballantine, 1982.

Hunt, Morton M. *Her Infinite Variety: The American Woman as Lover, Mate & Rival.* New York: Harper & Row, 1962.

International Publishers. *The Woman Question.* New York: 1951.

Jacoby, Susan. *The Possible She.* New York: Farrar, Straus & Giroux, 1979.

Janeway, Elizabeth. *Cross Sections from a Decade of Change.* New York: Morrow, 1982.

Janeway, Elizabeth. *Man's World, Woman's Place: A Study in Social Mythology.* New York: Morrow, 1971.

Jason, Philip K. *Anais Nin Reader.* New York: Avon, 1974.

Jenkins, Alan. *The Forties.* New York: Universe, 1977.

Johnson, Paul. *Modern Times: The World from the Twenties to the Eighties.* New York: Harper Colophon, 1983.

Jong, Erica. *Fear of Flying.* New York: Holt, Rinehart and Winston, 1974.

Kandel, Thelma. *What Women Earn.* New York: Linden Press/Simon & Schuster, 1981.

Kennedy, Florynce. *Color Me Flo.* Englewood Cliffs, N.J.: Prentice-Hall, 1976.

Kinsey, Alfred, Pomeroy, Wardell B., Martin, Clyde E., and Gebhard, Paul. *Sexual Behavior in the Human Female.* Philadelphia: Saunders, 1953.

King, Billie Jean. *Billie Jean.* New York: Harper & Row, 1974.

Klein, Ethel. *Gender Politics.* Cambridge, Mass.: Harvard University Press, 1984.

Komisar, Lucy. *The New Feminism.* New York: Franklin Watts, 1971.

Koedt, Ann, Levine, Ellen, and Rapone, Anita, eds. *Radical Feminism.* New York: Quadrangle, 1973.

Korda, Michael. *Male Chauvinism: How It Works.* New York: Random House, 1973.

Kraditor, Aileen. *The Ideas of the Woman Suffrage Movement 1890–1920.* New York: Columbia University Press, 1965.

Lenz, Elinor, and Myerhoff, Barbara. *The Feminization of America*. Los Angeles: Tarcher, 1985.

Lessing, Doris. *The Golden Notebook*. New York: Bantam, 1979 edition.

Levine, Suzanne Braun, and Dworkin, Susan. *She's Nobody's Baby*. New York: Simon & Schuster, 1983.

Levine, Suzanne, and Lyons, Harriet. *The Decade of Women*. New York: Putnam, 1980.

Lewis, Sinclair. *Main Street*. New York: Harcourt, Brace & World, 1920.

Lichtendorf, Susan S. *Eve's Journey: The Physical Experience of Being Female*. New York: Berkley, 1983.

Lichtenstein, Grace. *Machisma: Women and Daring*. Garden City, N.Y.: Doubleday, 1981.

Llewellyn-Jones, Derek, M.D. *Everywoman and Her Body*. New York: Lancer, 1971.

Lundberg, Ferdinand, and Farnham, Marynia F. *Modern Woman: The Lost Sex*. New York: Universal Library, 1974.

Maccoby, Eleanor E., and Jacklin, Carol N. *The Psychology of Sex Differences*. Stanford, Calif.: Stanford University Press, 1974.

Mailer, Norman. *An American Dream*. New York: Dial, 1965.

Mailer, Norman. *The Prisoner of Sex*. Boston: Little, Brown, 1971.

Manso, Peter. *Mailer: His Life and Times*. New York: Simon & Schuster, 1985.

Masters, William, M.D., and Johnson, Virginia E. *Human Sexual Inadequacy*. New York: Bantam, 1981 edition.

Masters, William, M.D., and Johnson, Virginia E. *Human Sexual Response*. New York: Bantam, 1981 edition.

McGinley, Phyllis. *The Province of the Heart*. New York: Viking, 1959.

Mead, Margaret. *Male and Female: A Study of the Sexes in a Changing World*. Westport, Conn.: Greenwood Press, 1949 edition.

Mead, Margaret. *Coming of Age in Samoa*. New York: Morrow, 1974.

Mead, Margaret. *New Lives for Old*. New York: Morrow, 1956; 1975.

Melamed, Elissa, Ph.D. *Mirror, Mirror: The Terror of Not Being Young*. New York: Linden Press/Simon & Schuster, 1983.

Mellen, Joan. *Women and Their Sexuality in the New Film*. New York: Dell, 1973.

Merriam, Eve, ed. *Growing Up Female in America: Ten Lives*. New York: Dell, 1971.

Mill, John Stuart. *The Subjection of Women*. Cambridge, Mass.: MIT Press, 1970 edition.

Miller, James. *"Democracy in the Streets": From Port Huron to the Siege of Chicago*. New York: Simon & Schuster, 1987.

Miller, Jean Baker. *Toward a New Psychology of Women*. Boston: Beacon, 1976.

Miller, Sue. *The Good Mother*. New York: Harper & Row, 1986.

Millett, Kate. *Flying*. New York: Knopf, 1974.

Millett, Kate. *Going to Iran*. New York: Coward, McCann and Geoghegan, 1982.

Millett, Kate. *The Basement: Meditations on a Human Sacrifice*. New York: Simon & Schuster, 1979.

Millett, Kate. *Sexual Politics*. Garden City, N.Y.: Doubleday, 1970.

Millett, Kate. *Site.* New York: Ballantine, 1976.

Mitchell, Juliet, and Oakley, Ann, eds. *The Rights and Wrongs of Women.* Harmondsworth, Middlesex, England: Penguin, 1976.

Moffat, Mary Jane, and Painter, Charlotte, eds. *Revelations: Diaries of Women.* New York: Vintage, 1975.

Morgan, Elaine. *The Descent of Woman.* New York: Stein and Day, 1972.

Morgan, Marabel. *The Total Woman.* New York: Pocket Books, 1975.

Morgan, Robin. *The Anatomy of Freedom: Feminism, Physics and Global Politics.* Garden City, N.Y.: Anchor/Doubleday, 1982.

Morgan, Robin. *Going Too Far: The Personal Chronicle of a Feminist.* New York: Random House, 1977.

Morgan, Robin, ed. *Sisterhood Is Global: The International Women's Movement Anthology.* Garden City, N.Y.: Anchor/Doubleday, 1984.

Morgan, Robin, ed. *Sisterhood Is Powerful: An Anthology of Writings from the Women's Liberation Movement.* New York: Vintage, 1970.

Morrison, Toni. *Song of Solomon.* New York: Knopf, 1977.

Murphy, Yolanda, and Murphy, Robert F. *Women of the Forest.* New York: Columbia University Press, 1974.

Myers, Henry, ed. *Women at Work: How They're Reshaping America.* Princeton, N.J.: Dow Jones Books, 1979.

Myrdal, Gunnar. *An American Dilemma: The Negro Problem and Modern Democracy.* New York: Harper & Brothers, 1944.

Naylor, Gloria. *The Women of Brewster Place.* New York: Penguin, 1983.

Olsen, Tillie. *Tell Me a Riddle.* New York: Dell, 1956.

O'Neill, Lois Decker, ed. *The Women's Book of World Records and Achievements.* Garden City, N.Y.: Anchor/Doubleday, 1979.

O'Neill, William, ed. *The Woman Movement: Feminism in the United States and England.* Chicago: Quadrangle, 1969.

O'Reilly, Jane. *The Girl I Left Behind: The Housewife's Moment of Truth and Other Feminist Ravings.* New York: Macmillan, 1980.

Ozick, Cynthia. *Art and Ardor: Essays.* New York: Dutton, 1984.

Paige, Connie. *The Right-to-Lifers: Where They Get Their Money.* New York: Summit, 1983.

Piercy, Marge. *The High Cost of Living.* New York: Harper & Row, 1978.

Pogrebin, Letty Cottin. *Among Friends: Who We Like, Why We Like Them and What We Do With Them.* New York: McGraw-Hill, 1987.

Pogrebin, Letty Cottin. *Family Politics: Love and Power on an Intimate Frontier.* New York: McGraw-Hill, 1983.

Pogrebin, Letty Cottin. *Getting Yours: How to Make the System Work for the Working Woman.* New York: McKay, 1975.

Pogrebin, Letty Cottin. *Growing Up Free: Raising Your Child in the 80s.* New York: McGraw-Hill, 1980.

Pogrebin, Letty Cottin. *How to Make It in a Man's World.* Garden City, N.Y.: Doubleday, 1970.

Radl, Shirley Rogers. *The Invisible Woman: Target of the Religious New Right.* New York: Delacorte, 1983.

Redstockings. *Feminist Revolution.* New York: Random House, 1978.

Reed, Evelyn. *Woman's Evolution: From Matriarchal Clan to Patriarchal Family.* New York: Pathfinder Press, 1975.

Rich, Adrienne. *Of Woman Born: Motherhood as Experience and Institution.* New York: Norton, 1976.

Rich, Adrienne. *The Fact of a Doorframe: Poems Selected and New 1950–1984.* New York: Norton, 1984.

Reich, Charles A. *The Greening of America.* New York: Bantam, 1971.

Reisman, David, Glazer, Nathan, and Denney, Reuel. *The Lonely Crowd: A Study of the Changing American Character.* Garden City, N.Y.: Doubleday, 1953.

Rix, Sara E., ed. *The American Woman: 1987–1988.* New York: Norton, 1987.

Robinson, F.N., editor. *The Poetical Works of Chaucer.* Boston: Houghton Mifflin, 1933.

Roiphe, Anne. *Up the Sandbox.* New York: Simon & Schuster, 1970.

Rollin, Betty. *Last Wish.* New York: Linden/Simon & Schuster, 1985.

Rosen, Marjorie. *Popcorn Venus: Women, Movies, and the American Dream.* New York: Avon, 1973.

Rossi, Alice S. *The Feminist Papers: From Adams to deBeauvoir.* New York: Bantam, 1974.

Ruddick, Sara, and Daniels, Pamela, eds. *Working It Out: 23 Women Writers, Artists, Scientists, and Scholars Talk About Their Lives and Work.* New York: Pantheon, 1977.

Ruzek, Sheryl Burt. *The Women's Health Movement.* New York: Praeger, 1979.

Sangiuliano, Iris, Ph.D. *In Her Time: Women, Crisis and Growth.* New York: Morrow, 1978.

Sayre, Nora. *Sixties Going on Seventies.* New York: Arbor House, 1973.

Schlafly, Phyllis. *The Power of the Positive Woman.* New York: Jove/HBJ, 1977.

Schickel, Richard. *Intimate Strangers.* Garden City, N.Y.: Doubleday, 1985.

Seaman, Barbara. *The Doctors' Case Against the Pill: More than 100 Medical Specialists Report How Love with the Pill Can Cripple and Kill.* Garden City, N.Y.: Doubleday, 1980.

Seaman, Barbara. *Free and Female: The New Sexual Role of Women.* New York: Fawcett Crest, 1973.

Seaman, Barbara, and Seaman, Gideon, M.D. *Women and the Crisis in Sex Hormones.* New York: Bantam, 1981 edition.

Seligson, Marcia. *Options.* New York: Random House, 1978.

Sennett, Richard, and Cobb, Jonathan. *The Hidden Injuries of Class.* New York: Vintage, 1973.

Shange, Ntozake. *For Colored Girls Who Have Considered Suicide When the Rainbow Is Enuf.* New York: Bantam, 1980.

Shepard, Don. *Women in History.* Los Angeles: Mankind, 1973.

Sontag, Susan. *A Susan Sontag Reader.* New York: Farrar, Straus & Giroux, 1982.

Stambler, Sookie. *Women's Liberation: Blueprint for the Future.* New York: Ace, 1970.

Spender, Dale. *Feminist Theorists: Three Centuries of Key Women Thinkers.* New York: Pantheon, 1983.

Stein, Jean. *Edie: An American Biography.* New York: Dell, 1983.

Steinem, Gloria. *Outrageous Acts and Everyday Rebellions*. New York: Holt, Rinehart and Winston, 1983.

Strainchamps, Ethel, ed. *Rooms with No View: A Woman's Guide to a Man's World of the Media*. New York: Harper & Row, 1974.

Strang, Jessica. *Working Women*. New York: Abrams, 1984.

Talese, Gay. *The Kingdom and the Power*. New York: New American Library, 1969.

Trahey, Jane. *On Women and Power: Who's Got It? How to Get It?* New York: Rawson, 1977.

Trilling, Diana. *We Must March, My Darlings*. New York: Harcourt Brace Jovanovich, 1978 edition.

Tripp, Maggie, ed. *Woman in the Year 2000*. New York: Arbor House, 1974.

Trudeau, G. B. *Dare to Be Great Ms. Caucus*. New York: Holt, Rinehart and Winston, 1973.

Unger, Rhoda K. *Female and Male: Psychological Perspectives*. New York: Harper & Row, 1979.

Wagner, Jane. *The Search for Signs of Intelligent Life in the Universe*. New York: Harper & Row, 1986.

Walker, Alice. *The Color Purple*. New York: Pocket Books, 1983.

Weitzman, Lenore J. *The Divorce Revolution: The Unexpected Social and Economic Consequences for Women and Children in America*. New York: Free Press, 1985.

White, Theodore H. *America in Search of Itself: The Making of the President 1956–1980*. New York: Warner, 1982.

Whyte, William H., Jr. *The Organization Man*. Garden City, N.Y.: Doubleday, 1957.

Wylie, Philip. *Generation of Vipers*. New York: Holt, Rinehart and Winston, 1955.

Willis, Ellen. *Beginning to See the Light: Pieces of a Decade*. New York: Knopf, 1981.

Wolfe, Tom. *The Purple Decades: A Reader*. New York: Farrar, Straus & Giroux, 1982.

Wollstonecraft, Mary. *A Vindication of the Rights of Women*. New York: Norton, 1967 edition.

Woolf, Virginia. *A Room of One's Own*. New York: Harcourt Brace Jovanovich, 1964 edition.

Woolf, Virginia. *To the Lighthouse*. New York: Harcourt Brace Jovanovich, 1964.

Yezierska, Anzia. *Bread Givers*. New York: Persea Books, 1925.

Zinn, Howard. *The Twentieth Century: A People's History*. New York: Harper Colophon, 1984.

ACKNOWLEDGMENTS

Before beginning what is bound to be a very long list of those who gave time and effort to this book, I would like to make clear that none of these generous souls should be held accountable for the choices that form its narrative. Consultations were extensive, it is true; hundreds of hours (perhaps thousands, if one took the time to tally) spent searching memories, retracing steps, and digging through files to retrieve personal papers. What is included in the text, however—the what, when, why, and especially who—is entirely my own responsibility. Some of these decisions, made at various sticking points over the six years since I first began the book, were painful. I worried about them into the late hours of many nights, especially when accounts differed, which, luckily and amazingly, only happened in a few instances and in very minor ways. In those few cases, I chose the one that seemed most likely and can only hope I was right.

I could not have even begun, of course, without the personal interviews that were my main resource. Most of them were taped and ranged widely in length. One—with Germaine Greer at her home in Tuscany—was conducted during most of each day over a period of four days; most others were shorter and took place at erratic intervals over the years. For their endurance of both the long and the short interviews, the one-time questioning and the repeated pestering, I thank:

Bella Abzug, Amy Adams, Jane Adams, Dolores Alexander, Curt Anderson, Ti-Grace Atkinson, Joanna Barnes, Marvin Barrett, Myrna

Blythe, Lillian Barnes Borton, Ivy Bottini, George Brockway, Helen Gurley Brown, Susan Brownmiller, Carrie Carmichael, John Mack Carter, Kay Clarenbach, Katherine Conroy, Catherine East, Mary Eastwood, Joanne Edgar, Brenda Feigen Fasteau, Jean Faust, Clay Felker, Mary Fiore, Milton Forman, Muriel Fox, Betty Friedan, John Kenneth Galbraith, Harry Goldstein, Lois Gould, Jeff Greenfield, Germaine Greer, Barbara Grizzuti Harrison, Harold Hayes, Richard Kaplan, Florynce Kennedy, Nancy Knaak, Michael Korda, Harvey Kurtzman, Leonard Levitt, Ajai Singh (Sonny) Mehta, Kate Millett, Robin Morgan, Nancy Newhouse, Jane O'Reilly, Barbara Nessim, Mary Perot Nichols, Richard Ottinger, John Pankhurst, Susanne Patch, Mary Peacock, Letty Cottin Pogrebin, Betty Rollin, Alice Rossi, Marlene Sanders, Barbara Seaman, Gloria Steinem, Sheila Tobias, Lyn Tornabene, Barbara Wyden, and Peter Wyden.

For the protection of those few who requested it, I have listed them all here rather than in the source notes relating to the specific chapter or chapters to which they contributed. It often happens, therefore, that my notes cite a source which is, in fact, only one of several. The incident in which Betty Friedan initially wrote the words and acronym "NOW" on a paper napkin, for example, can be found not only in several printed sources besides the one that appears in my chapter notes but was also confirmed to me personally by both Betty Friedan herself and Dr. Kathryn Clarenbach.

Also unmentioned in the notes are the many daily reporters who were the true chroniclers of this amazing movement. Certain bylines, I found as I studied the coverage, appeared faithfully again and again. Among these: Marylin Bender, David Behrens, Paula Bernstein, Helen Dudar, Judy Klemesrud, Lisa Hammel, Mary Perot Nichols, Jerry Tallmer, Lindsy Van Gelder. Their fine reportage was, obviously, essential to the telling of this story.

There is simply no way to thank Carol Rinzler sufficiently for legal and editorial advice—both equally superb and far beyond the call of duty. Or Sally Rose, whose sunny nature prevailed through her labors in the dark vineyards of research. Or Chris Bowen, for his rigorous attack on the newspaper morgue. Or that parade of energetic helpers who, on and off, filled in with a bit of typing here, some filing there, Xeroxing, retrieving, checking, all those endless details that are demanded in the weaving of a "true life" story such as this one. Laura Silver, Mary Ann Stackpole, Dana Underwood, Laura LaVille, Ruth Lese, Carol Brooks: thank you.

ACKNOWLEDGMENTS

The encouragement that Joni Evans gives to her authors is by now a publishing legend. For me, added to that absolutely correct report was a precious bonus—the unflagging loyalty of a true friend.

A profound appreciation is certainly due to my thoughtful and devoted editor, Bob Asahina. To my agent, Kathy Robbins, to the book's "godmother," Alice Mayhew, to the Simon & Schuster crew in general—Vincent Virga, Elizabeth McNamara, Rhonda Johnson, Mary Ann Tomasini, Marcella Berger, Dona Chernoff, Helen Niemirow, Frank Metz, Eve Metz, Joe Smith, Robert Anthony, and Debra Makay: thank you.

I would also like to express my gratitude to my long-suffering family, most especially—for reasons only she and I understand—my sister, Ceci Orman, and my nephew Peter Orman. To my daughter, Betsy Marrion, as well, who showered me with more enthusiasm and praise than I could ever deserve. To Jesse Cohen who gave me (*gave me!*) his IBM PC when, after several years of service, my poor Osborne died. To Larry Cohen, whose help included far more than his cheerful hoisting of boxes of books and files and clippings, and who in many ways bore the brunt of what seemed at times an unending project. To my niece, Julie Orman, for saving me dozens of trips downtown by transporting her cache of *Ms.* magazines all the way from Michigan, and to Felicia and Martin, as well.

I am in debt to more faithful and supportive friends than I can mention, but especially:

To Dick Kaplan for—among other immeasurably generous acts—his tireless help in securing all manner of clippings and books. And Carrie Carmichael, for popping into my working dungeon at regular intervals to tell terrible jokes and thereby keep me (relatively) sane. Two good buddies such as these only appear in one's lifetime by virtue of light waves from a rare and lucky star.

To Paula Bernstein for her books and good cheer, to Jane Adams for her periodic efforts to focus my eyes on the light at the end of the tunnel, to Bernie Mendik for the refreshment of his clear intelligence, to Phyllis Theroux, Ruthanne Koffman, and Judy Fireman, Nicky and David Bloom, Ursula Obst, Paul Deutschman, Lance Mald, Sharon Rosenthal, Phyllis Levy, Muriel and Ray Muldorf, The Auerbachs and the Roses, and all the rest.

To the librarians at the New York Public Library, the Barnard Women's Studies Library, the White Plains Library, and the miraculous Schlesinger Library at Radcliffe, my gratitude.

ACKNOWLEDGMENTS

And to a special group of friends in Binghamton, New York, who, during a time of my deep personal loss, behaved like—perhaps *are*, in some spiritual way—my beloved siblings. To all my friends and family who have been neglected over this long period of hibernation . . .

Thank you for your endurance and understanding. I hope you find the result is worth it.

Index

Friedan, Betty (*cont.*)
    lesbian issue and, 243, 247, 249–50,
        251, 271–72, 278, 369
    in mid-seventies, 368–70
    as "mother" of women's movement,
        309–10
    National Women's Political Caucus
        and, 313, 316–18
    NOW formed by, 130, 132–39
    as NOW president, 139, 141–42,
        270–71, 272–73
    physical appearance of, 18, 19–20,
        58, 60, 61, 135, 138, 269, 276–77,
        281, 282, 347
    in Plaza Hotel protest, 13–21
    political action as priority of, 311–12
    postgraduate studies of, 63
    in psychoanalysis, 64, 69
    sister's rivalry with, 60–61
    sixty-fifth birthday party for, 381–82
    at Smith College, 62–63, 83
    at Smith College fifteenth reunion,
        83–84, 89–90, 377
    Sneden's Landing house of, 69–70
    Steinem's commencement address
        and, 320–21
    Steinem's conflict with, 310–11, 336–
        337, 345, 347, 349–52
    as talk show guest, 98
    at Town Hall debate, 289, 297–98
    unfulfilled promise of, 83–84
    as wife and mother, 68–71
    on women's magazines, 94–95, 185
    on women's postwar return to
        homemaking, 76
    women's strike for equality and, 273–
        287
    writing career of, 64, 67, 69, 70–71,
        83–84, 89–99, 130
    see also specific writings
Friedan, Carl, 25, 66–67, 69, 96, 99
    divorce of, 266–69
    wife battered by, 17–18, 266–67
Friedan, Daniel, 67, 69, 382
Friedan, Emily, 70, 274, 275, 382
Friedan, Jonathan, 69, 70, 382
frigidity, 169
Furness, Betty, 138, 286
Future of Marriage, The (Bernard), 355

Galbraith, John Kenneth, 114–16, 320
"Gal Fridays," 87

Gallup poll, 153–54
Gandhi, Indira, 371
gay rights movement, 248–51
generation gap, 226–27
Germaine Greer versus the United States,
    290
Gilligan, Carol, 376
Ginsberg, Allen, 89, 122, 343
"Girl Talk," 98
Girodias, Maurice, 158–59
Gittelson, Natalie, 341–42
Goldsmith, Judy, 366
Goldstein, Al, 332
Goldstein, Amy, 54, 55, 56, 57–58, 59,
    60–61
Goldstein, Harry, Jr., 54, 55, 57, 58,
    84
Goldstein, Harry, Sr., 54–55, 56, 58, 59,
    64
Goldstein, Miriam, 54, 55, 58, 59–61,
    64, 68, 69
"Goodbye to All That" (Morgan), 187,
    215
Goodman, Ellen, 23, 376
Gordon, Mary, 331, 377
Gornick, Vivian, 170, 172, 206, 295,
    327
Gould, Lois, 331, 377
government, women in, 131–32, 171,
    313–14, 318, 348
Graham, Katherine, 329
Graham, Richard, 132, 134, 139
Graham, Virginia, 98
"Grand Coolie Damn, The" (Piercy),
    170
"Great Society," 130
Greening of America, The (Reich), 217,
    229–30
Greer, Alida Jane, 30
Greer, Barry John, 30–31
Greer, Eric Reginald, 29–30, 31, 33–34,
    37
Greer, Germaine, 25, 28–38, 72, 117–
    128, 255–65, 266, 305–6, 314,
    362, 364, 374, 379, 384–85
    as actress, 120, 121
    American women's movement
        criticized by, 367–68
    birth of, 28–29
    bohemian existence of, 118–19
    in Cambridge Union debate, 354
    childhood of, 29–34

PICTURE PERMISSIONS

Marcia Cohen
3 Conchas Pl.
Santa Fe 87508
505-5775119

CPSIA information can be obtained
at www.ICGtesting.com
Printed in the USA
FFHW022258031118
49181207-53393FF